THE WASHINGTON APPLE

The Environment in Modern North America

The Washington Apple

ORCHARDS AND THE DEVELOPMENT OF INDUSTRIAL AGRICULTURE

AMANDA L. VAN LANEN

University of Oklahoma Press : Norman

Publication of this book is made possible through the generosity of Edith Kinney Gaylord.

Portions of chapter 2 were published in an earlier form in "'Where Dollars Grow on Trees': The Promise and Reality of Irrigated Farming in Central Washington," *Agricultural History* 88, no. 3 (Summer 2014): 388–406. Portions of chapter 5 were published in an earlier form in "Reluctant Producers: The Struggle to Organize Cooperative Marketing for Washington Apple Growers, 1910–1930," *Journal of the West* 53, no. 1 (Winter 2014): 42–49.

Library of Congress Cataloging-in-Publication Control Number 2022003495
ISBN 978-0-8061-9066-2 (hardcover) ISBN 978-0-8061-9398-4 (paper)

The Washington Apple: Orchards and the Development of Industrial Agriculture is Volume 7 in The Environment in Modern North America series.

The paper in this book meets the guidelines for permanence and durability of the Committee on Production Guidelines for Book Longevity of the Council on Library Resources, Inc. ∞

Copyright © 2022 by the University of Oklahoma Press, Norman, Publishing Division of the University. Paperback published 2024. Manufactured in the U.S.A.

All rights reserved. No part of this publication may be reproduced, stored in a retrieval system, or transmitted, in any form or by any means, electronic, mechanical, photocopying, recording, or otherwise—except as permitted under Section 107 or 108 of the United States Copyright Act—without the prior written permission of the University of Oklahoma Press. To request permission to reproduce selections from this book, write to Permissions, University of Oklahoma Press, 2800 Venture Drive, Norman OK 73069, or email rights.oupress@ou.edu.

Contents

Acknowledgments	vii
Introduction	1
1. How the Apple Came to Washington	17
2. If You Build It, They Will Come: Railroads, Irrigation, and Early Settlement	40
3. One Bad Apple: Conforming to Orchard Management Practices	67
4. The Clamor of Bidders and Buyers: Getting Fruit to Market	96
5. An Apple a Day Keeps the Doctor Away: Advertising to Consumers	138
6. Weathering the Depression and War	171
7. Hyperindustrialization and the Future of Apples	206
Notes	231
Bibliography	267
Index	279

Acknowledgments

Writing can feel like a solitary experience, but as any author knows, it takes many people to bring a book to completion. I could not have written this book without archival resources from several institutions. Thanks to John Baule, archivist and director emeritus of the Yakima Valley Museum and Historical Society for his help in locating resources and illustrations. Trevor Bond, Mark O'English, and Cheryl Gunselman of the Washington State University Manuscript, Archives, and Special Collections offered valuable assistance as well. Cheryl was kind enough to let me work with a large uncatalogued collection, which I am happy to report has since been catalogued. Thanks also to the staff at the Minnesota Historical Society, the Wenatchee Valley Museum, and the Washington State Archives in Olympia.

Thank you to the Lewis-Clark State College Faculty Affairs Committee and Dr. Chris Riggs for providing funds to support my research. Faculty development grants and funding from the Idaho Higher Education Research Council enabled me to travel to the Washington State Archives, as well as the Minnesota Historical Society in St. Paul. Without this support, my project would not have been possible.

I am also grateful for the many friends and colleagues who have supported me over the years. Dr. Marlowe Daly-Galeano and members of the Lewis-Clark State Faculty Writing Group provided support and accountability. Ileah Bergman graciously served as my research assistant during the spring 2019 semester. She helped with newspaper research, and more important, she managed another project I was working on that semester, which freed up time to write. Tara Cross provided a listening ear whenever I needed it. Thank you also to the anonymous reviewers whose comments helped me make key revisions, and to the project editors and staff at the University of Oklahoma Press. They made this a smooth and enjoyable process.

Finally, thank you to my family for your support over the years. My grandparents, though no longer with us, cultivated my early love of history with trips to museums and historical sites. Thank you to my parents for supporting my educational journey, and to my brother Ryan, who is always ready for a nerdy conversation about food. Lastly, to Marc. Thank you for everything.

Introduction

In the late 1940s, Yakima, Washington, celebrated National Apple Week with an essay contest for the valley's schoolchildren. In a prize-winning essay titled "What an Apple Could Tell Us," eighth-grader Evelyn Revelli wrote, "Perhaps I'm not the only one who has thought of what stories an apple would tell if it could: Would it tell its life story? Would it tell of a bud that grew into a blossom, with petals protecting the seed inside, of the disappointment when the pretty petals dropped?"[1] I too have pondered this question. Apples accompanied Americans as they journeyed across the continent. We say that nothing is more American than apple pie. Someone precious to us is the "apple of our eye." We recount the story of Eve eating the apple—nature's perfect fruit nourishes our bodies while reminding us of our sins—or of Johnny Appleseed spreading the gospel of apples throughout a young nation. Orchards are places for romance, play, and mischief in countless short stories in the late nineteenth and early twentieth centuries. A few years before Revelli wrote her essay, the Andrews Sisters sang, "Don't sit under the apple tree with anyone else but me." Orchards provided trees to climb and apples for impish children to steal. Even today, apple picking is a popular fall activity, reminiscent of America's agrarian roots at a time when most of us are far removed from that past.

Apple trees could also tell us that romantic notions about orchards bear little resemblance to the realities of apple production. Americans' connection with apples, the role of orchards, and methods of apple production have changed over the centuries. In the nineteenth century, most farms had a small orchard, or at least a few trees. People grew their

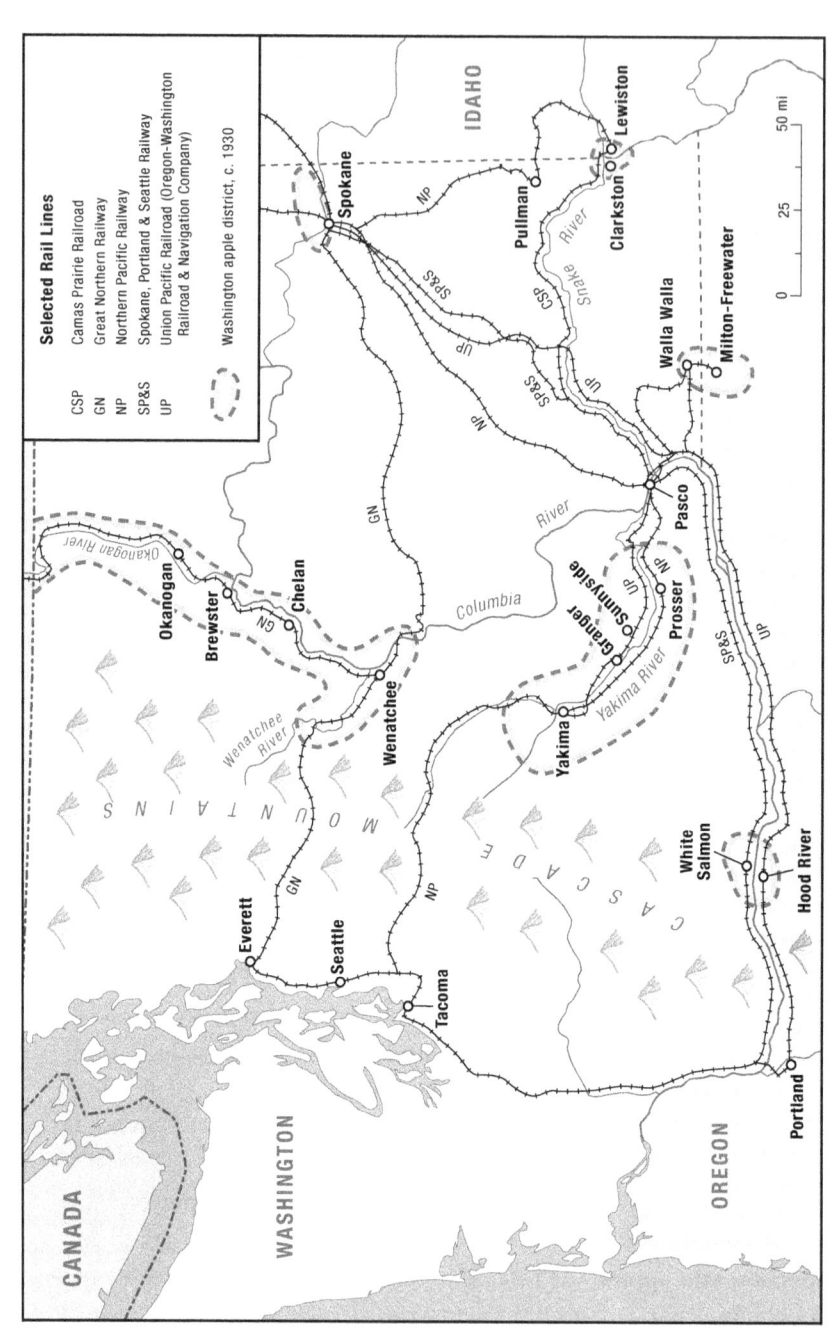

Washington's major apple-growing districts and rail lines. *Map by Erin Greb.*

own apples or purchased fruit grown within a few hundred miles of their homes. Today, we buy mass-produced apples in supermarkets. Regardless of where you live in the United States, you will likely find a Washington apple in your local produce section. In 2020, Washington State accounted for 69 percent of US apple production. As Washington State's leading agricultural product, apples are a nearly $2 billion industry.[2] Red apples with "Washington" stickers are as much a feature of American grocery stores as "Sunkist" oranges or "Chiquita" bananas. Most American consumers are familiar with these brands, so familiar that they may not even consciously think about them.

So why did Washington become the leading apple-producing state in the nation? That is the question this book attempts to answer. Washington shares some similarities with California. Historians Steven Stoll, Douglas Cazaux Sackman, Jared Farmer, and David Vaught have written about the origins of California's fruit industry. The California citrus industry emerged as rail transportation, irrigation, and marketing converged to become what Stoll calls "the industrial countryside." The Washington apple industry grew out of a similar convergence. As Sackman notes, California growers cultivated the idea of an "Orange Empire," a "quest for the recovery of Eden." Nonnative tree species transformed irrigated landscapes, and as Farmer writes, "tree planters staged a landscape revolution."[3] Early Washington growers also evoked Edenic imagery as they transformed the desert landscape. Rival districts vied to become the "apple capital" of the state. Though apples did not become embedded in the state's identity as oranges did in California, Washington and California fruit growers shared a cultural worldview. They were not mere farmers. They were "growers," who elevated the practice of horticulture by embracing science and business strategies. As David Vaught writes, the new horticulturists' goal was not only to enjoy personal gain, "but also to promote economic and social progress in their communities and throughout the state."[4]

But apples are not oranges. California's unique climate enabled growers to produce crops such as citrus and almonds that, unlike apples, did not grow everywhere. Citrus growers' only competition in the early 1900s came from Florida. Washington growers looked to California cooperatives like Sunkist for inspiration, but they faced a different marketing challenge. In the early 1900s, they had to compete with the nation's leading commercial orchards in New York, Virginia, Ohio, Indiana, Illinois, Massachusetts, Missouri, New Jersey, Pennsylvania, and California. Most commercial orchards had the added advantage of being within a few hundred miles of major urban populations, which reduced transportation costs.

Washington was also late to the game. While a few commercial orchards were planted in in the 1880s and 1890s, the bulk of the state's apple acreage was not planted until the twentieth century, decades after eastern states had developed commercial production. On the surface, taking on established eastern orchards seems preposterous. Washington apples cost more to produce than eastern apples. Irrigation and transportation to urban markets over three thousand miles away added to the cost of production. Why should a consumer pay three times as much for a Washington apple, when local apples could be purchased for a fraction of the price? A consumer might pay a premium for California oranges because they did not grow locally, but what distinguished one apple from another on the market? Despite these challenges, within two decades, Washington growers succeeded in not only creating but dominating the industry.

Today, Washington is synonymous with apples, just as Idaho is with potatoes, and Georgia with peaches. Thanks to clever marketing campaigns, product and place have fused in the nation's collective imagination. It is easy to assume that crops become connected with place because of natural suitability. Before I moved to Washington, I never thought about how apples grew, other than perhaps imagining some vague, green pastoral landscape, no doubt shaped by watching Disney's Johnny Appleseed cartoon as a child. My cartoon version of apple orchards could not be further from the truth.

Washington's primary apple-growing districts lie east of the Cascade Range in the Columbia Basin, a region of dry scabland bisected by the Columbia River. Historically, production centered in the Yakima and Wenatchee Valleys in the western part of the basin, but after 1960, new irrigation projects enabled acreage to expand east of the Columbia River. In its natural state, this is desert country, characterized by bunchgrasses and sagebrush. The imposing Cascade Range forms a scenic backdrop, but it blocks moist marine air from reaching Washington's interior valleys. Most of the region's precipitation, less than ten inches per year in some areas, comes in the winter. Ancient lava flows left the basin covered with thick layers of basalt. Tawny hills and exposed basalt outcroppings form a stark contrast to acres of green-leaved apple orchards. Irrigation canals cut through the landscape to deliver water for the many agricultural products grown in central Washington, including hops, pears, and cherries. Washington is the leading national producer of these crops too.

Washington possesses many characteristics that make it an excellent place to grow fruit. In the late nineteenth and early twentieth centuries, Washington promoters argued that natural advantages such as fertile volcanic soils, long summer days, and clear mountain streams to feed irrigation canals made apple production inevitable. The fact that central Washington is a desert did not deter railroad and real estate promoters. Experiments by early settlers had shown that central Washington's arid valleys had the ideal climate and soil for apple cultivation. To many, it was no surprise that Washington produced good fruit. All one had to do was plant trees and wait for nature to do its job. But Washington's apple growers faced many disadvantages as well: competition from established commercial apple districts, high production costs, and high transportation costs.

Though early developers argued otherwise, the apple industry was not a happy accident of nature. Apples are not native to Washington, any more than potatoes are to Idaho or peaches to Georgia. In the wild, plants evolved to survive specific geographies, connected to place through the whims of nature, but agriculture, the act of domesticating plants for human use, removes natural boundaries. The strong associations between foods and regions are often unnatural. They are the product of human intervention, transplantation, vision, and ingenuity. Humans have molded unsuitable environments to fit cultural and agricultural expectations. Poor soils are amended, fields are irrigated, and pests are killed. Washington's success in establishing an apple industry resulted from corporate investment, real estate promotion, science, technology, the construction of large infrastructure systems, and modern marketing methods. Nor did Washington's industrial agriculture develop in a vacuum. Many other agricultural products such as citrus and wheat developed into industries at the same time, all part of a national trend toward large-scale, standardized production.

Agriculture has not always been industrialized. Books such as S. A. Beech's classic *The Apples of New York*, Alice A. Martin's *All about Apples*, and Barrie E. Juniper and David J. Mabberley's *The Story of the Apple* examine early fruit culture in America and the global history of apples more generally. In her history of American fruit orchards, historic landscape architect Susan Dolan identifies four distinctive periods of orchard development: introduction and colonization, which lasted until about 1800; diversification and migration from 1800 to 1880; specialization and industrialization from 1880 to 1945; and monoculture and intensification from 1945 to the present. The trajectory of orchard development mirrored larger developments in American history. Colonists introduced apples to North America. Plants afforded sustenance and a physical connection with places colonists left behind. Each successive group of immigrants brought apples with them, most in seed form. Apples are heterozygous, meaning that seeds vary greatly from the parent plant. The only way to make sure an apple tree is true to the parent tree is to graft a scion from the parent tree to new rootstock. Variability can be useful in selecting for new traits, but it also meant that the trees in early orchards often produced inedible fruit used for fodder or cider making. Families had a few cherished trees with fruit suitable for baking, drying, or eating raw, and a few horticulturists experimented with grafts or purchased grafted varieties from nurseries.

In the second period, from 1800 to 1880, amateur plant breeders, horticultural societies, and western migration spread fruit to new locations and encouraged a proliferation of new varieties. Established orchards symbolized progress and permanency. As historian William Kerrigan explains, the seeds that John Chapman, a.k.a. Johnny Appleseed, distributed in the old Northwest established farmers' land titles, as it took up to five years for an apple tree to bear fruit. Although most orchards supplied apples for home use, the growth of American cities, coupled with improved transportation, fueled the development of commercial orchards planted from grafted trees. Upstate New York dominated commercial apple production in the nineteenth century thanks to the Erie Canal and its proximity to major urban centers. In 1862, the creation of the US Department of Agriculture (USDA) and the passage of the Morrill Act, which established land-grant colleges and universities,

INTRODUCTION 7

shifted orchard experimentation away from amateur horticultural societies toward professional scientific researchers, providing commercial orchards with valuable information on planting, pruning, pest control, and other relevant topics.

Washington and the Pacific Northwest were on the fringes of this second phase of development. Apples came to Washington in the 1820s and 1830s with Hudson's Bay Company employees and missionaries when Washington was still part of Oregon Territory. The first commercial nursery started in Oregon's Willamette Valley in 1847, and by the 1850s and 1860s, orchards had been planted throughout the Pacific Northwest. Farmers grew several varieties, mostly for home use. Small commercial orchards produced fruit for sale within the region. Oregon producers sold fruit in California's gold fields, but by the 1860s, California had developed its own commercial orchards. Competition proved too great, and growers ceased operation. Northwest farmers found some commercial outlets through mining booms in the 1860s and 1870s, but markets were undependable. A few optimistic souls held out hope that the Northwest might someday supply markets on the Pacific Rim, but that seemed unlikely, as California had already filled that niche.

In the third phase of orchard development, lasting from roughly 1880 to 1945, orchards shifted from commercial to industrial production. This book focuses on the period of industrialization, particularly the processes and institutions that contributed to the establishment and growth of the apple industry. Crops grown and sold for a profit can be classified as "commercial," but as Deborah Fitzgerald states in her book *Every Farm a Factory*, industrialization goes a step further, emphasizing "large-scale production, specialized machines, standardization of processes and products, reliance on managerial expertise, and a continual evocation of 'efficiency' as a product mandate."[5] These factors were evident in the production of consumer goods and agricultural commodities by the turn of the twentieth century. Washington apple production skyrocketed from 295,196 bushels in 1889 to over 2.6 million bushels in 1909 and 21.5 million bushels in 1919.[6] Handling that amount of fruit required specialized knowledge and technology, standardized processes, managers, and an emphasis on efficiency—all the factors that characterized successful factories applied to the production of fruit.

Farms in the early twentieth century achieved large-scale production of single crops, or monocultures. Traditional wisdom held that crop diversification protected farmers against the vagaries of nature and the marketplace. Monocultures, in contrast, encouraged farmers to put all their eggs in the proverbial basket. This was risky, but it could pay off. With monocultures, farmers achieved economies of scale to compensate for the additional costs of specialization, such as training and equipment. By the turn of the twentieth century, many viewed farms as businesses, a break from earlier conceptions of agricultural life. Rather than Thomas Jefferson's yeoman farmers, who formed the backbone of American democracy through landownership, farmers were trained professionals. As William Jennings Bryan proclaimed in his famous 1896 "Cross of Gold" speech, farmers supported society not through their landownership but through their ability to feed the nation. "Burn down your cities and leave our farms, and your cities will spring up again as if by magic," he intoned. "But destroy our farms and the grass will grow in the streets of every city in the country."[7] By the time Bryan made his speech, farmers not only fed America's industrial workers but were also part of the machine. Bryan himself compared farmers to other types of businesspeople—bankers, lawyers, shopkeepers—and argued that farmers were just as deserving of the title. Framing farmers as businesspeople redefined their place in the modern American economy. Farmers, or growers, as Washington orchardists preferred, were professionals with specific training and knowledge of their field, no different from any other professional occupation or business endeavor.

The shift from farmer to grower was not an easy one. In the 1890s, populists pushed for greater protections for farmers in the realms of transportation and finance. New federal regulations such as the 1906 Hepburn Act and the 1910 Mann-Elkins Act gave the Interstate Commerce Commission greater control over railroad rates and provided farmers some protection. Though echoes of old Jeffersonian ideals about independent yeoman farmers lingered, the larger problem remained—industrialized farming limited farmers' autonomy and placed them at the mercy of national and international market fluctuations. Old ideas clashed with the realities of the new industrial agricultural model. Newspapers and horticultural magazines of the late nineteenth and early twentieth centuries praised the farm as a place of traditional values in a changing world in one breath, while extolling the need for businesslike practices in the next. Nostalgic stories about the old apple orchard ran side by side with articles about the latest pesticide. In the early years of industrialization, Washington apple growers found themselves in the middle of this debate. Did orchards represent independence and self-sufficiency, or did they represent a new form of professionalism? Eventually, professionalism won out, largely for economic reasons.

Agricultural industrialization did not happen uniformly across the country; it depended on the crop's history, local environment, markets, and labor needs. It played out differently in established eastern orchards versus newly planted western orchards. Orchards in New York, though still very productive, were aging and in need of maintenance. As commercial production increased in the 1880s, apple prices fell, causing many New York growers to remove their orchards in the early 1890s. Those who continued to produce apples for the commercial market did so on diversified farms. A study of orchards from the 1920s found that "the permanency of western New York as a leading apple region may be explained partly by the conservatism of the New York grower."[8] This attitude served New York growers well, for a time. New York remained a leading apple-producing state into the 1920s.

Western orchards, except for previously established commercial orchards in California, came of age at a time when the industrialized orchard model was being established. While New York growers worked with outdated, aging orchards, western growers started from scratch in newly irrigated districts, planting orchards using the latest scientific advice for the express purpose of industrial production. Washington did not have a long history of commercial apple production to influence growers. Most growers were novices. Their naiveté led to mistakes, but it also contributed to a sense of community. Everyone had to learn together. At times growers resisted expert advice, but in the end, they conformed to industrial best practices to preserve their investments.

Hopeful prospectors planted new orchards on irrigated land throughout the West at the turn of the century—in Oregon, Idaho, Montana, Colorado, New Mexico, and Utah—but commercial orchard acreage in these states was dwarfed by developments in central Washington. By

1920, Utah and New Mexico each had a few thousand acres of commercial orchards that served local and regional markets. New Mexico growers often shipped their apples to neighboring Texas, for example. Colorado had roughly 10,000 acres in production, but by the 1920s, growers in the state had already lost an estimated 2,000 to 3,000 acres because of alkaline soils. At its peak, the Bitterroot Valley in Montana boasted 23,000 acres of commercial orchards, but by the early 1920s, most of this land, which had been in the hands of a few large developers, was in receivership, and the orchards neglected. Idaho had four commercial apple districts in the Payette Valley, Boise, Twin Falls, and Lewiston. Orchards in the Payette Valley and Boise struggled with frost damage. In Oregon, robust fruit districts developed in the Rogue River Valley and Hood River. In comparison, by the early 1920s, the Yakima and Wenatchee Valleys of central Washington had approximately 160,000 acres in production. Production data from the top-producing western districts show Washington's dominance. From 1916 to 1919, Wenatchee and Yakima combined averaged 14.68 million bushels a year, nearly twice the combined total production of the next largest western producers: Watsonville, California; southern Idaho; Hood River, Oregon; and Colorado.[9]

Western orchards, newly planted in the 1890s, started bearing in the early 1900s. Newcomers knew that they needed to grow quality fruit to be competitive, especially because two factors were working against them: the additional cost of irrigation and the distance from primary urban markets. The first western crops had fortunate timing. Reduced acreage in New York, combined with five years of consecutive crop failure in the Ozarks, provided an opening for western apples on the national market.[10] By the 1910s, New York growers, realizing the threat posed by western apples, began to adopt some of the grading and packing methods pioneered by western growers to stay competitive, but by then western apples had established themselves in the market. Change was not easy for established eastern commercial growers. New pruning and spraying methods added to production costs. Growers remained reluctant to replace old trees with newer, more commercially viable varieties. Trees take time to mature, and as long as older orchards were productive, growers lacked economic incentive to replace them.

INTRODUCTION

In many ways, the development of Washington's orchards mirrors that of other western districts. All were created at the point where transportation, land, and water converged. Railroads were vital to the development of the apple industry. They provided a link to distant markets, attracted new settlers, and invested money in apple-growing regions. "Agricultural advance," writes historian William G. Robbins, "was not inevitable" in the West. Western agriculture, from the ranchers and farmers of the High Plains to the orchardists in California and Washington, was tied to "an active capitalist class," namely railroads and eastern investors, who shaped western economic development.[11] As Richard White writes in his book *Railroaded: The Transcontinentals and the Making of Modern America*, railroads "lured settlers into places where they produced crops, cattle, and minerals beyond what the markets could profitably absorb." Railroads had to cultivate new markets to absorb western excess.[12]

The Northern Pacific Railway and Great Northern Railway arrived in the Yakima and Wenatchee Valleys in 1885 and 1893, respectively. The Northern Pacific generated revenue from the sale of its land grants. The Great Northern received no land grants, but railroad officials were involved in various real estate schemes. Land sales provided only short-term profit. Long-term profit came from encouraging farmers to settle the land and create a steady stream of freight. Western railroads and their executives engaged in a wide variety of business ventures. Some operated as direct subsidiaries of the parent railroad. In other instances, railroad executives served as board members or investors in companies that were at least nominally separate from the railroad. In central Washington, railroad officials invested in irrigation and land companies. Real estate developers wanted to capitalize on desirable land located near rail lines, but such land was worthless to prospective buyers without irrigation. Profitable land required transportation and water.

Irrigation systems were expensive to construct and maintain, so developers encouraged settlers to plant high-value crops. In many places, irrigation did not live up to its full potential. Historian Donald Worster writes that western farmers planted 75 percent of irrigated lands in low-value crops such as alfalfa or wheat.[13] Farmers planted small pockets of high-value specialty crops such as fruit, but except for citrus, fruit such as apples, pears, and apricots could be grown on nonirrigated eastern farms for a lower cost. In many places, plantings did not reach the critical mass necessary to support industrial infrastructure such as centralized packinghouses, warehouses, and marketing agencies.

Land in Washington may have offered some natural advantages over other locations—good soil, lots of sunshine, winters cold enough for trees to go dormant, but not so cold that frost was a significant worry—but growers faced many other obstacles. Orchards had high start-up costs. Trees did not bear until five to seven years after they were planted, leaving growers with no income in the interim. Irrigation systems were expensive to maintain, banks wanted returns on their loans, and railroads expected to make a profit from freight revenue. Environmentally, fungal diseases were not as large a concern for Washington growers as they were for growers in the humid East, but pests such as the codling moth and San Jose scale presented a formidable problem.

Orchards provided an idyllic backdrop for railroad real estate pitches that promised potential settlers independence and self-sufficiency, but, as Worster writes, the "untrammeled freedom" of the West was a myth. More typically, the West was "a land of authority and restraint."[14] Settlers who moved to central Washington found that they had to conform to industrial systems. To make a profit, even with high-value crops, they had to maximize economies of scale and produce flawless fruit that could compete on eastern markets. They had to cooperate on industry standards relating to orchard management, packing, and marketing. Those who ignored expert advice did so at their own economic peril. One of the hallmarks of the Progressive Era was a trend toward professionalization and the collection of data. It is perhaps no surprise that these trends affected agriculture as well. Despite nostalgic window dressings, farming was a business enterprise that required professional expertise.

Many of the settlers who purchased orchard lands had no previous farming experience. They were doctors, teachers, shopkeepers, and accountants looking for a change of pace. Novice settlers had to learn how to plant, irrigate, prune, thin, spray, fertilize, and harvest their trees. Then they had to figure out how to pack fruit, negotiate with buyers, and arrange shipments. While this book does not focus on labor, it is important to note that unlike California growers, Washington growers performed much of their orchard labor themselves. Before World War II, a family with a team could reasonably manage ten to twenty acres, with a few hired hands in early spring to help with pruning and additional help for harvest. California growers relied on a variety of labor sources, including contracted Chinese, Japanese, Sikh, and Mexican laborers. By contrast, most laborers in Washington's apple orchards were white, either local residents or migrant laborers. Many migrant laborers lived within a few hundred miles of central Washington and worked the harvest to supplement other sources of income. For Washington growers, learning the fundamentals of orchard care was not an intellectual exercise. They were vital skills.

Fortunately, an army of experts was on hand to help. Researchers at the USDA and land-grant colleges provided growers with the latest scientific knowledge about orchard management and marketing. Every aspect of the industry was scrutinized for improvements. Scientists studied the best methods for pruning, fertilizing, and planting trees, and for controlling pests. They scrutinized fruit varieties to determine which grew best in each climate, which ripened at the optimal time, which held up best during shipping. They evaluated marketing methods, prices, and economic trends.

Growers chafed against the constraints of industrialization, yet to make a profit, they had no choice but to accept industrial practices. Failing to follow recommended spraying regimens did not hurt just the individual orchard; it put all orchards in the district at risk. Shipping subpar fruit to customers damaged not only an individual reputation, but also the reputation of all growers in the state. Individual decisions had the potential to harm everyone in a district, and as the industry developed, decisions about orchard management moved from being made individually by growers, to being made collectively by the industry. County inspectors, employed by the Washington State Department of Horticulture, monitored orchards to ensure that growers applied sprays at the correct time, fining those who failed to comply. Apple-grading rules regulated size, appearance, and packing methods. For a time, many growers packed their own fruit, but eventually, many opted to send fruit to centralized packinghouses that provided better quality control and economies of scale. Growers worried that fruit brokers, railroad agents, and other intermediaries interfered with profits; however, it was impractical for growers to directly market their fruit to eastern consumers. They needed the transportation, cold storage, and marketing expertise the intermediaries provided. Ultimately, growers had to come together to form cooperative organizations because a single individual could not manage the complexities of marketing apples on such a large scale.

Even though western orchards were planted for commercial production, industrialization was a process. Some growers refused to join cooperatives, unwilling to give up their independence. But even those growers benefited from the construction of transcontinental rail lines, and trends toward urbanization that increased the need for commercially grown fruit to feed city dwellers. Some growers adopted scientific and technological advances faster than others. Modern marketing methods, such as branding, established stable market relationships with eastern and international buyers, even as competition between major growing regions thwarted efforts to form statewide marketing organizations. By the 1920s, the industry was not as orderly as some hoped, but nonetheless, an industry had been established. Apple production in other western states, except for Oregon and California, declined as growers in those districts struggled to match the industrial practices of Washington's growers. Likewise, apple production in Washington's nonirrigated districts declined as farmers, rather than conforming to industrial standards, chose to focus on other crops that were better suited to their local environments.

The Depression and World War II hurt Washington's fruit industry, though for different reasons. During the Depression, sales declined and the number of orchards in Washington decreased as banks foreclosed on properties, particularly orchards on marginal land. The economic devastation of the 1930s led to two additional developments that industry leaders had been urging for the previous two decades: a research station in central Washington close to growers, and the establishment of a statewide marketing commission. During the war, the US government requisitioned the best fruit, damaging consumer perceptions of the quality of Washington apples. After the war, the industry had to rebuild consumer confidence.

Since World War II, orchard development has been characterized by hyperindustrialization. In some parts of the nation, this has meant a move toward monocultures and greater intensification of orchard management practices. In Washington, these are not new trends, but rather a continuation of the industrialized processes that began over a hundred years ago. Hyperindustrialization has pushed the industrial mandates of efficiency, standardization, specialization, and large-scale production to their limits. Today's growers produce more than twice as many apples per acre as their counterparts did before World War II, thanks to advancements in tree varieties, rootstocks, and orchard management techniques.

Many Washington orchards are still small, family-owned operations, but consolidation had affected the industry in the last several decades. Today's orchards average one hundred acres, more than double the average a hundred years ago.[15] Mergers have decreased the number of cooperatives, packinghouses, sales firms, distributors, and retailers. Growers have fewer options for marketing and distributing their fruit than in the past. Perhaps one of the biggest changes after the war was the relationship that formed between railroads and the apple industry. The Great Northern and Northern Pacific played an integral role in creating the apple industry by providing transportation, financing irrigation, and investing in industrial infrastructure such as warehouses and icing facilities. After World War II, that relationship changed as modes of transportation shifted. Refrigerated trucks gave growers another transportation option, ending their dependency on railroads. For their part, railroad managers were frustrated by the shift but were unwilling or unable to accede to growers' demands to maintain the relationship.

In recent years, authors such as Michael Pollan and Eric Schlosser have critiqued industrialized agriculture. Publications such as the *New York Times* carry stories on the growing popularity of organic farms, the merits of eating locally grown produce, and the pitfalls of industrial farming. Consumers have become more conscious of the effects of their food choices on the environment. While industrial agriculture is often vilified, it is important to remember how different Americans' diets once were. Apples, and a wide variety of other fruits and vegetables, are now available year-round, something that was inconceivable in the nineteenth century. We do not have to worry about finding worms or rotten cores in our apples. Food is more accessible and affordable now than perhaps any time in history. On the other hand, critics are right to raise questions about the human and environmental consequences of industrial agriculture. As the story of Washington's apple industry demonstrates, industrial agriculture has its fair share of problems, not only for consumers and the environment, but for growers themselves. Growers in the late nineteenth and early twentieth centuries did not question the long-term environmental effects of chemical use. They did not think about food miles when shipping their crops across the continent. They did not worry about losing crop diversity. Those things were not in their vocabulary. From their perspective, industrial agriculture offered a promising future.

CHAPTER **1**

How the Apple Came to Washington

In June 2020, Washington's oldest apple tree died. The tree, planted on the grounds of Fort Vancouver, a Hudson's Bay Company outpost and later US army site, was reportedly 194 years old. Various retellings have muddled the details of how the tree came to Washington, but the basic story is that sometime in the mid-1820s, a young English officer, bound for Hudson's Bay Company's Pacific Northwest holdings, attended a farewell dinner in his honor. Toward the end of the dinner, the young lady seated next to him presented him with an apple. She asked that he keep the pips to remember her. The obliging gentleman gently wrapped the seeds in his handkerchief and placed them in his pocket.[1] Little did he know, the seeds would produce the first apple tree in the Pacific Northwest.

In this romantic telling, the seeds, and the ensuing tree, serve as a reminder of civilization on a new continent, a small piece of home stowed in a pocket, full of possibility. Whether they came from a lovelorn maiden or a more mundane source, the hope and symbolism embodied in those first seeds planted at Fort Vancouver in the 1820s became part of the creation myth of the apple industry in the Pacific Northwest. The story provided proof that the apple industry was destined for greatness at a time when specialized commercial orchards were developing. For apple growers attempting to professionalize, the Vancouver tree provided historical roots.

As the Pacific Northwest became more settled in the late nineteenth century, residents started to focus on their history. The hard pioneer days were over, and a more permanent prosperity was taking root. Newspapers across the region published pioneer reminiscences that highlighted the first to settle each town, the first to range cattle, or the first to plant wheat. Americans were relatively new to the Pacific Northwest, and their deepest roots went back to the arrival of the Lewis and Clark Expedition in 1805, and after that to the arrival of American missionaries in the 1830s. Historical narratives established legitimacy and a sense of belonging for people who were relative newcomers.

The nascent apple industry used historical narratives to establish a regional identity, build community among growers, and gain loyalty among consumers. Though the industry was new, growers were already framing their efforts in historic terms, tying historic precedent to future success. Dr. J. R. Cardwell, president of the Oregon State Horticultural Society, wrote in 1906 that "the intelligent foresight and patient labors of those who inaugurated this industry in the far-off wilds of Oregon are worthy a place in the archives of the State, and should be kept green in the memory of those who come after."[2] Though Cardwell specifically mentions Oregon, he could just as well have been talking about Washington. The commercial apple industry was in its infancy in both states, and many communities presented their own contenders for the title of "oldest" tree. Newspapers in Vancouver, Washington, rightly named the Hudson's Bay Company planting at Fort Vancouver. Papers in the Puget Sound area claimed two trees transplanted from Fort Vancouver to Nisqually in 1834 as the oldest in the state. Other papers reported that the oldest tree was planted by Nez Perce chief Red Wolf in 1837 on Alpowa Creek in eastern Washington. The seeds for Red Wolf's tree came from Henry Spalding, an early missionary. Lewis and Clark also traveled through the Alpowa Creek drainage, giving Red Wolf's trees multiple, though tenuous, connections to early American activity in the Northwest.[3]

In 1911, E. L. French, orchardist and former Washington State director of agriculture, asked district fruit inspector A. A. Quarnberg to take steps to preserve the tree at Fort Vancouver, located on US Army Reserve land. Quarnberg convinced the army to fence the tree. Shortly thereafter, someone marked it with a commemorative plaque. Since then, the Vancouver tree has held the undisputed title of "Oldest Apple Tree in Washington."[4] The timing of the tree's commemoration was not coincidental. By the 1910s, Washington's apple industry was more than an agricultural fad. It was beginning to offer serious competition to commercial apple districts in other parts of the country. The story of the tree provided growers with a foundational myth, historical roots to accompany the physical rootstocks that supported their orchards.

In hindsight, the story of the first apple tree seems foreordained, but that was not the case. Like most myths, the underlying story is far more complex. The line between this first apple tree and today's multibillion-dollar apple industry was not a linear march of progress. When Washington's first apple tree was planted, commercial orchards in New York were in their infancy, and few Americans considered apples a viable commercial crop, let alone an industrialized one. The Hudson's Bay Company planted apple trees at Fort Vancouver as an agricultural experiment to provide food for its employees, thereby supporting the fur trade, the reigning economic enterprise of the era. Nonetheless, growers at the turn of the twentieth century molded the past to their purposes. Newspapers carried not only accounts of those first apple trees planted in the Pacific Northwest, but also items about the first orchards in other states and histories of the commercial industry in New York. Though newspapers never directly connected Washington to these other histories, the fact that they were important enough to print implied a connection between Washington growers and other apple histories. Growers were not wrong in noting that Washington and the Pacific Northwest were part of a longer history of apple cultivation. Throughout its development, apple culture in the Pacific Northwest mirrored national trends. New settlers planted apples first for subsistence and later for commercial purposes.

Humans cultivated apples for centuries prior to the first plantings at Fort Vancouver. While the scientific genus *Malus* contains approximately forty species, apples consumed today are from the species *Malus pumila*, a surprisingly diverse species that varies in size, color, shape, and flavor.[5] Apples are highly heterozygous, meaning that they inherit different alleles, or versions of a gene, from each parent, unlike homozygous plants, which inherit the same alleles from each parent. More variation in alleles means greater variation between parent and offspring. A seed from a large, tart fruit, for example, might yield a tree that produces small, sweet fruit. Because of this genetic variability, horticulturists estimate that there are over twenty thousand separate cultivars of *M. pumila* worldwide, each with its own unique characteristics.[6] In a 1793 expedition to Kazakhstan, German botanist Johann Sievers became the first European scientist to encounter vast forests of wild apples, although his untimely death in 1795 prevented him from fully publishing his results. In his 1830 book *Flora Altaica*, Carl Friederich von Ledebour named the species *Malus sieversii* in Sievers's honor.[7] In the 1940s, Nikolai Vavilov's study on the Kazakh trees argued that *M. sieversii* was the dominant wild species responsible for today's domestic apple. Subsequent DNA analysis supports this theory.[8]

Human selection, migration, trade, and conquest spread apples from Central Asia to Europe and East Asia. The Chinese, Persians, Greeks, and Romans all cultivated apples.[9] Since apples do not grow true to seed, farmers learned to replicate desirable qualities, such as sweetness, through grafting. Invading Romans planted grafted apple trees throughout Europe, introducing sweet apples that were favored over the small, bitter, native European crab apples. Many orchards fell into disuse after the fall of the Roman Empire, but Europeans continued to grow trees, particularly at monasteries, which preserved knowledge of grafting.[10]

Europeans brought their crops and farming techniques to North America in the sixteenth and seventeenth centuries. Apples were one of many crops brought to America through the Columbian Exchange, a global movement of people, plants, animals, and diseases that followed European contact with the Americas. Europeans preferred the sweeter, domesticated *Malus pumila* to the bitter crab apples native to North America. While grain crops such as corn and wheat formed the backbone of agricultural production, the versatile apple filled many household needs. Apples could be stored for several months in cool cellars, dried, or cooked into butters and preserves. Cider vinegar was a common seasoning and a key ingredient in pickling foods for long-term storage. In an era of tainted water supplies, hard cider was the beverage of choice. Farmers let their livestock, usually hogs, forage for food in orchards. They also used pomace, the pulp left over after cider pressings, for animal feed.

Puritan settlers planted the first known orchard in the British colonies in Boston around 1625. Captain Edward Johnson, early colonial leader and founder of Woburn, Massachusetts, reported that by 1642, farmers had planted an estimated one thousand acres of orchards and gardens in New England. The success of orchards showed the bounty of the land

and the progress that Massachusetts Bay Colony had made in a few short years. Settlers had ample food. "Apples, pears, and quince tarts" had replaced "their former Pumpkin Pies," a notable observation because, as historian Cindy Ott explains, settlers considered pumpkins a food of last resort. The ability to replace pumpkins with other food signified an end to the early days of desperate survival. In addition to improved food supplies, orchards demonstrated mastery over the natural environment. The "wigwams, huts, and hovels the English dwelt in at their first coming" were transformed "into orderly, fair, and well-built homes, well-furnished many of them together with Orchards filled with goodly fruit trees."[11] Orchards provided a finishing touch to the Puritans' "well-built homes."

Colonial Americans, like the English, took great pride in local apple varieties. Colonists argued that the best local apples were hybrids of wild North American apples and European imports, thus asserting the supremacy of local farmland and their mastery over indigenous species.[12] Each successive group of immigrants brought their own orchard stock from their home countries.[13] By the eighteenth century, American orchards featured several varieties from all over Europe. Prior to the 1830s, most apples were planted from seed, leading to even greater diversity. Only wealthy horticultural hobbyists and a few professional nurseries practiced grafting.[14] In 1731, Robert Prince, a French Huguenot, established the first known nursery in British North America. Prince's nursery sold trees to wealthy landowners such as George Washington and Thomas Jefferson. Landed gentry planted grafted trees in formal fruit gardens, distinguished from the working orchards used for cider production or animal feed. Prince's nursery set the standard for horticultural catalogues during the first half of the nineteenth century; its 1845 catalogue featured 350 varieties of apples alone.[15] Nurseries like Prince's helped preserve and establish new varieties of fruit. They imported new varieties from Europe, expanding the types of trees available in America, and they supported horticultural hobbyists whose experiments aided later generations of orchardists.

In her history of American fruit culture, Susan Dolan argues that the introduction of new apple varieties to North America characterized the first phase of fruit culture. Continued migration and commercial development characterized the second phase, which started around

1800.[16] Americans carried apples west as the nation expanded in the nineteenth century. Apples became a symbol of national identity, evidence that America was taming new lands and embracing Thomas Jefferson's ideal of a nation of small, democratic farmers. At the same time, apples entered the economic life of the young nation as commercial orchards began to produce fruit to supply America's growing urban centers.

Of all Americans, John Chapman, better known as Johnny Appleseed, has the greatest association with apple trees. W. D. Haley's 1871 article in *Harper's* made Appleseed a household name at a time when apples had shifted from a subsistence crop to a commercial commodity. Haley's Appleseed symbolized a vanishing frontier and the hardships endured by early settlers before the "appliances of civilization" eradicated the true pioneer spirit.[17] Clad in nothing but a few cast-off rags, a cloak made from an old coffee sack, and a pasteboard hat, Appleseed roamed the countryside, sharing religious tracts and planting apple seeds brought from Pennsylvania in a sturdy leather sack. He had unbounded generosity and shared all his earthly possessions, no matter how meager. His nurseries extended credit to struggling farmers, but debts were never collected. Appleseed's tenderheartedness extended to all creatures, from mosquitoes to bear cubs to children.

Johnny Appleseed's story has become part of American mythology. It represents a different side of American conquest, one by the hoe rather than the musket. "At the heart of European conquest of the Americas," writes historian William Kerrigan, "was an agro-ecological revolution, one fueled by the spread of cultivated Old World crops."[18] Farmers planted trees to prove their land claims even as they cleared the land to make way for crops like corn or wheat. In the process, they changed the natural landscape. As Americans moved West, apple trees represented permanence and mastery over the new landscape because establishing an orchard took time. Even the most diligent farmer had to wait up to seven years before realizing a crop. Because of the time needed for trees to reach maturity, land grants in the old Northwest Territory required settlers to plant at least fifty apple or pear trees in exchange for the deed to the land, "encouraging homesteaders," write horticulturists Barrie Juniper and David Mabberley, "literally as well as metaphorically, to put down roots."[19]

The Chapman of Haley's story had no care for worldly possessions, but the real John Chapman speculated in land and operated nurseries, satisfying the demand for seedlings among settlers in Ohio and Indiana. By the mid-nineteenth century, nurseries like Chapman's became more common as farmers preferred nursery saplings to the unreliable quality of trees produced from seed.[20] From a commercial perspective, nurseries served two purposes. First, requirements for establishing legal title to land in the Ohio Valley drove nursery growth. To claim a one-hundred-acre plot in the "Donation Tract," formed in 1792 by the Ohio Company, settlers had to plant at least fifty apple trees and twenty peach trees within three years.[21] Saplings helped jump-start the claim process.

Second, nurseries provided stock for commercial apple production. Orchards underwent another change in the nineteenth century as the temperance movement made drinking less socially acceptable. Prior to this, hard cider was one of the most popular beverages in America. Cider provided farmers with a portable commodity for trade. Americans consumed it at most meals as well as at weddings, funerals, and political rallies. Cider consumption was so pervasive in American life that Gerrit Smith, a temperance advocate and landowner from New York, lamented that cider was "one of the grand difficulties in the way of the reformation of drunkards."[22] In 1775, 10 percent of New England farms had cider mills, and many others likely had small presses. In 1834, 388 commercial distilleries in New Jersey alone produced applejack.[23]

Temperance societies such as the American Temperance Society, founded in 1826, urged Americans to stop consuming alcohol. By 1836, over eight thousand temperance societies claimed an estimated 1.5 million members, about 10 percent of the American population. Membership was unevenly distributed throughout the nation. New Englanders signed more than a third of all temperance pledges, while southerners signed only 8.5 percent.[24] As markets for cider shrank, some farmers destroyed their orchards. Others turned to high-quality grafted trees that produced sweet table fruit.[25] In his community study of Worcester, Massachusetts, historian Ian Tyrrell found that farmers who took temperance pledges tended to have a greater interest in scientific advances and agricultural efficiency. They were more likely than their nontemperate counterparts to adopt new practices with an eye toward increased commercial development.[26]

Records show shipments of dried apples, brandy, vinegar, and cider from New England to the West Indies as early as 1741, but commercial orchards developed in earnest in the nineteenth century. New transportation networks and growing demand from urban centers like New York City made commercial apple production profitable. Because of its geographic proximity to East Coast cities and transportation corridors, upstate New York became a leading commercial apple producer. In 1821, the year the Erie Canal opened, New York exported 68,344 bushels of apples valued at $39,966. By 1850, the New York apple crop was valued at over $1.7 million. Commercial production exploded, outpacing US population growth. From 1850 to 1860, the US population increased 35.6 percent, while the value of orchard products increased 159 percent. New plantings in the 1850s and 1860s expanded commercial production, and by 1870, New York's commercial crop was valued at over $8.3 million.[27]

By the time *Harper's* published W. D. Haley's story of Johnny Appleseed in 1871, the nation was changing. Civil War had torn the country apart. Two years earlier, the first transcontinental railroad had connected California with the rest of the nation. Johnny Appleseed's stomping grounds in the Old Northwest had been settled. Those seeking fresh opportunities had to look farther west, and the Homestead Act of 1862 provided free land to willing takers. Farming was becoming more commercial. Improved plows, threshers, and harvesters increased efficiency. In 1862, the Morrill Land-Grant Act, which established land-grant colleges and created the Department of Agriculture, provided expert advice to farmers, bringing a new professionalism to farming. Cities were growing, populated by a landless working class, a worrisome trend for those invested in the idea of Jeffersonian agrarianism. Johnny Appleseed's story harked back to a simpler time of subsistence farming. Americans celebrated independence, self-sufficiency, community, and neighborliness, values that contrasted with the wage labor of industrialization and the faceless anonymity of urbanization that emerged after the Civil War.

The story of apples in the Pacific Northwest runs parallel to that of other regions as orchards shifted from subsistence to commercial production. The pursuit of fur, not agriculture, drove early commerce in the Pacific Northwest. Hudson's Bay Company (HBC) established some of the first settlements in the region for the purpose of collecting furs and outfitting suppliers. Through these settlements, HBC unwittingly played a key role in the development of agriculture in the region.

As HBC expanded its territory, the company encountered a significant problem. East of the Rockies, trappers had access to bison, Indian corn, and food shipped from eastern farms via canoe or steamboat. West of the Rockies, fur traders had difficulty obtaining provisions, or rather provisions that were to their liking. Euro-American trappers held strong cultural biases against salmon, a main staple in the region, and the supply of fish and game was not always reliable. HBC was forced to import food from eastern Canada and England. Shipping bulky commodities such as wheat flour around Cape Horn was expensive and impractical. The cost of transporting food from Europe and Canada was so great that George Simpson, governor of the Northern Departments, chastised his men for their poor management of provisions and remarked that they "may be said to have been eating Gold." Between 1822 and 1825, men at Fort Nez Perce (later Fort Walla Walla) ate seven hundred horses in addition to imported provisions when, according to Simpson, a good garden could have sufficed.[28]

In the Northwest, farm production became official company policy after George Simpson was appointed governor of the Northern Departments in 1821. A gifted administrator, Simpson determined to cut company costs by consolidating forts and trimming expenses. Many fur trappers resisted the idea of farming, fearing that it would detract from their main occupation, yet Simpson persisted. He believed that local food production would reduce company expenses, free up cargo space, and possibly create new commodities for export. In 1824, Simpson received permission to move the Northern Departments' headquarters from Fort George (Astoria), at the mouth of the Columbia River, to a site upriver at the confluence of the Columbia and the Willamette Rivers. The new site, called Fort Vancouver, was better suited to the agricultural experimentation Simpson hoped would feed his employees.

Fort Vancouver was not the HBC's first venture into farming. In 1811, the company founded an agricultural settlement on the Red River in present-day Manitoba, Canada. By the mid-1830s, the Red River Colony was producing a surplus. Fort Vancouver was soon equally successful. Simpson appointed chief factor John McLoughlin to supervise the farm.

In 1825, McLoughlin planted peas, potatoes, wheat, barley, oats, corn, and timothy. By the late 1830s, nearly one thousand acres were under cultivation, supplying fur trappers with a wide agricultural bounty including grains, fruits, vegetables, and forage crops for cattle and pigs.[29]

Sometime during these first few years, apple seeds arrived at Fort Vancouver. Multiple versions of the seeds' origins exist. One of the earliest comes from Henry Bingham, a missionary who visited Fort Vancouver in 1829 after sailing from Hawaii. According to Bingham, Captain Aemilius Simpson, head of HBC's Pacific coastal trade, planted the seeds himself sometime in 1827.[30] Narcissa Whitman, an early missionary, heard the story of the apple trees' origins when she visited Fort Vancouver in 1836. "Here I must mention the origin of these Apples and grapes," she wrote in her journal. "A gentleman twelve years ago, while at a party in London put the seeds of the grapes and apples he ate in his vest pocket and soon after took a voyage to this country and left them here. Now they are greatly multiplied."[31] This places the plantings as early as 1824. Other accounts place the first planting somewhere between 1825 and 1828. Simpson's own 1829 report to London mentions that in 1828, Fort Vancouver's garden contained small apple trees and grapevines. Extant correspondence shows that HBC ordered seeds from two London firms after 1827. David Douglas, a botanist from the Horticultural Society of London, provides another possible origin for the tree seeds. Douglas arrived at Fort Vancouver on a collecting trip in 1825. He assisted McLoughlin in the garden and asked the society to send seeds to Fort Vancouver. James Sabine, the head of the society, mailed at least two packages of seeds to McLoughlin. Unfortunately, the exact content of these shipments is unknown.[32] Yet another account says that the seeds came from six apples sent to Fort Vancouver, and that in 1826, Hudson's Bay Company chief trader P. C. Pambrun, who had helped grow the original trees at Fort Vancouver, planted a sapling from one of the seeds in Oregon City.[33]

Regardless their origins, the first trees at HBC produced fruit. The garden reinforced George Simpson and John McLoughlin's belief in the agricultural potential of the region. In 1833, HBC expanded farming to Fort Nisqually on Puget Sound. The following year, a clerk named Archie McDonald brought two saplings from Fort Vancouver and planted them at Nisqually.[34] Though official attempts to establish a company farm at

Nisqually failed, HBC granted land in the Willamette Valley to several employees who started their own farms with seeds and plants from Fort Vancouver.

HBC's successful experiments with European crops provided support for the next wave of immigrants: missionaries. Reverends Jason and Daniel Lee arrived in the Willamette Valley in 1834. Marcus and Narcissa Whitman, who established a mission at Waiilatpu near present-day Walla Walla, Washington, and Henry and Eliza Spalding, who established a mission near present-day Lapwai, Idaho, followed in 1836. Missionaries, as well as others who came in the late 1830s, marveled at the success of HBC's agricultural operations. Upon her arrival at Fort Vancouver in September 1836, Narcissa Whitman was pleasantly surprised by the garden, which she described in her journal: "Here we find fruit of every description. Apples peaches grapes. Pear plum & Fig trees in abundance. Cucumbers melons beans peas beats cabbage, taumatoes, & every kind of vegitable, too numerous to be mentioned. Every part is very neat & tastefully arranged fine walks, eich side lined with strawberry vines." The lush gardens at Fort Vancouver provided a welcome contrast to "the barren sand plains through which we had so recently passed."[35] Reverend Samuel Parker, who visited Vancouver the same year as the Whitmans, commented that fruits "flourish and prove that the soil and climate are well adapted to the purposes of horticulture." Reverend Jason Lee remarked that the orchards had "quantity of fruit so great that many of the branches would break if they were not prevented by props."[36]

The missionaries found not only fruit but a willing mentor as well. McLoughlin shared his knowledge and seeds with the newcomers. He gave Marcus Whitman seeds from the apple trees, which Whitman planted at the Waiilatpu mission.[37] After the Whitmans' death in 1847, Henry Spalding prepared an inventory of the Waiilatpu mission in preparation for its closure. The inventory included "one farm of 30 acres, fenced, cultivated, ditched; . . . Garden orchard of 75 apple trees, a few bearing, heavy ditch for irrigation, Nursery of apple & peach trees."[38]

Mission boards expected outposts to be self-sufficient rather than to purchase expensive supplies from HBC, but that was only part of the reason for starting farms. Early missionaries hoped to convert Indians to European-style farming practices. They considered farming and animal husbandry "virtuous (if not quite divine) occupations and lessons in Christianity," explains historian James R. Gibson.[39] Missions throughout the Northwest planted gardens and orchards in an attempt to induce the nomadic tribes of the Columbia Plateau to adopt sedentary lifestyles that would keep them close to the missions. The missions at Walla Walla and Spalding were drier than Fort Vancouver, receiving twenty inches of rain per year on average, compared to roughly forty inches at the fort. Marcus Whitman and Henry Spalding constructed rudimentary irrigation ditches to water their gardens and orchards. According to early Washington historians, water was a source of conflict between Whitman and the Indians. Indians wanted to use water from Whitman's canal for their own gardens. When Whitman refused, they dug their own ditch and, for a time, stopped the flow of water in Whitman's ditch.[40]

Like Whitman, Henry Spalding planted apple trees at his mission, using irrigation to grow successful crops. In 1837 or 1838, he gave seeds to the Nez Perce chief Red Wolf, who planted them on the Snake River at the mouth of Alpowa Creek in present-day Garfield County, Washington. Red Wolf's seeds likely came from Fort Vancouver, as McLoughlin supplied the Whitmans and Spaldings with seeds, although one account states that Henry Spalding brought the seeds from "the states." By planting trees at the mouth of the creek, Red Wolf ensured that the trees had enough groundwater to survive without irrigation.[41]

In 1852, Father Louis-Joseph d'Herbomez and Father Charles M. Pandosy founded a mission on Ahtanum Creek in the Yakima Valley, which would later become central to Washington's apple industry. The mission was reestablished in 1867 after burning during the Yakima War of 1855. Dates for first plantings at the mission vary. Some sources cite the 1850s and others the late 1860s. According to one source, the Ahtanum trees were shipped from France to Vancouver, and from there carried on horseback to the mission. Sources do not mention irrigation at the mission, but it would have been impossible to grow crops without it. A few Indians planted gardens in a slough, taking advantage of the natural moisture available. Sometime before 1864, Chief Kamiakin built a ditch off Ahtanum Creek to water his garden.[42]

Missionaries had limited success in convincing Indians to adopt sedentary agriculture. Indians tended to choose western crops that fit into existing food customs and seasonal migration patterns. They likely had a complicated view of orchards and trees. Some, like Red Wolf, adapted apples to Indian culture. Imported apples were sweeter than the native crab apples that grew in the Pacific Northwest and for some were a welcome addition to existing diets. On the other hand, the arrival of the fur trade and the influx of settlers on the Oregon Trail caused loss of life and land. Henry Spalding noted the fur trade was already causing changes to native diets by the 1830s. "The introduction of firearms frightened the game to a distance which called in the use of the horse," he wrote. "The absence of game food has been partially supplied, though at great expense and labor by an increased proportion of roots and fish." New settlers brought disease and put increasing pressure on Indian peoples' resources.[43]

In 1847, the pressure became too much, and a band of Cayuses killed Marcus and Narcissa Whitman and eleven other individuals at the Waiilatpu Mission, marking the end of the missionary period. Hostilities flared again in the 1850s. Isaac Stevens, Washington Territory's first governor and superintendent of Indian affairs, met with tribes at a treaty council in 1855. Further hostilities led to a second, more restrictive, treaty in 1856. Tribes of the Walla Walla and Yakima Valleys were forced to cede land to the US government and were relocated to reservations. The Yakama Nation moved to a reservation in the Yakima Valley, and Walla Walla area tribes relocated to northeastern Oregon on a reserve for the Confederated Tribes of the Umatilla.[44] The Nez Perce were also given a reservation. Congress ratified the treaty in 1859, opening eastern Washington for settlement.[45]

While missionaries did not achieve their goal of convincing Indians to adopt farming, their letters and other writings publicized the agricultural potential of the Pacific Northwest, ushering in a new period of settlement. Oregon Trail settlers bound for the Willamette Valley expected to find agricultural bounty and success. Instead, they found a foreign landscape devoid of familiar species. Early plantings by fur companies and missionaries, though successful, were largely symbolic. Trees provided sustenance for their owners, but early experiments did not ensure the availability of trees and fruit to successive waves of settlement. The unfamiliar landscape accentuated the distance from loved ones and their former homes. "Some of the earliest settlers in the Willamette Valley" thought that "nothing more thoroughly and painfully accentuated their isolated condition than the absence of fruit trees on their newly made farms," wrote J. R. Cardwell, president of the Oregon State Horticultural Society, in 1906.[46] Settlers in the Willamette Valley and other parts of the Pacific Northwest established orchards of their own as soon as they could obtain trees.

Although apples were an important crop, most families did not bring trees on the journey west. Saplings took up valuable room, and it was difficult to keep young trees alive on the six-month overland trip. Fortunately for settlers, an enterprising nurseryman named Henderson Luelling painstakingly transported scions, or grafted apple saplings, across the country and established nurseries that provided stock for subsequent commercial orchards. Born in North Carolina in 1809, Luelling followed the westward migration with his family, moving first to Indiana when he was thirteen, and later to Iowa before setting out on the Oregon Trail in 1847. A practiced horticulturist—his family included some of the first nurserymen in the Old Northwest—Luelling set out for Oregon with a wagon full of scions. Scions are easily transported when dormant, but they must be replanted before the tree emerges from hibernation. Since the young trees could not be held in hibernation for the duration of the voyage, Luelling planted seven hundred trees and shrubs, including twenty-one different apple cultivars, into what Luelling's biographer David Diamond calls a "botanical ark," a ten-by-four-foot box that fit atop a wagon.[47]

This was not the first attempt to transport trees to Oregon Territory. In 1845, William Barlow, another horticulturist, left Illinois with an assortment of grafted fruit trees, hoping to make his fortune in Oregon. Near Independence Rock, Barlow encountered several eastbound travelers who discouraged him from taking the trees any farther. According to the Oregonians, there were "old bearing orchards at Vancouver and in the French prairie." The most difficult portion of the road lay ahead, and the travelers doubted that he could move his wagon down the Columbia River without dismantling it. Barlow dumped the contents of his wagon. He later learned, much to his chagrin, that not only could his wagon have survived the trip, but there was also a large demand for grafted trees. Barlow made the best of the situation by planting his remaining seeds. The next fall he sold all fifteen thousand seedlings for fifteen cents apiece, a tidy sum, but a great deal less than he might have made from grafted trees. "When I say I lost $50,000.00, I mean just what I say," he later lamented. "I could have made a full monopoly of all the grafted apples and pears on the coast, as California [also] had nothing but seedlings. . . . Mr. Henderson Luelling, who crossed the plains in 1847, two years later than I did, with substantially the same kind of fruit trees . . . supplied the country as fast as he could," he concluded.[48]

Unlike Barlow, Luelling persisted in the arduous journey. He faced harsh weather, rough trails, and discouraging comments from other emigrants. The family, which included his pregnant wife, Elizabeth, and their eight children, traveled at a slow pace to preserve the trees. They soon fell behind the rest of the wagon train. Historians do not know how Luelling protected his trees from animals and inclement weather, but throughout the summer, the trees moved across mountain passes, river crossings, and arid lava beds. As the party ascended South Pass in late July, overnight temperatures dropped precipitously, costing hundreds of saplings. Luelling managed to save many, and by August some were over five feet tall. In September, the family crossed the Blue Mountains of Oregon, where they met Marcus Whitman, who had been scouting a new route from the Umatilla River to The Dalles. Whitman immediately realized the value of Luelling's trees and tried to persuade him to plant his stock at Waiilatpu, the Whitmans' mission, but Luelling declined.[49] Whitman returned to Waiilatpu after leading the party to The Dalles. While the Luellings proceeded to the Willamette Valley, Marcus Whitman met a different fate. That November, a band of Cayuse Indians killed Marcus and Narcissa Whitman, along with eleven others, at Waiilatpu.

Shortly after arriving in Oregon Territory, Luelling and his partner William Meek established an orchard at Milwaukie, Oregon, with the surviving trees. Between 1848 and 1851, they sold few trees because they lacked sufficient rootstock to graft new scions. The cherry trees Luelling transported took readily to wild rootstock, but he had little success grafting apples to the rootstock of wild Oregon crab apples (*Malus fusca*). Meanwhile Luelling purchased seeds from other emigrants to start new rootstocks. In 1850, Luelling's brother Seth arrived with more seeds, and by 1851 enough seeds had sprouted that the nursery was able to make eighteen thousand grafts. Four-foot-tall trees sold for one dollar each.[50]

Spurred by their success, the brothers started a second nursery in Salem, Oregon, in 1853 where they set out one hundred thousand seedlings and employed fourteen men as grafters.[51] By 1856, Luelling operated nurseries in four Oregon locations—Polk County, Milwaukie, Salem, and Albany—plus two nurseries in northern California and one in Steilacoom, Washington Territory.[52] The nurseries offered a wide selection of common varieties such as Red Astrachan, Summer Sweet, Gravenstein, Blue Pearmain, Gloria Mundi, Baldwin, Rambo, Winesap, Seek-No-Further, American Pippin, and Spitzenburg, all representative of the scions that survived the journey west. In addition to trees grown in his own nurseries, Luelling purchased trees from eastern nurseries and transported them to Oregon by ship.[53] The Luellings supplemented their profitable nurseries by selling fresh fruit to eager settlers whose own orchards were not yet bearing. Their first apple crop sold in Portland for one dollar per pound.

As the gold rush gripped California, Henderson Luelling opened new operations in California to profit from the "food rush" created by the demand for fresh produce in the mine fields. Miners were desperate for fresh food. "One day, while walking through the market of Marysville, I saw some pears for sale. I had seen no fruit yet in the country. All my boyish appetite was aroused," Charles D. Ferguson recalled in his account of mining in California. "I took one and ate it and was about to take another, when it occurred to me to ask how much they were apiece. It somewhat jogged the intellect when in a modest and innocent way I was told that they were only $2.50 apiece. I suddenly discovered that the one I had already eaten was sufficient for me at that time."[54] At these prices, Luelling and other Northwest growers saw the potential for profit.

During 1849, over 1,100 ships docked in San Francisco harbor bearing food and other supplies for the mines.[55] California had some established orchards, but not enough to keep up with demand. Oregon growers stepped into the void and profited from sending their agricultural surpluses south. Luelling sent his first shipment of apples, packed in boxes bound in iron straps to prevent theft, from Portland to California in

1853. He sent bimonthly shipments from Oregon to San Francisco until 1869, and his two California nurseries, which grew some of the first non-citrus grafted fruit trees in the state, supplied fruit to a burgeoning population of miners and other California emigrants.[56]

Luelling's early monopoly on nursery stock did not last; other emigrants soon started competing nurseries with their own stock. Nurseries made sizable profits because of the high demand for grafted fruit trees in the region. George Settlemier, who emigrated from California in 1850, established a nursery that eventually surpassed Luelling's in both size and variety of trees. David J. Chambers established the earliest nursery on Puget Sound with trees purchased from Luelling and Meek. Others started commercial nurseries throughout the region as well. "People in those days in this sparsely settled country knew what their neighbors were doing," J. R. Cardwell explains in his history of the Oregon fruit industry. "They came hundreds of miles from all over the country for scions and young trees to set in the little dooryard or to start an orchard so that the trees were soon distributed all over the settlements of the valley."[57]

Luelling laid the groundwork for commercial apple production in the Pacific Northwest.[58] He sold most trees to individuals in Oregon and Washington Territories for home use, but demand from the California gold rush led some Oregonians to plant commercial apple orchards. Prior to the Civil War, apples shipped to California sold for more money than any other Oregon commodity, and exports remained robust until the establishment of California orchards drove down prices. Food rushes initially brought great profits to suppliers, but profits diminished when markets became oversaturated. Apples that sold for one dollar a pound in San Francisco in 1853 brought just twenty-five cents a pound in 1856.[59] Although prices dropped, Oregon growers continued to ship apples to California well into the 1860s, especially late varieties such as Yellow Newtown Pippins and Winesaps that typically ripened after the California market had ended for the year. Without the lucrative California mining markets, however, Oregon growers had no outlet for their produce. As J. R. Cardwell explained, the downturn of California markets produced a "virtual paralysis" in the Willamette Valley:

The fruit could not be handled, and thousands of tons were left to rot, or taken to an unremunerative market, and dumped into San Francisco Bay. There was a flurry among fruit growers; outspoken, indeed clamorous expressions of alarm were heard on all sides. The timid prophesied wreck, ruin, and disaster. Newly planted orchards were given over to neglect; large tracts set aside for tree planting were left to native pasturage, or sown to wheat, oats, clover or grass. A vast, important, and promising industry was in great jeopardy.[60]

By the time Cardwell wrote his history of early orchards in 1906, the process of industrialization was under way. His presentism is on full display, as he talks of the "great jeopardy" facing the promising industry. While some farmers had commercial success, it was premature to speak of a Northwest apple industry in the 1860s or 1870s.

Early accounts of Pacific Northwest orchards are tinged with language that points toward the inevitability of industrialized apple orchards in the Pacific Northwest, perhaps because when those accounts were written, the apple industry was developing. Like other western commercial ventures, orchards were not immune from the boom-and-bust cycles of the economy. Oregon newspapers from the 1860s and 1870s rarely mentioned commercial apple production, although articles about raising apples for home use appeared regularly. Articles encouraged farmers to raise a variety of crops and livestock, not only to supply family needs but also to guard against market fluctuations. In California, though the number of orchards increased—by 1870, orchards totaled two million trees—commercial growth remained limited without access to new markets.[61]

Gold mining dwindled in California, but other mining rushes in the West produced corresponding food rushes. Gold was discovered in the Colville district in Washington Territory in 1855 and in the northern Rockies a few years later, fueling agricultural development outside the Willamette Valley. Mining booms offered the first true market for agricultural products in the inland Northwest, and as more miners arrived, stock owners drove herds from Oregon to Washington Territory to take advantage of the grass-covered Palouse hills, which were ideal for raising stock. Supplies for mining camps were shipped through Portland and conveyed by steamboat upriver to Walla Walla, Washington Territory. Walla Walla became the primary supply center for the mining camps, and stock owners and farmers capitalized on the demand created by successive mining booms. In Florence and Orofino, Idaho Territory, for example, apples sold for as much as one dollar apiece, a price that encouraged farmers to plant trees. Newcomers started growing wheat and planting orchards to meet local demands. Ransom Clark established the first nursery in Walla Walla County in 1859; two years later, Philip Ritz brought trees from Oregon. In 1862, Ritz started his own nursery about half a mile south of Walla Walla, and by 1872 he had an inventory of one million trees.[62]

As the discovery of gold in Idaho and Montana fueled agriculture in Walla Walla, it also spurred early settlement in the Yakima and Wenatchee Valleys. The mining booms of the second half of the nineteenth century boosted development across the Columbia Basin or Plateau, an arid region drained by the Columbia and Snake Rivers and characterized by basalt flows, rolling grass-covered hills, and sagebrush steppes. "Unlike California, mining was dispersed among a dozen important districts spread over a huge area," explains historic geographer Donald Meinig, "and the Columbia Plain lay between the mines and the sea, and thus became directly bound up in the whole maelstrom of development."[63] Early explorers referred to the Columbia River watershed as "the Great Columbia Desert" because the land appeared barren and seemed to offer little promise for agricultural development. In his memoir, Ezra Meeker, an early Oregon Trail settler and pioneer of the hops industry in the Yakima Valley, described his 1853 journey to present-day Yakima, Washington, a town that would later be at the center of Washington's apple industry:

> We all thought these lands were worthless, as well as the valley, not dreaming of the untold wealth the touch of water would bring out. The road lay through a forbidding sage plain, or rather an undulating country, seemingly of shifting sands and dead grass of comparatively scant growth. As the sun rose, the heat became intolerable.... The heated air trembling in the balance brought the question of whether or not something was the matter with my eyes or brain; whether this was an optical illusion, or real, became a debatable question to my mind.[64]

Writing in 1911, Meeker acknowledged that his initial impression of the land was incorrect, but one can hardly blame him for thinking the land worthless. Unlike the lush, green terrain of the Willamette Valley, central Washington did not have any visible economic or agricultural potential. Gold changed that perception. In 1855, an army scout found several gold nuggets in the Wenatchee area, luring eager prospectors. Later discoveries made on the Fraser River in British Columbia in 1858 and on the upper Clearwater River in Idaho in 1860 dwarfed the finding. Still, some decided to stay rather than chase the next big thing.

The Yakima Valley attracted cattle ranchers, eager to supply hungry miners with provisions. Most settlers focused on raising cattle. "At that time the bottom lands were covered with a dense growth of rye grass twelve feet high in many places," recalled early rancher Leonard L. Thorp, "while a luxuriant carpet of nutritious bunch grass made the sage brush hills a veritable paradise for cattle and horses."[65] Few planted fruit trees. Orchards at Ahtanum and Fort Simcoe on the Yakama Reservation date to the 1860s. Settlers knew that it was possible to grow good fruit; the problem was water, or lack thereof. Rather than constructing irrigation ditches, growers planted trees along river bottoms. This provided adequate water but also left trees susceptible to spring floods and winter frosts. According to one early local history, "the first attempts at fruit raising were ridiculed by stockmen," who thought growing fruit in the desert was a ridiculous notion.[66] Farmers lost many trees, but those that survived produced sizable crops. By the 1870s, encouraged by early success, growers started building small irrigation ditches and moving their orchards to higher ground.

As with the oldest tree in the state, there are many contenders for first apple tree in the Yakima Valley. By the turn of the twentieth century, Yakima was emerging as an apple-producing region. A strong provenance helped establish the region's identity, but defining "first" can be tricky. First tree to bear fruit? First tree from seed, or first grafted tree? First tree planted for commercial purposes? Newspapers and chroniclers of early state history did not agree on these distinctions. The trees at the Ahtanum mission are most likely the first bearing trees, although accounts differ as to when trees were planted at the mission. Newspaper accounts point to 1868 plantings on the Wiley ranch near Ahtanum as another early contender. Klickitat Peter, a Yakama Indian, is also credited with planting a commercial orchard in the Yakima Valley in 1877, although historian William Luce cites Henry Pichwell's plantings in 1887, and Fred Thompson's in 1889, as the first true commercial orchards. During the 1870s, several individuals constructed irrigation ditches, with varying degrees of success. Those who constructed ditches did not always plant orchards, but the histories of irrigation and apple cultivation are intertwined because orchards cannot exist without water.[67]

The Wenatchee Valley and fruit districts to the north also had their own firsts. Former prospectors in north-central Washington converted the flumes and channels for sluicing gold into irrigation canals for their orchards. Hiram "Okanogan" Smith is credited with planting the first trees in the Wenatchee district. Smith came to north-central Washington sometime after 1848. He tried his hand at mining, and when that failed, he opened a trading post. Accounts vary, but he planted his first trees in 1854 or 1858. After Smith was elected to the Washington territorial legislature in 1865, he brought several small apple trees from Olympia to his claim in Oroville, Washington Territory. While Smith is credited with planting the first trees, Philip Miller is credited with planting the first commercial orchard, in Wenatchee in 1872. Miller and his brother purchased trees from White Salmon, Washington Territory, on the north bank of the Columbia River, across from Hood River, Oregon, a place that would become one of Oregon's primary fruit districts. Miller likely also purchased trees from The Dalles, Oregon, and Walla Walla.[68]

In the examination of firsts, the distinction between trees planted for subsistence and those planted for commercial purposes is important. Most settlers in the Pacific Northwest planted trees for home use, as was common on farms across the country. The first trees planted for these purposes, like those planted by John Chapman and earlier generations of farmers in the Old Northwest, mark the beginnings of settlement. More than being proof of homestead claims, orchards marked the permanence of America's presence and advertised that settlers were there to stay. In contrast with the Jeffersonian ideal of the yeoman farmer, commercial orchards pointed to a different path, one of capitalistic development that tied growers to national and global markets. Pacific Northwest residents valued both narratives: the independent, democratic nature of small farms and the desire for greater economic success.

The Northwest's early attempts at commercial production were minor compared to those of New York, the Shenandoah Valley, or California.

Local markets were relatively small, and there was no efficient way to transport apple crops out of the region. Until the mid-1880s, Walla Walla lay at the center of commercial activity in Washington Territory thanks to its proximity to transportation networks. Located near the Columbia River, the town had steamboat access to Portland to the west, and it was home to the first railroad in the territory. Because of its direct connection with Portland and the coast, Walla Walla served as a supply center for the mining booms to the north and east.

Despite early optimism, farmers in the Walla Walla Valley were plagued with the same problems their neighbors in the Willamette Valley had faced a decade earlier: the demise of mining threatened their fruit markets. Without booming mining towns, farmers had little outlet for their produce. Local markets could not absorb the loss in sales, and it was difficult to ship fruit long distances. Then came the infamous winter of 1883. Temperatures dropped to minus twenty-nine degrees Fahrenheit, devastating orchards. Many growers decided that replanting was not worth the effort. Walla Walla remained a small but important fruit-growing district into the twentieth century. In 1900, Walla Walla pioneer Dr. Nelson G. Blalock boasted the largest orchard in the state at five hundred acres.[69]

Although the bottom dropped out of the market after each successive gold rush, some remained hopeful that apples could be a viable commercial commodity for the Northwest and looked to the Pacific Rim for new markets. An 1869 article in the *Albany State Rights Democrat* lamented that many orchards had decayed since the "orchard mania" of the previous years had passed. "Apple orchards are neglected because apples are cheap," the author wrote. "People acting upon the unreasonable presumption that it will always remain so, are virtually surrendering one of the most pleasant and profitable branches of industry." The author argued that even though prices fluctuated, apples were still an important commodity and "should always be one of the staple products of Oregon," especially considering the potential development of a northern transcontinental railroad.[70] In 1869, rail connections lay several years in the future, and transportation was no guarantee of viable markets for Northwest fruit. Commercial growers had good reason for abandoning their orchards and moving on to other pursuits.

The first apple tree planted at Fort Vancouver demonstrated that fruit trees could thrive in the Northwest, but whether a commercial industry could thrive remained to be seen. Land east of the Cascades had many natural advantages—sunny summer days, good soil, and relatively few pests and diseases compared to other commercial regions in the nation. Natural advantages amounted to little without consumer markets and irrigation. In the 1880s, markets remained local. Steamboats and stretches of portage rail connected communities along the Columbia and Snake Rivers, but much of the rest of Washington Territory was accessible only by mule or wagon. Apples grown in the few commercial orchards in the territory did not travel far. While many settlers had constructed small irrigation ditches for subsistence orchards, the large-scale irrigation systems needed for commercial production were expensive to construct and hard to justify given the lack of markets. Chroniclers of the first trees argued that the apple industry was preordained because of Washington's natural advantages. Instead, in the 1880s and 1890s the arrival of rail lines coupled with an influx of capital from outside investors revived commercial orchards and brought new industrial growth.

CHAPTER 2

If You Build It, They Will Come
Railroads, Irrigation, and Early Settlement

The wagon ride from the train station in Mabton, Washington, to Sunnyside, Washington, was less than ten miles, but for ten-year-old Roscoe Sheller, it was the culmination of a momentous journey. In 1898, Sheller and his parents left a prosperous hardware store in Iowa to seek their fortune in the deserts of central Washington at the Christian Cooperative Colony. Colonists hoped to create a utopian society from the ruins of an abandoned townsite called Sunnyside. Lured by the prospect of good farmland, mild winters, and plenty of sunshine, Sheller's father purchased an eighty-acre farm with an established orchard. Mr. Wentworth, the land's owner, sold out because his wife refused to move into what she termed "a Godforsaken Dust Hole." Who could blame her: Wentworth's house was a run-down shack, infested with bedbugs and coated in fine desert dust known locally as "blowsand." Wentworth had not bothered to clear the land between each row of trees, leaving the orchard dotted with sagebrush. Mr. Sheller was far more optimistic about the farm's prospects than Mrs. Wentworth. He wrote for his wife and son to join him on what was to be their "Rainbow's End." Fortunately for Mr. Sheller, Mrs. Sheller overcame her initial disappointment in the farm and made the best of the situation.[1]

By the 1920s, Yakima and Wenatchee vied for the title of "Apple Capital of the World," but at the turn of the twentieth century, they were still sparsely populated. The arrival of rail transportation and the construction of irrigation canals prompted new interest in settlement. Like other families, the Shellers moved to central Washington looking for new opportunities. Prior to the 1880s, most American immigrants overlooked central Washington in favor of the Willamette Valley, the Puget Sound, or the Walla Walla Valley. Early travelers in the Pacific Northwest referred to the area east of the Cascade Range as "the Great Columbia Desert."[2] The Columbia Basin, bisected by the Columbia River, is covered in basalt flows carved by glaciers and massive floods from ancient Lake Missoula. The landscape, in its natural state, is dominated by bunchgrass and sagebrush. In north-central Washington, the Wenatchee Valley follows the contours of the Columbia River with branches of lowlands along the Columbia's tributaries. The Yakima Valley, comprising an upper and a lower valley, is broader. The Columbia Basin lies in the rain shadow of the Cascade Range. The west side of the mountains receives ample rainfall, so much that early farmers struggled to beat back native vegetation. East of the Cascades, however, rainfall decreases dramatically. Mrs. Sheller would have had few opportunities to see real rainbows at "Rainbow's End." Depending on the location, most of the Columbia Basin received ten to twenty inches of rain per year. Early settlers were not wrong in their assessment of the area as a desert. Without irrigation, the arid valleys of central Washington had no obvious agricultural potential. Ranchers had some success, but by the 1880s, the land was overgrazed.[3] Though early settlers overlooked the region, by the 1880s, some were starting to rethink its potential. The region's soil, enriched from alluvial deposits and volcanic ash, was nonalkaline and drained well.[4] It proved to be quite productive with the addition of water. Orchards and gardens grown by settlers and by Indians on the Yakama Reservation demonstrated the fertility of the soil and encouraged investment in irrigation.

Washington's apple industry arose in the 1890s as large-scale irrigation projects, land speculation, and rail transportation converged. Irrigation systems, financed first by railroads and private investors and later by the federal government, provided the water to make agriculture possible. Real estate promoters worked with railroads and government officials to sell land and attract settlers. Railroads provided land, capital, and connections to distant markets for surplus produce. In theory, railroads, irrigation companies, and landowners worked toward the same goal—to turn the desert into an economically productive landscape. The reality was more complicated. Rather than serving existing markets, investors built expensive railroad and irrigation systems in advance of actual need. When private companies failed to profit from expensive irrigation infrastructure, the Northern Pacific and Great Northern Railways tried to salvage projects because railroad profits depended on settlers' success. Instead of the easy profits and independence promised by real estate agents, settlers found half-built irrigation systems and corporate entanglement. Many unsuspecting white-collar workers found their dreams quickly dashed. The transformation of desert lands into industrial orchards is a story of good intentions, greed, and an audacious vision for America's future.

Before the arrival of the railroads, central Washington was geographically isolated. The imposing Cascade Range lay to the west and arid scablands to the east. Stage service connected Yakima and Wenatchee to neighboring towns, and a ferry came up to Wenatchee once a week. As local land promoter Arthur Gunn complained, "The boat is poor and the service is bad, yet it is all there is."[5] Local promoters in Yakima and Wenatchee lamented the lack of transportation and schemed to bring rail service to their towns. Justifying rail service was a catch-22. Central Washington lacked the population and industry to warrant rail connections, but without rail connections, the population and commerce would not expand. As the Northern Pacific and Great Northern built mainline transcontinental routes through Washington, residents had no guarantee that the railroads would build through their townsites. Local promoters used all the connections at their disposal to ensure that the rails came to them, with mixed results. In Yakima, disputes over the Northern Pacific's land grant and right-of-way complicated construction. After town leaders refused to donate land for a station and right-of-way, the railroad platted a new townsite, North Yakima, four miles north. Though tracks passed through Yakima, trains did not stop. Washington Territory sued the Northern Pacific to force it to build a depot at Yakima. The territory won its case, but by that point, many residents had taken the Northern Pacific up on its offer of free lots in the new town.[6] Residents had mixed feelings about the move. Some resented the railroad's tactics, while others believed the move to the new town was necessary to meet growing infrastructure needs.[7]

Similarly, the Great Northern chose to build a mile south of Wenatchee, leaving the four-year-old town isolated. Real estate speculation along the line created complications. The Wenatchee Development Company (WDC), started by Seattle real estate investors but owned in part by James J. Hill of the Great Northern, speculated on land at the new townsite, while competing real estate companies had invested in the original townsite. Fearful of residents' reactions, the WDC and the Great Northern withheld the particulars of the proposed route and Hill's connection to the new townsite.[8] When the new town location was finally announced, early Washington historian Lindley M. Hull remarked that "a feeling of bitterness engendered that deeply stirred the emotions of the entire community."[9] In an effort to mend relationships, the WDC offered new lots to all the establishments willing to move to the new townsite.

Although local boosters took credit for bringing rail service to Yakima in 1885 and Wenatchee in 1893, the railroads chose those routes because they lay between the major destinations of Seattle, Spokane, and Walla Walla. By the 1880s, settlers had already claimed much of Washington's prime, nonirrigated farmland. The easternmost counties of Washington received just enough rainfall to make dryland wheat farming possible, and farmers had expanded north from Walla Walla into the rolling hills of the Palouse. The Northern Pacific connected the wheat-rich Walla Walla Valley to Puget Sound via Yakima. At the same time, the Great Northern connected Spokane, growing because of silver mines in northern Idaho and wheat farming in the Palouse, with Seattle via the Wenatchee Valley.

Railroads could make or break a town. In addition to transportation, railroads brought an influx of capital that financed infrastructure for local industry. Railroads had a vested interest in helping towns succeed because they needed revenue from freight and passengers. As one early promoter wrote, "It is worth more to the railways and the country to get one man to buy a farm and settle in Willamette Valley, than for us to haul fifty people through the west."[10] The same held true in central Washington. Profitable farms that supplied national and international markets led to an increased need for transportation, which in turn led to more revenue for railroad companies.

In 1870, there was one principal transcontinental route. By 1900, there were five. Railroad companies, hoping to generate profit for their shareholders, developed land along their lines through a variety of corporate ventures. Railroads did not leave the generation of freight to chance.

They assessed land for its economic potential and steered potential settlers into specific activities. Land sales from government grants provided one important source of revenue. The US government granted the Northern Pacific forty million acres, checkered along the rail line in alternating square-mile sections.[11] While the Great Northern received no land grants, it too invested in real estate. Both companies profited from direct land sales and from streams of freight revenue from farming, logging, and other economic enterprises. In some cases, the railroads started subsidiary corporations, or they invested in local corporations, becoming stockholders rather than owners. In other cases, railroad executives, as private individuals, purchased stock or founded companies. Regardless of the legal framework used to manage assets, many western companies could trace some connection to a railroad. Though Yakima and Wenatchee had transportation, they still lacked irrigation infrastructure to turn desert parcels into profitable farms, a problem the railroads could not afford to ignore. Railroads rarely held direct ownership of irrigation companies, but they did invest in several private irrigation ventures. Western railroads wanted irrigation to succeed.

On a national level, irrigated land offered a solution to the social and economic problems of crowded eastern cities. Between 1870 and the 1890s, the US population increased over 60 percent, while urban populations grew 123 percent, thanks to immigration and the labor demands created by industrialization.[12] Traditionally, Americans viewed the West as a safety valve for overpopulated cities that prevented some of the civic and labor unrest that plagued Europe. That changed when the superintendent of the 1890 census announced, "The unsettled area has been so broken into by isolated bodies of settlement that there can hardly be said to be a frontier line." In his famous essay "The Significance of the Frontier in American History," presented at the 1893 World's Columbian Exposition in Chicago, historian Frederick Jackson Turner argued that the frontier significantly shaped the American character, causing Americans to undergo a "perennial rebirth" at each new frontier. Westward expansion provided new economic, social, cultural, and intellectual opportunities.[13] For decades, historians have debated the merits of Turner's argument, but for all its flaws, it reflected prevailing cultural beliefs and fears of the time. Without a frontier, where would America turn its energy?

Imperialism provided one outlet for America's energy, and irrigation provided another. The United States did not need overseas imperialism, some argued, because it still had plenty of work to do within its own borders. The frontier was not really "closed." Available arable land had been settled, but there was still plenty of arid land in the West, ready for settlement and economic exploitation. As a writer for the *San Francisco Call* opined, "It will cost us more time, more money, and more labor to establish order in the Philippines than to irrigate the 70,000,000 acres of Western land."[14] Rather than directing America's energies overseas, supporters argued that irrigating the arid West provided a new safety valve. "The wage earners of the East want wider fields for labor. The manufacturers of the East want new markets for their wares," explained California lawyer and national irrigation advocate George H. Maxwell. "Where can either get what they want so fully as by the development of the great arid West which is capable, with irrigation for its irrigable lands, of sustaining a greater population than the whole United States holds today."[15] Desert lands in their natural state were not valued because of an apparent lack of economic use, but with water, these lands could be "reclaimed" and settled, turning wage earners into land owners and consumers of manufactured goods.

Proponents of irrigation tapped into cultural fears about the frontier. At the turn of the century, America was amid a crisis of manliness. Some worried that without a frontier, American men would lose their vitality and vigor. Supporters contended that farms built strong men and provided an antidote to the unwholesome effects of city life. Irrigation advocates targeted the professional management class that had arisen to support America's growing industrial machine. Farms built the last generation of business leaders. Opening land to irrigation provided the opportunity to instill similar values in the next generation, and to restore the vigor of those run down by city life. In a 1914 report, the Washington Irrigation Institute noted that many of the nation's top business leaders had been raised on farms, and "many nerve-racked, broken down, business and professional men have regained their health by getting back to the farm."[16] They framed irrigation as a democratic form of land use because farms would stay small and be available to many people. Irrigation systems required constant monitoring and specialized knowledge;

therefore, owners would have to be educated and present to oversee their systems, limiting farm sizes to what a single farmer could manage. The fact that white-collar workers lacked farming experience, or that absentee owners could hire others to manage their farms, did not factor into supporters' arguments.

Although irrigation supporters made persuasive arguments, they still lacked financial backing. Early irrigation experiments demonstrated the richness of central Washington's land, leading land speculators, investors, and communities to construct larger irrigation systems to bring more land under cultivation. Local entrepreneurs founded irrigation companies in dry locations across the state including Kennewick, Clarkston, Yakima, Sunnyside, Burbank, and Wenatchee.[17] Businesspeople established companies with funds from local water subscriptions, land sales, and investment partners from Seattle, Tacoma, and Spokane, who in turn obtained funding from eastern investors. The small, personal irrigation ditches of the 1870s transformed by the 1890s into a growing industry of locally owned corporations backed by outside investors. Companies promised steady water supplies and offered complex plans for irrigating more acreage, which was then sold to prospective orchardists.

Initial success was short lived. Private investors sank millions into irrigation schemes across the West, but it was difficult to make a profit from irrigation. Systems were expensive to construct and required ongoing maintenance. Irrigators planned to recoup costs from water users' subscriptions. Unsurprisingly, companies had trouble finding enough subscribers. Few people wanted to take a chance on unproven irrigation ditches or buy land when water was a mere promise. A few private companies eked out profits through land sales, but most were losing ventures that cut their losses before construction was complete. The financial Panic of 1893 further limited the willingness of private investors to support irrigation projects. When private irrigation companies failed, they left settlers high and dry.

Large-scale irrigation projects required capital: funds from private investors or money from state and federal coffers. The railroads, a major source of funding, watched these developments closely. The corporate papers of the Great Northern and Northern Pacific reveal a tangle of subsidiary corporations and nominally "independent" corporations with boards of directors consisting of railroad officials. Railroads and their subsidiaries owned and invested in a variety of western industries, but they were reluctant to finance irrigation directly. The Panic of 1893 hurt corporate finances, and the Populist Party was pressuring the government to address the problem of monopolies. Fearful that direct financing would lead to accusations of monopolies, railroads found other ways to invest. Central Washington provides examples of both direct and indirect financing. The Northern Pacific and the Great Northern, as well as officials from both companies, invested in private irrigation companies, keeping irrigation investments separate from the railroad, at least on paper. Both railroads also took control of irrigation companies after private efforts failed. As farmers settled the Yakima and Wenatchee Valleys in the 1890s and early 1900s, private irrigation companies continued to sell real estate and water rights. Some speculators sold land to prospective buyers and cut their losses before completing irrigation canals. Others, including those financed by the railroads, genuinely wanted their irrigation projects to thrive. Success was measured not only by corporate profits but by how many farmers settled the land.

Railroads and local town boosters used newly constructed irrigation projects to attract settlers to the thinly populated Yakima and Wenatchee Valleys. The mere suggestion of a new canal was often enough to set off rampant land speculation, but building functional systems was challenging, as projects in Yakima and Wenatchee demonstrated. The Yakima Land and Canal Company was formed in 1889 by Walter N. Granger and a group of St. Paul investors. Originally from New York, Granger had previous experience with several irrigation projects in Montana. After surveying the site, the company purchased land from the Northern Pacific. At the same time, the Northern Pacific acquired two-thirds of the stock in the new irrigation company. Though the irrigation company technically owned the land, the Northern Pacific was effectively in control.[18] In 1892, Thomas Oakes, president of the Northern Pacific, offered Granger an option on ninety thousand acres in the Yakima Valley at a price of $1.25 an acre. All Granger had to do was supply the water. Oakes and Granger consolidated their interests into a new venture, the Northern Pacific, Yakima, and Kittitas Irrigation Company. Granger remained as vice president, while Paul Schulze, head of the Northern Pacific Department of

Agriculture, became president. This time, they organized two corporate entities, one for the irrigation project and one for real estate development in two towns—Sunnyside and Zillah, the latter named after Oakes's daughter. The company planned to construct 550 miles of canals and laterals to irrigate forty thousand acres. Construction commenced in 1891, and by 1893, the canal, known as the Sunnyside Canal, had reached Sunnyside. Unfortunately, the Panic of 1893 took a toll on the company's finances. The Northern Pacific filed for bankruptcy and could not aid the failing companies. Unbeknown to Granger and other investors, Schulze had embezzled company stocks to finance personal expenses. Schulze left the company in disgrace and committed suicide in April 1895. Granger, facing a foreclosure suit, could not save either company. The Christian Cooperative Colony purchased the Sunnyside townsite, and in 1900 new investors revived the irrigation company as the Washington Irrigation Company, with Granger as manager. By 1905 the company operated over seven hundred miles of canals and laterals that watered thirty-six thousand acres, the largest irrigation project in the valley.[19]

Meanwhile in Wenatchee, rumors of railroad construction fueled speculation in irrigation companies. Seattle investor Judge Thomas Burke founded two land companies in Wenatchee, one at the original townsite and one at the new townsite. In November 1891, Burke merged the two holdings into a single company, the Wenatchee Development Company. Burke convinced Great Northern president James J. Hill to buy one-fourth interest in the company. "I need not tell you that it assures the future of Wenatchee," wrote Burke to a colleague. Several Great Northern executives also purchased stock in the company upon Hill's recommendation.[20]

Without water, Wenatchee Development Company lands had little value. In 1896, Jacob Shotwell approached Arthur Gunn, land agent for the Wenatchee Development Company, about extending the ditch he and his brother Harvey, both civil engineers, had constructed in the late 1880s. Shotwell's son later recalled that his father built five miles of ditch with assistance only "from W. E. Stevens, who furnished his groceries and took his pay in a water right for his land."[21] Gunn and Shotwell incorporated the Wenatchee Water Power Company and ten days later had secured an agreement with the Wenatchee Development Company, exchanging water rights for land.[22] Through his connection with Burke,

Gunn arranged to meet Hill in St. Paul, Minnesota. Hill agreed to advance the Water Power Company a $12,000 bond. "Hill evinces a decided desire, I believe, to aid the Wenatchee Valley," Gunn wrote Burke after the meeting, but he wished to conceal the Great Northern's involvement with the company so the project would appear "to stem from grassroots action and be more palatable" to the town.[23] When news of Hill's investment in the Water Power Company became public, it indeed met with mixed reviews. The prospect of the ditch excited most people, but Gunn believed that some opposed it "because it will not line their own pockets."[24]

The Water Power Company quickly spent most of its funds purchasing rights-of-way for the canal. Neither Gunn nor Burke was able to keep the company solvent. Understanding the importance of irrigation to developing lands in Wenatchee, the Great Northern reluctantly purchased the Water Power Company in 1898, the same year the ditch, known locally as the "Gunn Ditch," was completed. The company was organized under the auspices of its subsidiary the Lake Superior Company, which also held Great Northern's shares in the Wenatchee Development Company.[25] As historian Claire Strom notes, subsidiaries like the Lake Superior Company were common. Big business and monopolies came under attack in the 1890s, and the Sherman Antitrust Act, passed in 1890, fed corporations' fears of regulation. Hill had already come under fire in 1895 as part of a proposed merger between the Great Northern and the Northern Pacific. Subsidiaries hid companies' "involvement in the development of businesses integral to their success."[26] In the case of Wenatchee, the Development Company and the Water Power Company were integral to the prosperity of the Great Northern in central Washington. The Great Northern operated the Water Power Company at a loss until 1911, though it did see some indirect returns. "Its results from an irrigation (not a financial) standpoint probably made the other projects possible, resulting in a large traffic for our company," reflected Great Northern comptroller Robert Farrington in a letter to James Hill regarding the sale. "The loss . . . is a comparatively small amount for the company to pay for the results obtained."[27]

Private investors operated several other irrigation companies in central Washington. In 1901, Wenatchee business owners hired engineer William T. Clark to survey a new canal on the Wenatchee River. Clark, who had just finished surveying a canal in Yakima, found a financial backer in Portland, Oregon, and formed the Wenatchee Canal Company.[28] The Wenatchee Development Company contracted with Clark to provide water to at least six thousand acres of company lands in return for an annual water-use fee of $1.50 per acre.[29] The agreement promised a steady supply of water for Development Company lands, thereby increasing their value. Shortly thereafter, the Wenatchee Development Company agents recommended increasing the price of town lots by 25 percent because of the proposed canal.[30] Clark completed the canal, known as the "High-Line," in 1904. Like other early irrigation companies, it went bankrupt, and in 1915 it was later reorganized as the Wenatchee Reclamation District, a public utility governed by a board of commissioners in Chelan County.[31]

By the 1910s, many private irrigation companies started in the 1880s and 1890s had become public irrigation districts. High maintenance costs forced several private companies into bankruptcy and left farmers to take matters into their own hands. The federal government became involved with irrigation with the passage of the Newlands Reclamation Act in 1902, but the Reclamation Service was reluctant to take on projects in Washington because the state, as Reclamation Service director Frederick H. Newell argued, was "well covered with irrigation systems." The government investigated potential irrigation sites in the Wenatchee-Okanogan region, but it deemed them to be useless or of limited potential. In the Yakima Valley, the Reclamation Service did not want to fight private interests and contended that too much land was in private hands to justify government intervention. Conflict over water rights also slowed federal intervention, particularly on the Yakama Reservation. The federal government, spurred by white settlers who had purchased reservation lands, initially planned to open much of the reservation for settlement and tried to convince the Yakamas to sign away their water rights. The Yakamas refused. Local farmer Lucullus Virgil McWhorter helped publicize the Indians' cause. The government eventually gave up its plan and agreed to irrigate Indian farms. The Wapato Project, managed by the Bureau of Indian Affairs, watered 71,104 acres on the Yakama Reservation at Wapato. Similarly, the Reclamation Service eventually reversed its decision about the Yakima Valley thanks to lobbying by Washington legislators. In 1905, the Washington Irrigation Company sold the Sunnyside

Canal, which watered 85,290 acres, to the government for $640,000. By 1922, private companies watered 29 percent of irrigated land in the Yakima Valley, publicly held irrigation districts watered 24 percent, and government projects 47 percent.[32]

Despite the financial failures of private irrigation companies, developers argued that anyone could find success in central Washington's newly irrigated landscape. Irrigation did not guarantee farmers' financial future, but it raised land values more than any other improvement, especially if farmers grew the right crops. "As soon as water is put on this formerly worthless land it rises in value to a figure several times what the best non-irrigated land would bring," wrote James J. Hill in his 1910 book *Highways of Progress*, "prices justified by the profits from special crops of early fruits, melons, berries or vegetables to supply high-priced markets."[33] In the early 1900s, according to *Better Fruit*, the preeminent horticultural journal in the Pacific Northwest, unimproved irrigated acreage in Wenatchee sold for $300 to $500 per acre. Land planted with fruit trees, a specialty crop, sold for $700 to $1,000 per acre depending on the age of the orchard. Compared to the price of nonirrigated wheatland acreage, which sold for as little as $10 per acre, irrigated land was profitable for real estate companies but an expensive investment for farmers. Boosters argued that it was well worth the expense, citing profits of up to $1,000 per acre, far above typical orchard returns of $275 per acre.[34]

By the time the Shellers emigrated to Washington, many eager and often inexperienced settlers had purchased plots of land from railroads and real estate developers, lured by glossy brochures promising prosperity. The Shellers' experience in Washington was not unique. All the major transcontinental railroads had immigration departments to advertise land along their lines to prospective settlers. Local chamber of commerce leaders and real estate developers throughout the West worked with railroad sales agents to promote land sales through attractive photograph-laden advertising brochures. Advertising materials for western lands, regardless of location, shared similar themes. Communities competed for settlers and capital by claiming to have the most productive land, the friendliest citizens, and the closest ties to railroads. Brochures emphasized the land's fertility and the health and civility of local communities. In his study of Northern Pacific Railway advertisements in

Minnesota and the Dakotas in the 1890s and early 1900s, Sig Mickelson found that the most cited feature was land prices and values, followed by proximity to markets, rail lines, schools, and churches.[35] In essence, brochures told buyers how much land would cost, how much profit they could make, and what kind of community existed.

What worked to attract farmers to the Dakotas also worked to attract prospective orchardists to Washington. Brochures attested to each town's prosperity through glossy black-and-white photographs of multistory Victorian houses, schools, churches, and main streets lined with brick buildings and electric streetcars. One brochure produced by the North Yakima Commercial Club in 1912 noted not only the town's population—14,082 in 1910—but also postal receipts, bank deposits, and prominent brick and stone buildings as markers of economic success. It lauded the citizens of North Yakima for their "magnetic energy, vitality, optimism and abundant well-being" and their "confidence in the future that finds its warrant in the truly remarkable growth it has made and the prosperity it now enjoys."[36] How could one resist a town with such a positive outlook on the future? The articles of incorporation from the Wenatchee Investment Company illustrate the lengths to which real estate companies went to sell lots and increase property values. The founding charter allowed the company to lay out the townsite, build streets and bridges, purchase hotels, and construct dams, irrigation ditches, ferries, and a street railway.[37] More than a simple real estate company, the corporation engaged in the business of transplanting American civilization to a new environment.

While western land brochures shared many similarities, irrigated lands required a slightly different approach. "Irrigation was unfamiliar to most Americans," writes historian G. Thomas Edwards. Because of this, promoters had to sell prospective buyers on the idea of irrigation.[38] The myth of the garden, a popular theme in late nineteenth- and early twentieth-century America, was a continuation of Manifest Destiny. Boosters embraced the biblical injunction to subdue the land and be fruitful, and they used complex and frequently contradictory images to describe their landscape, mixing, as Mark Fiege explains, "organic and mechanical, female and male, secular and divine metaphors."[39] Metaphors abound in promotional literature. One particularly florid brochure for Granger, Washington, likened its irrigation project to the great cradles of civilization: the valleys of the Nile, Indus, and Euphrates. "The Supreme Ruler of the Universe never intended that man should depend entirely on rain to nourish his crops," it explained. "Truly Irrigation is the Handmaiden of Husbandry."[40] According to boosters, irrigation transformed the desert from "uncultivated prairies" to "acre after acre of broad cultivated domains, rich in fruit, hops, grain, and vegetables of every description," as one writer in the *Yakima Herald* proclaimed.[41]

Irrigation represented not only the ordered construction of the natural landscape, but the creation of new, wholesome communities populated by strong, healthy, and moral individuals. Photographs of budding trees, happy children, and tidy farmhouses provided visual evidence of the claims made in promotional brochures. Comically doctored photographs showed plump children next to oversized fruit to emphasize the health and fertility of the irrigated landscape. Many brochures for the Yakima Valley featured photographs by Seattle-based photographer and Yakima orchard owner Asahel Curtis. Curtis's photos of overladen trees, piles of fruit boxes, and stately homes highlighted the prosperity of Yakima's newly irrigated lands.[42] Boosters designed promotional literature to entice settlers to newly irrigated townships. While many brochures showcased fantastical images and prose, others contained straightforward, practical information for potential home seekers about such things as economic opportunities and community life. Promoters sold purchasers a lifestyle rooted in a modern take on Jeffersonian agrarianism, casting small farmers as businesspeople who could achieve independence and wealth through modern scientific farm management. Anyone with a keen business mind and a willingness to learn could make a fortune in the irrigated West.[43]

Profits from land sales were foremost in the minds of boosters. They were not interested in just any settlers; they aimed advertising at novice farmers—teachers, lawyers, doctors, and other professionals who had little farming experience. They had to convince buyers that they could learn how to farm. Towns desired upstanding citizens who could make positive contributions to growing communities; farming skills could be acquired, but a strong moral character could not. Town booster Walter Granger opined that newcomers had to "all be prosperous farmers where they came from and have brought with them ample means for the immediate improvement of the land."[44] Though not explicitly stated, the subtext is clear—only middle-class, native-born, white applicants need apply. Granger "had no intentions of his valley's serving as a haven for the discontented or the dispossessed," writes historian W. Thomas White. "Rather he looked forward to the creation of a moral, affluent society composed of already successful farmers who could assure the future of the Yakima Valley."[45]

Granger was not alone in his views on settlement. Brochures for irrigated orchard lands in California, Oregon, and British Columbia also asserted that irrigated farming was reserved for "higher" classes of people, or, as one British Columbia brochure noted, "a refined cultured class of people—the finest class of people on Earth."[46] Though race is not mentioned, the meaning is clear. Pseudoscientific theories like social Darwinism, with its emphasis on racial hierarchies, underlay conceptions about who was best suited to inhabit irrigated lands. Most landowners in central Washington were either native-born whites or immigrants who had been in the United States for several years and had acculturated to American life.[47] Japanese farmers established communities in Hood River, Oregon, and Wapato, Washington, in the Yakima Valley. By 1915, nearly five hundred Japanese immigrants had settled the Yakima Valley, where many leased or owned farms on the Yakama Indian Reservation. In the 1920s, Oregon and Washington passed laws prohibiting aliens from owning land. Consequently, many Japanese farmers lost their land or were forced to enter illegal leases.[48] Rather than stating their racial views explicitly, boosters focused on values that enabled settlers to transform the landscape. "The fact is, to Washington was transplanted all the sterling cardinal virtues—energy, industry, thrift, courage, respect for law, for women, and the home," observed an agriculturist who visited eastern Washington in 1908.[49] This view of farmers stifled diversity, but it also enforced narrow community standards that later helped growers conform to farming practices.

From the beginning, boosters emphasized the profits to be made from irrigated specialty crops, especially fruit, which, like irrigation, required specialized knowledge. Grain crops, such as wheat, grew more cheaply on dryland farms. Irrigated grain from central Washington could not compete with grain from the dryland farms of the Walla Walla Valley and Palouse region of eastern Washington, some of the best wheatland in the world. Instead, boosters praised the land's ability to produce the finest fruits and vegetables with little effort, and its proximity to Washington's growing urban markets. "This land is too valuable to be given up to grain," a newspaper reporter wrote in the *Yakima Herald*. "The railroads take the garden stuff raised in the Yakima Valley to the coast cities in a day, and there is never a time, from the middle of June to the end of October when the market is slow."[50] Although the writer overstated the ease of transporting and selling produce, his rhetoric exemplified the type of articles printed in local newspapers, agricultural trade publications, railroad literature, and locally produced town promotional literature.

Promises of easy wealth pervaded the pages of real estate brochures. Orchardist Charles Keiser, a transplant from Illinois, purchased an orchard in 1904 after seeing a brochure with the slogan "The Wenatchee Valley, Where Dollars Grow on Trees!" Keiser later recalled, "Somehow I had the delightful delusion that all an orchardist had to do was to pick apples in the fall and sit around the rest of the year."[51] One can hardly blame him for that conception. While Keiser ascribed the origin of the slogan to Leonard Fowler, editor of the *Wenatchee Republic*, many advertisers in Wenatchee and Yakima used this imagery. The cover of a brochure advertising the Yakima Valley features a drawing of a well-dressed man literally picking round, gold dollars off a fruit tree, while his wife and small daughter sit on the ground below, packing the orbs into an apple box.[52]

Apples had an advantage over other specialty crops because of their long storage time. With proper storage, fresh apples lasted for several months, and they were hardy enough to ship in the crude refrigerated railcars available in the early twentieth century. Settlers throughout the Northwest grew a wide variety of fruit. Many types, including berries, apples, and pears, grew exceedingly well west of the Cascades, and growers had great hopes for the region's potential. Berries and cherries developed commercially, but apples did not. Agricultural production competed with other, more lucrative industries. According to *Better Fruit*, the magazine of the Northwest Fruit Growers' Association, "Few people appreciate the fact that very little of the soil of Western Oregon and Washington is cultivated. Its people have been so busy clearing forests,

Brochures, like this one for Granger, Washington, circa 1910, touted the economic potential of orchards. *Collections of the Yakima Valley Museum.*

cutting lumber, catching and canning fish, besides building railroads and constructing houses that they have not had time to devote to agricultural pursuits." In central Washington, by contrast, economic opportunities were more limited. It was expensive to construct and maintain irrigation systems. Growers had to produce crops with high returns.[53] The region's fertile volcanic soils, warm summer temperatures, and, surprisingly, its lack of moisture, which discouraged fungi, scabs, and other moisture-related diseases, made apples and other fruit commercially viable crops.

Specialty crops offered the highest potential for return, but in much of the West, irrigation canals watered nonspecialty crops. This, writes historian Donald Worster, was one of the failures of western irrigation. Farmers planted 75 percent of irrigated land in "alfalfa, wheat, cotton, and pasture grasses . . . products that could be produced more cheaply elsewhere."[54] There were exceptions, such as citrus orchards in California, but most irrigated lands failed to live up to their full economic potential. Central Washington's boosters wanted to avoid this fate. They had a grander vision for the region that centered on high-value fruit crops. Settlers did plant alfalfa and other low-value crops in the early years while orchards matured, but such crops were never the end goal.

Boosters painted a compelling picture of central Washington's irrigated lands, but they failed to explain the challenges of working in an arid, irrigated landscape. Settlers soon discovered a vast gap between glossy real estate brochures and the realities of irrigated agriculture. Early settlers found sagebrush instead of verdant gardens. Worster writes that Americans were not prepared for the difficult consequences of irrigation, namely that far fewer people benefited from irrigation systems than expected. Systems "had to be organized into tight hierarchical and corporate entities which violated traditional rural culture."[55] This ran counter to the promises of easy wealth and independence promised in promotional literature. Irrigated farming required cooperation and specialized knowledge. Not only did farmers have to work with others in their irrigation districts to manage irrigation systems, but they also had to learn how to grow crops within the parameters of an irrigated system. Help came from land-grant colleges, such as Washington State College, founded in 1890. Although WSC did not establish a field research station in central Washington until 1937, research conducted by the college provided valuable information. Early cooperatives, such as the Northwest Fruit Growers' Association, founded in Hood River, Oregon, in 1894, disseminated horticultural information through publications, workshops, and grower meetings. Growers who weathered the first few years of orchard operation hoped for handsome returns, but a poor crop or low prices in a glut market might still lead to foreclosure. Farmers quickly learned that dollars did not grow on trees, and that success came at the expense of full independence.

Even successful families, such as the Shellers, struggled in the early years. Arriving in Sunnyside full of optimism for their new life, Mrs. Sheller initially referred to her anticipated western home as "Rainbow's End," a term she quickly abandoned after disembarking from the train in central Washington. It was difficult for her to remain enthusiastic when confronted with the reality of their new homestead. The house was a small, filthy, bedbug-infested shack. The few small peach trees resembled "little more than whips with bushy tops." Sand, sagebrush, and bunchgrass covered the property, and the irrigation canal needed substantial repairs. Sunnyside also failed live up to the Shellers' expectations. During their first few days, news of a dance held at the boardinghouse horrified Mrs. Sheller. Drinking, dancing, and card playing went against the Shellers' religious beliefs, and based on the Christian Cooperative Colony's sales pitch, they assumed that the townspeople shared their values.[56]

Many farmers found the barriers to irrigated agriculture impossible to overcome. Historian John Fahey estimates that "nearly three-fourths of original buyers of irrigated tracts sold their land within three years."[57] The historical record contains little information about those who sold out, why they sold out, or what their lives were like after selling their orchards. Accounts from the early years of settlement in central Washington were written by those who stayed. Some, like Mr. Wentworth, from whom the Shellers purchased their farm, must have found the land disappointing and moved on to other economic prospects. Others took jobs in nearby towns, falling back on their original professions or working in other apple industry jobs like sales or distribution. In the heroic narratives of local history, individuals who failed simply faded from the story, replaced by those who persevered. Still, it is possible to understand why many failed.

For starters, settlers had to obtain water. Because irrigation canals were costly to build and operate, many private companies went bankrupt before completing canals. Others failed to collect maintenance fees and went bankrupt because of costly repairs. Settlers had to pick up the pieces. Some landowners formed cooperative water districts to take control of water delivery. In other cases, new investors took over projects. If a company or cooperative did succeed, geography still posed a barrier, as it determined where water could be delivered. Acreage on a slope downhill from a river or creek offered ideal conditions. Water could be pumped from rivers to benchlands but pumping water uphill was impossible at the time. Even with advances in canal construction, natural water flows failed to keep up with demand, especially in the early years before the construction of storage reservoirs. Water frequently seeped out of early earthen canals before reaching its end user. Growers also found that they had to use more water than what experts recommended. If too little water ran through irrigation furrows, it mixed with soil to create a muddy goo known as "slickens" that rested on the surface and prevented water from soaking into the ground. Growers in Sunnyside, for example, had to put so much water on their fields that the local water table rose from forty feet below the surface to ten feet. In 1904, the water table rose so high that Roscoe Sheller recalled that the town's streets were "quagmires." Wagons sank axle deep into the muddy streets, and buildings with basements flooded.[58] Lining earthen ditches with concrete and constructing storage reservoirs solved some water delivery problems, but those solutions were expensive and took time to construct.

Growers also needed capital to start an orchard. Contrary to the claims in horticultural magazines, local newspapers, and promotional

Example of furrow irrigation in an orchard near Yakima, Washington. *Photograph by P. Wischmeyer. Collections of the Yakima Valley Museum.*

literature, orchards required a substantial outlay of capital to purchase land, trees, and water rights, in addition to the costs of building a house and other expenses. In the early 1900s, for example, the average settler who purchased a forty-acre farm on the Sunnyside Canal needed $3,500 for land, water rights, and housing.[59] A 1912 promotional brochure produced by the Yakima Commercial Club calculated the total expense of "developing from raw land to an apple orchard" at $34.50 per acre for plowing, leveling, purchasing, and planting orchard stock, and $55 per acre for four years of irrigation. Expenses from planting to bearing totaled $89.50 per acre, or $3,580 for forty acres that were not yet producing a fruit crop.[60]

Even if growers had start-up capital, they still had to master the skills necessary to run an orchard. Land had to be cleared, though pulling sagebrush and bunchgrass was easier than clearing stumps. Irrigation ditches had to be regularly inspected, cleaned, and repaired. Growers had to plant their orchards and plow furrows to deliver irrigation water to the saplings. After trees were planted, the yearly cycle of labor began. Trees were pruned each winter. In the spring, they were watered. The cycle of watering was repeated at least three or four times throughout the season.[61] Once trees started bearing fruit, growers had to monitor spring temperatures and set out smudge pots to protect trees against frost. In the spring, and again in summer, trees were sprayed with pesticides or fungicides to prevent damage to fruit. In July, trees were thinned to remove small fruit, ensuring that the remaining fruit would be a marketable size. As fruit matured, heavy branches had to be propped up to prevent breakage. In between caring for trees, a grower had to tend to any secondary crops—alfalfa, other fruit, vegetables, livestock. In the fall, growers harvested trees, packed fruit, found buyers, and hauled fruit to rail sidings for shipment.

A grower with a team of horses could care for a ten-to-twenty-acre orchard with a few hired hands to help with pruning, and extra labor at harvest. Washington did not have a large available labor pool because of its small population. Unlike in California where growers relied on contracted Chinese, Japanese, Sikh, or Mexican labor, in the Northwest most orchard labor before World War II was performed by whites: growers' families, neighbors, and seasonal workers. The Pacific Northwest has a history of racial exclusion, as reflected in booster pamphlets, and few nonwhite laborers were available. Washington was geographically distant from Mexico, and growers did not have the financial capital to hire crews of foreign workers, as raisin growers in California did, for example.[62] The Chinese Exclusion Act of 1882 barred Chinese immigration to the United States, and many Washington towns had evicted Chinese residents, sometimes forcibly, before central Washington was irrigated. A few Chinese workers may have harvested fruit, but they were not a major source of labor. Central Washington had a small Japanese population. Japanese laborers cleared land in places like Hood River and occasionally worked the harvest, but they tended to work their own farms.[63] Indians from the Yakama and Colville Reservations participated in the harvest in the early years, but "the evidence suggests that Natives did work in the orchard but only occasionally, preferring other subsistence activities," writes historian Tony Zaragoza, "and those who sought work in agriculture were not hired by apple growers, but instead by other industries."[64] As apple acreage grew, finding labor for the harvest would become more challenging, but since trees took up to five years to produce fruit, that was not an immediate concern. Hired labor was rarely mentioned in horticultural publications or growers' meetings. Most orchards were small enough that growers needed workers for only a few weeks at a time. In the early years, production was low enough that a family could harvest their own orchard, especially since most growers planted dozens of varieties of fruit that ripened over a two-to-three-month span.

The larger worry was finding alternative income sources while orchards matured. Some growers farmed part time while working full-time jobs in town. Others supplemented their income with seasonal employment, helping their neighbors with pruning, harvesting, and fruit packing. Wenatchee orchardist Charles Keiser acquired his 160-acre homestead along Wenatchee's Highline in 1904, and in 1908, he purchased another 100 acres. He later sold the second tract, saying that "to make that place pay, I almost literally sweat blood, but the debts mounted." Fortunately, Keiser had a degree in electrical engineering and landed a job with the Wenatchee Electric Company.[65] Fred Raymond, a business college graduate who ran grocery stores in Nebraska and New York before purchasing an orchard in Granger, Washington, gave up his orchard and opened a store in Yakima.[66] Like Keiser and Raymond, other orchardists sold their land or took jobs in town because they were unable to make a living from their orchards.

Absentee ownership offered another solution. For some, absentee ownership was an economic necessity. For others it was a fanciful dream encouraged by promotional literature. An exhibition at an Illinois fair persuaded Dr. Isaac Hubbard to buy twenty acres of fruit land from the Chelan Land Company for $9,000. Hubbard remained an absentee owner for eleven years and spent all his spare funds on the orchard. "Only one of those eleven years did we realize any cash whatsoever," remembered Hubbard, "and every penny of that had to go into improvements." Hubbard and his wife eventually decided to sell the land.[67] While some absentee owners eventually took up residence on their land, promoters worried that absenteeism hurt agricultural development and community growth. The Washington Irrigation Institute argued that recruiting novice farmers encouraged absentee ownership. "The lawyer, doctor, merchant, or the plumber, carpenter, or bricklayer . . . must abandon his only means of making a living if he goes to live on the land." This put novice farmers in a difficult position. If they stayed on the farm, they had no means to support themselves, but they did if they practiced their profession in town.[68] Being an absent but solvent owner was not ideal, but it was better than becoming a financial liability.

Secondary crops, such as alfalfa or vegetables, also provided income while orchardists waited for trees to bear fruit. George Batterman, who purchased land in Wenatchee in 1906, planted vegetables and melons between his rows of trees, a practice known as "intercropping." Novices received conflicting advice about what to grow in their orchards, with established growers, railroad executives, and college-trained horticultural experts weighing in on the problem. Critics argued that secondary crops distracted orchardists from producing the high-quality fruit that provided the best returns on irrigated land. A high-quality, standardized product was easier to market and would bring enough profit to subsidize the region's complex infrastructure. *Better Fruit* published articles promoting fruit monocultures. "Where land can be made to give returns that our fruit land can," wrote a *Better Fruit* reader from North Yakima in 1906, "the owner cannot afford to devote any of it to raising the few

Example of an intercropped orchard in Okanogan County, circa 1910. Growers often planted secondary crops between fruit trees to generate income while waiting for trees to mature. *Frank S. Matsura Photographs, Manuscripts, Archives, and Special Collections, Washington State University Libraries.*

tons of hay or the few sacks of potatoes he will need." The editors agreed, praising the letter "from a man after our own heart who came out of the crowded unhealthy wholesale business of the city and engaged in fruit growing on business principles."[69]

In Wenatchee, owners of the Highline Canal encouraged buyers to put their land in apple orchards. An investor approached William T. Clark, Thomas Burke, and Arthur Gunn, major stakeholders in the canal, with a proposition to diversify by establishing a sugar beet farm and factory. The men had divided opinions. Gunn supported the proposition because sugar beets would generate an immediate return for the Highline, but Clark opposed it, claiming that "the land would be more valuable for the raising of fruit."[70] Clark won the argument, and sugar beets were not planted. It was not simply a matter of one crop being more valuable than another. In addition to rail lines and irrigation canals, the region needed infrastructure to process crops, whether that be fruit packinghouses, sugar beet refineries, or grain elevators. It was more efficient to focus on one crop and one type of infrastructure.

College-trained experts presented a more favorable view of intercropping. They recommended planting alfalfa or peas for their nitrogen-fixing properties, especially as central Washington's soils tended to be low in nitrogen. Samuel Fortier of the USDA recommended planting alfalfa and plowing it under to enrich orchard soil, a practice that growers with young trees could not always afford. He conceded that if the soil was rich, berries and shallow-rooted vegetables could be grown between rows.[71] Washington State College professor Oscar M. Morris lamented the increasingly businesslike nature of farming. Single crops might be profitable in the short term but prove disastrous in the long term. Morris recommended diversifying in a way that protected orchards while providing alternative income to insulate farmers from volatile markets. Vegetables like potatoes, field peas, or string beans would grow between orchard rows without damaging trees, with the added benefit of enriching the soil.[72] In an issue on crop diversity, *Better Fruit* recommended keeping bees, dairy cows, hogs, sheep, or poultry. Rather than detracting from fruit crops, these secondary crops complemented orchard production. Bees provided pollination and honey. Dairy cows and sheep fed on alfalfa grown between rows of fruit trees. A sideline in poultry or hogs required very little space or investment.[73]

Farmers, especially in the early years of the twentieth century, had to face the hard realities of economic survival as they struggled to make sense of conflicting advice. Growing a secondary crop worked for some, but expert recommendations to diversify proved of no use to new orchardists who knew as little about dairy cattle as they did about orchards.[74] Instead, failure was possible on two fronts: in the orchard and with the secondary crop. Still, many turned to secondary crops because they needed to support their families. Some tried to follow expert advice, while others made poor choices, planting crops that choked out young trees. "I well remember the sight of an orchard which I saw not long ago which was so intercropped with rhubarb as to make it apparent that the owner was growing a rhubarb crop with trees between," recalled Arthur Bouquet, a *Better Fruit* contributor. Crops such as rhubarb and asparagus easily overran orchards. Bouquet argued that the problem was not intercropping, but rather farmers' inexperience in choosing crops.[75]

The question of diversification involved a deeper philosophical issue at the heart of American agriculture, beyond the necessity of supporting one's family. As the nation became more industrial and urbanized, Americans debated the future of rural life. Some believed that farmers would benefit from new technology and standardization, while others saw this as the degradation of the core values of rural America: hard work, independence, self-sufficiency. In his book *Highways of Progress*, James J. Hill outlined his vision for the agricultural future of the nation. Even as he argued that scientific processes needed to be applied to agriculture "as carefully studied and applied as are the details of manufacturing processes or manipulations of a chemical laboratory," he opposed the industrialization of farms. Farmers could increase production to meet the demands of the growing nation while maintaining small, independent, diversified farms.[76]

Pacific Northwest farmers weighed in on the issue through outlets like *Better Fruit*. One editorial cited a horticulturist who likened farm communities to nations. Nations with more diversity, "the ones where the people have blonde hair, black hair, brown hair; blue eyes, black eyes, brown eyes, etc.," were likely to be "the most prosperous, happiest, best educated, most cultured and intelligent nations of the world." Likewise, farming communities with a wide diversity of crops were prosperous, as demonstrated by "good roads, good schools, lighting systems, telephones and all of the other conveniences which go to make the life in the country one of pleasure and interest instead of one of monotony and drudgery." *Better Fruit*'s editors lamented Northwest fruit growers' lack of interest in diversity. They argued it led farmers to neglect family and civic duties.[77] Other Northwest growers took a more practical view. Relying on a single crop was too much of a gamble, like "roulette, racing, or rum," argued L. S. Smith before fellow growers at the 1913 annual meeting of the Washington State Horticultural Society. "There are perhaps some few individuals who can make a sort of a success growing nothing but apples," he conceded, but in general the prospect was too risky.[78]

The Washington Irrigation Institute saw the financial plight of farmers, especially those on irrigated tracts, as a national crisis. Starting a farm was an expensive proposition that left most farmers with large debts, but the institute believed careful management and efficient business practices could make farms more profitable. Modern technology such as trolley lines, phonographs, telephones, automobiles, and mechanized farm equipment such as tractors and power sprayers brought farmers closer together as communities and made rural life more attractive. As the institute concluded, "The many labor-saving devices remove a lot of the drudgery and enable the intelligent worker to get greater efficiency from his efforts than ever before."[79] Mechanization also allowed growers to manage orchard work with fewer hired hands. These arguments notwithstanding, farming, especially in irrigated areas, required specialized knowledge and skills, including the use of the latest technology and scientific methods. Increasingly, this would lead to specialization. Growers who lacked specialized expertise could not expect commercial success.

Throughout the 1890s and early 1900s, farmers and boosters continued to foster visions of wealth and prosperity in Washington's apple orchards. The increase in the number of bearing apple trees in central Washington shows that while individual growers may have struggled, the industry was growing. In 1890 there were 25,146 trees in central Washington, in 1900 there were 346,804, and by 1910 there were nearly a million trees of bearing age in the district.[80] Wenatchee shipped apples as early as 1900, but the first substantial crop of 587 cars shipped in 1904. By 1909 that number had grown to over 2,000 cars.[81] In 1907, growers shipped over one million dollars' worth of fruit out of the Yakima Valley.[82] While some orchardists failed, many others managed to survive the initial phase of development. For most, the quick wealth promised by boosters never materialized, and the fledgling industry still faced monumental challenges. Orchardists needed to become educated and trained in horticultural methods. They had to learn to adapt to the unique soil and the climate. They had to combat pests, tree diseases, frosts, and other dangers to orchards. Once they overcame those problems, they still faced the daunting task of selling and transporting their fruit to markets a continent away.

CHAPTER 3

One Bad Apple
Conforming to Orchard Management Practices

Many families who moved to central Washington quickly learned that growing fruit was far more difficult than they had anticipated. Roscoe Sheller recounted the day a noted horticulturist visited his family's orchard in Sunnyside, Washington. Sheller's father stood in shock as the stranger plucked several small apples from his trees. "I know exactly how you feel," the horticulturist explained. "I endured the same torture, when a total stranger gave me my first lesson in thinning. I felt like shooting him, certain he was destroying my crop." Thinning was necessary; otherwise the trees would not produce fruit of a marketable size. "Wouldn't you rather grow ONE extra fancy apple than a dozen culls?" he asked.[1] Sheller saw the error of his ways. He thinned the entire orchard, but even with help from the horticulturist, it took several attempts to learn the proper technique.

Like the Shellers, novice growers found that orchards were not idyllic respites from city life. Promotional literature boasted that anyone could profit from orchards, but it skimmed over the complexity of orchard management. Washington's small, fifteen-to-twenty-acre orchards resembled the Jeffersonian ideal of yeoman farmers, free landowners who supported their families through their own labor. But new settlers in central Washington were not farmers; they were growers. "Grower" denotes a professional, someone who produces crops for profit, not family consumption. Orchards were businesses that required a professional approach and specialized knowledge. Growers had to consider many factors to grow perfect, marketable apples. After choosing which variety to plant, they needed to know how to prune and thin trees, when and how to apply irrigation water, which sprays to use to address a host of orchard pests and diseases, and how to apply those sprays properly. Perhaps the two most important tools for creating a standardized product were orchard sprays and the selection of trees. Chemical sprays reduced negative effects from insects, fungi, and other diseases. Growers chose apple varieties for their marketable characteristics: consistency of production, appearance, and hardiness in transport.

Two factors set apple growers on a path toward industrialization: the need for a high-quality product to compete in distant markets, and pressure from the community of growers to conform. Standardization extended beyond using the latest scientific methods to reduce costs and maximize output. Though booster pamphlets promised independence and self-sufficiency, growers soon learned that they had to work together to establish industry standards and improve quality. As the saying goes, "One bad apple can spoil the bunch." Individual actions affected all growers, good or bad. Growers had to think beyond their own orchards. Insects and orchard diseases did not respect property lines. Those who refused to conform to standard practices could harm their neighbors' crops. Growers also had to consider market trends and consumer preferences, as consumers' experiences with Washington apples affected the reputation of the entire industry.

Many growers faced a steep learning curve in shifting from "farmers" to "growers." Washington's environment offered many natural advantages including winters cold enough to induce tree hibernation, long summer days to ripen fruit, and fertile soils. Irrigation allowed growers to control the timing of water delivery. The dry environment discouraged fungal diseases, which plagued eastern growers. But natural advantages alone did not ensure success. Wenatchee resident Jack Scaman recalled his early days working for orchardist S. A. Burbank. All of Burbank's trees died because of his "screwy" technique: "He'd dig a big hole, stick a tree into it, dump in some water, tramp down the clay around it, pour in more water and . . . tramp again," recalled Scaman. "A concrete wall around every tree, that's exactly what he made."[2] Jake Miller, another novice orchardist, nearly killed his trees in 1895 after applying too much aphid spray.[3] Many things could go wrong in an orchard. Trees had to be properly planted, protected from frost, fertilized, and pruned to ensure that adequate sunlight and nutrients reached the fruit. Growers had to monitor orchards for a host of insects, fungi, and other diseases and apply appropriate sprays. Any imperfection—worm stings, blisters, uneven coloring, misshapen appearance—rendered apples unsalable. As Sheller's horticulturist advised, extrafancy apples were worth something. Culls were not.

Research and education played a critical role in the developing apple industry. College-trained experts, horticultural organizations, and federal, state, and local agricultural agents provided scientific knowledge necessary for growers' success, as many growers lacked experience with central Washington's environment and with orchard cultivation in general. The Morrill Land-Grant Act of 1862 established land-grant colleges across the nation, including Washington State College (WSC), founded in 1890. WSC's Agricultural College opened two years later.[4] Like promotional brochures that attracted settlers to central Washington, the administrators at WSC advocated a higher purpose of shaping young people into model citizens. At the first WSC Farmers' Institute in 1892, George Lilley, experiment station director, explained that education at the agricultural college created well-rounded farmers who were conversant in the latest scientific methods and the arts. "It is the purpose of the school to teach those of the rising generation and prepare them for the industries, the responsibilities and the work of life," he remarked. Training "preserves habits of industry and manual exertion, and cultivates a taste for home and rural life."[5] At a time when the United States was urbanizing, such training aimed not only to preserve rural life but to elevate the importance of farming as a profession, a theme echoed in promotional literature.

Expert knowledge was important for new growers who planted specialty crops in irrigated landscapes. As in California, the natural landscape provided many advantages, but growers had to choose wisely. As historian Steven Stoll writes, "Precise planting exploited the virtues of land."[6] For growers in Washington, this meant choosing the most optimal apple varieties, a daunting task as there were dozens to choose from. Because trees took up to five years to produce fruit, choices mattered. Traditionally, farmers grew a wide variety of apples for home use. Some apples produced excellent cider or vinegar, while others worked in fresh

Orchards along the Columbia River below Brewster, as depicted by Seattle-based photographers Asahel Curtis and Walter Miller. Agricultural experts provided advice on a variety of topics including orchard layouts and tree spacing. *Box 132.G.9.2F, Advertising and Publicity Department, Great Northern Railway Company Records, Minnesota Historical Society.*

or dried applications. Farmers grew a mix of early- and late-ripening varieties to provide the household with fresh apples from August through November. Diversity had benefits for the home grower, but it presented challenges for the commercial grower. Commercial growers needed trees adapted to local growing conditions. Fruit had to be hardy enough to withstand transportation and several months of storage, and it had to have a pleasant appearance that appealed to buyers. Ripening time was important too, as growers considered when their fruit ripened relative to their competitors' fruit. William A. Taylor of the USDA, for example, observed that early-ripening apples sold well internationally, especially in Britain, because they were ready before the domestic British crop and after the Australian crop, which was shipped to Britain.[7] Later-ripening varieties sold for longer into the spring. For Pacific Northwest growers looking to market apples internationally and domestically, this was an important consideration.

Early Washington growers experimented with multiple varieties. In 1902, Charles Ray, a grower and warehouse manager for fruit shipper J. M. Perry, boasted that he was able to identify one hundred varieties by sight. Growers produced so many different varieties that other producers sought Ray's skills to identify their trees.[8] At a 1912 conference, F. A. Huntley, Washington's state horticultural commissioner, estimated that farmers grew well over two hundred varieties of apples. Of these, approximately fifty varieties of winter apples and ten varieties of summer apples were grown commercially. Huntley advised that twenty commercial varieties were adequate, and that "each locality should perhaps not have over a half dozen varieties of winter apples, and in some localities I am sure the number should be cut down . . . to two or three varieties."[9] Huntley surmised that growers' personal preferences and ignorance about local growing conditions drove the proliferation of varieties.

Commercial success depended on growing a few varieties to perfection. Experts encouraged farmers to raise high-performing commercial varieties with good market value. At the same conference, WSC professor Oscar M. Morris called for a study to produce a list of choice varieties for growers. He complained that many growers planted so-called old varieties—that is, apple varieties popular in the East. Farmers often ordered nursery stock from catalogues, with little regard for how the trees might perform for commercial purposes under local soil and climate conditions. Out-of-state mail-order nurseries offered farmers more choices, but scions might also arrive damaged or infested.[10] As early as 1892, the Washington State Board of Horticulture endorsed a selected list of twenty apple varieties chosen "by the leading growers of the state for general cultivation, having good qualities, productive and valuable for marketing."[11] Few varieties on the list were grown in large commercial quantities in central Washington.

Farmers planted many apples that are little known today, with colorful, descriptive names such as Red Astrachan, Blue Pearmain, Gloria Mundi, Rambo, Yellow Bellflower, Yellow Transparent, Waxen, Limber Twig, Seek-No-Further, and Twenty Ounce. Some varieties fell out of favor because of their susceptibility to frost damage. After a severe freeze in November 1896, the WSC experiment station began a study on the impact of weather on orchards in eastern Washington. The researchers learned that most damage occurred in damp areas, such as river bottoms or recently irrigated plots. Moisture in the soil and trees created ice, which broke down saplings from within. Apples at higher elevations fared better because of drier conditions. Trees were most susceptible to cold temperatures and frosts in spring when they started to bloom. Growers used smudge pots and other orchard-heating devices to prevent damage on cold spring nights, but choosing a hardy tree improved the odds of success. Some varieties resisted cold weather better than others. Yellow Bellflower, Fall Pippin, Esopus, and Yellow Newtown sustained the most damage, while hardier Ben Davis and Jonathan varieties survived.[12]

By the 1910s, several varieties had emerged as top choices. Ben Davis and Wagener apples matured faster than other varieties, giving growers early profits.[13] Other considerations included hardiness, appearance, ability to withstand shipping and handling, and a long storage life. For these reasons, experts recommended Winesap, Spitzenburg, Yellow Newtown, Rome Beauty, Grimes Golden, Jonathan, and Ben Davis. By the 1930s, this list had been further narrowed to four principal varieties: Winesap, Delicious, Jonathan, and Rome Beauty.[14]

Because market conditions determined which varieties were grown, some early commercial varieties eventually fell out of favor. Low-quality apples were not worth growers' time. To recoup growing, packing, and transportation expenses, growers charged prices two to three times higher than those of eastern apples. Consumers would pay higher prices only for top-quality fruit. "Shy-bearing" Spitzenburgs produced few apples, making the production cost per apple much higher than for more prolific varieties. They turned a profit only when prices were exceptionally high. Maiden Blush and Winter Banana went out of commercial production because their color, a cross between red and yellow, was not popular with consumers.[15] The thick-skinned Ben Davis, a popular early commercial variety, fell out of favor because it lacked flavor. Consumers tended to purchase Ben Davis apples when other varieties were unavailable.[16] "I don't raise Ben Davis apples to eat," remarked one Washington grower. "I raise them to sell . . . and I buy good apples to eat at home."[17]

As the industry developed, growers adopted new varieties to meet changing market demands. As a *Better Fruit* staff writer commented, "The problem of obsolescence applies to fruit growing the same as it does to manufacturing."[18] Medium-sized red apples sold particularly well, and growers sought new varieties with a deep, uniform red color.[19] Growers experimented with red strains of several established varieties including Jonathan, Winesap, and Rome, but the new Delicious varieties captured the market. Today, Delicious apples have become a symbol for everything that is wrong with industrialized agriculture. Their uniform shape and shiny red skins are visually appealing, but they lack flavor and often have a mushy texture. Headlines such as "The Red Delicious Apple Is an Atrocity" proclaim consumers' disdain for the variety, and the fruit is described as tasting like Styrofoam or cardboard.[20] Over the last few decades, new varieties have supplanted the Delicious, a trend that the *New York Times* greeted with the headline "The Long, Monstrous Reign of the Red Delicious Apple Is Ending."[21] But a hundred years ago, the Red Delicious offered Washington growers many benefits.

The Delicious apple, discovered by Iowa farmer Jesse Hiatt, came into widespread commercial use in the 1920s. Hiatt spent several years trying to promote his apple with little success. In 1895, he sold the variety to Stark Bro's Nursery in Louisiana, Missouri. The company registered the name "Delicious" with the US patent office. Stark Bro's used clever marketing campaigns to spur sales of Delicious trees, such as including free Delicious saplings with orders. One Stark brochure described the fruit as "an absolute king commercially; incomparable for dessert; with cream and sugar, like peaches; a good cooking apple. . . . In short, as a quality apple it stands pre-eminent."[22] In 1913, state horticultural commissioner F. A. Huntley assessed the variety's potential. At the time, it was untested commercially, but it grew well in the Yakima and Wenatchee Valleys. "The Delicious is a fairly good apple," he wrote, "but it does lack color."[23] It had other qualities that made it attractive to growers. The trees were sturdy, and the fruit stored well for several months.[24]

By the 1920s, new strains of Delicious with better color such as Richared and Starking became available. In 1910, G. T. Richardson of Monitor, Washington, discovered Richared, a bud sport mutation. A bud sport occurs when one bud of a tree produces apples different enough from the rest on the tree to be considered a new variety. The new apples achieved a solid, bright red color earlier than other Delicious apples. After observing the bud sport for several years, Richardson sold the variety to the Columbia & Okanogan Nursery Co. in Wenatchee, which began selling Richared saplings in 1926. The name "Richared" derived from Richardson's name and the apples' "richer red" color.[25] On average, trees produced 90 percent extrafancy fruit, whereas the regular Delicious variety typically produced 76 percent extrafancy apples. Grower Ralph Sundquist of Yakima planted Starkings in his orchard in 1925. When one of the trees produced its first apples in 1927, he was impressed by the "superiority of color." Someone agreed, because the apples were stolen before harvest. The next year, Sundquist exhibited his Starkings at the Washington State Fair, where they were praised for their superior texture, flavor, and size. By 1931, 40 percent of all trees in Washington were Delicious varieties. Growers still planted Winesap, Rome, and Jonathan trees, but as older trees were removed, they were generally replaced with a Delicious variety.[26]

Changes to federal law aided the development of new varieties. Advances in plant breeding, pioneered by horticulturists like Luther Burbank, led to hundreds of new varieties. After a failed attempt to protect cultivars in 1892, Congress took up the debate again in 1929. Proponents argued that asexually produced plant cultivars were like other inventions because such plants would not produce naturally without human intervention. In 1930, Herbert Hoover signed the Plant Patent Act, which allowed horticulturists to patent plants that produced asexually, including apples.[27] Patents allowed horticulturists to keep sole marketing rights of their cultivars for seventeen years. The Columbia & Okanogan Nursery Co. filed the first Washington apple patent in 1931 for a new variety of Jonathan dubbed "Blackjon" for its deep red skin.[28]

Washington was part of a national trend in the reduction of commercial varieties. In the forty states that produced apples commercially, ten varieties accounted for 60 percent of trees by the early 1930s. Relying on fewer varieties presented some problems. When growers produced dozens of varieties, they were able to stagger harvesting, packing, shipping, and storage, as some varieties ripened as early as August and others as late as early November. Specializing in only one or two varieties meant that most of the crop had to be processed at the same time.[29] Delicious trees were also susceptible to worm damage and collar rot and were more finicky to prune than other varieties. On the other hand, focusing on specific varieties offered market advantages. Washington had distinguished itself by producing higher-quality apples than other regions, but by the 1930s, eastern growers had caught up. To stay competitive, regions became specialized in commercial varieties most suited to their climates. For example, northeastern states produced excellent McIntosh apples, better than those grown in Washington. So why compete? Instead, Washington growers focused on varieties that excelled in Washington.[30]

Choosing a marketable variety was only the first step to success. Fruit not only had to have a marketable color, shape, and size but also had to be free from worms and rot. At first, growers in central Washington believed arid conditions spared them from the pests and diseases that plagued fruit growers everywhere else in the nation. Despite the promises made by promotional literature, insects were a problem for all fruit trees from the outset. Infested nursery stock shipped from out of state, improper spraying, and the transportation of infected fruit contributed to the problem. Transportation was a double-edged sword that made commercial fruit growing possible but also facilitated the movement of pests. One Washington State College study, for example, found that orchards near packinghouses were more likely to have infestations.[31]

Washington farmers struggled to battle insects such as codling moth and San Jose scale, two of the most feared insects because of the damage they inflicted. Codling moths lay their eggs on apples so that newly hatched larvae can feed on the fruit. San Jose scale attaches itself to trees and feeds on the sap. The yellow females live in colonies and secrete a waxy grayish-black coating, or "scale," over themselves. Untreated, colonies can grow large enough to cover an entire tree, making it look as if it has been "coated with fine ash-colored bran."[32] In later stages of infection, fruit becomes cracked or misshapen.

Fruit pests have been around as long as fruit trees. The codling moth came to North America on trees the first colonists brought from Europe. Their spread paralleled the expansion of apple and pear trees across the continent. San Jose scale, reported in Washington Territory as early as 1885, most likely arrived on nursery stock imported from California.

By the 1890s, it was widespread in eastern Washington. Unlike codling moths, scales are not very mobile. They spread through human activity such as fruit packing and transporting nursery stock.[33] During the 1850s and 1860s as the number of commercial orchards in upstate New York and California increased, growers had to combat a variety of infestations. Scabs and fungi became so rampant in New York orchards that by the 1880s and 1890s many farmers had no choice but to destroy their trees.[34] By the late 1890s, Washington growers also worried about the impact of insects and disease on the infant apple industry, as some growers lost 40 to 50 percent of their crops. Axel L. Melander, professor of entomology at Washington State College, reported that only half of Washington's 1904 commercial crop was shipped, 1,500 cars worth $600,000. He attributed at least $200,000 of lost profit directly to the codling moth.[35]

Growers could not afford such high losses, so they turned to chemical sprays. Before World War II, chemical sprays were ineffective, expensive, and of limited use in commercial agricultural production. Fruit was the exception. Growers and scientists in fruit districts across the country experimented with many solutions of varying toxicity and effectiveness to salvage crops, including manufactured pesticides and home remedies such as salt sprays, whale oil, kerosene, sour milk, tobacco, caustic soda, and oil.[36] Growers could choose from several commercial or homemade sprays, each with different application times and concentrations. Agricultural experiment stations tested these concoctions to determine their efficacy, and horticultural journals reported on scientific and anecdotal results. Scientists at the University of California, for example, published several bulletins on scale, codling moth, and other orchard insects in the 1890s.[37] Researchers in the Northwest built on this work. As Washington growers established commercial orchards in the early twentieth century, they were able to benefit from this growing body of knowledge.

Newspaper editors, horticultural magazines, local inspectors, and federal horticultural agents railed against insects, depicting them as mortal enemies to be vanquished. Industry leaders urged growers to spray pesticides, to turn pigs loose in orchards to eat the insects, and to monitor neighbors' actions. "There must be a live interest manifested in the subjection of these blood-thirsty Spaniards," wrote Orlando Beck, Yakima

County horticultural inspector, likening the war on pests to the recent Spanish-American War. "A few Dewey's is all we need," Beck concluded, and "the sun will soon be shining with full force as it used to do a few years ago."[38] Beck's attitude toward orchard pests was common. Growers described pests in apocalyptic terms, but they maintained unshakable optimism that a scientific solution was at hand.

By the early twentieth century, experts found that arsenic compounds with colorful names such as "Paris green" and "London purple" were effective against codling moths.[39] Arsenic-based pesticides were relatively cheap and easy to obtain. Paris green (copper acetoarsenite) was commonly used as a pigment in paint, wallpaper, fabric, and other consumer goods. In the nineteenth century, companies marketed Paris green and London purple (calcium arsenite), the by-product of aniline dye used in the British textile industry, as pesticides. Before the discovery of its insecticidal properties, manufacturers dumped London purple at sea. London purple was cheaper than Paris green, but it was more soluble and tended to damage plants. It fell out of agricultural use by 1900. By the 1920s, Washington growers had replaced both products with lead arsenate, as it caused less damage to trees. Lead arsenate remained the most popular pesticide until the introduction of DDT after World War II.[40]

Fungicides, such as Bordeaux mixture (copper sulfate), were also an important part of the chemical arsenal. French vintners popularized copper-based fungicides, sprinkling a copper compound called verdigris on crops that bordered roads to discourage pilfering. In 1878, an epidemic of downy mildew, a fungal disease that caused vines to drop their leaves, threatened French vineyards. Growers discovered that the verdigris-sprinkled vines remained healthy. By the mid-1880s, growers had replaced verdigris with the cheaper copper sulfate. Further experimentation led to the widespread adoption of Bordeaux mixture in vineyards and orchards.[41] In Washington, growers used Bordeaux mixture to combat apple scab, a fungus that attacked the leaves and fruit of apple trees. The fungal spores left dark olive-colored patches on the leaves and fruit. In mild cases, the fungus formed small spots on the apple. Though the fruit was edible, it could not be sold. In more severe cases, scab caused apples to crack open and fall off the tree. Copper fungicides offered effective prevention. A 1906 study by Washington State College

Spraying an orchard for codling moths. By the 1920s, most growers used mechanical sprayers for efficient application. *Collections of the Yakima Valley Museum.*

showed that a solution of copper sulfate and lime eliminated scab in 89 percent of the trees sprayed.[42]

Sprays existed in two forms: wet and dry. In early years, many growers sprayed trees with low-pressure manual hand pumps. Mechanized high-pressure sprayers mounted on wagons, tractors, or modified automobiles allowed faster application. Some high-pressure sprayers used canisters of compressed gas to create pressure. One model employed gears connected to a wagon; as horses pulled the wagon through the orchard, the turning gears created pressure in the pesticide tank. While this was creative, tests showed that the wagon had to drive down a row of trees nine times to build up enough pressure to spray on the tenth pass, hardly a time-saving design. Horticultural experts preferred spray pumps powered by gasoline engines, which produced the most reliable pressure for spraying trees evenly. Such experts provided growers with information on how to purchase gas sprayers and troubleshoot minor engine problems. As one Washington State College bulletin stated, it was "hardly necessary to forgo the advantages of modern methods" for lack of mechanical ability.[43]

Most growers preferred liquid sprays, but some used dry dust sprayers with bellows to blow dry poisons onto the trees. It was difficult to apply too much dust, and dust did not injure delicate blossoms. Dry sprays were also cheaper: E. L. Stewart, an orchardist in Yakima, paid $117 for seven dust sprayings, compared to $237 for six liquid sprays. Though spraying was expensive, it accounted for only 10 percent of growers' costs. Stewart's real savings would have come from the roughly 10 percent increase in marketable fruit that he claimed by using dust sprays.[44]

Dust sprays had drawbacks, as Roscoe Sheller wrote of the duster his family used at their orchard in Sunnyside. "It belched clouds of flour-fine dust of lime, sulfur, Paris Green, and other ingredients, intended to suffocate living insects and leave a coating of poison on young apples that would send any bug attempting to taste one to a violent death," he recalled. "If the stuff choked worms and bugs as effectively as it did us, we'd have the cleanest crop in the whole world."[45] According to entomologists at Washington State College, dust sprayers were "unsatisfactory" and "had no place in orchard spraying." Although dust sprays appeared to coat trees more thoroughly than wet sprays, the dust tended to blow away instead of settling onto the trees. Claims that dust sprays worked better were largely anecdotal.[46]

Though growers wanted to produce marketable fruit, some resisted spraying. For many, it was an unpleasant task. Donald Wheeler, son of a White Bluffs orchardist, recalled that everyone he knew hated spraying. The Wheelers first hauled their sprayer on a wagon and later a modified Model T. The chemicals' noxious fumes, combined with the desert heat, made the family dread this chore. Experts advised farmers to wear a mask and cover all exposed skin when working with pesticides. The county agent "told us we must wear masks but no one did that I know of," Wheeler recalled. "It was so hot already! Sometimes already getting up to 100 degrees. I tried a mask once and had to take it off right away; I would have fainted."[47] Even growers who used protection sometimes burned themselves or their trees. When researching caustic soda spray, A. B. Crodley observed that "every drop that strikes one's hands or face burns severely. Men declared they would not work for five dollars a day if required to use it."[48]

Growers resisted using sprays for other reasons, too. Sprays were expensive, and some growers skipped applications to save money. Others were skeptical because of their own bad experience with sprays. While some sprays were ineffective, growers' inexperience also led to poor results. If solutions were mixed improperly, sprayed at the wrong time of year, or sprayed in the wrong amount, they failed and left trees susceptible to further infestation. Other growers did not trust expert advice. Research on scientific orchard management was still in its infancy, and recommendations changed as researchers learned more about Washington's environment. Advice from USDA scientists or eastern researchers was not always appropriate for central Washington. Research done at land-grant colleges in the Pacific Northwest did not always address central Washington either. Campuses at Corvallis, Oregon, and Pullman, Washington, were hundreds of miles away from central Washington and had different climates. Because of these variations, neighbors and friends were often more trustworthy sources of information than unknown scientific experts. *Better Fruit* regularly published growers' observations alongside reports from scientific experts, sometimes warning growers to be wary of experts. In one *Better Fruit* article, for example, George Wright warned fellow growers about the accuracy of tests that measured nutrients in soil. A test might show that soil is high in potash, Wright explained, but it might be high in an insoluble form of potash not absorbed by trees.[49] The moral of the story depended on the grower—ask for clarification, or distrust expert results.

Like other consumer products at the turn of the century, commercial pesticides were largely untested and unregulated. Though researchers worked to verify pesticide efficacy, research was ongoing. Agricultural bulletins had to compete with trade publications and information from pesticide companies. Everyone had an opinion, but not every opinion was scientifically validated. *Better Fruit* published reports from the USDA and state college agricultural stations alongside anecdotal testimonials. The magazine also advertised sprays produced by companies across the nation, including Sherwin-Williams, the paint manufacturer. Manufacturers were not required to accurately label their products. Growers had no reliable way to evaluate most chemicals on the market, but desperation drove orchardists to experiment with various treatments, even those of questionable quality.

Without research and regulation, growers had no way of knowing whether they were eradicating orchard pests or wasting money on ineffective products. Experimentation debunked some sprays, but with scores of products and orchard pests, it took time for researchers to test the effectiveness of sprays for each specific need. Arsenic-based pesticides, for example, were generally effective against the codling moth, but they had little effect on San Jose scale. Experiments in 1904 and 1905 by A. B. Crodley of the Oregon Agricultural Experiment Station in Corvallis showed that lime, sulfur, and salt sprays were effective, but the formula mattered. Crodley's experiments highlighted the challenge growers faced in finding effective pesticides. He tested several homemade and commercial sprays. Of the three commercial sprays available on the market, two worked, but they were less effective than homemade sprays. The third commercial spray was ineffective. In this case, orchardists fared better by mixing their own sprays at home.[50]

Horticultural regulations evolved as the industry grew and new research became available. Unlike with other do-it-yourself spray solutions, growers could not mix their own arsenic-based pesticides. They had to rely on manufactured sprays and hope that they contained enough arsenic to be effective. In 1901, the Washington state legislature banned the sale of adulterated or low-grade sprays. State regulations required that Paris green contain at least 50 percent arsenic trioxide. The Washington Agricultural Experiment Station chemist provided free analysis of pesticide samples. Sellers who failed to comply faced a misdemeanor and a fine of $25 to $100.[51] By 1915, a state board analyzed all insecticides and fungicides marketed to commercial growers to ensure that sprays met purity standards.[52]

Scientific studies went beyond quality assurance. Experts had to consider the practical application of pesticides in the orchard and provide growers with clear instructions. Growers had to learn which sprays eradicated the dozens of insects, fungi, bacteria, and viruses that damaged fruit trees. Poor orchard management led to low yields and profits for individual growers, but consequences extended beyond the individual. Growers' choices affected their neighbors and by extension the whole district. Those who failed to spray undermined neighboring orchards' spray regimes. The quality and productivity of all growers relied on standardized methods of orchard management to keep orchards pest- and disease-free. Local counties tried to enforce the use of sprays in campaigns against the codling moth, San Jose scale, and other orchard pests, but voluntary efforts fell short. Instead, industry leaders turned to the state legislature for help with grower education and compliance.

California provided a model for Washington growers in their attempts to control pests. California's fruit industry was in full swing in the 1890s, while Washington's was still in the early stages of development. Like Washington growers, California growers had to produce superior fruit to make up for transportation costs. Because pest control was vital to the success of the industry, California growers began lobbying for regulations. The state passed its first horticultural inspection act in 1881. Under the act, three unpaid horticultural inspectors monitored orchards and cited owners who failed to address pest problems. Over the following decade, California revised the statute to implement more robust regulations. State laws eventually regulated the purity of pesticides, and in 1899, a horticultural quarantine law authorized agents to inspect all fruit that crossed California's borders.[53]

Washington followed suit in February 1891, creating a state Board of Horticulture composed of nine members, each of whom represented one of the state's agricultural districts. Although Washington had attained statehood only two years earlier, fruit was a large enough commercial concern to justify state regulation. The board set regulations for pest control, disseminated information to growers, investigated reports of insect infestation, inspected nursery stock, and raised funds for lectures and educational events. Board members also responded to complaints from growers who turned in their neighbors. Those who failed to respond to board recommendations faced fines of $25 to $100, plus the cost of any other actions the board might take, such as disinfecting an orchard by spraying it. Nurseries faced even stiffer fines of anywhere from $50 to $200 if their trees were not certified clean.[54]

At first, the state Board of Horticulture had little impact on the fruit industry. Board members were required to visit each county in their district only once a year, and they were limited to a maximum of sixty inspection days per year. Inspections varied from district to district. One member inspected 1,550 orchards in his district in "all towns of importance," while another did not visit all the counties in his district because he had received no complaints.[55] Such discrepancies ensured the continued spread of orchard pests. State inspectors were supposed to certify imported nursery stock because trees from out-of-state nurseries brought new pests into Washington. Because of a shortage of inspectors, many shipments slipped through without approval. In 1892, a shipment of trees from Stark Bro's of Missouri arrived in Spokane infested with woolly aphids. Authorities discovered the infestation only after the trees were distributed throughout eastern Washington. The fruit inspector tracked down the trees and destroyed all but one carload, which was never found.

Over time, state regulations governing the Board of Horticulture evolved from general proscriptions to specific policies. The hodgepodge system of inspections gave way to a professionally organized system. By 1897, the Department of Horticulture was headed by a professional commissioner with horticultural experience and a certificate from Washington State College. A state-level horticultural board still represented each growing district, but responsibility for inspections shifted to county boards, which had the power to appoint their own inspectors. By 1903, county inspectors had to have professional credentials, pass an examination, make monthly reports, and attend a yearly educational "Inspector's Institute" held at Washington State College. Inspectors who failed to attend the institute forfeited their jobs.[56] Across Washington, counties put their local inspectors to work. Yakima and Benton Counties authorized inspectors to "enforce compliance with [their] orders in all cases where it is necessary to spray, and to prosecute all cases in violation."[57] Walla Walla County's inspector scolded growers to spray with "something besides whitewash." Asotin County used $15,000 of municipal funds to purchase pesticides and spraying equipment, while Chelan County hired a fruit inspector at an annual salary of $1,500. In Prosser, Washington, authorities discussed the mandatory elimination of all infected trees.[58]

The Department of Horticulture took responsibility for educating growers about the insects, fungi, and bacteria that harmed their orchards. County inspectors' reports indicate that growers were eager for information about how to effectively control orchard pests. Inspector S. W. Maxey from Ellensburg reported in 1893 that of the twenty-four spray notices he gave, "all had made efforts to eradicate the pests from their trees; though many of these were not altogether successful, because directions had not been fully observed and carried out."[59] Growers wanted to eradicate orchard pests, but novice growers, even those with the best intentions, still had to learn how to mix complicated spray formulas and follow intricate spray charts. The state commissioner distributed bulletins and circulars with the latest spray formulas and recommendations based on research by scientists at Washington State College. Growers also had access to research bulletins produced by the USDA. County agents and college researchers attended community meetings and offered educational conferences and lectures to present the latest research and address growers' concerns. Publications such as *Better Fruit* generally endorsed the work of the USDA and agricultural colleges.

Most growers complied with Maxey's spray orders, but "in one or two instances it appeared that the spraying had been done only to evade the orders of the board."[60] County inspectors viewed growers who simply went through the motions with skepticism. Their actions threatened the health of the state's fruit industry and frustrated inspectors. A misapplied spray could be worse than not spraying at all because it could damage blossoms, burn foliage, and even kill trees. Misapplied sprays also failed to interrupt a pest's life cycle, allowing infestation to spread. State inspector D. M. Jessee of Walla Walla complained about "indifferent" growers: "I mean that class of men who will persist in trying to see how small a hole they can crowd a tree into, instead of digging a large, roomy hole, according to my instructions." From Jessee's perspective, "it is this class who deride fruit raising."[61] Inspection was not about protecting individual rights; it was about protecting the community. One infected tree could wreak havoc on everyone's orchards. Horticultural inspectors understood this, even if a few growers did not.

Not everyone approved of the state's top-down approach. Grower K. W. Shafford challenged the legality of Washington's fruit inspection laws. In 1905, Shafford loaded 825 boxes of infested apples onto an outbound railcar. When local inspector J. M. Brown discovered the shipment, he ordered the fruit destroyed, arrested Shafford, and held him on $200 bail. Shafford appealed the decision to Brown's boss, who agreed that the fruit was infested. Shafford sued the county on the grounds that the horticultural act was unconstitutional.[62] Three years later, the case made its way to the Washington State Supreme Court. Shafford argued that the state owed him damages for destroying his personal property. The court saw the matter differently. It ruled that the fruit inspector acted in good faith, and "the owner of the fruit evidently supposed the same." Since Shafford had appealed to Brown's boss, he seemed to acknowledge the validity of the law. As for damages, the court ruled that since the fruit was wormy, "the owners suffered no loss for which they could maintain an action."[63] Inspections would continue.

Though a few growers resisted, inspectors' reports were generally positive. Growers struggled to learn proper techniques, but sources indicate that they accepted state regulation because they saw the value of protecting their individual orchards and livelihoods. The state horticultural board's top-down approach defined the fruit industry in Washington State. It ensured a level of quality and standardization by enforcing inspections and spraying regulations. Growers would not ship wormy apples out of Washington if the horticultural department had any say. Legally, growers had to comply with standard orchard management practices, and neighbors pressured each other to comply.

Growers worked together to combat orchard pests, forming volunteer crews that sprang into action at the first sight of infestation. Most orchards were smaller than ten acres and were maintained by a few individuals throughout the year, except in the fall, when growers hired additional workers, often transient laborers who traveled to central Washington specifically for the harvest. The rest of the year, growers relied on labor from their family or a few hired hands. Volunteer associations provided emergency labor to deal with abnormal disease and pest outbreaks. Without community help, growers would not have enough labor to deal with emergencies. In 1913, for example, the Lower Nachez Valley Fruit Protective Association organized volunteer crews to fight an infestation of blight. Worried about finding enough labor to remove the blighted trees, one owner called the horticultural inspector and offered a dollar per day to any person the inspector could find. The inspector contacted the protective association, and within forty-five minutes a crew of fifteen volunteers arrived on-site. They cleared the orchard of blight by the next afternoon and refused payment, insisting that quick action was in the best interest of the community. Prosser, Grandview, and Sunnyside had similar volunteer organizations. Most volunteers were not orchardists; they were town businesspeople trained by the horticultural inspector in disinfecting orchards. Local businesspeople in Yakima even went so far as to raise money for a blight fund.[64] That local business owners volunteered for this type of work speaks to the economic importance of orchards to surrounding towns.

The state Department of Horticulture urged timely spray regimens to avoid emergency situations. Researchers at Washington State College published spray calendars showing when and how to apply sprays throughout the growing season. Yearly spray schedules depended on the pest or disease. To combat codling moths, for example, growers needed to spray arsenic-based pesticides as blossoms started to open, when the calyx and immature petals formed a "cup" where young codling moth worms crawled for shelter. The idea was to force pesticide into the calyx to kill worms early in their life cycle. A. L. Roberts, a contributor to *Better Fruit*, thought that some of his apple varieties were naturally wormier than others, until he realized that some calyces closed earlier than others. Roberts advised that trees "should be sprayed until there is not a dry twig or branch about it, and hardly a calyx on it that is not full of water [containing pesticide spray]."[65] Axel L. Melander of Washington State College recommended a three-spray regime for codling moth. Growers applied the first spray before the calyx closed, the second two weeks later, and the third after the first brood of moths hatched. Melander reported that some growers applied a fourth or fifth spray later in the summer.[66] Perhaps growers thought that if three sprays were good, more must be better. Scientific studies attested to the effectiveness of arsenic-based pesticides against codling moth. A study conducted in the Yakima Valley between 1903 and 1905 revealed that 85 percent of the sprayed fruit was worm-free. Of the wormy fruit, an estimated 40 percent showed evidence that the worms had entered through the calyx, meaning that growers had not properly applied the first, and most important, spray.[67]

Today, the image of apple trees dripping wet with pesticide or coated in toxic white powder is troublesome, but in the early 1900s, it represented progress. Most scientists and nonscientists alike saw promise in lead arsenate and other hazardous pesticides. The Food and Drug Administration did not exist until 1906, and even then, the agency set no limits for arsenic on fruit until the late 1920s. Growers worried about overspraying only if it wasted money or damaged trees. They gave little thought to consumer safety, even though arsenic was a known poison. Part of this laxity was a result of the extensive use of arsenic in many consumer goods including wallpaper, oil paint, fabric, children's toys, soap, and candy. Arsenic was used medically and cosmetically in the nineteenth century; flushed cheeks, an early symptom of arsenic poisoning, popularized its use as a health tonic and cosmetic.[68]

Growers were also unconcerned because they believed that arsenic residues blew or washed off trees before harvest. Early tests supported this view. Spray residue studies conducted by A. J. Cooke, an entomologist at Michigan State University, in the 1880s concluded that rain and wind removed most arsenic within three weeks of spraying, and risk was thus minimal. Other studies, however, found that some residue remained on the fruit, although the amounts varied depending on how recently the fruit had been sprayed. The problem with relying on studies of eastern orchards was that they received summer rain; western orchards did not. Scientists also based their studies on recommended applications of arsenic, but many growers sprayed more frequently than recommended, sometimes within the critical weeks before harvest.[69]

As early as 1891, the British journal *Horticultural Times* criticized the level of arsenic residue found on imported American apples. American growers brushed off these concerns. The apples were shipped in used flour barrels, they explained, and inspectors mistook flour residue for arsenic.[70] British inspectors were not mistaken, but the matter went no further. A few American agricultural experts warned about the dangers of lead arsenate, but they were the minority. In 1909, W. P. Headden of the Colorado Agricultural College reported on the death of trees from arsenic poisoning. He hypothesized that arsenic became soluble after mixing with Colorado's alkaline soils, causing the trees to absorb the poison. *Better Fruit* published his study, but with a caveat from the editor expressing skepticism about the findings.[71] E. D. Ball of the Agricultural College of Utah Experiment Station questioned the soundness of Headden's research methods and stated that "the publication is most unfortunate, as it will cause a decided reaction against a highly successful method of spraying and bring consequential financial loss."[72] A reader also wrote in, chastising the magazine for frightening people away from lead arsenate and claiming that his trees had suffered similar damage from cold, not arsenic.[73]

For growers and agricultural experts, the benefits of arsenical pesticides outweighed any hazards. They regarded sprays as essential scientific tools to overcome the whims of nature. Experts warned users of potential dangers. The Oregon Agricultural College Experiment Station, for example, warned against storing liquids in old lead arsenate barrels because livestock had died after drinking from old spray barrels. This information was not intended to discourage farmers from spraying; rather, it was a reminder to handle poisons with care. A 1919 study by the USDA Bureau of Chemistry warned that levels of arsenic on apples and pears could cause arsenic poisoning. The bureau warned growers to avoid overspraying and urged them to clean fruit before shipment. Growers countered that sprays were necessary, residue concerns were overblown, and cleaning fruit was cost prohibitive.[74]

Most American growers denied the potential hazards of arsenic residue until the 1920s, when complaints from British consumers forced them to reevaluate their position. In October 1925, a family in Hampstead became ill after eating American apples tainted with arsenic. A month later, British authorities fined a fruit merchant after his customers became ill from imported American fruit contaminated with arsenic. American growers dismissed the incident as an anomaly, but the story refused to die. Throughout the spring of 1926, British health inspectors arrested and fined additional grocers for selling American apples with arsenic levels above the legal limit of 1/100 of a grain per pound. Pacific Northwest fruit contained the highest levels of arsenic because the fruit was not washed by rain during the growing season, and growers often sprayed for codling moth right before harvest.[75]

Questions about consumer safety mounted during the 1925–26 season. On November 26, 1925, the *New York Times* reported that British authorities fined a fruit merchant for selling fruit that contained 20/100 of a grain per pound of fruit. Officials learned of the contaminated fruit after a customer became sick from eating an apple. Two days later, the *Washington Post* called the reports overblown. Each apple, reported the *Post*, had "less than a third of a medical dose. . . . A dozen would have had to be consumed at once before serious effects could follow." American commercial interests claimed that "English agitation was part of a movement to injure American trade."[76]

Reports of contaminated apples continued to surface. In January, authorities fined two retailers for selling imported Jonathan and Newtown apples with 1/35 and 1/30 of a grain of arsenic per pound of fruit, respectively. British authorities distributed pamphlets to fruit dealers about high arsenic levels on imported apples. In February, the *London Times* reported that inspectors charged four different grocers with selling apples with 5/100 of a grain of arsenic per pound and 56/100 of a grain of lead per pound. In March, another was fined for selling apples with 1/12 of a grain of arsenic per pound. Testifying at a trial, a medical officer from Hampstead reported that the levels of arsenic found were "absolutely dangerous." The *London Times* chastised American growers for failing to reduce their use of arsenic spray, and by April, British merchants refused to handle apples from the United States. The *New York Times* reported that demand for American apples declined 40 to 60 percent.[77]

As reports of contaminated apples increased, growers tried to counter the negative publicity. British growers, who also used arsenical pesticides, distanced themselves from the controversy. They argued that American growers used different application methods, and they perpetuated the myth that rain washed off excess arsenic residue. The National Federation of Fruit and Potato Trades Associations released a statement confirming the safety of arsenic sprays. Growers in all apple-growing countries had used sprays for over thirty years, and in that time "as far as could be ascertained no case of illness had ever arisen."[78] An anonymous correspondent to the *London Times* highlighted a report by the British Ministry of Agriculture from the previous year showing that samples of British apples had no arsenic residue.[79] British growers had good reason to defend the use of arsenical sprays, as they were the only effective method of combating codling moths. Commercial production relied on effective methods of pest control.

On the other side of the Atlantic, American growers tried to frame pesticides in a positive light. Washington growers could not argue that rain washed off residues. Instead, they focused on scientific studies and the lack of consumer complaints. The *New York Times* reported that "wholesalers, some of whom had had scientific investigations made, contend there is absolutely no danger to the public from arsenic-sprayed apples."[80] Despite assurances of safety, the British government threatened to embargo American apples unless the US government acted. Bowing to pressure from Britain and wanting to avoid the awkward situation of having apples confiscated, the USDA agreed to uphold the British limit of 1/100 of a grain of arsenic per pound. They ordered horticultural inspectors to comply with the new limits.

To uphold British standards for export, USDA inspectors seized several carloads of fruit with high levels of arsenic. The first legal test came in November 1926 when Suncrest Orchard Company of Medford, Oregon, challenged the seizure of five carloads of its apples and pears, found to have fruit with 1/9 of a grain of arsenic. The court ruled in favor of the federal inspectors. Though the USDA would not set domestic tolerances until 1928, the British tolerances effectively applied to all commercially grown apples.[81] Consignment firms or marketing cooperatives handled western fruit destined for eastern markets. Firms shipped fruit to Britain irregularly, whenever New York and other Atlantic markets were glutted. Growers had no way of knowing which apples were sold domestically and which were shipped to foreign markets. In 1925, before the scare, Great Britain accounted for 80 percent of the US apple export market. That year the United States exported over 2.5 million boxes of apples to Britain, of which over 1.1 million were from Oregon and Washington. Although this was only a fraction of the nearly 34 million boxes of apples Oregon and Washington produced that year, it was still a significant number.[82]

Publicity from the arsenic scare also had the potential to harm domestic sales. Western apple growers, fearing heavy-handed federal regulations, offered to cooperate with the USDA with the hope of shaping new regulations. In the spring of 1926, western growers formed the National Spray Residue Committee to investigate the problem of spray residues. At a conference that November in Portland, Oregon, the group adopted a series of resolutions reaffirming its commitment to cooperate with government officials. Wanting to avoid a trial in the court of public opinion, the committee went "on the record decisively as opposed to any form of publicity or otherwise airing this problem before a political, judicial, or any other public forum." They praised the press in western states for "suppressing articles which might prove detrimental to the industry."[83] Growers had no intention of giving up arsenic-based pesticides, because there were no effective alternatives. Perhaps it is not surprising that the conference focused on damage control and public relations rather than reducing lead arsenate usage.

Growers promised cooperation, but reducing arsenic on apples was more complicated. J. W. Hebert, chair of the National Spray Residue Committee, summed up the problem: "The successful growing of fruit requires the use of insecticides which leave a residue on the fruit at harvest time; therefore, the residue must be removed as the final and only satisfactory solution of the problem if the industry is to enjoy permanent security and stability and the confidence of the public."[84] Researchers at Washington State College and Oregon Agricultural College studied new methods for eliminating lead arsenate residue. Lead arsenate is not water soluble, and growers often mixed it with oil bases to make it adhere to trees. This made residues difficult to remove. Researchers focused on two methods of cleaning apples after harvest: dry and wet. The dry method was already in widespread use. Automatic brush or rag machines removed dust and surface grime before apples were packed for shipment. While this improved the aesthetic appearance of fruit, it did not remove lead arsenate. The wet method involved soaking or spraying apples with a wet solution. Researchers tried several acidic and alkaline solutions, looking for a substance that would remove residue but not damage the apples or decrease storage life. After testing dozens of solutions, they found that a 1 percent solution of hydrochloric acid removed arsenic and lead residue to acceptable levels.[85] Hydrochloric acid was accessible and relatively inexpensive, and it had the added benefit of improving apples' appearance, a marketing bonus. Finding a silver lining, the editor of *Better Fruit* quipped, "Looks as though it took a near-calamity to disclose that our superior fruits could be made more attractive than ever before."[86]

By late 1926, the *Washington Post* declared the arsenic scare over, but controversy over arsenic and lead residues persisted through the 1930s as growers, the USDA, and the FDA continued to debate tolerance levels. The *London Times* published information from new studies about the use of hydrochloric acid to remove arsenic residue, but the discovery of hydrochloric acid did not end consumer fears about arsenic.[87] In 1927, twenty-seven people in Los Angeles suffered arsenic poisoning after eating apples from a boxed-lunch company, and in the early 1930s Poland

and Romania banned the import of American apples because of concerns about arsenic levels.[88] In 1934, Seattle papers reported that one woman died and several others became ill after eating homegrown pears sprayed with an arsenic-based pesticide. Although the death turned out to be from an unrelated medical condition, newspapers were quick to blame arsenic.[89] A 1936 health column in the *Washington Post* cited a recent report that claimed arsenic poisoning was more common than previously thought. Readers may have been frightened by the column's discussion of a Connecticut family who became violently ill after consuming washed, baked homegrown apples, but the columnist assuaged readers' fears. The benefits of eating healthy fresh fruits and vegetables outweighed any remote possibility of arsenic poisoning. "Fruit and vegetable growers are compelled to use insecticides," the columnist concluded. "Otherwise crops would be ruined and there would be no fruits or vegetables for human consumption."[90] Herein lay a central conflict of the industrial apple. The production of healthy food required the use of dangerous chemicals. Industrial production enriched consumers' diets but came with an environmental cost.

The apple industry never fully confronted the danger of the pesticides it used to create perfect apples. At the annual meeting of the Washington Horticultural Association in 1926, one member dared to question the safety of lead arsenate at the end of a presentation on hydrochloric acid:

MR. NICHOLS: This question is a little bit off the subject, one of the men who is selling wiping machines told me that arsenate of lead was accumulative, and if you ate one one-hundredth of a grain every day for ten years, it would be in your system at the end of that time. I do lots of spraying and eat lots of it, and I am wondering how long I am going to live.

PROF. HARTMAN: A perfectly logical question. You should consult medical authorities at once (laughter).

VOICE: I think Mr. Nichols will live as long as the rest of us.[91]

The crowd laughed off Mr. Nichols's question, perhaps because it touched on a difficult line of inquiry. Regardless of the danger, commercial apple production relied on pesticides. Downplaying health concerns was easier than confronting the possibility of losing one's livelihood.

At a spray conference in 1933, attendees raised the question of safe lead tolerances. This time the question was taken seriously, and the conversation turned to available scientific evidence on lead poisoning. Studies varied as to how much lead had to be consumed and in what form. "We don't know how much lead is required to cause chronic lead poisoning," stated presenter Dr. W. A. Buick. "The attempt to determine the minimum chronic poison dose over a long period of time for drinking water, for various foods containing lead, for various individuals, and other complicating factors make it extremely difficult to arrive at a true estimate of the amount of lead." Buick informally interviewed physicians in Wenatchee, reasoning that if lead arsenate caused chronic lead poisoning, those living in and around orchards would be prime candidates. Aside from some workers who sickened several years earlier from inhaling lead residue near a wiping machine, the doctors knew of no lead poisoning cases from ingestion.[92]

A more rigorous study by the Division of Industrial Hygiene of the National Institute of Health in 1938 investigated the effects of ingesting or inhaling lead arsenate and confirmed Buick's anecdotal evidence. For fourteen months, the study monitored 1,231 men, women, and children who worked in orchards and lived in areas where lead arsenate had been used since 1900. Only seven participants "had a combination of clinical and laboratory findings directly referable to the absorption of lead arsenate." Despite showing signs of absorption, none of the seven met the minimum criteria for lead intoxication set by the Committee on Lead Poisoning of the American Public Health Association. On the consumer side, the study found traces of lead in consumers who ate apples and in the control group. Levels of lead were slightly higher in the apple group, but this was not attributed to anything other than the "usual dietary and atmospheric sources."[93] Studies like this confirmed growers' belief that lead tolerances were too rigorous and that consumer fears were overblown.

Even as growers pushed for higher lead tolerances, they complied with federal policy by removing residue, reducing pesticide use, and seeking alternatives to lead arsenate.[94] Growers protested the new lead and arsenic tolerances, but they could not afford to ignore them. After the 1926 scare, the Yakima Valley Growers' Spray Residue Committee urged growers to use preventive measures against codling moths, such as setting traps in heavily infested areas, pruning trees, destroying infested fruit, and using proper spraying techniques. Since codling moths breed several times each year, growers who eradicated the crucial first brood could avoid late-season spraying. Researchers searched for safer alternatives to lead arsenate, but substitutes such as calcium arsenate, zinc arsenate, and manganese arsenate damaged trees, failed to eradicate codling moth, or were more harmful to humans than lead arsenate. In the early 1930s, fluorine compounds appeared to be a promising solution. While fluorine compounds were effective at killing orchard pests, early toxicity reports showed that they were as harmful to humans as arsenic. In 1933, the Food and Drug Administration alerted growers that any trace of fluorine on fruit would be "regarded as a basis for action under the food and drug act." As an article in the *Big "Y" Bulletin* lamented, "hope of growers for arsenical substitute is once more shattered."[95]

As concerns about lead residue continued into the 1930s, some growers felt that apples were unfairly targeted since other consumer products had higher levels of lead or arsenic. In January 1933, the Food and Drug Administration detained six hundred cars of Yakima apples for lead and arsenic testing. Most cars were within acceptable levels, but the shipping delay led to spoiled fruit and lost sales. Industry leaders claimed the FDA discriminated against Washington because 40 percent of growers used alkaline solutions to clean apples rather than hydrochloric acid. The FDA denied this claim, but its actions left growers frustrated. They were trying, though grudgingly, to comply with spray residue regulations. Growers were in a bind. At the height of the Depression, few could afford new washing equipment to remove residues. Nor could they afford losses from wormy or spray-contaminated fruit. Several years later, William H. Horsley recalled an incident in a letter to fellow cooperative managers. Quoting from a consumer research bulletin that found that cigarettes contained lead and arsenic "in amounts from 5 to 25 times greater than the 1935 government tolerances for spray residues on fruits," he cynically opined, "I haven't seen where the Department of Agriculture has held up any cigarette shipments like they did on our apple shipments a few years ago."[96]

Growers used lead arsenate until after World War II, when DDT came on the market. Like lead arsenate, DDT had problems, as have subsequent generations of pesticides. Researchers continue to search for safer pest control methods. Washington's early growers found that the natural environment conferred some advantages such as fewer fungal diseases and ample sunshine. But those advantages were not enough to produce marketable, worm-free apples. Growers still had to manipulate their environments, starting with the irrigation ditches constructed to deliver water to orchards. They had to select trees with fruit that had optimal ripening, hardiness, color, and yield. They had to fight biological infestations. Research conducted at land-grant colleges, at the USDA, and even by nonscientists provided some solutions, as did cooperation and conformity to state regulations. They also learned that orchard management alone would not solve every problem in the industry. Chemical sprays had environmental consequences, and growing the perfect apples did not matter if consumer sales lagged. In addition to managing their orchards, growers also needed to understand marketing.

CHAPTER 4

The Clamor of Bidders and Buyers
Getting Fruit to Market

In 1912, C. L. Durkee, a disgruntled grower in Meyers Falls, Washington, wrote to Louis Hill, president of the Great Northern Railway, for help finding storage facilities for his apples while they awaited shipment. The only storage warehouse near the railroad belonged to the local fruit cooperative. Other storehouses located farther from the tracks were not acceptable alternatives because Durkee would have to pay additional fees to have his fruit hauled from the warehouse to the railroad. In his letter, he argued that the railroad should take responsibility for farmers because railroads had settled farmers on the land. Growers like Durkee were lured to central Washington with promises of independence. The fees and rules imposed by the local cooperative represented a loss of independence, and even though membership would have solved his storage problem, he refused to join. "What this country needs is settler[s] not orchardists," complained Durkee. "Self-sustaining people. Not paupers. Contented homes. Not a lot of specialists & sore heads."[1]

Washington growers like Durkee clung to the idea of farmers as independent business owners, but they soon learned that apple marketing, like growing, required cooperation, specialized knowledge, and a complex infrastructure of packinghouses, sales networks, rail transportation networks, and storage facilities. Just as growers learned that failure to spray caused harm to neighboring trees, so too did they learn that shipping inferior apples harmed the reputation of the entire state industry. Growers had already standardized some aspects of orchard management, but for the industry to succeed, they had to address the complex logistics of moving a perishable good to distant consumer markets. This required advances in cold storage and railcar technology, robust transportation networks, managerial and record-keeping expertise, connections with distant buyers, knowledge of national and global markets, and consumers willing to pay for a premium product, tasks beyond the capacity of an individual grower.

Prior to the twentieth century, commercial orchards sold fruit seasonally through a system of decentralized distributors. Farmers either marketed their own produce or sold it to a buyer with whom they had an established relationship. As early as 1741, New York growers shipped apples to the West Indies, and records dating from the 1750s show shipments to Britain. Real commercial growth started after the opening of the Erie Canal in 1825.[2] Between 1850 and 1900, the value of commercial orchard products in the United States grew nearly 1,000 percent. In 1890, New York State had the largest commercial industry and the most bearing apple trees in the nation, just over 15 million.[3] Eastern commercial growers had the advantage of proximity to major urban areas. Though New York growers engaged in a robust export trade, most apples did not travel far from where they were produced.

Washington's first million-bushel crop, in 1895, encouraged new settlement and orchard plantings, but new orchardists gave little thought to fruit marketing. Orchard management dominated horticultural conversations as growers waited for trees to bear fruit. Local markets absorbed most available fruit, and traveling brokers purchased any excess. In the early 1900s, recalls John Gellatly, Wenatchee historian and early resident, "there were no oiled roads, and obviously the flying dust, plus the stain of the spray material made the fruit look very unappetizing—still it sold like hotcakes."[4] Market gluts in the 1880s led to low apple prices, and in the early 1890s, many growers in New York pulled up their trees. Prices had just begun to improve in the early 1900s as Washington growers sold their first crops outside the region. Luck and timing were on their side. Five consecutive crop failures in the Ozarks of Missouri, the nation's fifth most valuable apple commercial district in 1900, provided an opening for western apples.[5] Buyers showed up on growers' doorsteps, sometimes far in advance of harvest. Unfortunately for Washington growers, early luck did not last.

By the turn of the century, the map of commercial fruit production was changing. Railroad construction and irrigated western fruit tracts began to disrupt distribution systems. Irrigated western lands were well suited for growing a variety of fruit including apples, peaches, pears, cherries, and plums. Production quickly outpaced local and regional markets. Western growers sought to compete in national markets, especially urban markets on the East Coast, several thousand miles distant. Transportation and refrigeration technology made access to national and international markets possible as consumers demanded fresh produce. This meant, however, that growers no longer had a corner on their regional markets. They had to compete with other apple-growing regions and other types of fruits, such as citrus. By 1900, California led the nation in fruit production, in large part because of the state's burgeoning citrus industry, with orchard products valued at over $14 million. New York ranked second, with orchard products valued at $10.5 million. In total, twenty-one states reported orchard products in excess of $1 million, but California and New York dwarfed most states. Combined, they accounted for 29 percent of the nation's orchard production.[6]

In 1900, Washington ranked a modest twenty-second in the nation with orchard products valued at just under $1 million.[7] Sales of dusty, tired fruit boosted growers' hopes, but local markets were already saturated. Eastern buyers had their pick of orchards, and they had no incentive to make the long trek west if closer crops were available. Buyers also used growers' ignorance of general market conditions to drive prices lower. As orchard production grew in the early 1900s, Washington's marketing problems became more pronounced.[8] Some years, gluts drove prices down, leaving growers with little profit. Other years weather ruined crops. Even in years with healthy crops and favorable marketing conditions, growers could not always get their fruit to market because of problems with storage or transportation logistics. Experts predicted that increased production would exacerbate the marketing problem.

Distance from consumers compounded Washington growers' marketing problems. Eastern commercial growers had much lower transportation costs than western growers since they shipped fruit a few hundred miles at most. Western fruit, on the other hand, was shipped thousands of miles, and growers had to charge higher prices to recoup shipping costs. On average, consumers paid three times more for western boxed apples than for eastern barreled apples. "The Northwestern apple is a specialty product, not a staple," explained the Northwest Fruit Exchange in 1913. "For every carload of apples grown in the Northwest, there are 20 carloads grown elsewhere."[9] Washington growers hoped that they could gain an edge over eastern competitors and justify higher costs by producing high-quality fruit. By the mid-1910s, Washington apples began to compete with those grown in New York and other eastern districts. Eastern growers struggled to adopt the scientific growing methods used in western orchards. They slowly made costly orchard "renovations," as one agricultural bulletin called the new spraying, pruning, and thinning regimens.[10] Many were understandably reluctant to make drastic changes because their orchards were still profitable. Plus, they knew they had one key advantage over western growers—proximity to markets.

High transportation costs were not the only problem. Because of Washington's distance from the primary consumer markets on the East Coast, growers had no choice but to trust their profits and livelihoods to a series of intermediaries. Growers were suspicious of such go-betweens, but they could not market apples nationally without them. Individualized marketing worked for farmers who loaded their goods onto their wagons and sold them to consumers in the nearest town. Northwest growers, however, could not replicate this model. Instead, they relied on bankers, railroad officials, and commission agents who purchased fruit wholesale to sell to grocers.

In the early years, cash buyers purchased most fruit outright, usually at the time of harvest. In good years, buyers offered growers cash advances on their crops as early as June or July, although this did not guarantee a sale. If growers were unhappy with prices, they could break their contracts. Cash buyers offered the advantage of up-front payments. Buyers also relieved growers of responsibility for shipping and marketing fruit. Some cash buyers were local businesspeople who owned warehouses and assembled carloads of fruit or vegetables to sell to established business partners. Others came from eastern cities to purchase apples directly; however, eastern buyers did not purchase Northwest fruit if the eastern crop was good, much to the chagrin of Washington growers.[11]

Occasionally, growers lost their profits by selling to disreputable buyers who failed to pay for the fruit after receiving it. The major drawback to the cash system was that growers received lower prices by selling at the peak of harvest rather than waiting until later in the season when demand might be higher.[12]

Consignment or commission houses provided an alternative to cash buyers. Eastern fruit houses in cities such as Chicago and New York acted as brokers between growers and eastern consumers. Rather than purchasing fruit outright, consignment houses held fruit in storage and sold it when the market seemed most favorable. Consignment houses deducted freight, icing, and warehouse fees, and a sales commission of 10 to 15 percent from the final sale price. Like cash buyers, some houses gave growers an advance early in the season so they could purchase spraying and packing supplies.[13] Advertisements for commission houses featured in *Better Fruit* touted their connections in eastern markets, expert knowledge of fruit markets, and past successes in disposing of fruit. After taking possession of the fruit, consignment houses decided when and at what price to sell; the grower no longer had control. Most consignment houses were honest and worked to develop strong relationships with growers, but there were swindlers. Growers could never be sure. An agent might falsely claim that fruit was damaged and had to be sold for a low price. Consignment houses tended to blame growers for low prices, citing problems with packing or damage to fruit. Industry experts, such as Oregon State College horticulturist C. I. Lewis, reminded growers to make sure that their fruit was properly packed and graded at delivery to avoid such conflicts.[14]

A revision to state law in 1907 provided growers with greater legal protection. Senator W. H. Paulhamus, a prominent fruit grower from western Washington and president of the Puyallup and Sumner Fruit Growers Association, introduced legislation to strengthen existing codes relating to commission merchants. The Commission Merchants Act, or Paulhamus Bill, as the press called it, repealed an older 1895 law that required commission houses to keep records of sales. The new law required commission houses to obtain a license, provide growers a receipt of the condition of fruit at the time of delivery, give notice within forty-eight hours of any sale, and pay growers within ten days instead of thirty. It also limited commission agents to a 10 percent commission fee, not including transportation costs.[15]

In general, growers favored the new regulations, but commission houses were divided. Some, such as J. B. Powles & Co. of Seattle, felt that if houses were following the 1895 law, the required bookkeeping should be largely in place, although as Powles noted, it would be difficult for the firm to report the names of all purchasers to growers. The law forced smaller firms out of business because they could not finance the required $3,000 bond or secure a line of credit to pay growers within the mandated ten-day window. For large firms like Powles, this was a net benefit. Other commission houses objected to the bill and refused to comply. The Seattle Produce Association, which represented several commission houses in Seattle, planned to ignore the bill, claiming that the cost of extra clerks made it impossible for merchants to profit on a 10 percent commission. Six weeks after the bill passed, the state had issued only twenty-five licenses, although an estimated fifty firms fell under the law. To circumvent the law, some merchants stopped taking goods on commission, limiting themselves to cash-only transactions, which were not governed by the new law. The *San Juan Islander* expressed the sentiments of growers with the headline "Commission Pirates Will Ignore the Law." Paulhamus, in an open letter to the press, advocated enforcement and urged growers to do their part by patronizing merchants who complied. At least one firm, W. H. Jones & Co. of Seattle, advertised its compliance with the law by touting its $20,000 bond.[16]

Despite the controversy, consignment houses and their regulation were important for the development of the apple industry. Several companies established long-term relationships with Washington growers and successfully used their business connections to open new markets. James S. Crutchfield, a commission agent from Pittsburgh, Pennsylvania, became one of the most diligent promoters of Washington apples. He first traveled to Wenatchee in 1903 to purchase fruit. Eventually, his company, Crutchfield, Woolfolk & Gibson, hired local commission agents and opened sales offices in Portland and Seattle. Two of Crutchfield's agents, W. F. Gwin and Alfred Z. Wells, later formed successful commission houses of their own. Crutchfield advocated "quality fruit produced by careful growing and quick harvest, rapid transportation, and cold-storage," and at times he criticized growers for not maintaining high enough standards.[17] In 1912, as glutted markets drove down prices and threw the industry into crisis, Crutchfield complained that growers had no concept of how markets worked. "They count everybody a middleman," he stated. "If they can deliver the goods direct to the consumer, then they do not need any middlemen, but that is just as impossible as it is for them to carry their products to market in automobiles, or without the railroads, for instance."[18] In other words, times had changed. Growers no longer had direct links to consumers. Like it or not, intermediaries played a necessary role in marketing fruit.

Crutchfield was not the only person to recognize the deep flaws of Washington's marketing system. By the 1910s, growers, railroads, and agricultural experts agreed that the apple industry was in crisis unless it solved its marketing problems. In an address before the International Apple Shippers' Association in 1913, U. Grant Border admonished growers to change their business methods. "His annual custom at crop time has been to seek the cool of his porch, smoke his pipe contentedly, and listen to the clamor of bidders and buyers," he declared. "Between crops he spends his time perfecting his fruit, perfecting his pack, and making two apples grow where one grew before, giving no thought to that other most important factor of likewise increasing consumption."[19] This mythical producer, like so many real producers in Washington, could no longer assume that the high quality of his fruit would attract wholesalers. As production in Washington's apple districts increased, so too did competition for that fruit on the market. A more sophisticated strategy was necessary. H. C. Hampson of the North Pacific Fruit Distributors argued that "just as *scientific manufacturing* cannot succeed without scientific advertising, distributing and selling organization, so *scientific production* alone will result in failure without *scientific advertising, distributing and selling machinery.*"[20]

As growers examined marketing strategies, a third option developed: the growers' cooperative. Growers may have been able to rely on cash buyers and commission agents in the past, but now they needed a more proactive approach to create demand in eastern consumer markets and address grower complaints about freight rates, damage to fruit in transit, and broker commissions. California provided a blueprint for how cooperatives could improve marketing. While commercial orchards date to the 1840s, the citrus industry took off in California during the 1870s.[21] By the 1890s, the state had 4.5 million orange trees and 1.3 million lemon trees. As in Washington, growers faced market gluts and declining prices.[22] Fruit packing and grading were not standardized, and a decentralized distribution system left individual growers with little leverage against eastern fruit brokers who took advantage of growers' ignorance to drive prices lower.

Cooperative marketing offered a solution for controlling surpluses and distribution, disseminating information, and coordinating sales to reduce competition. Throughout the early 1890s, dozens of organizations sprang up in California, each with a slightly different method for attacking marketing problems. Some operated cooperative packinghouses, some sold fruit, while others attempted to regulate both sales and packing. By 1893, overproduction—or, as argued by many clever boosters, underconsumption—pushed prices downward to a point where local cooperatives in California's major citrus districts agreed to unite under one umbrella, the Southern California Fruit Exchange. During its first two seasons, the exchange allowed individual cooperatives to continue selling fruit. This system was confusing and did little to alleviate growers' marketing problems. Finally, in 1895, the exchange required that all members sell through exchange representatives.[23] In 1903, the Southern California Fruit Exchange reorganized as the California Fruit Growers Exchange and settled into a formula that worked relatively well. Local associations took responsibility for picking, grading, packing, and loading the fruit onto railcars. The central organization maintained a sales agency that collected market data and coordinated sales and shipments from the various local districts. By 1932, the California Fruit Growers Exchange had 210 local associations with thirteen thousand growers in twenty-six districts.[24]

In the early twentieth century, members of the Country Life Movement promoted cooperatives as means to improve farmers' lives and alleviate the burdens of rural life. While hints of that rhetoric seeped into discussions about forming cooperatives, like their counterparts in California, growers in Washington focused on financial gain.[25] Cooperatives improved sales. California fruit growers were on the cutting edge of industrialized horticulture. Fruit and vegetable production was becoming oriented to national markets, and Washington growers were paying attention. Newspapers and trade publications featured articles on the activities of the California fruit growers, accompanied by editorial asides urging Washington growers to adopt a similar organization.[26] Industry leaders and horticultural experts cited California as the example of successful cooperation. Agriculture, like other fields, was becoming more professionalized in the early twentieth century. Participating in national and international markets required professional knowledge of market conditions and sales outlets. Forces beyond growers' control affected sales whether they liked it or not. They could follow expert advice and band together for mutual protection, or they could continue to go it alone and hope for the best.

In 1894, a group of growers representing Oregon, Idaho, Washington, and British Columbia founded the Northwest Fruit Growers' Association, one of the first cooperatives in the Northwest. The group's publication *Better Fruit*, started in 1906, became one of the primary forums for the apple industry in the Northwest. In the first issue, W. H. Paulhamus, president of the Puyallup and Sumner Fruit Growers Association in Washington, extolled the "importance of fruit growers associations." With good soil, ideal climate, and hard work, "any person with a good common sense and a reasonable amount of energy can produce a most excellent crop," he wrote, but that did not matter if there were no markets to absorb it.[27] Paulhamus estimated that the actual production of fruit accounted for only one-third of the business; growers should focus the rest of their energy on marketing. He believed Northwest growers could produce noncitrus fruit superior to that grown in California if they cooperated on packing, shipping, and marketing.

Cooperatives had the potential to generate larger profits by enforcing quality standards, decreasing competition, and opening new markets. Hoping to reap the benefits of cooperation, several organizations sprang up across the region, many with bylaws based on those of California cooperatives. Cooperatives advocated packing arrangements that lent themselves to uniformity and easy inspection. They purchased supplies such as pesticides and spraying equipment in bulk to distribute to their members at a reduced cost. Cooperatives also adopted rules to reject any fruit that failed to meet association standards. By 1907, the list included the Hood River

Apple Growers Union, Hood River Fruit Growers Union, the Wenatchee Valley Fruit Growers Association, the Spokane Fruit and Vegetable Growers Association, and Yakima County Horticultural Union. Some cooperatives were successful, but others were short lived. They either disbanded from lack of members or merged with other cooperative organizations.[28]

Through cooperatives, growers hoped to gain leverage against intermediaries and keep a greater share of profits. In a 1913 essay on the need for cooperation, E. H. Shepard, editor of *Better Fruit*, argued that growers of perishable products were not getting their due. Nationally, farmers received 46.5 percent of the final retail value of their crops, with the remainder divided among jobbers, retailers, waste, and railroads. Relying on anecdotal evidence, he claimed that growers of perishable produce received only 13 percent of the final retail price. Unlike some critics, he did not deny intermediaries their fair share. "The railroad is entitled to a freight rate that will pay a satisfactory return on the investment. The wholesaler and the fruit dealer are entitled to a profit that is reasonable on the amount invested in his business and for his services," Shepard explained. "I believe that many fruit growers today are indiscriminately condemning many wholesale dealers who are purchasers of our fruits. We need the good ones; we should eliminate the bad ones."[29] Shepard's view on intermediaries was somewhat surprising since *Better Fruit* was a vocal outlet against such go-betweens and loss of profits. But by 1913, apple growers were shipping thousands of carloads to national consumers and could no longer avoid intermediaries. The goal was to establish a system that maximized trust and grower control.

Although cooperation offered several benefits, just as in California, growers were initially cool to the idea of cooperative marketing.[30] Joining meant giving up a degree of control. Cooperatives did not send payment until they sold all fruit in that season's pool, so growers received payments for fall crops the following spring. Growers balked at the fees and dues cooperatives charged. To some, this was another example of intermediaries depriving the grower of hard-earned profits. Even by the 1920s, when the industry was better established, many growers continued to deal independently with commission houses and cash buyers.

Those who favored cooperatives tried to convince fellow growers of the benefits of organization. *Better Fruit* editor E. H. Shepard used the magazine as a platform to persuade growers of their merit. Shepard acknowledged growers' concerns about intermediaries, but he knew it was not practical to eliminate go-betweens entirely. He advised growers not to "censure" those who were against cooperatives. "I believe I am justified in saying that a large part of the fruit growers who believe the middleman should be eliminated are people who have never been engaged in any commercial business of any importance," he explained. Instead, he encouraged patience and education to bring growers around.[31]

Despite growers' reluctance to join, strong local and regional cooperatives developed across the state. By the 1920s, Washington had four major apple cooperatives and several smaller organizations. The oldest, the Yakima County Horticultural Union, was founded in 1902 at a time when Yakima shipped few apples east. The union established a business relationship with a cash buyer named J. M. Perry, who handled the union's fruit exclusively in the first year. Later the union handled its own distribution under its Blue Ribbon brand. By 1910, the union had constructed a stone warehouse, and by 1919, it owned cold-storage facilities.[32] In a 1923 study on Northwest apples, business professor Harold Maynard wrote that the union was the only cooperative with a waiting list. He attributed the union's success to its conservative business practices. It never accepted more fruit than it could market, and it sold only the highest-quality fruit.[33]

The Yakima Fruit Growers Association, known as "Big Y," formed in 1911 as a loose confederation of smaller cooperatives that maintained their own warehouses and accounts. Big Y served as a clearinghouse for reporting sales. The structure never worked well because growers worried that other members might be getting better prices. In 1918, Big Y restructured with a centralized, top-down administration. Like the Horticultural Union, Big Y handled its own distribution through sales representatives who worked directly with buyers. They placed all fruit into a single pool and paid members the average pool price. To maintain quality, Big Y used a central packing system whereby Big Y employees packed all members' fruit in Big Y facilities.[34] The Horticultural Union and Big Y governed from the top down through boards of trustees. At times they solicited member input, but final control lay with the board.

Unlike Yakima, Wenatchee developed decentralized cooperatives formed from confederations of local associations. Each association acted independently, operating its own facilities and choosing when and at what price to sell its fruit. As Maynard explained, "Under this plan, the local does not sell its fruit to the central association, but merely uses the central association as its selling agent."[35] The Skookum Packers Association and the Wenatchee-Okanogan Cooperative Federation (Wenoka) followed this model. The Northwest Fruit Exchange began advertising apples using the Skookum brand in 1914, and in 1916 it decided to turn the brand over to Wenatchee growers, thus forming the Skookum Packers Association. Several local cooperatives joined the new association. The cooperative allowed members to sell apples under the Skookum brand, provided they maintained high-quality standards. The association inspected fruit, arranged for bulk purchase of packing supplies, and set sales policies, while the Northwest Fruit Exchange continued to distribute Skookum fruit. In 1922, eight associations canceled their contracts with the Northwest Fruit Exchange. By doing so, they also canceled their membership with the Skookum Packers Association. The eight associations formed a new organization: the Wenatchee-Okanogan Cooperative Federation. Two associations, the Okanogan Growers Union and the Wenatchee-Skookum Exchange, remained loyal to the Skookum contract.[36]

As cooperatives developed, growers learned that what happened to apples after harvest was just as important as orchard management. All the work of pruning and spraying was for naught if apples were damaged during or after harvest. Scientific experts offered growers advice for optimizing harvest. The industry had to train pickers and packers in proper methods of handling and shipping. High-quality fruit was not enough to entice buyers. Fruit also had to be attractively packaged and arrive at its destination in pristine condition, none of which could happen without expert handling at harvest and beyond. Cooperative associations offered a solution to these problems by helping growers pool their knowledge and resources, enforcing quality standards, and negotiating with shippers and buyers.

Apples began their journey from orchard to consumer at harvest time. The specialized knowledge used to grow apples extended to harvesting and packing. The Northwest grew a variety of crops, and each crop had its own labor needs. Hops and fruit destined for canneries could be picked

Orchard crew picking and packing apples, circa 1912. In the early years of production, many growers boxed apples on their farms. *Collections of the Yakima Valley Museum.*

by inexperienced workers because a little damage or bruising to the fruit had little impact on the final product. Apples, on the other hand, were shipped fresh. They had to be handled with care or the crop would be ruined. *Better Fruit* offered picking and packing advice to growers based on information from agricultural research stations and experienced growers. C. I. Lewis, horticulturist at Oregon State College, advised growers to "handle the apples as though they were eggs," never dumping them in piles or dropping them into deep picking bags.[37] This was sound advice, but it was not always easy to enforce, depending on the labor available for harvest. For most of the year, growers maintained their orchards themselves, or with the assistance of a few hired hands, making it easy to monitor the quality of work done in the orchard. During harvest, a grower and family could pick a small farm, one in the five-to-ten-acre range. Large orchards required additional labor.[38]

In the early years, friends and neighbors aided each other with harvest, and entire families picked fruit. As orchard acreage expanded in the 1910s, growers had to find additional labor sources. Most industries in the Pacific Northwest required seasonal labor at different times of year with differing skill levels. Except for logging, seasonal labor requirements for most industries peaked in the summer months. Fruit harvests started in June with berries and lasted into October and November when the last apples ripened. Labor needs for fruit canneries followed shortly behind fruit harvest. In August, farmers required additional hands for wheat harvest. Fish canneries required extra labor to can summer fish runs. "That is one of the great faults of our industrial life here," lamented Washington state labor commissioner E. W. Olson. "We have so much intermittent employment that men and women are not employed in the same industry but a short time, when they have to seek work in other lines." Though Olson was talking about the fishing industry, he could well have been talking about any other industry in the Pacific Northwest. Not only were jobs seasonal, but each fruit harvest provided only a few weeks of employment at a time. Many Washington State residents picked up seasonal jobs to bolster household finances. Secretaries or shopkeepers might take a few weeks in the summer to work a fruit or hops harvest. Women and children traveled to work berry harvests while their husbands held down urban jobs. Farmers supplemented their incomes with jobs that complemented the seasonal patterns of their own crops.

For the apple industry, labor needs peaked in September and October during harvest. Though the number of laborers varied from year to year, a 1936 study of the Yakima Valley estimated that an additional five thousand to six thousand workers were needed for harvest. Workers comprised a combination of residents and migrants. Resident workers had their own farms or jobs. One study of Yakima estimated that 65 percent of resident workers lived in town, presumably working other jobs throughout the rest of the year. A study of Chelan County found that 24.5 percent of fruit workers were also part-time farmers. Studies conducted in the 1920s and 1930s do not specify what kind of work fruit harvesters did the rest of the year. One 1926 study interviewed female workers about the work the men in their families did during other times of the year and found that over 25 percent reported work in agriculture,

17 percent in lumber, 10 percent as undefined "laborers," and the rest in a variety of occupations including transportation, building trades, machining, fishing, firefighting, public service, metal trades, mining, clerical work, and professional jobs.[39]

As discussed in chapter 2, Washington had a small population and therefore a smaller labor pool. While some Indians and Japanese immigrants worked the harvest, most laborers were native-born whites or European immigrants who "with few exceptions are English speaking and literate."[40] Growers were reluctant to hire the few nonwhite laborers who were available. By contrast, Indians from across the Pacific Northwest traveled to Yakima for the hops harvest each September, about the same time as the apple harvest or slightly before. The hops harvest in Yakima required nearly three times more labor than apples, so hops growers needed all the labor they could find.[41] In the 1930s, Filipino laborers harvested hops as well. Unlike hops, apples had to be handled carefully, and growers did not trust nonwhite labor. A 1937 labor study noted that "neither growers nor experienced fruit workers seemed to believe that these groups, particularly Indians, were physically capable of picking apples. Nor do their habits of work fit the situation."[42] Racial attitudes of growers shaped hiring patterns, but workers themselves also made choices. Hops picking offered flexible hours and more autonomy in the field and required less skill than apple picking. For these reasons, apple harvest was less appealing to some workers.

Because apples required special handling, growers hired fewer women and children for harvest, unlike berry and hops growers, who tended to employ many women and children. Picking apples required handling heavy fruit ladders and canvas or burlap fruit sacks that fastened around pickers' waists and necks. A 1926 study by the Women's Bureau found that "many ranchers consider the work too onerous for the average woman."[43] A study from the same year on child labor found that only one-third of children surveyed had picked apples. "Picking apples, pears, and peaches, particularly in orchards where fruit is carefully graded for shipping, is usually regarded as too difficult for children, at least those under 14 years."[44] Younger children could not manage the weight of fruit sacks, nor did growers trust them to pick fruit without bruising it. Women and children did harvest apples, however, especially in years when there were labor shortages. Women teamed up with male pickers, often a husband or relative. The women would harvest the lower half of the tree, while the men would harvest the top half, which required more climbing. Female pickers worked around the weight issue by emptying their picking sacks before they were full. In the same way, older children helped with the harvest. Some school districts delayed the start of school or adjusted the school calendar to include a two-to-three-week "apple vacation" so children could help with the harvest. Some parents appreciated the break, as it enabled the entire family to work. Others opposed the break, particularly mothers who had to work the harvest but lacked childcare for younger children.[45]

While local workers performed most orchard labor throughout the year, in September and October, growers had to supplement local labor with migrant labor. Depending on the year, half or more of the harvest labor force consisted of migrant labor. "The reputation of apple orchards for steady work and good pay has spread far," noted a study by the US Department of Labor Women's Bureau, "and it is customary for many pickers and packers to come long distances, with their own camp equipment, to the famed orchards."[46] Growers generally did not provide housing, so migrant laborers had to bring their own camping equipment. Most harvesting jobs lasted only a week or two, but because different apple varieties ripened at different times, a picker could move from orchard to orchard and find employment for several weeks. Growers did not have an organized system to procure labor, nor did they use formal contracts. A few growers advertised in newspapers, but many workers found their jobs through word of mouth or by asking at an orchard.[47] Some years this left growers scrambling for labor, and other years there were more workers than jobs.

Migrant laborers could be further divided into two categories: those who worked only one crop per season, and those who "followed the fruit." A 1936 study of labor in the Yakima Valley found that 38.1 percent of migrant laborers lived permanently in Washington. Like residents of Yakima and Wenatchee, many families in the Northwest worked fruit harvests for additional income, and some just happened to live closer to orchards than others. Society pages of Northwest newspapers noted the comings and goings of single-crop migrants, as in an announcement in the *Vashon Island News-Record* that Mr. and Mrs. Middlehoff had just returned from picking apples in Wenatchee.[48] The apple harvest paid comparatively well, and it provided many people with a nest egg to help survive the rest of the year. One thirty-year-old widow, for example, supported herself by working the apple harvest each fall and working as a store clerk the rest of the year. The apple harvest paid an average of $3.42 per day in 1926, more than she could make as a store clerk. The apple harvest also followed grain harvest, so it was common for families who worked the August grain harvest to spend part of September harvesting apples.[49]

The other group of migrants, those who "followed the fruit," cobbled together longer stretches of employment by moving from crop to crop. These workers were known by many names—"fruit tramps," "fruit hoboes," or "fruit transients." The Northwest produced a wide variety of fruit. From strawberries in June through apples in October, migrants could find work harvesting fruit and hops. At the end of the fruit harvest season, some migrant workers found winter work in lumber camps or as laborers in cities like Portland or Seattle. Others traveled south to California to spend January and February working in citrus orchards. While growers relied on migrant labor, communities in central Washington urged workers to move on at the end of each season. Not only were migrant laborers disconnected from the communities they worked in, but residents also worried about having large numbers of unemployed laborers in their communities over the winter. Every year, some migrants were unable to move on. This was "doubly hard for the fruit hobo with a family," observed a 1926 study by the US Department of Labor Women's Bureau, "which is never long enough in a place to be part of a community and its organization to know what the friendship of old neighbors means."[50]

After the harvest, apples were packed and either shipped or placed in storage. In the early years, packing and grading methods varied from district to district. Growers packed their own apples on the farm, but as the industry developed, more complex packing systems and rules emerged. From the outset, it paid to ship only the highest-quality fruit. As James S. Crutchfield, a prominent distributor, explained to Northern Pacific Railway officials, "The Northwestern districts that cannot grow fine apples had

GETTING FRUIT TO MARKET

Workers in 1910 packing apples in a small outdoor shed typical of those used by growers in the early years of apple production. *Collections of the Yakima Valley Museum.*

better quit the apple business right away, they have no chance whatever."[51] To maintain quality, Washington growers established strict grading systems to ensure uniform quality. Improper packing could ruin good apples. Although growers wanted to maintain their independence, fruit quality affected the reputation of the entire industry. Marketing even a small amount of damaged fruit could damage the region's reputation and sales.

Establishing uniform grading standards and packaging was an important step toward standardization. In the early years, each shipper or cooperative maintained its own grading rules. In 1908, the Yakima County Horticultural Union, the Yakima Valley Fruit Shippers Association, and the Zillah Fruit Growers Association collaborated on grading standards for the entire Yakima Valley in response to criticism of a "lack of uniformity in pack."[52] By the 1910s, central Washington growers had adopted three grades: extrafancy, fancy, and "C." Grades were very specific as to size, color, and defects allowed. Grades adopted by the North Pacific

Fruit Distributors in 1914 specified that extrafancy apples had to be "smooth, matured, clean, hand-picked, well-formed apples only; free from all insect pests, disease, blemishes, bruises and other physical injuries." The fancy grade permitted some blemishes such as scratches, if they were small, while "C" grade apples could be "slightly misshapen" with "slight sunscald" and have no more than two pest-inflicted blemishes. By contrast, a 1911 manual by horticulturist Liberty Hyde Bailey Jr. advised growers to separate their apples into two classes. First-class apples were ripe, while second-class apples were overripe or wormy.[53]

Standards aided marketing, but they were part of a larger trend toward food regulations. Consumers and progressive reformers worried about sanitation and food safety, especially as Americans purchased more of their food from distant producers. Consumers had no guarantee that their canned beef was actually beef. Unscrupulous merchants cut pepper with sawdust and watered down their milk. Horror stories of tainted milk or rotten meat abounded, most famously in Upton Sinclair's 1906 book *The Jungle*, which uncovered the unsanitary practices of Chicago's meatpacking plants. Without regulations, consumers had no guarantees of food safety. Some manufactures took matters into their own hands, such as H. J. Heinz, who gave tours of his famous sauce factory where white-clad workers demonstrated the purity of the factory and the product.[54] The Pure Food and Drug Act, passed in 1906 after Sinclair's shocking exposé, began to offer consumer protections. Consumers came to expect higher standards of quality from all their food. Apples were different from manufactured foods because consumers could inspect the product and make their own judgment about quality, but fruit jobbers who purchased carloads of fruit could not inspect every box. Statewide standardization gave jobbers confidence and helped the fruit industry police itself since poorly packed or low-quality fruit could be traced back to its source.

Many states enacted laws related to apple grading, but few had the financial resources to enforce regulations. Washington and New York did more to enforce grading rules than other states. In 1914, New York enacted apple-grading legislation with language similar to that of Washington cooperatives. Fancy grade apples had to be "of good color for the variety, normal shape, free from dirt, diseases, insect and fungus injury, bruises and other defects."[55] Rather than passing specific, fixed grading legislation, Washington took a different approach.[56] In 1915, state law mandated a yearly "State Grade and Pack Conference" where growers reviewed statewide grading standards. Standards were a moving target, set by growers each year. This system fostered communication among growers and allowed them to adjust grades based on the natural variations of each crop year. It encouraged growers to buy into the system because they had a voice rather than having standards imposed by the state legislature. The law also required growers to label all packed boxes with the variety of fruit, the place it was grown, the name of the grower or association, and the grade.[57] Labels helped keep fruit growers honest. In 1920, the state amended its horticultural statutes to require certificates of inspection, with fees covering the cost of inspection services. Those who failed to properly label or grade their apples faced misdemeanor charges and fines ranging from $50 to $500.[58]

Grading rules maintained quality standards, but each year, they prevented up to 50 percent of Washington's apple crop from reaching the market.[59] Small, wormy, misshapen, discolored, or blemished fruit was thrown on the cull pile. In New York, processors evaporated, or dried, cull apples, up to 75 percent of the crop in some years. Evaporated apples were not as profitable as fresh apples, but markets in eastern cities or in Europe offered a good outlet for low-quality fruit. Cull apples were processed into cider or vinegar as well.[60] Industry leaders in Washington urged the construction of similar cider-making or evaporation plants. In theory, salvaging culls seemed like a recipe for profit, but the evaporated apples were not economically viable in the Northwest. First, processing plants required a substantial capital outlay, and it was difficult to find investors. At an agricultural meeting in 1913, an inventor named Michener solicited $23,000 for a new evaporation company using his patented "Everfresh" process. Growers at the meeting were skeptical of the originality and profitability of this process. E. F. Benson, a grower at the meeting, noted that "his method of promotion appears to be the rankest graft or rather the most ridiculous proposition that I ever heard of."[61] The new technology offered no clear savings over existing plants. Michener tried to gain support by offering to pay six to ten dollars per ton for cull apples, well above the five dollars per ton paid by similar plants. The company would never have turned a profit at Michener's proposed rates.

Financing evaporation facilities was only the first hurdle. Plants could never be certain how much fruit would be available because of natural crop variations. Successful evaporating and canning plants never relied exclusively on apples for this reason. Plants usually did not pay enough to make it worth a farmer's time and effort. Most years, five dollars per ton did not cover the expense of picking and transporting poor-quality fruit. It was less expensive for growers to dump fruit than to haul it to a processor. Finally, processed fruit products faced the same marketing hurdles as fresh fruit: distance from markets, high transportation costs, and competition from other regions. Canneries in Washington did brisk business in peaches, pears, and berries because these fruits were highly perishable, and, because most of the crop was grown specifically for canning, canneries received top-quality fruit. Some canneries handled apples, but canneries, like growers, had to produce a high-quality product to compete against other products on the market. Growers shipped almost all high-quality apples fresh, leaving canneries with low-quality cull apples in which they had little interest. As one Yakima cannery proclaimed, "The dry yard is the only place for culls."[62] Most culls were thrown away or used as animal feed. Culls were an unfortunate industrial by-product. The real money was in high-quality fresh fruit.

Grading rules standardized fruit shipped from Washington, but standardization did not end there. Packing was equally important. Until the 1920s, two main types of packing arrangements predominated. Cooperatives such as the Yakima Horticultural Union, or large cash buyers such as Conrad Rose of Wenatchee, operated centralized packinghouses located near railroad tracks for ease of loading. Growers unaffiliated with a cooperative or cash buyer packed their own fruit in small, on-site packinghouses. As late as 1941, 40 percent of fruit in Yakima was still packed "on ranch."[63] Both methods had advantages and disadvantages. Growers who packed in the orchard maintained direct control over their fruit and did not have to pay packing fees to a third party. Large packinghouses, on the other hand, offered greater efficiency through economies of scale by purchasing packing materials in bulk. They also found it easier to attract skilled laborers. A small packinghouse might provide a few days' work, but a large packinghouse offered several months of employment, a better proposition for expert packers. Large houses invested in specialized machinery for washing and sorting apples; machinery was cost prohibitive for individual growers. The arsenic scare of 1926 brought an end to many on-site packing operations because packers had to wash apples to remove arsenic residues. Although some growers resisted joining cooperatives because of fees and lack of control, packinghouses packed fruit more cheaply and achieved greater standardization than individual growers.[64]

Packinghouses relied on skilled packers to pack apples correctly. As with orchard management, professional training and experience mattered. After struggling to find experienced workers, the Hood River Apple Growers Union opened a packing school in 1907. By 1910, it boasted an enrollment of two hundred men from across the United States. In 1909, Yakima, Wenatchee, and Walla Walla started packing schools.[65] While men initially dominated packinghouses, by the 1920s much of the sorting and packing was done by women. Some skilled packers migrated from California to Washington with the fruit harvests, but most warehouses employed nonmigrant labor. Packers had to be able to grade apples, wrap them, and pack them into apple boxes quickly and accurately, and women were very adept at this task. Packing paid roughly 70 percent more than sorting, and it paid more than picking. One Medford grower complained about women being paid more for "lighter tasks" while men toiled at more demanding jobs, especially because women spent their money on "luxuries" rather than supporting a family. A 1926 study of women in fruit and canning industries in Washington presents evidence to the contrary. Over half of women reported working to meet basic household expenses. Others worked to afford upgrades for their homes, such as household appliances. Over a quarter of women who worked in fruit warehouses supported themselves.[66]

Grading rules dictated minimum sizes for each variety grown. Packers used wooden grading boards with holes of various sizes to sort apples. By the 1920s, larger packinghouses, such as the Yakima Fruit Growers Association, installed mechanical sorters.[67] Apple sizes corresponded to the number that fit in the standard Northwest box; therefore, size 88 apples were larger than size 175 because only 88 fit into a box.[68] Packers wiped apples clean of any visible grime, wrapped them in paper printed with

Packing apples at the American Fruit Growers packinghouse in Wenatchee, Washington (date unknown). By the 1920s, many apples were packed in centralized warehouses equipped with mechanized washing and sorting machines. *Photograph by Simmer Studio. Box 133.F.3.1B, Advertising and Publicity Department, Great Northern Railway Company Records, Minnesota Historical Society.*

the grower's name or logo, and packed them into wooden apple boxes.[69] *Better Fruit* carried diagrams of packing arrangements for different-sized fruit. The type of packing depended on the grade of apples, with the most elaborate packing methods reserved for apples destined for fairs, demonstrations, or high-profile customers.[70]

Western growers adopted packing methods different from those of their eastern counterparts. From Colorado to the West Coast, growers packed apples in boxes. East of Colorado, growers packed apples in barrels. There were some exceptions. Eastern growers sometimes used bushel baskets or boxes for loose apples, and midwestern growers, particularly in the Ozarks, shipped apples in bulk in straw-lined boxcars.[71] In a 1911 manual, horticulturist Liberty Hyde Bailey Jr. explained how to pack a barrel. After carefully placing two or three layers of apples on the bottom, a process known as "facing," packers poured apples into the barrels. Packers then shook the barrels to pack fruit as tightly as possible. "It is better to jam these apples severely," he wrote, "than to allow those in the interior to rattle." Bruised apples were part of the process. Bailey did not worry about the layer of crushed apples at the top of the barrel because the lid, made of soft wood, would absorb any resulting juices.[72] Eastern growers had lower production and transportation costs, so they could afford to write off the cost of damaged apples.

Western growers, however, could not afford such losses. Consumers were not going to pay more for western apples if they were rotten, bruised, or blemished. California growers pioneered the use of new packing methods by developing smaller fruit boxes as early as 1885.[73] Barrels were constructed of hardwoods, which were in short supply in western forests. Boxes, by contrast, could be easily manufactured from pine, which was cut into pieces called "shooks." The best box makers could assemble one hundred boxes per hour. Boxes stacked easily and fit into boxcars more efficiently. Growers also found them easier to market because boxes had ample space for labels.[74] While box dimensions varied among fruit districts, all had approximately the same volume; three western boxes were the equivalent of one eastern barrel.

Boxed apples typically sold for three times as much as barreled apples, regardless of their origin. Unscrupulous commission buyers sometimes purchased barreled apples and repacked them in boxes to attain higher profits. New York grower F. A. Waugh tried the experiment on his own apples. His barrels sold for two dollars each, while boxes also sold for two dollars each. "In other words," he concluded, "one bushel of apples nicely wrapped and packed in boxes brought just as much as three bushels of the same fruit in a barrel." Even though his boxed apples sold for more, Waugh remained skeptical that boxes would replace barrels for eastern growers. He recommended that eastern growers reserve boxes for their fanciest grades. "The person buying a package of this kind expects it to contain something good," he explained. "If the purchaser buys a box of apples and finds the fruit inferior, his resentment is much greater than if he has been cheated on a barrel of apples. Most purchasers have grown accustomed to being more or less swindled on apples in barrels."[75] In

Lidding apple boxes at the Wenoka Packinghouse in Wenatchee, Washington (date unknown). *Photograph by Simmer Studio. Wenatchee Valley Museum and Cultural Center, 87-42-76.*

other words, boxes did not pay unless the fruit was top quality. For eastern growers, barrels achieved a greater economy of scale, and consumers were willing to tolerate the occasional bruised or damaged apple.

In 1902, the Northwest Fruit Growers' Association adopted a standard box measuring 10½ × 11½ × 18 inches, though not without some controversy.[76] Eastern congressional representatives pressured Congress to regulate the size of apple boxes for interstate trade. The 1908 Porter Bill and the 1910 Lafean Bill proposed a 2,342-cubic-inch bushel-sized box, slightly larger than the standard Northwest box. Northwest growers opposed both bills. Though the standard Northwest box was smaller, they argued that boxes contained over a bushel because of the tight packing and slight bulge in the boxes. In 1912, Congress fixed a standard size for apple barrels, but not boxes. Rather than waiting for eastern congressional representatives to introduce new box legislation, Washington growers went on the offensive. In a demonstration at the New York Land and Irrigation Show, E. F. Benson of Tacoma unpacked a box of Washington apples and heaped the fruit into two half-bushel baskets, demonstrating that Northwest boxes held over a bushel of apples.[77] In a 1914 circular letter clarifying recent amendments to the Pure Food and Drug Act, the US Department of Agriculture stipulated that the Northwest apple box, measuring $10½ \times 11½ \times 18$ inches, contain a minimum of one bushel, in compliance with the law.[78]

Cooperative packing saved growers money by using trained laborers and purchasing materials in bulk, but that was not the only service that cooperatives offered. On the other end of the spectrum, groups like the Northwest Fruit Exchange, a private marketing organization affiliated with the North American Fruit Exchange formed in 1910, acted as a sales agency for Northwest cooperatives. Members benefited from experienced agents' knowledge of markets. Exchange offices in eastern cities and in Europe monitored prices and market conditions 365 days a year.[79] Marketing cooperatives claimed that by eliminating competition within Washington, growers could focus on competition from other states. Collective marketing shielded growers from volatile markets by spreading the risk across the group. Growers received payments based on market averages rather than prices on the day of sale. Profits were slightly lower, but they were steadier. The most important argument for marketing cooperatives was that growers maintained control of the system. Cooperative sales agents were not eastern strangers; they were people of the growers' choosing. An individual grower could not afford an agent in every city. Nor did individuals have the collective bargaining power necessary to negotiate with shippers. Since sales agents worked for all cooperative members, growers could be assured that agents represented their interests.[80]

Cooperative membership gave growers an edge because cooperatives built reputations for quality. "Every mercantile business, every factory standardizes its output," explained E. H. Shepard. "If we are to succeed we certainly should have the common sense to adopt methods of business that have evidenced their value."[81] H. C. Sampson of the North Pacific Fruit Distributors shared a story that illustrated the importance of a cooperative's reputation. A Yakima peach grower asked permission to put the "Big Y" brand label, used by the Yakima Fruit Growers Association, on the inside of his box and his own labeling on the outside. The association granted permission. The peaches were graded, inspected, and shipped as normal; the only difference was that the "Big Y" was on the inside of the box. When the Portland purchaser received the shipment, he demanded to know why he had not received "Big Y" peaches. The cooperative assured him that he had, but the purchaser insisted on a price reduction of five cents per box. The labels on the inside of the box "made no difference at all, as his retail customers had built up a trade for 'Y' brand peaches . . . and nothing but 'Y' brand peaches would satisfy them."[82] Consumers associated a certain level of quality with the Big Y brand, but not with the individual grower's label.

The success of regional cooperatives spurred ambitions for a statewide organization modeled after the California Fruit Exchange. In 1907, a group at the annual Washington State Horticultural Society meeting proposed an organization called the Federation of Washington Fruit Growers to promote uniform shipping and packing practices and to disseminate current scientific and marketing research to growers. It never got off the ground.[83] Four years later, growers met in Walla Walla, Washington, to form a regional organization encompassing Washington, Oregon, and Idaho. They debated the proposal's merits through the summer and fall of 1911, but ultimately, cooperatives in Hood River, Oregon, and Wenatchee refused to join.[84] Not only were growers wary of losing control of their fruit, but strong regional rivalries, born out of the booster spirit, made regional cooperation difficult to achieve. Local cooperatives succeeded because growers built relationships with their neighbors, not with growers from rival districts. They could see exactly where their dues and membership fees went. In 1937, the state legislature authorized the Washington State Apple Advertising Commission, later called the Washington Apple Commission, which finally provided a statewide body to serve as a hub for marketing information and advertising, but the fragmented system of marketing through a network of cash buyers, consignment houses, cooperatives, and distributors remained. Local cooperatives represented a compromise between growers' need for independence and modern marketing strategies.

Even without statewide marketing, industry leaders leveraged the cooperative power of growers in other ways. They shaped state legislation relating to the apple industry. They served in national organizations such as the International Apple Shippers' Association. More importantly, they maintained relationships with the railroads. Standardized packing and organized marketing practices mattered little unless railroads transported fruit to consumers in a timely fashion. Apple growers in central Washington had a complex relationship with the railroads. On the surface, the relationship appeared contentious. Newspapers printed editorials against perceived injustices including high freight rates, damage in transit, lack of storage facilities, car shortages, and transit times. *Better Fruit* occasionally published antirailroad articles that framed railroads as the enemy of growers. Correspondence between apple industry leaders and railroad executives, however, reveals a much different relationship. Both sides expressed frustration about shipping logistics. Growers' complaints often stemmed from the lack of infrastructure or the cost of freight. Though growers and railroads disagreed about who was responsible for constructing important infrastructure such as rail sidings, warehouses, and icing facilities, both sides had to contend with problems in the distribution system that were outside their control. For their part, the railroads had their own business interest to protect, which included revenue from apple shipments. Railroad agents monitored apple traffic and maintained regular contact with cooperatives, distributors, and shippers to head off potential problems.

Freight rates were the most contentious issue between growers and railroads. Railroads could not change freight rates without the approval of the Interstate Commerce Commission (ICC), a government agency created in 1887 and expanded in 1906 to regulate transportation. At ICC hearings, railroads and growers had the opportunity to present evidence for adjustments to freight rates. Though the ICC often ruled in railroads' favor, railroads preferred to avoid hearings because they were time consuming, and there was always the possibility that the ICC would approve lower rates. Growers used the threat of rate changes to gain other concessions from the railroads. While railroad executives could not lower freight rates, they could finance packing facilities, donate to marketing campaigns, or build new sidings. At times, railroad executives gave in to grower demands, hoping to avoid the dreaded ICC hearing. In the 1920s, for example, the Northern Pacific and Great Northern considered financing industry advertising campaigns to avoid discussions about freight rates, even though this went against standard company policy.[85]

As the apple industry grew, transportation logistics became a greater problem. Northwest fruit industries relied on railroads and refrigerated boxcars. "The refrigerated railroad car," wrote historian William Cronon, "was a simple piece of technology with extraordinarily far-reaching consequences."[86] Refrigerated cars allowed farmers to ship produce from the West and South, some of the nation's most productive agricultural areas, to urban markets in the Northeast, changing Americans' diets in the process. Refrigerated railcar technology evolved throughout the nineteenth century. In the 1830s, railroads shipped fruit and other delicacies in insulated or ventilated cars that circulated outside air to cool the car without ice or mechanical refrigeration. In 1869, the year the first transcontinental railroad was completed, the Union Pacific shipped a carload of fruit from California to New York in a ventilated boxcar. Until the 1870s, perishable shipments were limited. Without refrigeration, any delays led to spoiled shipments. That changed when meat and dairy producers began investing in refrigerated railcars. Gustav Swift, a Chicago meat packer, was one of the first to send large-scale shipments of dressed beef to eastern markets. At first, Swift shipped carcasses during the winter in ventilated cars; the cold winter air kept the beef frozen. Swift later worked with engineer Andrew J. Chase to develop an insulated refrigerated car with compartments to hold ice and cool all parts of the railcar. Later designs placed bunkers on each end of the car, leaving cargo space in the center of the car.[87]

New refrigerated car technology was expensive, but a sensible investment for private firms like Swift and Armour that shipped products year-round. Fruit, however, was seasonal. Growers did not have the capital to invest in their own railcars, and railroad companies were reluctant to invest in equipment that would be used only a few months a year. In 1880, railroads owned only 310 refrigerated railcars. By contrast, private lines owned over 1,000 cars.[88] In the 1880s and 1890s, railroads continued to ship fruit in ventilated cars known as baggage, express, or passenger fruit cars, attached to passenger trains that delivered fruit coast to coast

Loading boxes of Skookum apples onto a Fruit Growers Express refrigerated railcar. *Photograph by Asahel Curtis. Box 133.F.3.1B, Advertising and Publicity Department, Great Northern Railway Company Records, Minnesota Historical Society.*

in about fifty hours.[89] By the early 1900s, fruit shipments were profitable enough that western railroads decided to invest in refrigerated cars. In 1906, the Southern Pacific and Union Pacific purchased a share of Armour's business and formed a subsidiary, Pacific Fruit Express. Other refrigerated car companies followed such as Fruit Growers Express, an Armour subsidiary founded in 1920, and Western Fruit Express, a subsidiary of Fruit Growers Express and the Great Northern, formed in 1923.[90]

In the early 1900s, unrefrigerated cars carried Washington apples to Northwest markets such as Seattle and Portland. For short distances, railroads used standard boxcars with added ventilation. They reserved refrigerated express cars for shipments east. Ventilated boxcars kept fruit cool, but they could not keep apples at the optimal temperature of forty degrees Fahrenheit for the entire transcontinental journey. Engineers experimented with different designs for ice-cooled railcars, and by 1910, railroads had adopted a standard refrigerated car design that included tight-fitting doors, insulated walls, large ice bunkers at each end of the car, and mechanical fans powered by the car's axle to circulate air while the car was in motion. Cars also included heaters to keep the temperature above freezing when necessary. Because of these modifications, refrigerated cars cost about twice as much as ordinary boxcars.[91]

As the apple industry grew, express cars could not keep up with demand. Increases in fruit and vegetable production across the West put additional pressure on the small fleets of refrigerated cars owned by the railroads and their subsidiaries.[92] As thousands of trees planted in Yakima and Wenatchee began bearing in the 1910s, refrigerated car shortages intensified. In Washington, carload shipments increased from an average of a few hundred cars per year in the early 1900s to over ten thousand cars per year in the 1910s, and roughly thirty thousand cars per year in the 1920s.[93] Rather than connecting fruit express cars to passenger trains, the railroads began to operate "fruit blocks," trains consisting exclusively of fruit cars.

Even though railroads increased the size of their refrigerated fleets, it was not enough to keep up with demand. Cars did not make many trips in a year, which limited profitability. In 1912, the average refrigerated car took seventy-three days to make a round trip, including loading and unloading. At this rate, each car could conceivably make five round trips per year. However, apples were shipped only in the fall and winter, in the weeks immediately after harvest. This meant that each car made only one round trip during the shipping season, a significant underutilization of available rolling stock since refrigerated cars were not easily adaptable to other purposes. Since crop size varied from year to year, railroads tried to estimate car requirements well in advance of the next shipping season. In 1912, the Northern Pacific, which served the Yakima Valley, owned 1,500 refrigerated cars. It ordered an additional 1,125 for the 1913 season. By 1915, managers estimated they would need another "4,000 cars, if the refrigerators make only one trip."[94] In 1915, the Great Northern estimated that Wenatchee would ship approximately 9,000 to 10,000 carloads of fruit. At that time, the Great Northern owned only 3,600 refrigerated cars, although not all of these were available to handle the Wenatchee crop. General manager J. M. Gruber recommended the

GETTING FRUIT TO MARKET 127

Loading Fruit Growers Express railcars at the American Fruit Growers packinghouse in Wenatchee, Washington. *Photograph by Asahel Curtis. Box 133.F.3.1B, Advertising and Publicity Department, Great Northern Railway Company Records, Minnesota Historical Society.*

purchase of an additional 1,000 cars and commented that "it seem[s] too bad to have to buy refrigerator cars because the only time we have use for them is during the apple and potato crops."[95]

The 1913 car shortage in Wenatchee provides a window into the challenges of railcar operations. On November 1, 1913, the *Wenatchee Daily World* reported that all warehouses in the valley were full, and that at least 600 carloads of apples were ready for shipment. Warehouses notified growers to stop delivering fruit until more cars were available. According to the paper, the shortage arose from the Great Northern's assumption that cars used early in the season would make two or more trips hauling fruit. Unfortunately, many of the cars had not yet returned.[96] Railroad agents monitored the situation closely, reporting the number of cars needed and the number of cars available. The next day, Wenatchee received 125 cars. "There would have been no shortage but for the unprecedented rapidity of loading this year," complained railroad agent A. A. Piper.[97] For the next ten days, the number of cars needed exceeded the number of cars available, although new cars arrived continually to meet demand. At the end of a hectic few weeks, agent W. C. Watrous reported that to date, the Great Northern had loaded 3,525 cars, fewer than the 3,708 loaded the previous year. Growers still needed another 400 cars by the end of the year.[98] The immediate crisis had passed, but car shortages continued. Railroad agents tried to anticipate transportation needs, but it was difficult to pin down the exact number of cars needed in any given season, especially since railroads had to account for refrigerated car usage across their entire system.

In addition to purchasing and maintaining refrigerated cars, railroads also had to maintain icing facilities along the route to replenish each car's ice supply, which added to logistical challenges. Ideally, fruit was precooled in a storage house and loaded into a car that had been precooled and iced. The Northern Pacific, for example, began precooling cars in Yakima as early as 1908.[99] Depending on conditions at the time of shipment, cars were re-iced en route to keep fruit at an optimal temperature. Until the late 1910s, railroads in central Washington relied almost exclusively on natural ice to cool cars. Investors in Yakima and Wenatchee constructed artificial ice plants in the early 1900s to provide cold storage for local dairies, butchers, and breweries. Railroads occasionally called on local plants to supplement ice supplies, but artificial ice was not consistently used for fruit shipments until the early 1920s because of cost.

Natural ice was cheaper than artificial ice, but it had some drawbacks. Central Washington produced little natural ice. Railroads sourced some ice from Loon Lake, north of Spokane, but most years, the ice on Loon Lake did not reach the minimum twelve-inch thickness required for harvest. Instead, the Great Northern obtained most of its ice from British Columbia and Montana, while the Northern Pacific sourced ice from Montana and North Dakota. Natural ice was produced on artificial lakes, specially dammed for this purpose. During the winter, workers kept the lakes clear of snow, since snow acted as insulation and prevented ice from thickening. At harvest, mechanical saws broke the ice into four-hundred-pound blocks, and conveyor belts moved the ice into storage facilities.

In 1913, a group of investors, known as the Wenatchee Natural Ice Company or the Three Lakes Improvement Company, approached the Great Northern about harvesting ice from a lake six miles from Wenatchee. After two years of discussions, the Great Northern turned down the offer. The investors provided weather reports and affidavits from local residents attesting to the depth of the ice, but the railroad's own investigators discovered that the lake had not frozen solid enough to permit the operation of an ice-skating rink. If the ice was not thick enough to skate on, then it certainly was not thick enough to harvest.[100] The Great Northern chose to honor its contracts in British Columbia. The ice was better, and infrastructure for harvest and storage was already in place.

As fruit production increased throughout the 1910s, the lack of local ice supplies created headaches for the railroads. They had to transport ice several hundred miles and construct storage facilities at both the point of ice harvest and the point of car loading. Moving ice long distances was costly and tied up railcars that could haul paying freight. Natural ice shrank up to 20 percent in storage, and it lost more volume as workers broke four-hundred-pound blocks into smaller pieces to load into refrigerator bays.[101] Artificial ice offered many advantages over natural ice. It freed up railcars and eliminated shipping costs, and less ice was lost to shrinkage. The major drawback was that artificial icehouses required a substantial capital outlay. In 1916, the Great Northern considered constructing an artificial ice plant. Although production cost fifty-nine cents more per ton than natural ice, the plant would save the railroad eighty-one cents per ton in handling fees. The proposed plant would produce two hundred tons of ice a day, and plans included a ten-thousand-ton storage facility to stockpile ice for the harvest rush, as the Great Northern had used nineteen thousand tons of ice the previous season. The outbreak of World War I scuttled plans because of increased machinery costs and a shortage of ammonia needed as a coolant. Instead, the Great Northern started negotiations with the Columbia Ice and Cold Storage Company. W. J. Mooney, the railroad's icing inspector, argued that an arrangement with Columbia Ice benefited all parties. It shifted responsibility for storing ice to the private firm, and it freed railcars normally used to haul ice for other purposes. Finally, consolidating icing operations at one location, Wenatchee in this case, created greater economies of scale by reducing the need for additional natural ice facilities. Growers were not happy with the news of a contract. Columbia Ice had connections with the Northwest Fruit Exchange, and growers feared a monopoly.[102] Nonetheless, the Great Northern's contract with Columbia Ice provided a critical service to growers.

By the early 1920s, the Northern Pacific also turned to artificial ice. Unlike the Great Northern, the Northern Pacific had competition. The Oregon-Washington Railroad and Navigation Company (OWR&N), a subsidiary of the Union Pacific, also vied for business in the Yakima Valley. It had access to refrigerated railcars through the Pacific Fruit Express, a subsidiary of the Union Pacific formed in 1906 to ship California citrus.[103] The Pacific Fruit Express had the largest fleet of refrigerated cars of any American railroad, it had been in the refrigeration game longer than the Northern Pacific, and it had a more robust infrastructure. Northern Pacific officials worried that without a secure supply of ice, they might lose customers. Northern Pacific president Charles Donnelly was initially skeptical of artificial ice, which he called a "leap in the dark." He chastised his managers for not providing a comparative cost analysis with natural ice. Managers quickly responded. Artificial ice was more cost effective if the railroad factored in costs of handling, transporting, and storing natural ice. Company experts calculated that, depending on variable overhead costs, natural ice cost between $3.91 and $5.33 per ton, while artificial ice cost between $3.60 and $4.00 per ton. By this time, the Northern Pacific's icehouses needed costly renovations, which added to the overhead costs. Donnelly balked at the ten-year contracts offered to ice plants in Yakima, but as his managers pointed out, the Great Northern granted ice plants in Spokane twenty-year contracts. The Northern Pacific was lucky that Yakima icehouses accepted a shorter term. The arguments about competing railroads proved most persuasive. The Northern Pacific ultimately signed ten-year icing contracts with J. M. Perry and Co., the Yakima Fruit Growers Association, and Yakima Artificial Ice & Cold Storage Co. By contracting with all three entities, it blocked the OWR&N from obtaining that ice, and it attracted business from growers who used the storage facilities at these locations.[104]

Steady supplies of ice did not always prevent damage to fruit in transit. Sometimes train crews failed to follow icing instructions. Delays or misrouting might add hours to transit time, causing temperatures in the car to rise. Once the fruit left their hands, growers had to rely on communication with the carrier and commission agent. Growers accused railroad companies of giving them the "runaround" and not settling damage claims promptly. Railroads answered by blaming growers for sending poor-quality and improperly packed fruit. Both sides had valid concerns and a desire to protect their profit margins. Neither side was solely to blame. The logistics of moving fruit long distances with crude refrigerated cars meant that some damage was inevitable. Growers and the railroads needed each other to ensure the success of their businesses, so they worked to find acceptable solutions.

Publications such as *Better Fruit* advised fruit shippers to foster better relations with the railroads. They printed instructions for making damage claims. They recommended that growers have at least two witnesses to inspect the car contents, condition of ice, state of vents, temperature, and door seals—all factors that, if faulty, could lead to damaged shipments. Apples needed to be stored at thirty-two to forty degrees Fahrenheit during shipment to maintain freshness; this required ten thousand pounds of ice for each refrigerated car over the course of a transcontinental journey. Giving carriers icing instructions was "not only wholly unnecessary and dangerous, but absolutely suicidal." Icing was the carriers' responsibility, and shippers had no way of knowing what kind of delays or other problems the car might encounter during shipment.[105] If the fruit was damaged in transit, the railroads could claim to have followed the shippers' directions precisely.[106]

Cooperative associations, large cash buyers, and individual growers actively petitioned the railroads for better facilities and the government for better legal protection. Organizations such as the Yakima Valley Traffic and Credit Association, formed in 1917, lobbied for lower rail rates and voiced concerns about railroad practices. Associations held their members to strict packing standards. By policing themselves on the front end of the process, growers made sure that fruit left their hands in good condition. Growers also petitioned the Northern Pacific for a fruit inspector. In 1912, the railroad hired an inspector hoping to reduce the number of damage claims. Traffic manager J. G. Woodworth strongly objected to the hire; he argued that an inspector increased the railroad's liability regardless of the nature of the damage. If the inspector failed to notice a problem, it would be hard to avoid paying damages.[107] Growers soon changed their minds about the railroad inspector as well. The Yakima Fruit Growers Association called for the removal of inspector Fred Thompson because of a conflict of interest with his connections in the fruit business. Northern Pacific attorney Ira P. Englehart believed that Thompson had avoided any conflicts and surmised that the association wanted him removed because it suspected him of "not being friendly to them."[108] In spite of Woodworth's fears, having an inspector reduced the number of damage claims, and Thompson "earned his salary many times over in deterring persons from attempting to ship frozen apples."[109] By 1915, the state began regular inspections when Washington passed a law requiring horticultural inspectors to certify that fruit was pest-free, graded, and properly packed.[110]

During World War I, when the US Railroad Administration took control of the nation's railroads, Northern Pacific hired the Moorhead Inspection Service to inspect fruit shipments. Growers complained about "incompetent" inspections "made in a manner injurious to products."[111] The Yakima Valley Traffic and Credit Association complained to R. H. Aishton, regional director of the US Railroad Administration, that inspectors damaged fruit by climbing on boxes and prying off slats. He asked the Northern Pacific to share copies of inspection reports and offered to share the cost of inspection with the railroad. The Northern Pacific declined both requests.[112] From the railroad's perspective, savings from reduced damage claims more than compensated for any ill will created by the inspection process. Railroad inspections continued after the war.[113]

Damage in transit remained an ongoing problem, but new storage facilities alleviated car shortages. Apples differed from other commercial fruits. Citrus was harvested nearly half the year, which reduced pressure on transportation systems. Soft fruits (pears, peaches, apricots, cherries) were shipped immediately after harvest or canned. Though growers harvested apples within a one-to-two-month period every year, they could store apples for several months. Placing apples in short-term storage reduced market gluts by spreading sales over a longer period. Growers could wait to sell when conditions were most favorable. Storage took pressure off the transportation system by spreading apple shipments over months instead of weeks.

In the early years of apple production, central Washington had few storage facilities. Western Cold Storage Company of Chicago opened the first ice-cooled storage plant in the country in 1878. The first fully mechanical refrigeration plant opened in Boston in 1881. By the 1890s, several US cities had mechanized cold-storage facilities that generated year-round profits from storing meat, dairy, and produce. The American Warehousemen's Association, organized in 1891, listed twenty-nine cold-storage companies in twenty cities in its first directory; Portland, Oregon, had the only storage facility in the Northwest. Though early statistical information on cold-storage plants is incomplete, by 1914, the United States boasted 898 cold-storage warehouses, mostly in New York and Chicago.[114] Eastern growers were the first to make extensive use of these facilities.[115] Cold storage made it possible for consumers to purchase apples harvested in October well into the spring, but because facilities were located in eastern cities, the railroad had to transport Washington's apple crop east within a very narrow time frame in the weeks after harvest.

Until the 1920s, mechanically refrigerated warehouses were prohibitively expensive. Yakima had an ice plant and cold-storage warehouse as early as 1904, and Wenatchee had similar facilities by 1907.[116] Early cold-storage facilities were small and not designed specifically for the apple industry; anyone who needed storage could rent space for personal or business use. By 1915, cold-storage warehouses in Washington, Oregon, and Idaho had a capacity of about one million apple boxes. The crop for that season was over seven million boxes, meaning that local cold storage handled only 14 percent of the crop.[117] The rest had to be housed in "common warehouses," which relied on insulation and ventilation to keep fruit cool. Cheaper to build than mechanically refrigerated warehouses, they ranged in size from small cellars at individual orchards to large warehouses owned by growers' cooperatives or fruit shippers, such as the 50 × 180–foot warehouse owned by the Wenatchee Valley Fruit Growers Association.[118] Large warehouses, located on or near rail lines, often doubled as packinghouses and served as temporary storage for apples awaiting shipment to cold-storage facilities in the East. Ideally, apples need to be kept between thirty-two and forty degrees Fahrenheit, but it was difficult to achieve consistently low temperatures in common storage warehouses. Much depended on the weather. Cool fall nights and cold winters helped maintain satisfactory temperatures. To maintain lower temperatures, warehouses were insulated with double walls filled with sawdust or straw. Many warehouses used fans and ventilation shafts to circulate air, and some used ice to lower temperatures further. While common storage warehouses were not ideal, they provided crucial temporary storage.

The shortage of local storage facilities frustrated industry leaders. Growers looked to the railroads for assistance. Some, like C. L. Durkee, wrote to railroad executives directly. In his letter to Louis Hill, president of the Great Northern Railway, Durkee argued that it was the railroad's responsibility to provide storage facilities because the railroad was responsible for settling farmers on the land.[119] Hill took Durkee's letter seriously. The Great Northern sent an agent to Meyers Falls to investigate Durkee's claims, even though he shipped only one or two carloads of apples per year. The Great Northern investigator found that Meyers Falls had several storehouses available for rent, but the fruit growers' union warehouse was the only warehouse located on the tracks. Durkee refused to join his local fruit growers' union because he objected to the twenty-five-dollar membership fee and the 10 percent commission collected by the association. He would have to bear additional costs to transport his fruit from the warehouse to a rail siding.

Durkee's dilemma raised fundamental questions about who was responsible for storage. Small, independent growers argued that they were shut out of the system. Their refusal to join a cooperative left them with fewer storage options and higher costs. Since they could not fund the construction of their own facilities, they expected the railroads to fill the gap. Likewise, cooperatives, though they were in a better position to construct warehouses, argued that the railroads should bear some of the costs because storage helped the railroads too. Railroad experts agreed that growers needed to store one-third to half of their crops on-site to relieve pressure on the railroads' refrigerated car fleets, but they were reluctant to accept responsibility for the problem.[120]

The 1912 apple crop, the largest to date, put tremendous pressure on railroads and local storage facilities. One Northern Pacific official estimated that the industry could have saved $96,000 in storage fees if more facilities had been available.[121] Given the shortage of storage warehouses, growers asked for storage-in-transit privileges, meaning that the railroads would store fruit in refrigerated cars on sidings rather than ship it directly to a final destination. Railroads were wary of storage in transit because it took cars out of service, and they wanted to avoid any perceptions of favoritism. The Interstate Commerce Commission required railroads to treat all shippers the same. Storage in transit was an expensive, temporary solution, and the railroads did not want to offer this service to everyone.[122] Growers were desperate for these privileges because without local storage, they lacked leverage against eastern buyers who controlled eastern warehouses. In the end, the railroads resorted to storage in transit because the national crop was so large that eastern storage warehouses filled and had no room for western crops.[123]

Storage in transit was a Band-Aid, not a permanent solution. In 1913, several investors in the Yakima Valley petitioned the Northern Pacific for assistance with financing cold-storage warehouses. Northern Pacific executives debated the issue. Some, like Thomas Cooper, argued that "it is better in the long run for business generally that the railroads stick to the particular business for which they are organized."[124] In other words, stick to transportation. Building storage warehouses seemed like a slippery slope. If the railroad financed a warehouse for one cooperative, what about others? Railroad-owned storage facilities could lead to serious conflicts of interest and open the door for additional damage claims or charges of discrimination in car availability and rates. "The position that we would like to take and to maintain," wrote Northern Pacific president Howard Elliott, "is that we will provide the cars and the transportation, and that the fruit grower will provide the fruit and the storage at the shipping points."[125]

While Elliott preferred to limit the Northern Pacific's role to transportation, he also recognized that "the success of our line in the Yakima Valley depends so largely on the care and marketing of fruit that we may in self-defense have to stand responsible for some investment in storage plants, just as we have in cars, so as to keep this business on its feet." Elliott estimated that the Northern Pacific grossed $2 million from fruit shipments alone, a profit that gave the railroad a keen interest in promoting the industry's success.[126] Without fruit shipments, the Northern Pacific's business in the Yakima Valley would have been negligible. Though the railroad wanted to stay out of the storage business, it might have no choice, especially if its rival in the Yakima Valley, the OWR&N, decided to construct storage. To avoid potential conflicts of interest, Elliott suggested that the Northern Pacific aid growers by funding warehouse construction through local banks or trusts. The railroad could stand behind the banks' investment without growers' knowledge. Alternatively, the railroad could construct storage facilities and then rent or sell them to growers.

Finally, the Northern Pacific and its competitor the OWR&N, in cooperation with the Yakima Fruit Growers Association, began construction on a warehouse at Zillah, Washington, in 1914.[127] Aside from this singular joint venture, railroads did not finance new construction, although they did lease railroad rights-of-way for this purpose. Private interests, including individual cash buyers, commission houses, and cooperatives, raised the capital to construct enough warehouses to meet industry needs. A survey of the geographic distribution of cold-storage warehouses showed that by 1927, the Pacific region had 14,260,661 cubic feet of storage, a 190 percent increase over the previous decade and 24.9 percent of the national total. Washington ranked fourth after New York, Illinois, and Kansas as the state with the most cold-storage capacity. Apple storage constituted the majority of this space.[128]

Railroads and growers clashed over issues such as freight rates and infrastructure, but for the most part, they established strong business relationships. Even though growers complained about rail service, they depended on the railroads for their livelihood. Some historians have contended that cooperatives formed as a response to the overbearing pressure placed on growers by big business—namely the railroads. By forming cooperative organizations, the argument goes, growers could stand up against corporate bullies. This narrative pits railroads and growers against each other in a struggle for supremacy.[129] Correspondence in the Northern Pacific and Great Northern archives reveals a more complex story. While growers and business leaders in Washington were publicly critical of railroads, in private they actively sought railroad support. As California and other western districts also learned, the system worked more efficiently when growers and railroads cooperated.[130] Several industry leaders formed lasting friendly relationships with railroad executives.

Railroads actively encouraged growers to form cooperative associations because they made the industry stronger, which in turn benefited the railroads. Problems with car shortages, transit times, and freight rates persisted largely because of the complicated logistics of moving a perishable product across a continent. Railroads made determined efforts to keep abreast of market conditions so they could transport crops as efficiently as possible, but they needed the apple cooperatives to address issues of storage and marketing. In solving these issues, cooperatives further standardized industry practices related to picking, packing, and storing fruit. They constructed packinghouses and storage warehouses, facilitated bulk purchase of supplies, centralized packing operations, and produced newsletters informing their members of the latest spraying techniques and market conditions. By working with railroads and eastern buyers, they built distribution networks for domestic and foreign markets that helped growers receive higher prices for their fruit. By the 1910s, cooperatives would also begin to turn their attention to advertising to increase sales.

CHAPTER 5

An Apple a Day Keeps the Doctor Away
Advertising to Consumers

Improved packing, storage, and distribution fixed part of Washington growers' marketing problem, but another key factor remained—creating consumer demand. By the 1910s, industry leaders preached that slow sales resulted from underconsumption, not overproduction. "Don't talk to me of overproduction when there are 20,000,000 wage earners and 30,000,000 school children who leave home every day without an apple in their lunch baskets!" an apple booster wrote with dramatic flair in a 1913 *Better Fruit* editorial. "History records but one year when there were too many apples, but that is harking back to Adam."[1] Growers might have been convinced of the superiority of their apples, but consumers had not gotten the message. Improving the quality of the fruit through careful grading and packing helped, but growers needed a more sophisticated means for creating consumer awareness and loyalty. Growers had to induce the "apple-less masses" to change their shopping habits and eat more Washington apples. The continued success of the apple industry hinged on establishing a large, stable consumer base through advertising.

In the early twentieth century, Washington apples, like California citrus and Central American bananas, were a luxury item. But by the 1910s, that was changing. Thanks to refrigerated railcars and ships, seasonal boundaries no longer dictated the availability of fresh produce. Railroads and shipping companies had effective systems in place to handle large volumes of produce, achieving economies of scale that placed produce prices within consumer reach. "I can well remember a time when in

Chicago, Cincinnati, St. Louis and other cities the people got along very nicely with old potatoes, onions, cabbage, etc., grown in Illinois, Ohio, Missouri, etc., till new crops came in, but that is no longer so," a grower, resentful of western fruit, complained in 1923. "Now they have got so high toned . . . that they start during midwinter using these same commodities from far off Southern climes and paying about double the price for them."[2] Farmers who had grown food for local markets found themselves in competition with imported produce, often of higher quality. Although this grower felt that fresh vegetables were an imprudent waste of money, consumers felt differently. "By World War I," writes historian William Leach, "Americans were being enticed into consumer pleasure and indulgence rather than work as the road to happiness."[3] Items like food and clothing, which had once been viewed as objects of sustenance, became items for consumers to enjoy. The word "consumption" itself shifted from a negative meaning of wasting or destroying, to a more positive meaning that implied the satisfaction of desire.[4]

For most of the nineteenth century, farmers and manufacturers had little reason to advertise food products. Most people purchased perishable foods such as fruit, vegetables, meat, and dairy near the point of production. Many nonperishable staples like flour were also produced locally and sold in bulk at dry goods stores, except for a handful of canned and processed foods. By the turn of the twentieth century, American shelves held a growing number of branded items. Companies such as Heinz, Campbell Soup Company, Quaker Oats Company, Nabisco, and others manufactured food for national markets. Improved transportation networks made it possible to ship processed foods and highly perishable foods across the country, changing established methods of wholesale marketing. Manufacturers and retailers adopted new national marketing campaigns with illustrated labels and print ads, colorful billboards, electric signs, and artistic shop displays, a stark difference from older black-and-white print ads. Between 1870 and 1900, American businesses increased advertising spending tenfold, from $50 million to $542 million. By 1910, businesses were spending approximately $600 million per year.[5] The new advertising was colorful and spoke directly to consumers' needs and desires. Stores and manufacturers had to convince consumers that their products, whether jewelry, lamps, hand creams, or fruit, were not frivolous luxury goods but things necessary for everyday life. Creating demand for apples was no different.

As consumers encountered new choices, department stores and mail-order companies like Sears revolutionized shopping by providing consumers with a wider array of goods than was available in local dry goods stores. Department stores carried some food items, but the real revolution in grocery shopping started in the 1910s with the rise of grocery store chains like A&P, Safeway, and Piggly Wiggly. A&P, founded in the 1850s, originally sold tea. Over the years, it added additional dry goods to its product lines, and in 1912 it opened its first "economy" stores, no-frills stores that sold a broad range of groceries at low prices. Safeway opened its first store in 1915, and Piggly Wiggly started the first self-service grocery store in 1916.

Like department stores, chain grocery stores represented a new type of shopping. Before chain grocery stores, consumers visited several different merchants to purchase their groceries, going to separate stores for dry goods, meat, dairy, and produce. Mom-and-pop grocery stores were everywhere because it was easy to get into the grocery business. All a person needed was a little space and some money for inventory. What mom-and-pop stores lacked in inventory, they made up for in service, offering free delivery and building personal relationships with customers. Chain stores changed the model. Unlike small, independent grocery stores, chains had the retail and warehouse space to purchase in bulk, and they passed those savings on to consumers. Corner markets could not compete. After World War I, chain grocery stores added refrigerator cases to carry meat, dairy, and produce in addition to dry goods, an expense that many small grocers could not afford. Chain stores offered one-stop shopping and lower prices for consumers looking to stretch their food budgets.[6]

Historian Alan Trachtenberg writes that "advertising arose as a functional institution linked to the great shifts in the spheres of production and distribution, to new technologies of communication, to the growing empires of the big-city, and to the rise of the department store."[7] California citrus growers set the standard for fruit advertising. In 1907, the California Fruit Exchange created the Sunkist brand as an experiment to market oranges. Orange sales rose 17.7 percent as a result, and the brand became a permanent fixture of fruit advertising.[8] Washington marketers emulated Sunkist. Many campaigns focused on consumer education. Print ads, pamphlets, recipe booklets, and posters explained the healthful properties of apples, the flavors of different varieties, and the best methods for storing and cooking apples. Apple industry leaders argued over the best way to advertise their product. Advertising could target consumers, distributors, or retail outlets. Those who pushed for advertising to distributors argued that they were important because they sold to small groceries and chain stores alike. Those who advocated consumer advertising argued that consumer demand would force grocery stores to carry Washington apples and drive purchases from distributors. In the end, the apple industry advertised directly to all three.

Initially, apple marketing revolved around railroad promotions. The Great Northern and the Northern Pacific invested in advertising apples because they wanted to attract prospective growers, sell real estate, and increase apple traffic. Railroad executives and local commercial clubs sent complimentary boxes of apples to high-ranking politicians, foreign dignitaries, and celebrities such as Presidents Theodore Roosevelt and William Howard Taft and actress Sarah Bernhardt. Local newspapers reported on these shipments and the reactions of the recipients.[9] James J. Hill, president of the Great Northern Railway, and his son Louis had a standing Christmas order with growers in the Wenatchee Valley. Hoping to find new purchasers, they distributed apples to friends and business associates in New York, Boston, and Europe.[10] Railroad executives touted the superiority of apples from their region, but recipients sometimes got confused, as Howard Elliott of the Northern Pacific discovered when Robert Jones, a personal friend, wrote to inquire about purchasing Wenatchee apples. "I wish very much you would switch all of your apple business to the Yakima Valley," Elliott replied, "as when you buy from the Wenatchee Valley, the Northern Pacific gets no revenue at all, as that is on the Great Northern."[11] Elliott salvaged the situation by asking Jones to distribute Yakima apples exclusively, but the difficulty in making a distinction among Washington districts remained. For most consumers, one Washington apple was much like any other.

While the railroads had a strong interest in promoting Washington fruit, there was a limit to their involvement. They tended to broadly advertise the districts in their territory—Wenatchee for the Great Northern, and Yakima for the Northern Pacific—rather than individual growers or cooperatives. Cooperatives kept the railroads apprised of their advertising campaigns to coordinate publicity, though they rarely received direct support. Northwest Fruit Exchange, for example, had a long-standing relationship with the Northern Pacific, and exchange officials regularly corresponded with railroad officers. Despite the cordial relationship, when the exchange asked the Northern Pacific in 1913 to use its fruit exclusively in dining cars, the Northern Pacific declined. "For the railway company to pick out a particular brand and feature it either in their advertising or on their dining cars . . . would be criticized by those who did not belong to your association," explained Jule M. Hannaford, second vice president of the Northern Pacific.[12] The Northern Pacific agreed to place Northwest Fruit Exchange advertisements in its ticket offices, but using the cooperative's fruit exclusively in the dining cars was a step too far.

Refusing to associate with a specific brand did not prevent railroads from advertising Washington apples more generally. Both railroads featured Northwest produce on their dining car menus and advertised fruit at ticket offices. They worked with local commercial clubs and newspapers such as the *Wenatchee Daily World* and the *Yakima Herald* to support fairs, exhibits, and media coverage. One of the largest promotional events was Spokane's National Apple Show, first held in 1908. Spokane businesspeople originated the idea of a national apple show to bring attention to their city, educate growers, and promote commercial apple production. Few apples were grown in Spokane, but Spokane hoped the show would help establish its position as a regional center of trade, finance, and transportation.

In the late nineteenth and early twentieth centuries, fairs were a means of showcasing American progress. Part education and part entertainment, world's fairs such as the Pan-American Exposition (1901), the St. Louis World's Fair (1904), and the Alaska-Yukon-Pacific Exposition (1909), as well as smaller regional fairs, provided a platform for exhibiting western agriculture. Run by the Spokane Chamber of Commerce, the National Apple Show aimed to "encourage the growing of high-class commercial apples" and "bring to the attention of the East the great possibilities of the West in apple growing."[13] The ambitious twofold purpose of educating Northwest growers and eastern buyers had mixed results. It left many wondering whether the true purpose of the show was to promote the apple industry or to promote Spokane.

Show organizers planned exhibits to appeal to commercial growers and interested amateurs. Carload exhibits, consisting of 630 boxes of perfectly packed apples lined up in rows 7 boxes tall by 90 boxes long, formed the show's centerpiece. Carload contests appealed to large commercial growers, but smaller orchards could participate in categories such as the ten-box, the five-box, best keeper, or biggest apple. Two hundred fifty varieties, most not grown commercially, were eligible for the plate competition in which contestants presented five single apples on a plate. Homemade apple products such as jelly, marmalade, vinegar, and pie had their own prizes and categories. The show also featured educational talks for commercial growers, a packing school demonstration, and a lunch counter run by the Washington State College Department of Domestic Economy that served apple dishes.[14]

Show organizers enlisted financial support from local businesspeople and the railroads. In a shrewd move, they asked Louis W. Hill, president

H. M. Gilbert's carload exhibit at the Spokane National Apple Show in 1908. *Collections of the Yakima Valley Museum.*

of the Great Northern Railway, to be president of the first National Apple Show, thus ensuring the railroad's support. Organizers hoped to make this a truly national show by seeking exhibitors from New York and other major apple-growing districts. To encourage participation, the Great Northern offered a 50 percent refund on fares for all carload exhibits transported to the show. Hill contributed personal funds to the show, communicated with other railroads to solicit donations, and encouraged growers along the Great Northern line to submit exhibits. Hill's father, James J. Hill, contributed $1,000 to purchase one hundred prize-winning boxes of apples. Although ten dollars for a box of apples that would sell for three to four dollars was a small prize, it came with bragging rights. James Hill was a very respected figure among Northwest growers.[15]

Over one hundred thousand people attended the first show, held in December 1908. Growers took home over $35,000 in prizes. Efforts to make the show national failed; it remained a regional affair, with most exhibits and attendees hailing from Washington. Except for a few prize categories specifically reserved for eastern and southern apples, Northwest apples took every prize. Of the 248 exhibitors listed in the program, only 21 came from states outside the Northwest. According to organizers, lack of interest was not a reflection on the show; rather, it was because of a poor crop year in the East. That was a plausible excuse, but the larger problem was that it was expensive for eastern growers to transport apples to an untested regional show that offered them no benefits. Washington's apple industry was still in its infancy and did not yet present real competition to New York's apple growers. Some Northwest districts also refused to participate. Growers from Hood River, Oregon, one of that state's major districts, refused to participate over a rule disagreement, foreshadowing problems that would plague the show for the next few years.[16]

Yakima and Wenatchee's participation in future shows remained questionable as each district fought over prizes and rules. After the first show, Yakima believed that favoritism toward Wenatchee apples had pushed Yakima out of contention for major prizes. "I am convinced the intention when the rules were adopted, and the intention from that time since has been to count Wenatchee 'in' no matter what showing was made by the other districts," complained H. M. Gilbert, one of Yakima's largest growers, to Northern Pacific president Howard Elliott.[17] The *Yakima Herald* had predicted that Gilbert's carload of Winesaps would take first prize, and the city was disappointed when Mike Horan of Wenatchee took the prize instead. Horan reportedly spent $2,000 over typical growing costs to produce his prize-winning car. He employed four expert pickers who scoured his orchard for perfect apples. Gilbert, on the other hand, picked and packed his apples as he would any other carload.[18] Horan's methods were widely known, reported the *Herald*, "and indicate how hard Wenatchee is willing to battle for its scoring at every fruit display that is given, and how that section would probably be beaten if they did not use every crook and turn to perfect their exhibits."[19] With unintentional irony, an editorial on the same page stated that "no one can say that Yakima is a poor loser . . . there will be no one who can point their finger and say 'Sour Grapes'"—except for the Wenatchee paper, which announced, "Yakima Man Sore Because He Lost Prize." Horan argued that he won fair and square because he took greater care in packing his apples, taking three to four months to fill the car, while Gilbert reportedly "packed 80 boxes a day."[20] Whether Horan's efforts represented an excess bordering on "cheating" or an attentiveness to detail that would propel the industry to greater heights was open to interpretation.

While the results of the first National Apple Show disappointed Yakima, Wenatchee celebrated. News of the win covered nearly the entire front page of the December 12 issue of the *Wenatchee Daily World*. Headlines proclaimed, "Wenatchee Apples Supreme" and "Wenatchee Goes Wild with Enthusiasm." Local businesspeople arranged an impromptu "nightgown parade." Residents marched through the street cheering with torches, drums, horns, and flags. Someone started a large bonfire, and when that grew "so hot that it was feared that the telephones would be melted," someone else started a second fire farther away with a pail of kerosene donated by the local grocer. One business owner predicted that the apple show results would lead transportation lines to vie for access to the city, buyers to clamor for the best apples regardless of price, and manufacturers to rush to build factories to process cull apples into vinegar and jellies.[21] For boosters eager to gain publicity for their towns, winning mattered. Washington apples were not known on a national level, and growers were keen to prove the superiority of their product.

In the end, Gilbert and Horan both marketed their prize-winning carloads. Gilbert sold his apples to an English buyer who shipped them to London for display, providing additional publicity for Yakima Valley fruit, and Horan sold his to a New York buyer.[22] By this time, plans were under way for a second apple show. Louis Hill declined to serve a second term as show president, arguing that it would be better to rotate presidents each year to avoid the appearance of favoritism. He recommended Northern Pacific president Howard Elliott to fill the position. Elliott reluctantly agreed. Growers in Yakima believed show organizers had treated them badly, and Elliott did not want to create ill will for the Northern Pacific by accepting the position.[23] Disagreements over show rules and financing persisted for the next few years, putting Elliott in the difficult position of trying to balance Northern Pacific's interests while creating a level playing field for the show. After complaints about the 1908 carload contest, the show's board of trustees convened to draft new scoring rules. They adopted the American Pomological Society's rules for rating quality; however, as the 1909 show approached, both Yakima and Wenatchee complained that the rules discriminated against the primary commercial varieties in their sections. Growers in Montana were reluctant to exhibit because they thought the rules were too strict, and growers from New York declined because of the distance and cost.[24]

The show needed Yakima's and Wenatchee's participation if it was to continue. Yakima growers wanted to change the carload rules to allow growers to enter the competition as a team. The distribution of Howard Elliott's donated prize money created additional tension. The show's organizers had designated Elliott's donation the "Howard Elliott Delicious Carload Prize." The problem was that Yakima did not grow this variety commercially. It would be impossible for Yakima growers to enter the category named after their railroad president. H. M. Gilbert relayed his concerns to Elliott, who contacted show organizers to let them know he was "considerably disturbed" that his prize left out Yakima growers. Matters came to a head in October 1909, when the Yakima Commercial Club passed a resolution stating that Yakima would not participate unless the rules changed. Show officials E. F. Cartier Van Dissel and Ren Rice, who were present at the meeting, explained that it was too late to change the rules for the 1909 show, but they assured members that they would hold a meeting of growers after the show to revise the rules. Organizers resolved the matter of the Howard Elliott Carload Prize by dividing his $1,000 contribution four ways to sponsor carload prizes for Winesap, Rome Beauty, Wagener, and Spitzenburg varieties. At the show, Yakima Valley apples took first place for the Winesap carload and second place for the Rome Beauty and Spitzenburg carloads. Elliott later lamented that "the Apple Show seems to be producing as much trouble in the West as Eve did in the Garden of Eden."[25]

Elliott agreed to serve as president of the show for the 1910 season, despite continued tension over rules and exhibit locations. Growers did not trust Spokane organizers. Once again, Wenatchee and Yakima threatened to withdraw from the show. Rumors circulated in Wenatchee that the Hills had withdrawn their support because of organizers' treatment of growers.[26] One faction wanted to move the show to an eastern city where consumers could be introduced to Northwest apples, but Spokane business owners were not eager to finance a show that did not directly impact their city.[27] According to H. M. Gilbert, many Yakima growers preferred to exhibit in Chicago against eastern apples, and they participated in the Spokane show only out of loyalty to Elliott.[28] Organizers finally reached a compromise by planning show dates in Spokane and Chicago. The Chicago portion of the show was a fiasco. The National Apple Show had to share rented space in the Coliseum with a land show. The land show promoters used false advertising to funnel attendees away from the apple show and into their show. When confronted, they refused to remove their advertising. The situation was resolved only after the Northern Pacific threatened to withdraw its business from an advertising agency owned by one of the land show trustees.[29] Attendance improved for the last few days of the show, but the damage had been done. Chicago was expensive for growers and organizers, and the railroads were losing interest in financing a show that produced little national recognition for Northwest apples.

By this point, the National Apple Show was national in name only. Organizers tried to meet their original goal of education by hosting meetings of the Washington State Horticultural Society, but by 1911 the show had morphed into a festive community event rather than a serious trade show. Jule M. Hannaford, who became president of the Northern Pacific in 1913, did not share Howard Elliott's enthusiasm for the show, and by

1914, the Northern Pacific and other lines had significantly reduced or ended their subscriptions. By the mid-1910s, railroads were cutting back on contributions to fairs and shows because they wanted to save on costs and because they believed that the shows were not sustainable models for advertising. In a 1914 letter, Hannaford wrote that "the Apple Show at Spokane has outlived its usefulness as a national event." Louis Hill concurred, as did J. D. Farrell, president of the OWR&N.[30] George Reid, assistant to the Northern Pacific president, had even harsher words for the show, calling it a "fake" and stating that "it has no more influence on the apple industry than a dog show, in my judgement."[31]

The National Apple Show continued until World War I before fading into obscurity. Northwest apple districts never fully trusted the intentions of Spokane organizers, and the show never became an outlet for fruit buyers. The major Northwest districts never felt that Spokane was the appropriate place to celebrate apple culture. As Waldo Paine, chair of the Publicity Bureau for the Spokane Chamber of Commerce, explained, "Practically all apples in the northwest are marketed through the various selling agencies and very few, if any of the growers sell their apples direct."[32] In later years, the show took on a carnival atmosphere. The 1916 show, for example, featured attractions such as a baby pageant, a mind reader, a vaudeville horse act, and free Charlie Chaplin films.[33] Ultimately, a local celebration of apple culture developed in Wenatchee, which hosted the first Apple Blossom Festival in 1919, an event that still exists today.

As an editorial in the *Yakima Valley Progress* opined, the National Apple Show "died in a little while of inanition without leaving any friends or any estate." An exhibition "which few people saw and of which not a tenth of 1 per cent of our possible consumers ever heard or ever will hear" was a waste of time and resources.[34] In effect, the National Apple Show marked the end of fairs and shows as a serious marketing and advertising outlet. Though growers made showings at a few fairs in the 1920s, such as the 1922 Pacific Northwest Fruit Exposition in Seattle, most concluded that it was better to focus on advertising methods that offered more tangible returns.

Apple industry leaders realized the need for new and innovative advertising, but implementing national marketing campaigns required cooperation. By the 1910s, Wenatchee and Yakima had emerged as the preeminent growing districts in the state. Washington growers had confidence in their apples. They believed their product was superior to that of other apple regions in the United States. The real competition came from other districts in Washington. These two rivals used every advertising tactic at their disposal to compete for shares in eastern and foreign markets. "Many of us remember the methods used by our old friend P. T. Barnum whose skill in 'transferring' half dollars made him famous," wrote grower J. C. Roth in a letter to the Yakima Commercial Club. "Advertising a Circus and advertising apples require somewhat different means, but we can and should advertise our apples in the same persistent manner as do our friends in Wenatchee."[35]

To most consumers, one apple looked much like any other, regardless of where it was grown. Washington growers had to overcome this perception and convince shoppers that their apples were different from those grown in other areas. Continuous advertising through catchy slogans, moving-picture slides, billboards, advertisements in metropolitan newspapers, and plays featuring "apple cookery" helped keep Washington apples in the consumer spotlight. In the 1910s and 1920s, advertising happened through a variety of channels. Regional cooperatives and national trade organizations such as the International Apple Shippers' Association developed their own advertising. Additionally, independent growers, still reluctant to join cooperatives, developed their own unique box labels and brands. The financial losses of the Great Depression would finally push growers to accept unified district and statewide advertising, but until then, several advertising campaigns vied for consumers' attention. Some strategies were simple; the Washington Fruit Company, for example, included a special poster for retailers to hang with each box of apples.[36] Others were more complex, such as the national $10,000 newspaper ad and window display campaign proposed by the Northwest Fruit Exchange in 1913. The exchange tested the campaign in Duluth, St. Paul, and Minneapolis before a national launch.[37]

Letters and free samples helped build relationships with distributors and retailers. In 1912, for example, the International Apple Shippers' Association distributed twenty thousand posters and mailed letters to thirteen thousand retailers asking them to support the apple industry by keeping prices low to encourage volume sales. Fourteen hundred retailers replied to pledge support, such as one grocer in Philadelphia who offered apples at a lower price, as a regular grocery item rather than as an exotic specialty. Much to the grocer's surprise, sales jumped from three to five boxes per day to fifty boxes per day, which greatly increased his profits.[38]

Consumer education was another advertising tool. Recipe booklets created interest by encouraging women to try new products or recipes. One of the most famous examples of a consumer education campaign is Betty Crocker. Introduced in 1921 by the Washburn-Crosby Company, later part of General Mills, Betty Crocker, a fictionalized home economist, sold flour and other products through a radio cooking show and cookbooks. Many brands such as Sunkist oranges, Sun-Maid raisins, and Jell-O published cookbooks and recipe pamphlets. Major railroads and the fruit exchanges published their own apple cookbooks. In addition to recipes, booklets included articles on the production of Northwest apples, nutritional information, and detailed descriptions and uses for different varieties of apples. Union Pacific distributed a booklet with 150 recipes for apple dishes that represented the best recipes submitted by Northwest cooks. The recipes, which included cakes, salads, jellies, marmalades, and pies, demonstrated the "plain, simple and practical, and . . . pleasing variety of forms in which the 'King of Fruits' may be served."[39] *Two Hundred and Nine Ways of Preparing the Apple* by L. Gertrude Mackay, acting head of the Department of Domestic Economy at Washington State College, was sold at the first National Apple Show in 1908 and republished by the International Apple Shippers' Association in 1912. The association circulated an estimated half million copies to customers through retail outlets.[40] In her introduction, Mackay urged readers to stop thinking of apples as a "luxury" good and to appreciate their nutritional qualities.[41] Despite the emphasis on health, Mackay's book included many desserts, ranging from the familiar apple pies, dumplings, and fritters to the more decadent recipes such as apples à la Parisienne, an orange juice–soaked sponge cake covered with cooked apples and meringue; or Delmonico apples, possibly named after Delmonico's restaurant in New York, a layer of baked applesauce sprinkled with ground almonds, butter, and crushed macaroons and served as a side dish with meat.[42]

Advertisers were always looking for new ways to increase sales, and branding created instant product recognition in a competitive marketplace. At a time when there were few regulations on consumer goods, consumers had little to go on other than the manufacturer's reputation for producing recognizable, dependable products. Through advertising campaigns, consumers associated brands such as Ivory soap, Campbell's soup, and Heinz ketchup with a high level of purity and quality. Branded characters took this one step further by giving a voice to products. Today, consumers are familiar with Tony the Tiger and the Keebler Elf, but branded characters were new to consumers at the turn of the century. Early branded characters evolved from comic strips in the late 1890s. Richard Outcault created one of the first nationally recognized comic characters, the Yellow Kid, while working for Joseph Pulitzer's newspaper, the *World*. The *Yellow Kid* comic gained tremendous popularity as it was serialized in newspapers across the country. Realizing his character's monetary potential, Outcault tried to copyright the Yellow Kid. The courts ruled that Outcault could copyright the name, but not the drawing, as there was no precedent for such copyrights. Without exclusive rights to this character, Outcault stopped drawing the Yellow Kid in 1898. By this time, many people had imitated the character and used it to promote products ranging from chewing gum to ladies' fans.[43]

Although the Yellow Kid was never used to market apples, Outcault's next cartoon creation was. In 1902, Outcault hit on another winning combination: Buster Brown. The format of the stories was simple. Every week Buster, dressed in a sailor suit and sporting angelic curls, found his way into some kind of innocent mischief with his sidekick pet dog Tige. Each panel ended with a resolution in which Buster contemplated his actions. Buster Brown was an instant success, and by 1908, the comic appeared in at least twenty-four newspapers nationwide. Buster Brown's broad appeal made him popular with advertisers. At the St. Louis World's Fair in 1904, Outcault sold the rights to Buster Brown to several manufacturers, including Outcault's most famous client, the Brown Shoe Company. The US Copyright Office recorded over ten thousand individual copyright applications for products using the Buster Brown brand.[44]

Comics provided a perfect marketing vehicle because the American public was already familiar with the characters. Advertisements became extensions of the comic strips themselves. Licensed Buster Brown ads featured the same recognizable characters from the comic strip. In 1912, Outcault and his son licensed the character to the Wenatchee-Columbia Fruit Company to sell one hundred carloads of fruit, according to the *Wenatchee Daily World*. That fall, in ads mimicking the comic's "resolution" panels, Wenatchee-Columbia urged growers to sell their apples with the company under its Buster Brown label. In contrast to advertisements that would have appeared for eastern consumers, the ads in the *Wenatchee Daily World* were designed to build grower confidence in modern marketing methods. "Resolved: That I am sharpening my pencil to book orders for 100 carloads of the finest Wenatchee apples," read the first advertisement. "I want them so I can give a few of my friends in my hometown of New York just one little 'taste.' My friends in New York don't know much about Wenatchee apples yet but they will before Tige and I get through with them."[45] The advertisement contained many hallmarks of the comic strip. Buster appeared with his sidekick, Tige the dog. Buster's resolves were not apologetic, despite his naughty deeds. Rather, Outcault used these panels to provide social commentary or to give Buster an opportunity to defend his good intentions. In the advertisement, as in the comic strip, Buster resolved to "fix" the problem—in this case a New Yorker's unfamiliarity with Wenatchee apples.

While the Wenatchee-Columbia Fruit Company attached itself to a nationally recognized brand, other growers' associations developed their own brands. The Skookum brand, adopted by the Northwest Fruit Exchange in 1914, was one of the best known. Initially, the brand used a totem pole logo to evoke the Pacific Northwest, but in 1916 the exchange changed its logo to a smiling cartoon Indian. Like other brands of the era such as the Gold Dust Twins and Aunt Jemima, the Skookum brand played on racial stereotypes. According to early advertisements, "the word 'Skookum,' belonging to the Indian jargon, is a word expressing 'Quality is the best.'"[46] In the wake of the Alaska gold rush, Northwest and Alaska imagery became popular with Americans. The *New York Times*, for example, carried advertisements for novels that featured rugged outdoorsmen pitted against the Pacific Northwest wilderness, such as "Skookum Chuck," a man looking for adventure.[47] The word "Skookum" and the use of the Indian logo implied that these apples were from a rugged, exotic place, and they could imbue consumers with strength and vigor. One early Skookum ad featured a picture of a man that vaguely resembled Theodore Roosevelt with the slogan "Skookum . . . It means 'bully' in Indian."[48] By hinting at Roosevelt, the ad played to ideas about manhood and strength. Prior to the adoption of the cartoon Indian, ads depicted a young boy, a woman, or an Indian eating a Skookum apple with the word "bully," or slogans such as "she can't speak Indian, but she knows what 'Skookum' means" and "Skookum apples are the bulliest product of the great Northwest apple orchards."[49]

By 1916, the Skookum brand was so successful that Wenatchee orchardists formed a new organization, the Skookum Packers Association, to regulate the trademark. The Northwest Fruit Exchange remained the exclusive distributor of the apples, but control of the brand shifted to the new organization. Growers connected with the Skookum Packers Association retained some autonomy. Newly designed labels left room in the lower corner for growers to add their individual orchard's brand.[50] Advertising went beyond labels. The exchange spent an estimated $70,000 to $100,000 per year on a national ad campaign with advertisements in publications such as *Good Housekeeping*, the *Saturday Evening Post*, and the *New York Times*.[51] The Skookum Packers, like other manufacturers, offered consumers premiums like apple slicers, dolls, or booklets for a small shipping fee. In a 1927 coloring book, the Skookum Indian mascots, Ki and Lo, walk children through the process of picking, packing, and shipping apples. The book describes the most popular varieties of apples with detailed accounts of their appearance and instructions on how to use them. While most of the book focuses on apple production, the story of Ki and Lo has many racist elements. The origin story of apples in the Northwest, for example, explains that before white men came, Indians hunted game, "but they had no fruit," until "at last the paleface settlers came / And planted orchards there, / Until the hills and valleys / Now grow apples everywhere." The text elevates white culture while ignoring the fact that though Indians may not have had apples, they had access to other fruit before white settlers arrived in the region. Another part of the story explains that Skookum did not want consumers to think all apple varieties were the same, even if their mascots "look so much alike it's hard to tell them apart."[52]

In recent years, many brands have come under scrutiny for their racist roots. Quaker Oats, for example, retired the Aunt Jemima brand in 2020 because of outcry over the brand's racial stereotypes. Similar protests from Indian civil rights activists challenged Skookum's racist Indian character. The brand was retired in the early 1970s. Still, the legacy of the Skookum brand remains an important part of Wenatchee's history. A fourteen-foot-tall, mechanized billboard of the Skookum mascot, created in 1921, remains a prominent feature in Wenatchee. It sits atop the roof of the local Office Depot, the former site of a Skookum packinghouse. In 2016, the Wenatchee Valley Museum and Cultural Center mounted an exhibit on the Skookum brand to start a conversation about the brand's role in the community's history. The museum invited members of the Wenatchi Advisory Board to planning meetings to share their views. Some expressed nostalgia or indifference regarding the Skookum Indian character, viewing it as a generic character that had nothing to do with local Indian tribes. After all, "Skookum" is Chinook jargon, from western Washington, and not representative of the peoples of the Columbia Plateau. Others expressed opposition to the brand and felt that it was not only a caricature but represented the modern agriculture that forced Indians off their lands. In its final form, the exhibit featured presentations from members of the Colville Confederated Tribes.[53]

Though one of Washington's better-known apple brands, Skookum was one of many brands that developed in the 1910s and 1920s. Other large cooperatives had their own brands, including the Yakima Fruit Growers Association's "Big Y" brand, the Yakima Valley Horticultural Union's "Blue Ribbon" brand, the American Fruit Growers' "Blue Goose" brand, and the Wenatchee Cooperative District's "Jim Hill" brand." None of these brands featured cartoon characters, and the names of the brand are descriptive of the logos. Big Y featured a big blue *Y*, for example, and "Jim Hill" featured a picture of James J. Hill's head. In addition to the large cooperatives, individual growers, many of whom were not cooperative members, created hundreds of different colorful apple box labels, such as Richey & Gilbert, which patented the brand "Yakima Apples" in 1911.[54] Some cooperatives focused on advertising to dealers. Others, such as Big Y, ran national advertising campaigns aimed at consumers. In 1920, for example, Big Y ran advertisements in the *Saturday Evening Post* with "an illustration of three Jonathans hanging on the limb, in natural colors, with an orchard and distant snow-capped mountain in the background," the cooperative explained in its member newsletter. "A small panel will show a plate of apples, with an apple cut in sections, as a test made by the advertising and the sales departments showed that the cut apple made the strongest appeal for quick action by the apple-hungry."[55] Big Y did not consistently advertise to consumers. Some years, it focused on dealer advertising. In other years, when the quality of the crop did not justify the expense of national advertising, it relied on more generalized, industry-wide campaigns.[56]

Washington growers were not competing against only eastern growers; the various associations, cooperatives, growing regions, and individual growers remained at odds with each other. As the volume of yearly crops increased, Yakima and Wenatchee vied for the title of "Apple Capital" of the state, and later the nation. In some ways, regional recognition was more important than individual brand recognition. If consumers identified Skookum or Big Y apples with Washington, all growers benefited, but that did not further a district's interest. Although Wenatchee grew small crops of pears and peaches, apples dominated. While apples were also the leading crop in Yakima, they were not the only crop in town. The Yakima Valley produced a wide variety of fruit and led the nation in hops production. Commercial clubs in both regions worked to promote local industry. Wenatchee had a greater advantage in creating regional and brand recognition because it focused all its efforts on apples, whereas Yakima marketed its hops, pears, plums, peaches, and cherries along with its apples. In 1912, the Wenatchee Commercial Club hired a sales manager and proposed making the "Big Red Apple" a Wenatchee trademark for the exclusive use of growers in the valley.[57] Yakima might have produced more apples, but Wenatchee held claim to the "Apple Capital" title.

A 1914 study of the market standing of Wenatchee and Yakima apples completed by the Northern Pacific showed the impact of Wenatchee's aggressive sales techniques. Seattle and all other cities on Puget Sound favored Wenatchee apples, not surprisingly since these towns were served by the Great Northern. Likewise, Butte and Helena, Montana, and Jamestown, North Dakota, served by the Northern Pacific, favored Yakima apples. Buyers in New York City, Pittsburgh, Cleveland, and Detroit showed no preference for either district's apples. Wenatchee apples were favored in St. Louis, San Francisco, Cincinnati, Philadelphia, Milwaukee, Duluth, Billings, and Kansas City. Outside of cities served by the Northern Pacific, only two had a clear preference for Yakima apples: Boston and Winnipeg. When asked why they preferred Wenatchee apples, buyers cited the high quality. As distributor James S. Crutchfield explained, competitors in Wenatchee fared better because "an absent buyer knows just as well what he is getting when a four tier Wenatchee Winesap is described to him on paper as if he were personally looking at the fruit."[58] The study agreed, observing that "wholesalers advise that they can always depend on good stock from Wenatchee while occasionally a portion of the Yakima stock is poor." Wenatchee also had an active sales presence and ran aggressive advertising campaigns in cities that showed a preference. "The Yakima fruit shippers are simply supplying a demand," reported a St. Louis buyer, "while the Wenatchee are continually creating one."[59] While this study was no doubt a blow to Yakima growers, "these reports confirm our previous impression that the Wenatchee people," wrote Jule M. Hannaford, president of the Northern Pacific, "having nothing else to market, have specialized in the packing and marketing of apples to a greater extent than the Yakima Valley people."[60]

As regional competition continued, many industry leaders argued that statewide advertising would be far more effective than the dozens of advertising campaigns currently in place. The Northwest Fruit Exchange, which distributed apples for the Skookum Packers Association, encouraged statewide advertising in a new journal, *Northwest Fruit Grower*, introduced in 1920. If growers did not take a more proactive role in marketing their fruit, the exchange argued, then who would? Wholesalers focused on their own financial gain, and retailers had no incentive to stock expensive apples if consumers did not demand them. It was up to growers to cultivate demand. J. A. Warman, president of the Skookum Packers Association, characterized Washington growers as hardworking, independent businesspeople—"the finest class of people in the world"—who, if they failed to take action, would "sit idly by and see the very thing they have been striving for swept away from them by their own independence, by failing to work and cooperate with their fellow growers."[61]

Northwest Fruit Grower published examples of successful advertising campaigns used for other products, and general information about marketing and distribution trends in the industry. The journal also reported on the exchanges' advertising efforts including print ads in magazines and newspapers, subway and streetcar placards, recipe booklets, calendars, and promotional items for children. In the 1919–20 season, for example, the Northwest Fruit Exchange distributed 79,503 pieces of display materials, excluding print ads.[62] These announcements showed members exactly what the exchange was doing to help growers increase sales. The journal also published testimonials such as a letter from Mr. Vaughn, a customer who described Skookum apples as "the golden droplets of frozen sunsets wherein copy hides the ambrosial nectar more fragrant than the spices of Araby . . . so luscious, so fragrant, so beautiful in its ruby gown of waxen sheen."[63] While often melodramatic, letters demonstrated to growers that at least some consumers believed in the superiority of Skookum apples. The magazine encouraged members to share copies of the *Northwest Fruit Grower* and talk to their nonmember friends and neighbors to dispel myths and spread the word of what the cooperative could accomplish.

In addition to the *Northwest Fruit Grower*, the Skookum Packers Association ran ads in the *Wenatchee Daily World*, the largest daily newspaper in the Wenatchee-Okanogan region. In one advertisement, the Skookum Indian drives an automobile toward "higher returns, better sales service, stabilized markets, and organized industry," while an "independent grower," dripping sweat, walks behind. Another ad shows a Skookum grower under the "umbrella" of cooperative protection, while the independent grower stands in the rain of tight credit, low prices, speculation, and market instability. The market leaves the independent grower out in the cold, while the cooperative helps members weather the storm. Membership in the cooperative protected growers against the whims of a complex market. As one article argued, rather than making new arrangements with a different broker each season, like the "Tom, Dick, and Harry of the independent variety," growers needed "one strong growers' organization which will dominate the industry and which will be managed and operated by men of ability so that mistakes of the past will not occur again."[64] In other words, growers needed to avoid the competitive and fractured market environment of the past. The exchange envisioned an organization that could assist growers at every step of the way—from obtaining bank loans, to finding the best prices for crops, to creating consumer demand through national advertising campaigns.

The Northwest Fruit Exchange aspired to create a regional Skookum brand that encompassed growers in Washington, Oregon, Idaho, and Montana, but its plans fell apart because of regionalism within the Pacific Northwest. When the Skookum Packers Association became a satellite organization of the Northwest Fruit Exchange in 1916, it included members from all five of Washington's major apple-growing districts. In 1922, divided by regional loyalties, two-thirds of Skookum Packers Association members dropped their memberships, leaving only a small core of members from the Wenatchee-Okanogan region. The association rebuilt its membership from growers in the Wenatchee-Okanogan region, but the dream of a Northwest-wide marketing organization was not to be realized.

Although the Northwest Fruit Exchange's plans fell apart, by the 1920s, Washington growers were fully invested in advertising campaigns through local cooperatives. They also participated in the National Apple Week campaign sponsored by the International Apple Shippers' Association. James Handly, secretary of the Mississippi Valley Apple Growers' Association, originated the idea for a National Apple Day to promote sales. In 1905, he persuaded the International Apples Shippers' Association to support National Apple Day, although celebrations did not occur on a national level until 1913. The event took off in 1920 when the association voted to change National Apple Day from the third Thursday in October to Halloween. National Apple Day kicked off a weeklong celebration called National Apple Week, with a stated goal "to bring this splendid product of our orchards to every man, woman and child in the apple eating world."[65]

What made National Apple Week more successful than other national advertising attempts was that participation was voluntary, participants could choose their level of involvement, and they could use their own branding in conjunction with the event. The International Apple Shippers' Association provided publicity and made advertising swag such as recipe booklets and stickers available for purchase. More importantly, it served as an information clearinghouse so that organizations were aware

ADVERTISING TO CONSUMERS 159

A National Apple Week display in the window of the Yakima Hardware Co. featured some of the many different apple brands and labels used by growers. *Collections of the Yakima Valley Museum.*

of each other's efforts. Association newsletters highlighted planned activities and offered suggestions for promotions, such as contests or special talks. Railroads, steamship companies, cooperatives, chambers of commerce, retailers, and distributors participated by promoting apples through advertising in newspapers, window displays, giveaways, radio programs, and other publicity stunts. In 1923, for example, the Great Northern published advertisements in newspapers in every town served by the railroad, a total of 460 papers.[66]

The Great Northern, Northern Pacific, and other railroads featured apples prominently on their dining cars in support of National Apple Week. Northern Pacific, copying its signature dining car dish the "Great Big Baked Potato," sold a "Big Baked Apple." Great Northern National Apple Week menus from the 1920s featured a "Wenatchee Eating Apple" for ten cents and a "Baked Wenatchee Apple with Cream" for thirty cents.⁶⁷ For the 1925 National Apple Week, the Great Northern went a step further and featured a menu consisting entirely of apple-based dishes.⁶⁸ In addition to special apple menus, some years, the railroads gave free apples to passengers. In 1922, for example, the Northern Pacific distributed between five thousand and ten thousand apples packaged in small cartons printed with a short history of Northwest orchards and an explanation of how apples were being featured on dining cars. Local chambers of commerce also distributed apples to passengers at rail stations.⁶⁹

In preparation for the 1923 National Apple Week, Washington growers ordered forty thousand recipe booklets and eighty-five thousand stickers from the International Apple Shippers' Association in addition to the recipe booklets, blotters, pins, menu cards, and other Apple Week advertising distributed by the railroads. That year, the Union Pacific published 144,000 copies of a thirty-five-page recipe booklet, *150 Recipes for Apple Dishes*.⁷⁰ The Great Northern and Northern Pacific also published booklets with recipes, articles about apple nutrition, histories of apple-producing regions, and photos. One Great Northern pamphlet from 1925 featured actors Billie Dove and Jack Holt of the Famous Players-Lasky Corporation in their latest film *The Ancient Highway*, a romance story filmed in Wenatchee. Though little remembered today, Jack Holt was a well-known action film star of the silent era, and Billie Dove's popularity in the 1920s was on par with that of Mary Pickford or Clara Bow.⁷¹ The pamphlet featured photographs of the stars eating baked Wenatchee apples on a Great Northern dining car and picking apples in an orchard. As with products today, celebrity endorsements added glamour and allure. Billie Dove's proclamation that she wanted to "pick apples all by myself, climb a tree like a kid again, fill my hat," speaks to the wholesome, healthful image apple advertisers tried to attach to their product. Dove, posed with a large apple in each hand, looks the very picture of health and youth.

Apple giveaways were a popular way to generate publicity. In 1923, the Great Northern delivered apples to orphanages and children's hospitals in St. Paul, Minnesota. As part of the 1938 National Apple Week celebration, Great Northern officials presented apples to Coach Bernie Bierman and his University of Minnesota Gophers, who had been eating

Wenatchee apples that season as part of their training. The *Wenatchee Daily World* reprinted the photos with a caption about the publicity efforts the Great Northern made on behalf of Washington growers.[72] After presenting apples to the team for the publicity shots before their big game with Northwestern, the Great Northern distributed 350 Delicious apples in cellophane bags at the Quarterbacks Luncheon in St. Paul. As Great Northern official C. W. Moore recounted, "I purposely selected the huge 48-pack size so that they could not be comfortably carried in coat pockets—and the result was that practically all the quarterbacks returned to their offices carrying apples."[73]

In perhaps the most elaborate National Apple Week stunt, Yakima baked the largest apple pie on record at that time. The Southern Pacific baked a record-breaking three-hundred-pound apple pie in its commissary during National Apple Week in 1923, but in 1927 Yakima planned an even larger pie.[74] The National Apple Week Committee, led by the Yakima Valley Traffic and Credit Association, first considered baking an enormous apple cake since cake was easier to serve. They changed their minds because no dessert is more associated with apples than pie. Unaware of the Southern Pacific's earlier stunt, they decided "to make a pie just like mother used to make them, all in one piece, with a bottom crust and plenty of fruit and sugar, and a top crust appropriately decorated." A local hardware company built a custom pan that measured ten feet in diameter and eight inches tall. Another local company constructed a five-foot-long knife to cut the pie. Since the pie was too large to bake in any local oven, the town constructed a special brick oven just slightly larger than the pie, with a system of cables and winches to pull the pie into and out of the oven. Four local bakeries developed the recipe, and students from the high school home economics class constructed the pie on the day of the event. Libby, McNeill & Libby, which had a fruit cannery in Yakima, steam cooked the apples, as fresh apples would not fully cook in a pie that large.

The completed pie took two thousand pounds of apples, which cooked down to four hundred gallons, and a hundred pounds of sugar. Volunteers pushed the filling into place with garden rakes. Nine high school students rolled out the crust with six-foot-long rolling pins on custom-built twelve-by-four-foot tables before draping the crust on the

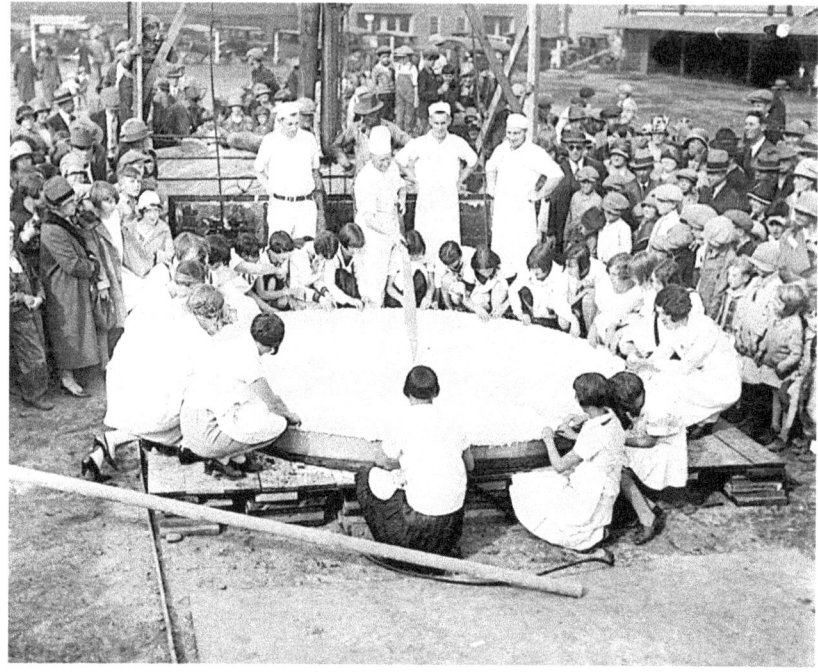

Putting the top crust on Yakima's 1927 National Apple Week apple pie. A volunteer holds the five-foot-long knife custom-made for the occasion. *Collections of the Yakima Valley Museum.*

pie. Metro-Goldwyn-Mayer, Pathé, Fox News, and International Newsreel filmed the event. Even though apples were already prepared, the filmmakers asked event organizers to peel apples for the camera. An estimated two thousand people were on hand to eat the hot pie. After five hours of serving pie, volunteers abandoned it to the town. People came with milk jugs, kettles, and other containers to scoop up the gallons of leftover filling. Stories of the event appeared in newspapers and on movie screens across the country. Yakima's hard work was nearly undone when the *New York Times* mistakenly captioned the event as having taken place in Seattle. Several newspapers reprinted the *Times* photo before organizers realized the mistake. Yakima's Apple Week organizers, with support from the Seattle Chamber of Commerce, requested corrections and restored proper credit for the pie.[75]

Yakima almost did not participate in National Apple Week events in 1927. During the 1925–26 season, Washington apples came under scrutiny when British health inspectors found several shipments contaminated with arsenic. This was not the first time British authorities voiced concerns. In the spring of 1892, the *Times* of London reported on a recent seizure of arsenic-contaminated apples by the New York Board of Health. Both British and American authorities dismissed the reports as exaggerated, stating that the amount of arsenic on apples was "infinitesimal" because most arsenic residue washed off or with rain or was wiped off with one's fingers. The American press framed the issue as an attempt to denigrate American exports. That summer, the *Washington Post* commented that "it is satisfactory to know that the attempt made some time ago to prejudice the minds of English consumers against the American apple . . . has utterly failed."[76]

As detailed in chapter 3, the arsenic scare of 1925–26 was different. News of contaminated American apples featured prominently in major American newspapers, and the British government threatened to embargo future fruit shipments if the USDA did not uphold British arsenic limits of 1/100 of a grain per pound. American growers were first skeptical, then defensive. Orchardists had used arsenical insecticides since the 1890s and widely believed that they were safe for consumers because they "washed off" during summer rains. Growers in the Pacific Northwest, the largest apple-producing region in the nation, found themselves on the front line of a controversy. Wary consumers feared arsenic, and bad publicity could ruin consumer markets. Yet arsenical insecticides were the only effective method to combat orchard pests, particularly the codling moth. The commercial production of apples, the very symbol of health, required the use of a deadly poison.

How growers responded to the charges of poisoning leveled against their industry illuminates the complex relationship among consumers, marketing strategies, and the realities of industrial agriculture. Research scientists quickly developed methods for removing arsenic-based sprays from fruit, growers purchased new equipment to wash apples, and two new advertising campaigns competed for growers' attention and railroad financing. Apples for Health was led by Paul Stark, president of the American Pomological Society and treasurer of Stark Bro's Nurseries in Louisiana, Missouri, a nursery best known for commercially developing the Delicious variety. R. H. Kipp, a marketing specialist for the Portland Chamber of Commerce, developed the Kipp Plan, proposed by the Washington State Chamber of Commerce.

With Apples for Health, Stark proposed a nationwide advertising campaign focused on the healthful properties of apples. Founded in October 1926, the organization planned to spend $1 million a year for four years on advertising, financed by contributions from growers and corporations. It set a goal to raise at least $100,000 from the railroads, with $75,000 coming from western railroads that directly served apple districts, and the other $25,000 coming from eastern railroads. Board members included representatives from the International Apple Shippers' Association, Pacific Northwest Boxed Apples, Hood River Apple Growers Association, and Western Fruit Jobbers. Initially, the plan had broad support from many in the apple industry.[77] In correspondence to the presidents of the Northern Pacific and Union Pacific, Great Northern president Ralph Budd shared his optimism about the plan. It seemed that apple producers across the country were finally organizing a modern advertising scheme. Budd's assistant William P. Kenney informed him that the campaign had the potential to "bring back the apple to the place of its former occupancy" at the breakfast table.[78] As the strongest proponent of the plan, Kenney argued that national advertising campaigns for products like raisins, bananas, and citrus had proven track records. Furthermore, the railroad provided monetary support for opening new districts for apple production, "and we should feel it more important to protect the country that we have already developed and brought to fruitful production and which we know will continue to produce if properly handled."[79]

Apples for Health was not the first advertising to link apples with good health. Nutrition had always been an important message in apple advertising. The old phrase "an apple a day keeps the doctor away," or some variation thereof, appeared regularly. In the early 1900s, nutritional science was in its infancy. Scientists completed some of the first chemical analyses of common foods in the American diet in the 1890s, and they had only rudimentary knowledge of fats, carbohydrates, and proteins. Home economists and fruit advertisers alike latched on to new advances in food science and used them to promote the consumption of fruit and vegetables. Wilbur O. Atwater, professor of chemistry at Wesleyan University in Connecticut, created nutritional tables with the carbohydrates, fats, and proteins of all known foods, which served as basic references for home economists across the nation. Atwater particularly emphasized proteins, and he and other home economists initially saw fruit and vegetables as luxury items because fruit did not provide as much nutrition as meat. But fruit's high carbohydrate content still made it a good source of food energy.[80] Pamphlets and recipe booklets included tables on the nutritional composition of apples and lauded them as a good source of carbohydrates.

As scientists began to discover vitamins, amino acids, and other nutritional building blocks in the 1910s and 1920s, advertisers incorporated new findings into promotional literature and print ads. One popular fruit pitch was that acidic fruits such as oranges, lemons, and apples could prevent "acidosis," a condition characterized by lethargy and general malaise. Acidosis is a real, but rare, medical condition caused by factors such as kidney failure, liver failure, diabetes, or drug overdoses, none of which can be cured by eating fruit. The fact that it was a rare condition did not stop advertisers from turning it into a marketing gimmick. According to advertisers, eating acidic fruit produced an alkaline condition in the body, thereby restoring natural balance and health.[81] One apple recipe booklet flaunted organic acids in apples as being beneficial for maintaining "balance," thus "overcoming constipation and intestinal putrification" and removing "poisonous products" from the blood.[82]

Invented health scares were not the only way to promote the healthful benefit of apples. More commonly, advertisements featured healthy people, especially children, eating apples. An early Skookum ad, for example, shows a drawing of a young boy, grinning widely and greedily clutching an apple. The ad states, "This youngster is happy. He's healthy too. 'An apple a day keeps the doctor away.'" The youngster is healthy because he is eating a Skookum apple. This is no ordinary apple; he is eating an apple imbued with the health and strength of the Northwest. The implication is that this apple provides more nutritional punch than an ordinary apple.

While the railroads debated the merits of supporting Apples for Health, R. H. Kipp of the Portland Chamber of Commerce approached the railroads with a second plan. This plan systematized selling and distribution channels by organizing growers into one group, and dealers and shippers into a second group. Growers would sell only to dealers who had signed on to the plan, and vice versa. Both groups would share advertising costs and be regulated by a central clearinghouse monitored by an agent from the US Department of Agriculture. Supporters argued that the Kipp Plan provided a solid framework to manage marketing on a regional basis and avoid gluts. "Right now Mr. Apple himself is in need of a doctor, or something," opined the *Seattle Post-Intelligencer*. "He is as big and red and world-famous as ever, but for the last three years has become something of a drug on the market." In order to work, at least 75 percent of apple tonnage needed to be part of the plan. Two hundred fifty growers, shippers, and dealers attended the planning meeting and unanimously accepted the plan.[83]

Faced with two competing plans, the railroads had to decide which, if any, they would support. Union Pacific president Carl R. Gray agreed that Apples for Health had potential if advertising remained general and all districts participated, but he was reluctant to commit to the campaign for two reasons shared by other railroads. First, Apples for Health placed a greater financial burden for advertising on the railroads rather than on the growers. Under the plan, growers would pay one cent per box, a total that Gray calculated to be $13,000. Meanwhile, his railroad was asked to contribute $25,000. Railroad executives expressed similar concerns about the Kipp Plan as well. The plan did not seem financially sound, the marketing plan was unproven, and there was no guarantee that a single infusion of cash from the railroads would be enough to guarantee success.[84]

Second, railroads worried about accusations of bias. Although the railroads had contributed to advertising campaigns in the past, it was no longer current policy. Not only did they open themselves to charges of favoritism within the apple industry, but they also faced charges of favoring one industry over another. The Union Pacific, for example, had recently refused to fund advertising for Northwest timber, and "this matter was bitterly resented."[85] It may have been resented even more if the railroad had financed either apple advertising scheme. On the other hand, the apple industry was in trouble after the arsenic scare. As George Reid, assistant to the president of the Northern Pacific, pointed out, a loss of Washington's apple industry "would be a hard blow to the railroads."[86] Saying yes to one industry's advertising campaign while saying no to another put railroads in a difficult position.

The main reason the Northern Pacific and the Great Northern entertained the idea of subscribing to either marketing scheme was to appease growers who were pressing for a reduction in freight rates.[87] Growers complained that freight rates to midwestern cities were too high. Railroad officials countered that growers did not understand rate structures. As William P. Kenney explained, "It's not that the Toledo, Chicago or St. Louis rate is too high. It is the fact that the New York rate is made lower than would ordinarily be the case." Because New York State had a robust apple industry, western apples had stiff competition, and high transportation costs affected growers' profits. The railroads subsidized freight rates to New York and calculated rates for points between Washington and New York on the New York rate. In 1925, New York City distributors received 4,589 cars of Northwest apples, versus 6,611 cars of New York apples.[88] Even though New York orchards were much closer, the Northwest had captured a significant portion of the market share. More Northwest apples were shipped to New York City than any other city in the United States. National advertising aimed at increasing apple consumption would maintain, or even increase, the Northwest's market share, and railroad officials calculated that support for advertising might temper talk of freight rates.

Growers were divided over the plans. The big question was, who would benefit from a national advertising campaign? In July 1926, a few months before the creation of Apples for Health, a group of cooperatives formed a new organization, Pacific Northwest Boxed Apples, for the purpose of advertising Northwest boxed apples. J. Walter Hebert, general manager of Big Y, served as the group's president. The thirty-eight-year-old Hebert had worked for Big Y since 1914. He was a strong believer in the power of advertising, but he thought that advertising should be "intelligently administered and unanimously supported . . . over a period of years." After running Big Y's national advertising campaign, he "eliminated it as impractical for an organization the size of Big 'Y.'"[89] In his view, small national campaigns run by individual distributors or cooperatives did not yield sufficient results. The industry needed to cooperate on a larger scale. Perhaps it is not surprising that in addition to working for Big Y and serving as president of Pacific Northwest Boxed Apples, Hebert also served on the board of Apples for Health. He supported any organization that might lead to unified advertising. Hebert saw a clear need for both plans, but the differences between Pacific Northwest Boxed Apples and Apples for Health confused growers. They questioned the necessity of having two organizations. Hebert tried to clarify the matter in an open letter. The difference was that one was specifically for boxed apples, while the other was for all apples, including those of eastern competitors who still packed in barrels. Hebert was hesitant to fully endorse Apples for Health because it was still raising money and had not yet formulated an advertising plan, but he advised cooperation with the group, provided that Apples for Health split any funds raised with Pacific Northwest Boxed Apples.[90] From his view, cooperation with a national campaign was possible, but not if it came at the expense of advertising boxed apples.

By 1928, it was clear that neither plan would succeed. The Yakima Valley Traffic and Credit Association decided not to contribute to Apples for Health because boxed-apple states would bear a disproportionate amount of the cost.[91] Big Y urged its members to ignore a fund-raising plea from Apples for Health because it had limited impact on Northwest growers. "Ours is a unique, highly specialized quality product," explained an article in the *"Big Y" Bulletin*, which "lends itself to an advertising and merchandising campaign with promise of more direct and early results than can possibly be secured by merely advertising the merits of apples generally."[92] Railroad officials expressed frustration with growers' lack of cooperation, and it appears they did not contribute to Apples for Health.[93] Growers expected a large crop and correspondingly low prices in 1928, and traffic managers feared that growers would not take action until it was too late. "This is the same old story," wrote J. L. Burnham of the Northern Pacific. "Every time there is a large crop of apples in Washington and low prices, the growers and dealers in Yakima get together and form some kind of an organization to further the sale of same, the thing is strung along and it invariably happens that there is an improvement in price, when the whole matter is dropped."[94] Burnham had already witnessed this cycle three times, and he was not surprised that cooperation did not work this time.

While the arsenic scare of the 1920s damaged the reputation of apples, growers had other concerns. Eastern growers had improved their growing methods and begun to produce higher-quality apples, making Washington apples less distinctive. Apple consumption was declining across the country as consumers turned to other fruit such as oranges and bananas. Between 1917 and 1926, Washington shipped an average of 103,822 carloads of apples per year to US markets, while an estimated 105,496 carloads of bananas entered the United States in 1926. This equated to 58,550,364 bunches of bananas, an estimated fifty-one bananas for every man, woman, and child in the country. With consumers purchasing more bananas than apples, one writer in *Better Fruit* questioned whether the apple was still the "King of Fruits."[95]

Washington fruit growers were not the only ones using large-scale advertising campaigns to sell fruit. They had to compete with the California Fruit Exchange and the United Fruit Growers, which also used print ads, recipe booklets, and other promotions to introduce consumers to their fruit. Ads touting the health benefits of fruit were common, and consumers were familiar with brands like Sunkist. "To have raisin growers, orange growers and the corporation selling bananas giving health talks to the public," wrote the editor of *Better Fruit*, "while a better fruit than any one of them is given little publicity is not good business for the apple growers."[96] In 1928, the Bureau of Agricultural Economics, with the cooperation of the New York Food Marketing Research Council, surveyed 3,100 consumers in New York City. This poll found that most housewives identified apples only by color: red, green, or yellow. Almost fifteen years after the introduction of the first brands, most consumers could not name a single favored brand. When pressed, one out of ten consumers named "Skookum," one out of sixteen named "Blue Goose," and one out of twenty-five named "Hood River." These apples were from Wenatchee and Yakima, Washington, and Hood River, Oregon, respectively, although consumers could not name these regions. African American women were the most familiar with brand names, even though they did not purchase brand-name apples. This was likely because, as household domestics, they shopped for upper-class white households who demanded the finest produce.[97]

Washington growers' advertising campaigns during the 1920s had mixed success. Although only 10 percent of consumers could name

"Skookum," that was a mark of success. There were hundreds of brand names on the market; shippers used at least 210 different brand names in Washington in 1928.[98] This does not account for shipping companies based in Chicago and New York, or brand names employed by growers in other parts of the country. With so many different brands competing for consumers' attention, only a few like Skookum, Blue Goose, and Big Y gained widespread recognition. It is significant that New York consumers could name only Northwest brands.

On the other hand, internal competition and jealousies prevented the development of a statewide marketing plan in the 1920s, despite several attempts. Growers might have sold more apples with cooperative advertising, but cooperative marketing was antithetical to the spirit of independent business fostered among Washington growers. Growers cared about profitability, but cooperation had its limits. Throughout the 1920s, advertising continued to center around individual cooperatives and districts. In good years, growers remained confident that their fruit would sell itself, and they were reluctant to decrease their net profits by relying on another intermediary. In bad years, they resumed discussions about the formation of marketing cooperatives. Ultimately, the radical economic realignment caused by the Great Depression provided the catalyst for statewide marketing. Only after the Depression nearly destroyed the apple industry did growers agree to a mandatory, grower-funded organization to promote mutual interest.

CHAPTER 6

Weathering the Depression and War

By the late 1920s, Washington's apple industry had matured. Cooperatives managed shipping, storing, and advertising campaigns, and independent growers benefited from the infrastructure created by the large co-ops, which included Big Y and the Yakima Horticultural Union in Yakima, and Skookum and Wenoka in Wenatchee. Then the Great Depression hit. "Apples are nitrated, freight-rated, and berated. They are thinned, washed, rinsed, sized, labeled and selected," wrote C. R. Miller, a West Virginia apple grower in a piece titled "Broke and Broker," reprinted in the *"Big Y" Bulletin*. "After the grower does all this . . . he turns them over to a broker. This man sends them 2,000 miles away and has them looked at by a color-blind confederate who telegraphs back that they 'can't handle ours at any price account lack of color. Try to get half dollar off per barrel.'"[1] Miller summed up the desperation felt by many growers across the nation during the Depression. Prices collapsed, making it impossible to recoup production costs. Expensive apples were a luxury most consumers could not afford. Over the course of the Depression, even the most ardent promotors of the industry had moments of doubt about the future success of Washington apples. Though the Depression forced many growers out of business, the industry stumbled on, supported by federal loans and, by 1937, a new research station and state advertising commission. Growers clung to the hope that if they could survive the Depression, consumers would resume purchases. While World War II brought economic recovery, it created new problems. Growers had to contend with labor and supply shortages, as well as wartime regulations. War contracts bolstered growers' finances, but they siphoned off the best apples, leaving civilians with poor-quality fruit that damaged Washington's reputation.

The Depression eventually forced many growers out of business, but in the early years, growers remained hopeful for strong sales. Nationwide, the 1929 apple crop was 20 percent smaller than the 1928 crop. Yakima, for example, shipped 1,900 cars in November 1929, 900 fewer cars than the previous November.[2] Apple shortages kept prices high in the fall of 1929, but by 1930, growers began to feel the pinch of the Depression. The Northwest, unlike other parts of the country, had a record crop year in 1930. That year the United States produced 30.8 million barrels of apples, 2 million fewer barrels than the previous five-year average. Other deciduous fruit crops were also smaller than average. Under normal conditions, apple prices should have been high, but low fruit and vegetable prices plagued growers across the nation. "A much smaller part of the population than usual is able to buy just what it wants," wrote Charles Durst, a contributor to *Better Fruit*.[3] Consumers had limited budgets, and fruit and vegetable sales suffered as a result.

Growers found creative ways to market their fruit in 1930. The Washington Boxed Apple Bureau conceived a national apple sale. The bureau ran newspaper advertisements in 71 cities and distributed over 100,000 window posters to 262 cities in 43 states.[4] The New York Apple Week committee, headed by Joseph Sicker, devised the unorthodox plan of letting unemployed men sell apples on the street.[5] The New York Police Department agreed to permit this practice without the usual vendor licenses. Five to six thousand unemployed men showed up every day to sell apples. Since potential apple sellers had no money, distributors trusted them to bring back profits from their first box of apples, which almost all did. While wholesalers in New York City had offered growers $1.75 per box, unemployed men sold them at an average of $2.25 per box. During the first week, they sold four thousand boxes of apples each day, including at least one carload of Wenatchee apples and one of Yakima apples. The promotion was so successful that Sicker extended it beyond the original week. The men made "an immense amount of profit," Sicker wrote. "In addition to this, they have saved the apple market and are buying clothes, shoes, goods, etc. and in their small sphere." Moreover, this innovative marketing venture was "bringing about prosperity such as has never been shown in such a short time."[6] Critics claimed that the unemployed were being exploited for a publicity stunt, but as an article in the *"Big Y" Bulletin* stated, "If giving cold and hungry men, many with families, an opportunity to work and earn a few dollars be exploiting the unemployed, let's have more of it whether they sell apples or cod-fish balls."[7] A Pittsburgh paper reported that at one welfare agency, eighty-seven families reported that they no longer needed assistance thanks to their apple earnings. Closer to home, distributors made plans for men to sell apples on the streets of Yakima.[8]

As successful as Sicker's plan was, selling apples on street corners could not save growers from the onslaught of the Depression. Growers had experienced bad years before, but losses were usually short term. Most growers recouped their expenses the following season. During the Depression, however, growers faced years of successive losses. American Fruit Growers, for example, reported losses of $544,572 in 1932 and $416,422 in 1933. As the Depression deepened, growers debated the cause of their misfortunes. Some blamed the inflated cost of shipping, utilities, insurance, and taxes for cutting into profits. Freight rates, which reportedly accounted for 45 percent of the market value of apples, were the worst offender, and growers wanted rates reduced to their pre–World War I levels.[9] Others in the industry saw other problems. "Call it underconsumption if you please; the effect is the same," shippers Gwin, White & Prince reminded their customers. "Fact remains that we have continued to produce a high-cost, necessarily under-priced article of luxury on a scale geared to the nearly universal prosperity of the late 1920s in face of the fact that our potential luxury-market has been severely contracted by the loss of millions of former consumers, reduced by the depression to a state of financial impotence."[10] Industry leaders had sounded the underconsumption alarm before, but this time no amount of advertising would convince struggling consumers to purchase more fruit.

The industry faced assaults on several fronts: low consumption, competition from other regions, and saturated markets. Old marketing problems were compounded by the Depression. For two decades, industry leaders had preached that cooperation would lead to stability, lower production costs, and better marketing practices. A few months before the stock market crashed in 1929, Congress passed the Agricultural

Marketing Act to encourage cooperative marketing. The act created a Federal Farm Board to oversee the establishment of "stabilization corporations" to bring producers of a commodity under a single marketing umbrella. The Farm Board was also charged with investigating marketing conditions and providing loans to cooperatives for marketing, storage, handling, or processing.[11] Northwest growers formed a new organization, the Northwest Council of Apple Cooperatives, as the Farm Board would deal only with "established cooperative organizations representing agricultural industries, either regionally or nationally." This excluded independent growers. The four largest cooperatives in Washington—the Big Y, Yakima Horticultural Union, Skookum Packers Association, and Wenatchee-Okanogan Cooperative Federation (Wenoka)—and the Hood River Apple Growers Association joined the council.[12]

Northwest growers had a mixed opinion of the act. Some hoped that federal legislation would solve marketing problems. Others were skeptical of national commodity corporations and worried that the Northwest would not have enough representation on the Farm Board. On the one hand, the law was in effect, so why not give participation a try? On the other, the law had limitations. Farm Board loans were available only for new facilities. The law made no provisions for loans to refurbish aging infrastructure or leased properties, a problem for Northwest growers since many storage and packing facilities were on land leased from the railroads. Northwest growers stalled efforts to organize the apple industry at a national level after finding that their midwestern and eastern counterparts had little experience with cooperative marketing. Northwest growers were strongly opposed to any organizational structure that lumped barreled apples with boxed apples. Because Northwest growers relied more on exporting smaller apples that had no domestic outlet, they worried that market stabilization plans would harm export markets and thus hurt their profits.[13]

By 1930, export markets were a growing concern. From 1923 to 1928, fruit exports nearly doubled. Nationwide, growers exported about 20 percent of the total commercial US apple crop. By comparison, growers in Washington, Oregon, and California exported an average of 25 percent. Changes to federal law at the beginning of the Depression, however, led to severe export declines. To address the economic havoc created by the stock market crash, Congress passed the Smoot-Hawley Tariff Act in 1930, with disastrous consequences for Northwest growers. Historian Joseph W. Ellison writes that Smoot-Hawley raised such nationalistic trade barriers that "while the bill was still before Congress, thirty-three nations protested against the contemplated rates."[14] After the bill passed, many countries passed their own duties on American products or added trade barriers such as licenses or quotas that effectively banned American imports. Canada doubled duties on American apple imports from thirty cents a box to sixty cents a box. Britain, the largest importer of American apples, adopted a policy of self-sufficiency, effectively boosting Canadian growers, who could label their apples as "Empire Grown." From the 1930–31 growing season, before Smoot-Hawley went into effect, until the 1934–35 season, US exports to Great Britain declined 50.6 percent, and global exports declined 61.5 percent. The American International Apple Association protested Smoot-Hawley, as did the Washington Boxed Apple Bureau and several cooperatives. Big Y lamented that "tariff walls built high enough and wide enough between two erstwhile friendly nations are but the forerunner of hatred and jealousy engendered by the clash of economic interests." Relations with Great Britain did not devolve to that point, but the decline in exports hurt growers' economic interests.[15]

The 1929 Agricultural Marketing Act provided little relief to Washington growers as the Depression worsened, but it was not the only federal intervention. Like farmers in other parts of the country, growers typically took out loans each spring to cover planting costs, and they paid the loans back each fall as apples sold. Depressed commodity prices in the 1920s led the federal government to take an interest in agricultural financing. The Agricultural Credits Act of 1923 built on earlier federal legislation to create a system of credit for rural farmers. The act established twelve Federal Intermediate Credit Banks, which were housed within existing Federal Land Banks. Congress authorized Intermediate Credit Banks to make short-term loans to cooperatives. Under the law, cooperatives could borrow funds at a discounted rate to distribute to members through their own credit corporations.[16] In 1930, cooperatives such as Big Y arranged financing through the Intermediate Credit Bank in Spokane.[17] This allowed cooperatives to keep production costs lower because they had funds to purchase supplies in bulk and could extend those savings, and credit, directly to grower-members.

By the 1931–32 season, the credit situation had deteriorated. Bank failures, compounded by successive years of poor crop returns, severely limited the credit available to growers. At least four banks in the Wenatchee District failed, freezing $2 million in assets. Growers in Wenatchee needed an estimated $1.5 million in crop loans to ensure full production, but because of bank failures, only $250,000 was available.[18] Growers in Yakima were in a slightly better situation, but financial institutions still needed an additional $500,000 to back crop loans.[19] By the spring of 1932, the situation was critical. Growers delayed pruning and spraying because they lacked funds, potentially compromising the productivity of not only their own trees, but all trees. Ignoring the spraying regimen—spraying too little or at the wrong time—would change the environmental equilibrium the industry strove to maintain. Meanwhile, industry leaders discussed financing options, especially one new option: federal funding from the Reconstruction Finance Corporation (RFC) through locally organized agricultural credit corporations.

The RFC, established in February 1932 under President Herbert Hoover, received $2 billion in appropriations to distribute to seventeen regional loan agencies. Individuals could not receive RFC funds, but agricultural credit corporations could. By mid-February, the RFC agency in Spokane had begun reviewing applications from Yakima and Wenatchee. Growers needed funds urgently, but there was a snag.[20] New credit corporations had to be backed by private funds. Apple cooperatives did not have enough liquid assets to back their own credit corporations, so they turned to railroads, public utilities, and spray companies for support. They rationalized that these companies benefited from their business with apple growers. Support for agricultural credit cooperatives ensured that growers could continue to ship apples, pay for water, and purchase spray. Industry leaders stayed in close communication with the railroads as plans for agricultural credit corporations developed.

Financial requests placed the railroads in a difficult position. They did not want to fund Washington growers because their own cash reserves were low, but they also realized that without apple shipments, their own financial position might deteriorate further. Railroad officials and apple industry leaders initially planned for one credit corporation to support all Wenatchee growers, but the Northwest Fruit Exchange, one of the largest shippers, which handled between one-fourth and one-third of Wenatchee's fruit, was reluctant to join, despite its need for RFC funding. Instead, the plan shifted to two credit corporations—one for the Northwest Fruit Exchange and another for independent growers—both backed by money from the railroads, local water-power companies, and growers. The Northwest Fruit Exchange needed $400,000 to finance its agricultural credit corporation, of which 75 percent was to come from the RFC. By early March, growers were not sure they could count on the RFC for any amount.[21]

Hope for RFC funds for growers began to evaporate as the spring of 1932 wore on. While the local board in Spokane approved credit corporation applications, the federal board in Washington, DC, denied or delayed applications. The federal RFC board took the position that "any organization to which money is loaned must have a substantial cash capital," complained Great Northern vice president Luthene C. Gilman, "which is just what does not exist in Wenatchee."[22] The apple industry was stuck in a catch-22. Great Northern president William P. Kenney was frustrated that banks received more consideration from the RFC than growers' credit corporations. After all, he argued, since the assets frozen in failed banks were largely agricultural assets, why was funding growers' credit corporations any different? If industrial agriculture were more solvent, it followed that the banks would be more solvent as well. Kenney had no respect for RFC head Eugene Meyers, a Hoover appointee and former chair of the Federal Reserve. "You cannot put him down as obstructionist," wrote Kenney, "but you can mark him as an ultra-conservative and never in sympathy with the Government's intention in an institution of this kind. In other words, he treats it purely as a banking institution without regard to needs or interest the new corporation is supposed to protect."[23] Kenney's sentiments were a common refrain among RFC critics. "Bankers viewed the RFC not as a way to expand the volume of credit but as a means of preserving their own and other institutions from bankruptcy," writes historian William Leuchtenburg. "The RFC virtually ignored its role as a public works agency."[24] The apple industry's experience with the agency bears out this observation.

By mid-March, Washington growers expected a sizable crop with minimal competition as trees east of the Rockies were damaged by a late frost. Growers remained optimistic for the outcome of the next year's crop, but they still needed financing. Railroad representatives and industry leaders lobbied the federal government to expedite aid, leaning on personal connections anyone had with members of the RFC and the Hoover administration.[25] Gwin, White & Prince, the marketing agency for the Wenatchee-Okanogan Cooperative Federation (Wenoka) in Wenatchee, gave up on RFC funding and began negotiating with First National Bank in Seattle. Gwin wrote to Luthene C. Gilman, vice president of the Great Northern, that eight hundred growers needed financing within the week, or it might be too late. He pleaded with the railroads for financial support, writing that "the time for hesitation is past. The time for decisive action is here. Dormant sprays must be applied within a few days. We repeat: the whole matter must be settled this week if we are to get the results aimed at."[26] If growers missed the first critical sprays of the season, the entire crop would be in jeopardy.

In Yakima, the situation was slightly better because the valley had suffered fewer bank failures.[27] Big Y and the Yakima Horticultural Union both applied for funds through Intermediate Credit Banks. Combined, the two cooperatives served about a third of growers in the Yakima Valley.[28] Big Y used reserves and cut expenses wherever possible, giving growers only the barest amount of money for spraying, pruning, and personal expenses. Overall, growers reduced production costs between 30 and 50 percent. Even though apple prices were low, Big Y repaid its bank loans for the 1932–33 season thanks to cost-cutting measures.[29] The Yakima Credit Corporation, financed through the RFC with $50,000 contributions from the Northern Pacific and Union Pacific, served independent growers.[30]

In the end, the Great Northern financed four separate agricultural credit corporations in the Wenatchee District. It had tried to limit its support to two corporations, one for the Northwest Fruit Exchange, to which the Great Northern contributed $50,000, and one for independent growers, which received just over $32,000. The Great Northern hoped these two corporations would serve most growers in Wenatchee. Because of lack of support from the RFC and growers' increasing desperation, the Great Northern funded two additional cooperatives—the Okanogan Agricultural Credit Corporation and the Wenoka Agricultural Credit Corporation. The latter, formed by Gwin, White & Prince with assistance from First Seattle Bank, received $50,000 from the Great Northern and Burlington. The railroad had not intended to fund this group, but as Luthene C. Gilman explained to Great Northern president William P. Kenney, "I think this is a better proposition than could be worked out through the RFC." Wenoka was a good producer, he continued, "and is, I think, the best managed organization that Wenatchee has."[31]

While the Great Northern assisted credit corporations, it turned down many other requests. Beyond their initial commitments, railroad officials were reluctant to invest in the apple industry because they were skeptical that they would see any returns. The Wenatchee District Cooperative, for example, had been financed through a credit corporation since 1925, under the 1923 Agricultural Credits Act. The law stipulated that loans could be used only for agricultural purposes, although in previous years, the co-op had used some funds to cover administrative costs. In 1932, officials informed the co-op that this practice was prohibited, which "naturally left us embarrassed," explained manager C. W. White, "especially since our previous banking connection, the Commercial Bank and Trust Company, is now in the process of liquidation."[32] White requested $15,000 from the Great Northern. After vice president Gilman denied the request, he made his plea directly to president Kenney, who also turned him down. That same summer, the Great Northern granted a $2,500 request from Okanogan. Kenney objected, "I have a very distinct recollection of advising you that under no circumstances would we give a nickel more to any financing proposition in the Wenatchee Valley." Gilman responded, "It does not seem possible to avoid this being done, particularly in cases where the parties have had long and friendly relations with you."[33]

Financing strained long-standing personal relations between railroads and shippers, especially in Wenatchee. The problem of funding some growers but not others was apparent, as Kenney wrote in a coded telegram: "I have not the slightest doubt but that ultimate end will be that we still have more Dempsters (enemies) in Thorium (Wenatchee) than we ever would have had if we had Dipteral (financed) nothing."[34] By May, the RFC still had not released funds to Wenatchee growers. Kenney's frustration turned toward those organizations the Great Northern had agreed to help. "I doubt if they ever intended to get any money from the R.F.C.," wrote Kenney of James S. Crutchfield of the Northwest Fruit Exchange and Gwin, White & Prince. From his perspective, pleas for help were attempts by cooperatives to use railroad funds to shield their own assets. In the face of financial hardship, the once mutually beneficial relationship between the railroad and the Northwest Fruit Exchange cracked. "Crutchfield is a dangerous, sneaking sort of a man," groused Kenney. "I never liked him, and I never felt he was on the square."[35]

By July, RFC money, albeit less than anticipated, started flowing into Yakima and Wenatchee. The Wenatchee Fruit Credit Corporation, comprising independent growers, received $70,000, and the Northwest Fruit Exchange Credit Corporation received $180,000, far less than the $300,000 requested. Though "impatient" with delays, vice president Luthene C. Gilman reported that "on the whole it may have been a good thing, as the inability to get money resulted in the growers doing a good deal of their own work, which they might not have done in case plenty of money had been forthcoming." In other words, growers had to economize whether they wanted to or not. Yet even with RFC money, there was still a shortage of funds. In Wenatchee, growers had pruned their trees, but spray applications were patchy, leading to concerns about infestation. The lack of capital meant that ancillary industries such as box manufacturing had not prepared for the upcoming harvest season, and growers worried about box shortages.[36] In Yakima, many growers had enough assets to manage spring operations, but by fall they were low on resources and needed loans to complete the harvest.[37]

Without assistance from the railroads, the apple industry would not have had enough capital to survive the 1932 season. Nonetheless, the relationship remained strained. Growers, led in part by Rufus Woods, editor of the *Wenatchee Daily World*, agitated for lower freight rates.[38] *Better Fruit*'s new editor, Volney T. Boaz, a son-in-law of prominent Yakima grower H. M. Gilbert, also used his platform to criticize the railroads for high rates. In his inaugural editorial, Boaz compared railroads to medieval butchers who used to bleed patients as a cure. "We've bled to the point where we have very little but ice water in our veins," he fumed.[39] Growers had a long history of protesting rates, especially in bad crop years. Apple prices were low, and growers wanted freight rates to decrease correspondingly. While growers could control costs by skipping a spray cycle or hiring fewer workers at harvest time, they had no control over freight rates, which were set by the Interstate Commerce Commission (ICC). Growers saw the railroads' seeming failure to lower freight rates as an extension of their reluctance to provide financial backing for credit corporations. Rufus Woods argued that the railroads were gouging growers and contributing to the downfall of the industry. In a letter to railroad executives, he argued that high freight rates were "killing off the orchardists here" and benefiting eastern growers.[40] Ralph Budd, president of the Chicago, Burlington & Quincy Railroad and former president of the Great Northern, urged Woods to see matters from the railroad's perspective. "I believe you know that the railroads are between the deep sea of poor net income if they cut their rates too much, and the devil of losing the business if they do not cut the rates," Budd explained.[41] Great Northern vice president Luthene C. Gilman was forgiving in his assessment of the situation; growers were frustrated by red tape involved in getting government loans.[42] It seemed understandable that some of that frustration be aimed at the railroads. In a response to Woods, Gilman also pointed out that the railroads were transporting apples at a rate over 16 percent less than the rate set by the ICC. Given that the ICC had to approve all rate changes, Gilman thought a rate reduction was "extremely doubtful."[43]

Financing remained a problem throughout the 1930s. In 1933, Reconstruction Finance Corporation rules changed. The Regional Agricultural Credit Corporation in Spokane, one of the seventeen regional credit corporations established by the RFC, could now make loans to individuals, but the program was cumbersome and restrictive. It required growers to choose a packer and marketer before receiving the loan. Sixteen hundred growers signed a petition to separate financing for production from that for marketing.[44] The loan amounts were also too small to cover growers' production costs. In a joint telegram to the RFC, the presidents of the Great Northern, Northern Pacific, and Union Pacific explained why growers urgently needed larger loans. Orchards were a long-term investment, and delays in spraying, pruning, or irrigation would decrease returns not only in the current season, but for years to come. If orchards failed, people who worked directly with the industry would be "rendered destitute," and entire towns in the region might collapse as well.[45] In response, the RFC agreed to raise its loan rate from fifty cents per box to fifty-five cents per box, still far below the sixty-two cents per box that growers requested.[46]

As the financial crisis deepened, industry leaders worried about the rising number of abandoned orchards. By 1920, Washington had 7.9 million trees of bearing age. In the 1920s, the number of bearing trees declined by 2.7 million, a 34.7 percent decrease, although yields continued to increase thanks to improved growing methods. During the Depression, the number of bearing trees in the state declined another 34 percent, from 5,193,571 to 3,404,140.[47] Some removals occurred because of the age of the trees, changes in consumer taste, and the fact that during the boom of the 1910s, orchards had been planted on marginal land. Others during the 1930s resulted from bankruptcies. Neglected orchards threatened the entire industry by harboring pests; therefore, state law mandated tree removal if orchards were not sprayed. County agent A. B. Chase estimated that about a third of trees in the Wenatchee District needed to be removed.[48] Removing trees was also a way to cut production costs and keep orchards solvent. Yakima District inspector A. C. Rich advised growers to remove stunted, low-producing, or badly infested trees to reduce spray costs, which could run from seventy-five to one hundred dollars per acre.[49]

As growers struggled for funding, some began to question the value of industrial agriculture. The great irony of American agriculture was and is that many farmers cannot feed themselves. Many growers had to borrow money for essential items like groceries. Twenty years earlier, experts encouraged growers to think as businesspeople, but now that mindset was ridiculed. An editorial in the *"Big Y" Bulletin* asked, "Is the orchard a factory or a farm?" The author argued that specialization cost farmers their self-sufficiency. The grower who plants a garden, keeps chickens, and "believes his orchard is also a farm and home and must make him a living whether Europe buys apples or not" is in a better position to survive than the grower who is "accustomed to cleaning up a nice fruit crop and taking a little trip to California."[50] The advice might have changed, but college-trained experts continued to drive the conversation. For example, a study by Washington State College showed that a home garden was healthy and cost effective, resulting in a net gain of $2.55 for each hour spent in the garden.[51] Unfortunately, the study did not account for how much this might detract from working in one's orchard, and it presumed that growers had free time to dedicate to the task.

Home gardening might put food on the table, but it could not save farms. Growers needed more government assistance, which came in the form of several New Deal programs. In March 1933, President Franklin Roosevelt issued an executive order creating the Farm Credit Administration, which consolidated the functions of the RFC and other federal farm loan programs. The Farm Credit Act, passed in June 1933, provided a new framework of local production credit associations (PCAs) through which growers could get loans. In March 1934, growers started submitting loan applications to the new PCAs, and by June, the government had loaned $1.8 million to four hundred growers. In 1935, the Wenatchee Valley was declared an "economically stricken area," which allowed it to receive emergency loan funds typically reserved for drought-stricken areas. A severe frost damaged the apple crop in October 1935, and the following spring, Washington received $250,000 in loans from the Resettlement Administration to assist growers with damaged trees. This patchwork of funding helped, but by 1936, 15 percent of growers still did not qualify for relief. Concerned that trees would not be sprayed on time, Chelan County commissioners appropriated $10,000 for an emergency spray fund. Industry leaders continued to lobby for additional Resettlement Administration funds.[52]

Agricultural supports were only one facet of the New Deal. The Pacific Northwest had larger ambitions. In 1934, a group of citizens formed the Pacific Northwest Regional Planning Commission to represent the interests of Washington, Oregon, Idaho, and western Montana. Funded by the National Planning Board, the group prepared reports about the region's resources to "develop the economy of the region integrated with national interests."[53] Regional planners had a vision of harnessing the natural bounties of the Pacific Northwest for national good. They looked at the region's undammed rivers as sources of power and irrigation, farms and fisheries as food for the nation, forests as places of recreation and sources of building materials. The planning commission, in the words of chair Marshall N. Dana, sought a "sustained yield of food and the means of material sustenance, all in order that we may bring about the most important objective—the sustained yield of life."[54] Despite the planning commission's intensive work, the Northwest would not experience the full results of some New Deal programs until after the Depression. For Washington's apple growers, New Deal programs did little more than help maintain the status quo.

During the Depression, the federal government and the Pacific Northwest Regional Planning Commission worried about resettling displaced Dust Bowl refugees. In 1936, an estimated ten thousand families moved to Washington, Oregon, Idaho, and western Montana from northern plains states affected by drought. Though far fewer than the estimated one hundred thousand families who migrated to California from the Great Plains, this was still a significant influx into the region.[55] The Resettlement Administration hoped to find farms for the new arrivals. A Farm Security Administration survey of the Northwest in the late 1930s found that of 20,917 recent settlers, 24 percent had settled on abandoned farms, 48 percent were hoping to settle on unimproved land, and 28 percent were working on farms.[56] While the survey covered the entire Northwest, migrants to central Washington found it hard to find farmland. Very few people took over abandoned orchards, which were often on marginal land and in need of costly rehabilitation because of seasons of neglect. Given the low price of apples, such orchards were not profitable, nor did newcomers have capital to invest in necessary improvements.[57]

Unimproved land did not offer opportunities either. Some historians such as Donald Worster argue that federal irrigation did not fully develop until the Depression, but that was not the case in central Washington. No new irrigation projects were completed in the state during the 1930s, meaning that unimproved land was not a viable resettlement option. At the beginning of the Depression, the Bureau of Reclamation had two active projects in Washington: the Yakima Project and the Okanogan Project. Both had successfully watered land since the early 1900s and continued to do so throughout the Depression. In 1935, Congress authorized funds to construct a new division of the Yakima Project, the Roza division. The storage dam was completed in 1939, but irrigation water was not available until 1941. Although construction on the Grand

Coulee Dam on the Columbia River began in the 1930s, the dam was not completed until 1941. The Columbia Basin Project came under the auspices of the Bureau of Reclamation in 1939, but construction of the irrigation system did not begin until 1945 and irrigation water was not available until 1948.[58] Irrigation projects started during the Depression did not provide immediate relief to farmers, but they would later open new lands to farming.

Many Dust Bowl migrants who found their way to central Washington found work picking fruit. Historian Richard Lowitt writes that conditions for migrants in the Northwest were not as "severe or as publicized as those in California, nor were there racial or ethnic dimensions to their plight."[59] Labor disputes were not as serious in Washington as they were in California. Washington growers, supported by local law enforcement, suppressed union activity. In the 1910s and early 1920s, the Industrial Workers of the World (IWW) attempted to organize workers in the Yakima Valley with no success. Police raided IWW meetings and prevented public gatherings. In 1933, the IWW again tried to organize farm labor in the Yakima Valley, with disastrous results for the union. Conflict between the IWW and Yakima Valley growers began in May when hundreds of IWW workers began picketing hops farms for higher pay. Prohibition had just ended, and hops prices had nearly doubled. The IWW argued that pickers should receive thirty-five cents an hour rather than the ten to twelve cents workers typically received. Local law enforcement, sympathetic to growers, quickly arrested picketers, ending the IWW's protest. Throughout the summer, the IWW continued to hold meetings to plan its next move. Likewise, over the summer hops growers and fruit ranchers formed "farmers' protective organizations" to prepare for expected union activity. IWW protests resumed in August at the start of peach season when workers at Anna Mitchell's Sunnyside peach orchard went on strike. Word of the strike spread, and neighbors rushed to Mitchell's defense. Outnumbered, the strikers dissipated. The final confrontation occurred on August 24, when a group of sixty to one hundred people gathered at the Congdon Orchard three miles west of Yakima to picket the pear harvest. Before long, a group of somewhere between one hundred and three hundred farmers bearing clubs, baseball bats, sticks, and other homemade weapons confronted the picketers in a bloody clash known as the "Congdon Orchard Battle." The farmers marched picketers into Yakima and left them at the courthouse. The National Guard and the sheriff's office restored order. Authorities held most picketers in the Yakima jail until the following December, when they were released on charges of vagrancy and told to leave town.[60]

IWW leaders failed to gain support for several reasons. At its peak strength in the 1910s, the IWW had the greatest appeal with transient single men. In the 1930s, most workers in the Yakima Valley had families or were permanent residents in the valley. A study of the 1935–36 season found that 70.6 percent of transient laborers lived in a family unit. The same study found that from August 1935 to July 1936, growers hired the equivalent of 34,881 days of labor. Yakima Valley residents accounted for 17,632 days of that labor, transients for 9,042, and unclassified days, meaning that the type of work was unknown, for 8,207. Even if transient laborers accounted for all unclassified days, residents performed at least half of all seasonal hired labor.[61] Workers with families would not have wanted to jeopardize their jobs, and residents had ties to the community that would have discouraged participation in IWW activities.

Second, IWW leaders underestimated the organization of Yakima Valley growers and local law enforcement. "Wobblies were engaging adversaries whose collective strength was so great that only the most naïve or deluded contemporary observer of the contest can have failed to foresee its eventual outcome," writes historian Cletus E. Daniel. He argues that government officials supported growers rather than labor, in part because growers were able to capitalize on the myth of the independent farmer to highlight their own suffering, obscuring the fact that these were industrial farms.[62] While growers did use this myth to their advantage, Washington's orchards were in fact small family farms, despite their industrialized trappings. In the Yakima Valley, over 60 percent of fruit farms were twenty acres or less, with 32.5 percent under ten acres.[63] "A majority of the growers are small owners," observed a publication by the Northwest Regional Council. "Dealings between them and their employees often are direct and on a personal basis." Though the council criticized the lack of union organization, it explained that "frequently the owner is in a tough spot and unable to provide better living quarters and higher wages."[64]

Despite their violent treatment of IWW protestors, some growers were sympathetic to labor's demand for higher wages. Because of high production costs, growers could not afford to increase wages from ten to twelve cents per hour to thirty-five cents per hour as the IWW demanded. Unlike hops prices, apple prices had not increased. In 1929, an average bushel sold for $1.39, but in 1933, an average bushel sold for only $0.68. Apple prices barely covered the cost of production. Federal loans provided enough money to scrape by, but growers still struggled to pay expenses such as property taxes and utility bills. Most owed money on loans taken out the previous year, in addition to loans coming due for the 1933 season. Growers in the Yakima Valley paid wages on par with national averages at the time, and most did not have the money to raise wages even if they wanted to.[65]

Some hoped that New Deal programs would provide relief for workers, but help did not materialize until late in the Depression. Transient labor peaked during harvest in September and October. Little work was available for laborers the rest of the year, and local officials encouraged transient labor to move on. A 1937 study of the Yakima Valley found that 38 percent of transient harvest workers were from nearby Washington counties, 23 percent were from drought states, 18 percent were from Oregon or California, and the remainder from other states. Those from drought states were most likely to establish permanent residence. Workers from Oregon and California were professional fruit pickers who followed the West Coast harvests. Surprisingly, growers preferred to hire drought-state refugees because of their previous farm experience and willingness to work. As the study notes, living conditions were "perhaps worse among farm laborers than among any group of farm population in this part of the country." Nearly 68 percent of single transient laborers and 43 percent of families lived in tents. Only 6.8 percent of single transient workers and 11 percent of families had permanent dwellings. The remainder lived in shacks or tourist cabins. The Farm Security Administration eventually started a farm labor camp program in 1939 to provide safe, sanitary housing to transient farm workers in the region. The camp in Yakima housed an apple-packing school run by the Works Progress Administration to train harvest workers.[66]

The problems of Dust Bowl migrants and transient workers received less attention because of larger concerns over the state of the apple industry. Despite low prices, industry leaders remained firmly convinced that they could solve the apple industry's problems by focusing on the quality and marketing of key varieties. The number of commercial varieties had declined during the 1920s, and the Depression limited commercial varieties to the four or five most popular apples, varieties such as Winesap and Delicious that would sell for a small profit.[67] Growers still had to pay attention to the quality of their fruit. The Delicious variety, for example, could be flavorless if picked too early, or mushy if picked too late. At a meeting in Wenatchee sponsored by the Skookum Packers Association, growers were reminded to make sure that "every Delicious a consumer received was 'irresistible'—fresh, crisp, snappy, juicy and full-flavored—so that it would not have to take second place" to apples from other districts.[68] This view, shared by others in the industry, was that diminished consumer purchasing power was not the issue. Instead, growers needed to provide consumers a quality product with advertising campaigns to grab their attention. To that end, growers revived discussions about industry-wide marketing cooperatives by soliciting funds from the railroads, lobbying for new state laws, and pleading with growers to join cooperative marketing plans.

In 1933, *Better Fruit* devoted an entire issue to the marketing problem. The Washington Boxed Apple Bureau presented a plan to create a central sales exchange to replace the over two hundred shippers and sales organizations currently operating in the state. The bureau set up subcommittees to lobby for lower freight rates, work on tariff issues, advocate for industry financing, craft a research agenda, promote trade through advertising, and coordinate sales.[69] Another plan, from William Berney of the Walla Walla Produce Company, proposed a "Surplus Crop Corporation." Berney thought it would be impossible to get everyone to agree to a unified marketing plan, so instead of arguing over specifics, growers would simply agree to let the corporation sell half their crop for a minimum price, thereby stabilizing the market and generating fairer prices.[70] Neither plan was adopted.

Growers continued to argue over freight rates, tariffs, and fruit quality. Lowering freight rates was not a viable solution, as the railroads were able to make a strong case with the Interstate Commerce Commission that rates were already low. Protests of foreign tariffs led the Roosevelt administration to reconsider the issue. The Reciprocal Trade Agreements Act of 1934 allowed the United States to negotiate tariff rates with individual countries, rather than have a blanket policy. By 1937, the government had negotiated sixteen separate agreements. Some agreements increased quotas; others lowered tariffs for all or part of the year. In the 1935–36 season, apple exports increased 86 percent over the previous season.[71]

The issue of whether and how to sell low-grade apples remained a topic of debate. In the early 1930s, growers discussed eliminating the "C" grade to improve quality, meaning that only the top two grades, extra-fancy and fancy, would be marketed and shipped. Growers in Wenatchee favored the change, while those in Yakima did not. Hearings held in July 1934 after the passage of the Washington Agricultural Adjustment Act provide a window into the problem of low-grade fruit. Based on the federal Agricultural Adjustment Act, the state act attempted to restore farm commodities to pre–World War I levels by setting minimum prices, regulating production levels, and issuing licenses to processors and wholesalers.[72] Under the proposal, minimum prices on high-grade fruit would be set by a committee of growers from each district, while culls and "C" grade apples would sell for a minimum of fifteen dollars per ton. Culls generated the most conversation. Those in favor of the minimum argued that it cost fifteen dollars per ton to grow and harvest low-grade apples. While growers would not profit, at least they would recoup production costs. Those against the minimum countered that the price was too high. Processors had been purchasing culls for as little as ten dollars per ton. Higher prices might increase the cost of goods such as canned apples or cider vinegar, cause factories to purchase apples from neighboring states, and deprive growers of income received from culls. As O. K. Conant of the Yakima County Horticultural Association reasoned, some money was better than no money. Despite the fervor over cull apples, less than half a percent of Washington's apple tonnage went to processing plants. Most growers treated culls as garbage. A. L. Brockway, a grower from Hanford, Washington, reported that his district had sold no culls in the past twelve years. A. L. Strauss, a grower from Yakima, likened culls to slaughterhouse leftovers. "I imagine such things are made into glue," he stated, "and I believe that the cull business is not nearly as important to the apple industry as it has been made to seem during this hearing."[73] If anything, the discussion of culls distracted from larger marketing problems. In the final regulations, the Department of Agriculture removed any specific references to minimum prices on cull apples.[74]

Although growers protested cull prices, they were overwhelmingly in favor of a marketing code that would set prices and provide industry-wide advertising. H. C. Bohlke of Grandview, Washington, testified that 90 percent of growers in Grandview and Sunnyside were in favor of a code. Representatives from three of the major cooperatives—Yakima County Horticultural Union, Yakima Fruit Growers Association, and Wenoka—stated that while the law had major flaws, they supported a marketing code in theory.[75] One disgruntled grower asked whether "this was a free country any more or not?" "It is not," replied Walter J. Robinson, director of the State Department of Agriculture. "As all countries become settled and developed," he continued, "we lose certain of our freedoms."[76] A few growers chafed under the constraints of industry, but the Depression had finally forced growers to reconsider their views on cooperative marketing. After years of false starts, Washington growers seemed to be moving toward a unified, statewide marketing system.

A statewide marketing campaign was ready to launch for the 1935 season, when the Washington State Supreme Court declared the state's Agricultural Adjustment Act unconstitutional, throwing the future of statewide marketing into question. At that point, it was too late to organize any alternatives. H. G. Hawkins, manager of Washington Deciduous Fruits, a group organized under the act to coordinate marketing and advertising, urged "voluntary action of growers."[77] In Wenatchee, a group of growers began to raise advertising funds, while major cooperatives in the state waited to see what would develop, and whether it would be more advantageous to advertise their own brands or join a statewide initiative.

With no statewide advertising campaign in 1935, another avenue opened for promoting Washington apples. Safeway grocery stores launched the "Farmer-Consumer Campaign" to advertise apples and other farm commodities. Since the 1910s, Washington growers had debated whether to spend advertising dollars on consumers or distributors. Advertising to consumers worked only if Washington apples were available in grocery stores. Grocery store displays were part of earlier campaigns, but the Safeway campaign was different because chain grocery stores were relatively new. Average American consumers in the nineteenth century would have purchased their food from several purveyors such as greengrocers, who sold fresh fruits and vegetables, and butchers and bakers. By the 1920s, American consumers could purchase all their food from a single grocery store chain such as the Atlantic & Pacific Tea Company (A&P), Kroger, or Safeway. A&P, one of the first grocery chains in the United States, built its empire on tea and coffee, later adding other dried, tinned, and perishable goods. In the early 1920s, few grocery chains carried fresh produce because slow supply chains led to spoilage. In 1924, A&P started a subsidiary, the Atlantic Commission Company, to manage purchases and distribution of fresh produce for its stores. Other grocery chains soon added perishable produce to their shelves.[78]

For its Farmer-Consumer Campaign, Safeway set a goal of selling four million pounds of apples during the Christmas season. Safeway had used similar campaigns for dairy, beef, nuts, and other products. "The need for such a Safeway Farmer-Consumer campaign for the apple industry is greater than it has been in some time," said R. W. Doe, Safeway vice president, "and we are going to do everything possible to help apple growers throughout the country move this surplus into consumption before Christmas."[79] During the six-day campaign, Safeway sold 63,981 boxes of apples in 2,900 stores, an average of 22 boxes per store. Stores increased sales by an average of 100 percent. In some districts, stores exceeded the average: Yakima increased by 219 percent, Portland by 378 percent, and Seattle by 401 percent.

Though Safeway's promotion was a rousing success, growers recognized that the patchwork system of cooperative and store campaigns was not enough. The industry needed consistent and coordinated marketing; the question was how to accomplish that while maintaining growers' and shippers' autonomy. "While most industries reached the pit of the depression in 1932 and have been on the upgrade since," remarked C. A. Leedy, president of the Skookum Packers Association, "I am convinced that the grower is at his low point in 1935."[80] The apple industry needed to take drastic action. In early 1936, four of the largest cooperatives in the region—the Yakima Fruit Growers Association, Skookum

Packers Association, Wenatchee Okanogan Federation (Wenoka), and Hood River Apple Growers Association—combined to form a "supercooperative" called Pacific Northwest Fruits (PNF). Under the plan, each cooperative continued to sell its own apples, but they would engage in a joint advertising and marketing campaign.[81]

As low prices and slumping sales continued in the 1930s, cooperatives struggled to pay back Reconstruction Finance Corporation loans taken in 1932 and 1933. After 1933, government loan programs favored individual growers. This left cooperatives in a bind. In normal years, crop sales brought in enough profits to cover spring outlays, but cooperatives could not sustain successive years of losses. Skookum Packers, for example, had been under the umbrella of the Northwest Fruit Exchange and its Columbia Agricultural Credit Corporation, formed with funds from the Reconstruction Finance Corporation and the Great Northern. By 1936, the credit corporation's finances were in dire straits. Skookum Packers had realized that "federal relief financing has built nothing permanent and has resulted in the disorganization of the industry," wrote M. S. Foster, president of the credit corporation.[82] Sales had become a free-for-all, and PNF hoped to restore order to the industry through coordinated advertising and distribution. Under PNF's plan, each cooperative contributed two cents per box to a joint marketing fund. Cooperatives hoped that coordinated sales and advertising would rebuild the market and lead to higher apple prices.

At the same time, a "Committee of Fifteen" in Wenatchee and a "Committee of Ten" in Yakima, both consisting of growers, shippers, and local business owners, were drumming up support for a statewide marketing organization to advertise Washington apples nationally. The committees interviewed hundreds of people involved in the apple industry and determined that growers' top concerns were the poor returns of the last five years, the lack of credit, and the lack of consumer demand. Growers preferred marketing solutions to reduced production, such as destroying orchards. "I don't believe we have an over-production, but we do have under-consumption," explained C. E. Chase, a member of the Committee of Fifteen, "due almost entirely to the fact that we have not made efforts to keep our consumption up to somewhere near what it used to be and also to improve our marketing and distribution of our apples all over the United States." Like PNF, the group also proposed funding advertising through a two-cent-per-box charge to growers.[83]

Some industry leaders were confident that a unified advertising campaign would aid growers, but others had concerns. Statewide advertising was not possible without the support of the major cooperatives that formed PNF. Editors of *Better Fruit* pointed out that there was "some apprehension" that PNF would stymie plans by maintaining a separate organization.[84] Northern Pacific vice president W. E. Coman feared that unless the two groups cooperated, "the apple industry from an advertising and sales standpoint will be seriously handicapped."[85] Meanwhile, railroad officials refused to finance any new cooperative schemes, including PNF's request for $200 for a thirty-minute promotional film on the apple industry. As Northern Pacific official J. M. Crawford opined, "There isn't much likelihood of the Pacific Northwest Fruits, Inc. operating successfully when each one of the member co-operatives may act independently in all matters."[86] Growers had discussed cooperative marketing schemes since the early 1920s, and railroad officials were skeptical that this latest iteration would work.

Committees in Wenatchee and Yakima moved quickly to build support for their marketing plan. They knew success depended on signing the majority of growers and shippers; they set a target of 85 percent of growers from each district. Many growers supported the plan, but the position of the big cooperatives remained uncertain. Skookum and Wenoka, comprising a loose confederation of small local cooperatives, left the issue to their members.[87] Big Y took a top-down approach to management, but it also put the question to a vote of the membership and agreed to join the plan if 85 percent of its members approved. Fifty-three percent of Big Y members voted against the plan, possibly because Big Y was already affiliated with PNF.[88] The Yakima committee was able to sign 82 percent of other growers, but without Big Y, they could not meet the 85 percent target. The committees decided to move ahead with the plan anyway.[89] By mid-August, Wenatchee and Yakima had signed 85 percent of growers and 95 percent of shippers to the plan. The group, incorporated as Washington State Apples, selected a board of four growers from Wenatchee and three from Yakima. One of their first actions was to hire J. Walter Thompson Co., a renowned New York advertising firm.[90]

Both Washington State Apples and PNF mounted successful advertising campaigns in 1936. George W. Coburn, vice president in charge of sales for the Northwest Fruit Exchange, reported that "the success of this industry lies with the growers *collectively* not individually," and that the success of PNF "should give just the necessary encouragement and furnish the demonstrations necessary to convince us of the efficacy and benefits of collective work."[91] In addition to posters and print ads, PNF produced a film about apple production and held contests for the best grocery store window. It also introduced a new mascot during National Apple Week, "Doc Apple," a dapper tuxedo-clad cartoon character with an apple for a head.[92]

Washington State Apples estimated that grower profits had increased by $4 million over the previous season, a result it attributed to improved advertising. In addition to print and radio advertisements, J. Walter Thompson conducted market research in Chicago, Dallas, Los Angeles, and St. Louis. Forty percent of women interviewed said they bought Washington apples because they had seen advertising, and 34 percent of all consumers remembered a print or radio ad, an "excellent showing" because a month had elapsed since the advertising campaign ended. J. Walter Thompson also used cross-promotional campaigns with other clients, a practice that Washington State Apples could not have afforded on its own. The Bing Crosby Kraft Cheese radio program, for example, featured recipes for Delicious apples and Philadelphia cream cheese and Old English cheese. General Mills' Betty Crocker radio program aired a recipe for a "Delicious Bisquick Apple Roll," and Pillsbury advertised a "Steamed Apple Sauce Pudding" with Washington apples.[93] A cross-promotion with Swift & Co.'s Formay shortening increased Formay sales by 15 percent and apple sales by 30 percent in markets where the advertisements ran, "the largest increase Swift & Co. ever had in connection with using another commodity in conjunction with their product."[94]

Washington State Apples started its campaign drive in January 1937 with high hopes for nearly unanimous grower participation. It had reason to be optimistic, given the advertising success of 1936. In early February, however, the Skookum Packers Association and Wenoka abruptly withdrew their support, citing their membership in PNF. They were happy with the PNF advertising and saw no reason to support both organizations. Washington State Apples board members expressed disappointment that a "small minority" could block the work of statewide advertising.[95] The "Committee of Fifteen" who launched Washington State Apples continued to hold public meetings to discuss options. The committee preferred voluntary participation but agreed that "if the sign-up under the voluntary plan could not be definitely concluded at least two weeks prior to the adjournment of the legislature, then immediate consideration would be given to the compulsory plan."[96] On February 25, the legislature's horticultural committee, chaired by Robert French of Okanogan, introduced a bill to create a statewide apple advertising commission.[97] Growers reacted positively to the announcement of the bill. The *Yakima Morning Herald* interviewed thirty-three growers, and all but one expressed strong support.[98]

A week after its introduction, House Bill 667 passed with no opposition.[99] Two days later, the senate passed the bill by a vote of 28 to 11. Two senators from western Washington questioned the financial structure outlined in the bill. Funds came from a two-cent levy on each one hundred pounds of apples shipped, collected through "Apple Advertising Stamps" affixed to boxes, invoices, or inspection documents. The money stayed with the advertising commission rather than going to the state treasury. A senator from King County opposed the bill on different grounds, arguing that advertising apples would divert consumer spending away from other goods. Both objections were overruled, and on March 17, Governor Clarence Martin signed the act into law.[100] Washington State Apples became the Washington State Apple Commission, an independent corporate entity charged with overseeing advertising, marketing, and scientific research into the health properties of apples. "Washington grown apples are handicapped by high freight rates in competition with eastern and foreign grown apples," the bill stated, "and this disadvantage can only be overcome by education and advertising." The bill aimed to stabilize the industry, which was "necessary to assure the payment of taxes to the state . . . , to alleviate unemployment . . . , and increase wages for agricultural labor."[101]

In an editorial following the passage of the law, *Better Fruit* expressed skepticism. Although the publication was "sincerely eager to see the apple industry go forward," it had reservations about how the law would be enforced and whether it would hold up to a legal challenge. Large cooperatives supported the bill, but regardless of its outcome, they were already engaged in strong marketing efforts and had "shown they can take care of themselves." The question was whether large cooperatives and independent growers could work together.[102]

Although Wenoka had precipitated the bill by withdrawing from Washington State Apples, it praised the bill. "Despite all attempts made in the past on industrial advertising campaigns, there have always been quite a number who chose to ride free, by not contributing toward the campaign but sharing in the benefits derived," stated an announcement in Wenoka's newsletter. "This has always been a weakness because it naturally caused accelerated resentment among the paying growers until the campaigns bogged down from non-support."[103] The new bill solved this problem because everyone would contribute. Even though Wenoka was a member of PNF, it told members that the bigger industrial advertising budget that would result from commission fees was a positive development.

A few months later, *Better Fruit* reported that the old Washington State Apples was "merging without delay or friction into those of the new state body."[104] Washington State Apples had fifteen board members, while the commission had only eleven. Four members voluntarily tendered their resignations, and the governor appointed the rest the new commission. Advertising work started by Washington State Apples in 1936 carried on seamlessly as the state commission retained J. Walter Thompson.[105] In its first year, the State Apple Advertising Commission placed advertisements in 32 newspapers in 28 cities, reaching an estimated 40 million people. Radio ads on 538 radio programs in 25 cities had a combined audience of 25 million. The commission sent 72,000 telegrams and bulletins to tradespeople, provided retailers with 304,000 pieces of store display materials, and made 17,000 phone calls to dealers and merchants. Cross-promotions with products such as Kraft cheese, Pillsbury flour, Mazola oil, Borden's, and Bisquick continued.[106]

Washington growers finally had a unified advertising campaign. In another victory, after over fifteen years of lobbying, the state legislature appropriated funds for an agricultural research station in Wenatchee in 1937.[107] Researchers at Washington State College (WSC) in Pullman had always supported growers. Pullman, however, was nearly two hundred miles east of Yakima and Wenatchee, and it had a different climate. Since the early 1920s, growers had lobbied for an agricultural research station in central Washington. Scientists and researchers at WSC, responsive to growers' needs, sent researchers to conduct fieldwork in Wenatchee. Wenatchee also had a USDA Cooperative Research Extension, founded in 1918. USDA researchers routinely cooperated with scientists from WSC. While this was helpful, growers argued that as apples were the number two industry in the state, the state should provide additional resources to address industry problems, particularly research on new pesticides for codling moths, alternatives to lead arsenate, and soil studies. As growers struggled to make ends meet during the Depression, insect infestations and worn soil contributed to losses. Codling moths alone cost an estimated $1 million in losses each year. Years of lead arsenate contamination were taking a toll. In older orchards, legume cover crops to fix nitrogen in the soil did not grow well, because of lead arsenate residues in the soil. Scientists needed to experiment with new fertilizers to address this problem. As Ben A. Perham, regent of WSC, stated, an experiment station was necessary because of "the increasing menace of pests, spray residue removal, soil depletion and innumerable other problems, troubles and difficulties."[108] The Tree Fruit Experiment Station, later renamed the Tree Fruit Research and Extension Center, purchased a fifteen-acre farm near Wenatchee and later acquired additional land. In 1939, the Works Progress Administration built a large machine shed, planted two hundred fruit trees, and helped install a stationary spray system with over five thousand feet of pipe. At the time, it was the only system of its kind in the United States.[109]

It is no coincidence that the state legislature created the Washington State Apple Commission and the Tree Fruit Experiment Station within weeks of each other. The apple industry had been lobbying for statewide marketing and additional research support for years. The stress of the Depression finally convinced the state legislature and reluctant growers that the apple industry could not survive without cooperation and professional expertise. Writing about the Dust Bowl, historian Richard Lowitt says that those "who survived the disaster best were in the habit of conducting their affairs with the aid of what had been learned through scientific study and experiment."[110] The same was true of apple growers in Washington. Many already followed expert advice, but the low apple prices during the Depression left no room for error. Meticulous orchard management and marketing made the difference between financial solvency or financial ruin.

Even with a statewide marketing commission and new research station, growers struggled to remain financially solvent throughout the rest of the 1930s and early 1940s. In 1937, growers in the Wenatchee-Okanogan region averaged $500 per acre in debt. The reasons for the high level of indebtedness were twofold, explained county extension agent E. H. Sargent. First, rapid expansion during the first twenty-five years of the apple industry drove up land prices, sometimes as high as $2,000 to $3,000 per acre. Many growers purchased land at peak prices. Fruit prices did not stay high enough to provide a return on growers' investments. Second, growers were not adequately financed during the Depression. Sargent argued that government programs such as the Farm Credit Administration and the Regional Agricultural Credit Corporation actually hurt growers. Loans were based on a grower's ability to repay. Low fruit prices meant low loans. Throughout much of the Depression, fruit prices hovered below the cost of production, forcing growers to economize in other areas, such as skipping fertilizer or pesticide applications or falling behind on mortgage payments.[111] This hurt orchard health and made it more difficult for growers to recoup costs in good years.

Growers received financing through government programs until the end of the Depression. By 1938, 60 percent of growers were once again obtaining financing through regular, private credit channels. The remaining 40 percent continued to limp along on federal aid.[112] Industry leaders continued to lobby government and railroad officials for funds to bail out the industry. In 1938, for example, James S. Crutchfield telegrammed Great Northern president William P. Kenney, pleading for support. Half of orchards lacked sufficient funds to spray. Without "immediate heroic action taken by railroads power companies and others vitally interested in supplementing good help being received from government," the industry would once again be in crisis.[113] "Our relationship for quarter century has been so intimate and mutually satisfactory reaching back to birth of this great industry that I feel free to urge upon you most liberal consideration this matter. I have confidence [in the] future prosperity this industry and we are backing it up with our capital and credit," Crutchfield continued, playing to the long-standing relationship between the two men.[114]

By this point, the Great Northern regretted that it had ever become involved in grower financing. Kenney blamed growers for not economizing enough.[115] He reserved some especially harsh words for Wenatchee growers in a letter to his vice president, Thomas Balmer. "Either Wenatchee is going to continue to raise apples as a business or it is going to give it up and there is no reason why the Government, the railroads, the power companies and others should be assessed for a continuance of the conditions that have applied the past few years," he wrote. "They did not worry where they got their spray money nor did they care who gave them the money to do the usual spring and fall work. They expected it to come to them and they did not expect to have to pay it back. We have all paid a large part of their bill and nothing has been accomplished to their benefit and it has been a large loss to all the rest of us."[116] Crutchfield and other industry leaders disagreed with Kenney's assessment. Growers had not taken loans in bad faith, nor had they expected years of depressed prices. Crutchfield and others held hope for recovery. Growers had to hang on just one more year. For Kenney, the refrain of "one more year" had soured.

By the late 1930s, railroads and other stakeholders started dissolving the credit corporations created under the RFC in 1932. The liquidation process took several years and was not completed until 1943. In the meantime, growers shifted their attention from the Depression to the war in Europe. "When the first shells exploded in Poland," indicated an article in *Better Fruit*, "prices and markets for fruit men exploded as well."[117] Even though it was too early to know how the war would affect growers, J. Walter Hebert of Big Y speculated that "it will materially affect the lives of all of us in many ways. . . . Those of us who experienced the last great war of 1914 will accept this as a foregone conclusion."[118]

The Depression dealt a blow to Washington's apple industry, but World War II brought hope of recovery. After the struggle to find a market for apples during the Depression, military contracts provided a steady outlet for fruit. During the war, the US military requisitioned approximately 20 percent of Washington's crop; the army purchased twelve million boxes in 1942 alone. Demand was so high that growers could sell anything they picked, including culls, which were processed into jams, jellies, and dehydrated apple products for military use.[119] Apples, unlike more perishable fruits, were one of many foods classified as essential for the war effort.[120] Coca-Cola, for example, was exempt from sugar rationing because of Coke's ability to boost morale and remind soldiers of home. Fresh apples did the same, and they broke up the monotony of canned and dehydrated rations. As Colonel McKenzie of the Quartermaster Corps reminded members of the International Apple Association, "To the fighting lads, battling on the beaches of France or the jungle islands of the Pacific, I can imagine no more pleasant reminder of homes from whence they came than a good, crisp American apple."[121] Former Big Y employee Alva L. Gwin became homesick at the sight of boxes of Big Y apples delivered to his ship in Guam. He reported that the apples "were in as good shape as when shipped."[122]

Because fruit was shipped long distances, the military preferred varieties that stayed crisp, such as the Winesap. Delicious apples, which by the 1940s were over 50 percent of Washington's crop, tended to go soft and mealy if picked too ripe or stored improperly. Mealy apples would not help morale. Typically, growers marketed Delicious varieties first because Winesaps held well in cold storage. Because of military demand and a shortage of refrigerated railcars, Winesaps took priority, while Delicious languished in storage until they could be transported to civilian markets.[123] Civilians had to make do, while the government shipped the best of the crop to soldiers overseas.

Military purchases were not a panacea for all the industry's problems. Growers still faced high transportation costs, fluctuating prices, lack of storage space, competition from other apple regions, and competition from other fruit. The war created additional complications: labor shortages, railcar shortages, and lumber shortages for apple boxes. Labor shortages were the most immediate problem. Prior to the Depression, growers and their families took care of orchard needs for most of the year, supplemented by a few year-round hands and transient labor at harvest. Cooperatives such a Big Y required hundreds of workers in their warehouses and gave preference to returning workers and their family members. In 1932, for example, Big Y boasted that 100 percent of its workforce was local.[124] During the war, many people left the region. Young men enlisted or were drafted. Young women, who typically worked in packinghouses, found more lucrative jobs in war industries in Portland or Seattle.

By the fall of 1942, central Washington needed an estimated thirty-five thousand workers for the harvest season. The apple industry called for volunteers. That spring the USDA War Board and the US Employment Service started registering potential farmworkers, including students and women. The Washington State Apple Commission advertised in seventeen newspapers across the state. Local committees from Yakima and Wenatchee appealed to school boards in Seattle and Spokane for student volunteers. The US Employment Service sent 460 workers from Chicago, and thousands of novice pickers arrived from around the state. A group of four hundred high school students from Seattle spent a four-day weekend picking fruit, while the University of Washington and Washington State College sent students to pick the crop. In Wenatchee and surrounding towns, all businesses except hotels and restaurants closed every other day so that all able-bodied workers could pick. In Yakima, grade school, high school, and college students joined the volunteer force, along with civic clubs, women's clubs, and churches. Reuben Benz of Yakima's Emergency Harvest Committee estimated that students alone picked two thousand of the twenty-five thousand carloads harvested in state.[125] A. F. Hardy, state director of the US Employment Service, stated that the harvest was "almost miraculous," as there was "virtually no migratory labor to depend on." Novice volunteers were able to harvest 95 percent of the crop.[126]

Labor shortages continued throughout the war. Washington growers had to compete with war industries and other agricultural commodities in the region. By the end of 1942, war industries in the Northwest employed over 235,000 workers. The US Labor Department estimated that war industries needed another 100,000 workers by the end of 1943, while the region needed an additional 69,000 agricultural workers for the 1943 harvest.[127] Federal agencies provided the apple industry some assistance. The US Employment Service called for volunteer pickers in 1943 and 1944. Expert packers and sorters were in such high demand that the service urged employers to "consider mutual arrangements to free them for this emergency duty."[128] The Bracero Program, started in 1942, brought guest workers from Mexico to the United States, but apple growers had to compete with other agricultural industries, such as potatoes and sugar beets, for a limited number of laborers. In 1943, the government promised Wenatchee growers six thousand Bracero workers for harvest, but because of labor shortages in Mexico, the Mexican government only sent three thousand. In the first year of the Bracero Program, workers signed six-month contracts that ran from April through September, meaning workers left at the start of the apple harvest. The government sent some Japanese internees to aid in the harvest, and volunteers filled the remaining gap. Braceros aided with the harvest in 1944 and 1945, and the federal government sent German prisoners of war to Yakima in 1944, but growers could not rely on the federal government to provide labor. Though the Bracero Program was vital for Northwest agriculture, during the war, Braceros harvested only 2 percent of Washington's apple crop.[129]

Anticipating the labor shortage in 1943, the Yakima Valley Food-for-Victory Farm Labor Committee enlisted volunteers for the harvest. The committee met with students at thirty-one Yakima Valley high schools. They asked local business owners to participate and organized childcare to encourage women to join the workforce. Everyone was asked to do his or her part. On a tour through the valley, Reuben Benz, chair of the committee, found workers from age fourteen to a seventy-three-year-old grandmother whose grandson was in the army. The committee enlisted pledges from fifteen thousand volunteers, short of their goal of twenty thousand but still an impressive number.[130]

While local communities volunteered enthusiastically, growers worried that novice pickers, especially women and children, would not be physically able to bring in the harvest. Working with the state extension service, Wenatchee grower Leo Antles began a series of time-motion studies on the mechanics of apple picking. He found that middle school girls could easily move the large orchard ladders used for picking, provided they used proper technique. To prove the point, *Better Fruit* ran a photo of fourteen-year-old Jean Olson of Wenatchee. A smile on her face and a picking bag slung over her shoulder, the 5'2", 110-pound teenager easily lifted the 37-pound picking ladder.[131] Volunteers did not pick as fast as more experienced workers, but they were more than physically capable of performing orchard work.

Labor was not the only shortage during the war. Many products needed for growing and harvesting apples were in short supply: ladders, packing papers, fertilizers, pesticides, and nails for box making. In 1943, the imported pesticides rotenone and pyrethrum were unavailable. Most other sprays were available that year, but the steel barrels used to transport pesticides were in short supply. Big Y asked growers to return their barrels for refilling as quickly as possible. Paper wrappings, which provided cushioning for apples packed in boxes, were not always available, and when they were, government shipments received priority. Timber for boxes was in short supply too. Before the war, apple box production consumed 90 percent of the lumber logged in north-central Washington, but the wartime construction boom diverted supplies. The industry saved 27 million board feet of lumber by cutting thinner box shooks, the individual pieces used to build boxes. Even with modifications, Washington's apple industry used between 80 million and 90 million board feet of lumber to produce apple boxes in 1943 alone, enough lumber to build 11,500 five-room homes.[132]

As costs for materials, labor, and transportation increased, wartime regulations added another layer of administrative bureaucracy to the state laws and cooperative rules that regulated the industry. The Office of Price Administration (OPA) placed a price ceiling on apples in October 1943 to check inflation. Growers could add a fourteen-cent markup per box to the OPA base price to offset expenses such as cold storage. Initially, the OPA agreed to a variable price ceiling that changed throughout the season to reflect the types of apples being shipped. Price increases soon became mired in red tape, frustrating industry leaders. J. Walter Hebert, sales manager of Big Y, called the OPA a "befuddled administration" that was incapable of correcting its own mistakes. "Either that, or like the old Missouri Army mule, they 'just don't give a damn,'" he complained.[133] Conflict between Washington growers and the OPA escalated after the San Francisco OPA office charged seventeen apple shippers, including Big Y, with violating the price ceiling order by shipping underweight boxes. Hebert vigorously defended Big Y's practices, calling the accusations a "smear type of publicity," as the OPA issued press releases about the issue before it served Big Y an injunction. Hebert maintained that all Big Y's boxes were weighed and labeled with a net weight. He blamed the problem on how OPA offices interpreted their directives, not on Big Y practices.[134]

Big Y confidently defended the quality of its apple shipments and questioned the need for the OPA, but other shippers deserved the OPA's criticism. Once the price ceiling was in effect, some tried to cut costs by shipping apples in bulk to increase profits. Bulk shipping eliminated the cost of boxes and labor for packing. Bill Brown, a Texas-based dealer-representative for the Washington State Apple Commission, reported that bulk carloads of apples arrived damaged and underweight. After hearing complaints from retailers, Brown visited the local rail yard to investigate. There he found men shoveling fruit out of boxcars into bushel baskets. They stacked the baskets so high that juice ran out the bottom. A car that was supposed to contain 33,000 pounds of apples was over 1,500 pounds short. In addition, over 2,000 pounds of fruit was "rotten beyond salvage."[135]

California retailers complained of similar problems. F. E. Boekenoogen, general sales manager of Consolidated Produce Co., wrote to the Apple Commission that most of the bulk-loaded fruit was bruised or punctured and had to be thrown away. "We think that if the shippers who loaded this fruit could have seen the condition of some of it on fruit stands in Los Angeles, they would have been very much ashamed of themselves for having loaded some of their finest apples in bulk," he chided. Consumers and retailers were so disgusted with the quality of shipments that many were "through with Washington apples." Growers who elected to ship bulk apples undid years of marketing campaigns designed to gain consumer trust and loyalty. "The Washington Apple growers, over a period of years, have built up a reputation for well packed, fine quality apples. They are certainly not doing this any good with the housewife when she sees a Washington Apple sign on a bin of bruised Jonathans, Delicious or Winesaps," Boekenoogen continued. C. E. Chase of the Apple Commission shared concerns that the apple industry was damaging its reputation, which might have long-term consequences after the war.[136]

To compensate, the Washington State Apple Commission continued to advertise throughout the war to encourage consumption and educate consumers about the health benefits of apples. Even though high-quality apples were not available, the industry wanted to keep Washington apples at the forefront of consumers' minds. The commission was not alone in its thinking. Many companies, such as Ford, Frigidaire, Campbell's, and the National Dairy Council continued to advertise their products throughout the war, even when products were not available or were in short supply.[137]

Changes in the grocery store industry compounded Washington's challenge in advertising apples during the war. Many grocery stores discontinued delivery services because of gas and tire rationing. Fewer canned goods were available because of tin rationing. Frozen foods were not rationed, so stores installed freezer units to handle new stock. As men were drafted and civilians took higher-paying war production jobs, grocery stores did not have as many employees at their disposal and began to move to a self-service model. Shoppers selected and packaged their own purchases rather than having a store clerk do it for them. "The men this method saves are free to help build planes and ships—and to work on farms," explained one Safeway advertisement, but for the apple industry it had a downside.[138] Inexperienced retailers did not know how to properly handle apples. Rough handling and lack of refrigeration at the point of retail further degraded apple quality. Grocery stores piled apples in bins instead of displaying them in boxes. Apples suffered damage as shoppers dug through bins looking for the best fruit.[139] Growers could do little about the labor and supply shortages that hurt fruit quality. All they could do was look forward to the end of the war and hope to regain consumer trust after years of supplying the market with less than perfect fruit.

CHAPTER 7

Hyperindustrialization and the Future of Apples

In a 1946 National Apple Week editorial contest, sponsored by the Yakima Valley Traffic and Credit Association, D. L. Mansell of the *Canton (Ohio) Repository* summed up the major problem facing the apple industry. During the war, consumers were subjected to low-quality foods cooked in institutional settings by "blacksmiths masquerading as pastry cooks" and cooks who were "able to get away with murder." Mansell described a recently purchased piece of pie as "criminal handiwork." The small portion was "a typical example, a pallid wedge of anemic dough thinly upholstered with a sickly yellow paste of what purported to be apple, but might have been almost anything." Although it tasted like "watered-down applesauce encased in cardboard," Mansell still maintained faith that apple pie might someday be returned to its rightful place in American life.[1] Of course, that required not only better cooks but better apples as well. After World War II, the apple industry had to repair its damaged reputation, while dealing with changes to distribution systems and consumer tastes.

In the second half of the twentieth century, the US economy shifted from industrial to postindustrial. Coined in the early 1970s, the term "postindustrial" describes the shift from manufacturing jobs to a service economy, a trend that accelerated in the late twentieth century thanks to automation. Yet "postindustrial" does not adequately explain postwar changes to agriculture. The prefix "post-" implies that the economy moved beyond industrialization. Instead, agriculture, and other manufacturing, became hyperindustrialized. In orchards, as in other areas of American agriculture and manufacturing, industrialization accelerated after World War II. Technology streamlined the work of "manufacturing" apples. Computers replaced armies of sales agents. Improved machinery eliminated jobs in packinghouses. Farms became larger, and distributors consolidated. The characteristics of industrialization—an efficiency mandate, an emphasis on standardization, specialized technology, and large-scale production—were pushed to the fullest possible extent.

Hyperindustrialization changed the way Americans ate, as new processed foods offered low-cost convenience. Washington apples had to compete with this new food landscape. Meals did not appear at the push of a button, as on the 1960s cartoon *The Jetsons*, but in self-serve supermarkets, shoppers could choose from a variety of frozen, canned, and powdered foods designed for maximum ease. Technology allowed consumers to purchase previously seasonal foods year-round. Some preservation technology pre-dated World War II. Clarence Birdseye, for example, pioneered flash freezing in the 1920s, but frozen foods did not catch on until affordable home freezers became available in the 1950s. Other technologies, such as new juicing processes developed in the 1940s, improved the flavor of canned goods. New refrigerated technology extended the life of fresh produce and allowed more foods to be transported out of season. "Many producers may not be aware of the competition that will come as a result of importation of tropical fruits which, because of inadequate refrigeration facilities, have heretofore appeared infrequently in our markets," wrote C. E. Chase, secretary-manager of the Washington State Apple Commission.[2] The apple industry was used to competing with oranges and bananas, but not with such a wide range of fresh, canned, and frozen produce. Growers could not afford to fall back on old production methods. Overall apple consumption dropped roughly 30 percent, from sixty pounds a year per capita in 1930 to forty-one pounds a year in 1947.[3] Growers had to rebuild the public trust so carefully cultivated in the 1920s and 1930s, and they had to fight for space on consumer tables.

Though growers looked for new methods to maximize efficiency and profits in a changing world, they faced the same fundamental challenges as previous generations, namely managing the environment and marketing fruit. On the surface, the postwar apple industry experienced many changes. The Columbia Basin Project opened new lands for irrigation, average farm sizes increased, packing machinery reduced labor needs, and immigrant labor replaced the native-born transient workers who harvested the crop before the war. The apple industry's long-standing relationship with the railroads dissolved as trucking provided a competitive transportation option. Cooperatives and distribution networks consolidated, limiting growers' autonomy within the system. Chain grocery stores altered distribution networks and consumer habits. Yet many of these challenges would have been recognizable to growers in the 1920s. Growers had always struggled with orchard management, marketing, and transportation. Even as times changed, most farms remained family owned, and growers continued to rely on experts to develop everything from new pesticides to new packing materials.

The apple industry started with irrigated lands, and its expansion since World War II has also been shaped by irrigation. For years, regional boosters such as Rufus Woods, editor of the *Wenatchee Daily World*, pushed for the development of the Columbia Basin. Critical of Wenatchee's reliance on apples, Woods envisioned Wenatchee as the economic center of new diverse industrial and agricultural activities in the Columbia Basin. Congress finally authorized the Columbia Basin Project in 1933. The project's centerpiece, Grand Coulee Dam, was completed in 1941. Contrary to Woods's expectations, power generated by Grand Coulee Dam did not fuel industrial growth near Wenatchee. Instead, the dam sent power to Spokane and the Hanford Engineer Works, which processed plutonium. In 1945, the Bureau of Reclamation began construction on the Columbia Basin Project to irrigate the region. The project delivered the first water from Grand Coulee Dam in 1952, opening thousands of acres east of the Columbia River for farming.[4]

To celebrate, local business owners planned a "Farm-in-a-Day" stunt to highlight the opportunities of the region. In one day, volunteers constructed a house and outbuildings and planted an eighty-acre farm with alfalfa, corn, clover, oats, beans, and potatoes. They gave the farm to World War II veteran Donald D. Dunn. Unfortunately, boosters' vision of settling the Columbia Basin with small farms was not to be. Crop prices dropped after World War II as wartime price controls ended and European farmers began to produce again. American agriculture had changed during the 1930s and 1940s, writes historian Paul C. Pitzer, as "accelerated mechanization, greater use of fertilizer, improved conservation practices, better plant varieties, and superior insecticides . . . suddenly revolutionized farms." Fruit growers were already familiar with these practices and their associated costs. For other farmers, the costs, combined with low commodity prices, were insurmountable. Farmers could not profit from eighty-acre plots, and as Pitzer notes, a quarter of settlers left the Columbia Basin Project within the first three years, including Dunn.[5] While the economic costs of irrigated land in the Columbia Basin made it unsuitable for small farms, larger agricultural operations flourished. Today the Columbia Basin Project waters 671,000 acres for agricultural production, with apples accounting for 9.6 percent of irrigated acreage. The Columbia Basin Project has shifted apple production within the state. In 2017, the Yakima Valley led the state in apple acreage, but the Columbia Basin led the state in apple trees, with 42 percent of the state's 126 million bearing trees.[6]

The new orchards in the Columbia Basin did not start producing until the late 1950s. From 1930 to 1950, the number of bearing trees declined 66 percent, from 7.96 million trees in 1930 to 2.69 million trees in 1950. Yet 1950 yields were 8 percent higher than in 1930.[7] The Depression forced growers to abandon marginal lands and unproductive trees. Growers used the latest scientific research to maximize the efficiency of remaining trees. Today, the Tree Fruit Research and Extension Center (TFREC) leads the search for new varieties and improved orchard management techniques. Founded in 1937 and operated by Washington State University, TFREC, in collaboration with the USDA, has conducted scientific research into topics including pome fruit diseases, pest management, and plant breeding. Today it operates over four hundred acres of research orchards and facilities.[8]

As new orchards came into production in the 1950s, growers adopted the latest technology, including the use of dwarf rootstocks, which produced smaller trees, allowing growers to plant dense orchards with greater production per acre. The adoption of semidwarf and dwarf rootstocks revolutionized orchard management. Dwarf rootstocks have many advantages. Rootstocks are clones, so growers can choose them based on desired traits such as disease resistance or cold tolerance. Dwarf trees are smaller and shorter, so fruit is easier to pick. Standard apple trees reach heights of thirty feet and are up to forty feet wide. By contrast, dwarf trees reach a height of six to twelve feet.[9] Because dwarf rootstocks tend to be weaker than full-size rootstocks, trees are grown on trellises, as in vineyards. As orchard plantings become denser, researchers are exploring new solutions for trellises that can withstand the weight of additional trees and fruit.[10] Trellises also provide a framework for netting used to protect trees from sun or insect damage, and they make trees easier to harvest.

The greatest advantage of dwarf rootstocks comes from high-density planting. In the 1920s, experts advised growers to plant 30–40 trees per acre. In 2017, Washington orchards in Wenatchee averaged 571 trees per acre, and in Yakima 690 trees per acre. Orchards in the Columbia Basin average 825 trees per acre. Some orchards have over 1,000 trees per acre.[11] Denser plantings lead to higher yields. Between 1921 and 1929, growers averaged 13,000 pounds per acre. In 2018, yields averaged 35,000 pounds per acre.[12]

Insects, fungi, and bacterial diseases will always be a problem for industrial agriculture in its drive for standardization and increased yields. Over time, organisms can develop resistance to chemical sprays, and finding a balance between standardization and safety remains a challenge. Lead arsenate created public scandal for the industry in the mid-1920s and continues to plague older orchards across the country. Even though growers stopped using lead arsenate in 1948 with the advent of DDT, residues remain in the soil. In Washington, an estimated 115,000 acres of historic orchard land are potentially contaminated with lead arsenate. Problems arise as old orchards are converted into subdivisions, schools, and business lots. The Washington State Department of Ecology's Toxic Cleanup Program has developed remediation protocols that include removing soil, capping soil, or mixing existing soil with new soil. The program has prioritized remediation for sites where children may be exposed, such as schools and parks.[13]

The advent of dichlorodiphenyltrichloroethane, or DDT, first synthesized in 1874, provided an alternative to lead arsenate. Paul Hermann Müller discovered DDT's insecticidal properties in 1939, and in the 1940s, the US Army used it to control mosquitoes. TFREC scientists W. J. O'Neill and L. J. Lipovsky experimented with DDT from 1943 to 1946. Initial trials against codling moth showed that "DDT promises better control with three or four applications than generally results from lead arsenate or cryolite in seven to nine sprays."[14] DDT seemed like a miracle—an effective pesticide that appeared to have no significant health impact for humans and that saved money because it required fewer applications. DDT had another unexpected benefit: it did not leave a visible residue, unlike lead arsenate, which coated leaves and fruit with a gray film.

DDT seemed almost too good to be true. While Rachel Carson's 1962 book *Silent Spring* is credited with drawing attention to the ecological damage caused by DDT, historian Elena Conis argues that consumers had concerns from the start. DDT "posed an unparalleled paradox," she writes. Older insecticides like lead arsenate or copper sulfate were very toxic to humans. It seemed incongruous that a substance that killed insects on contact had no effect on humans.[15] Washington growers quickly found other contradictions. DDT upset the biological equilibrium that had been established with lead arsenate. It eliminated codling moths, but it led to mysterious outbreaks of mites.[16] Perhaps lead arsenate had kept mites in check, or perhaps DDT killed predatory insects that fed on mites. Either way, it created a new insect problem. Growers used DDT until 1972, when the EPA banned its use following public outcry regarding its effects on the environment and human health. According to apple historian Al Bright, the Washington Horticultural Association initially resisted the ban on DDT but later admitted that codling moths were developing resistance to the pesticide, reducing its effectiveness.[17]

Growers continue to use a cocktail of chemicals to prevent damage to trees and fruit. In 2019, the Environmental Working Group listed apples on its "Dirty Dozen" list of fresh produce with the highest chemical use. Apples ranked fifth after strawberries, spinach, kale, and nectarines. Residues fall well within established EPA limits, and the Environmental Working Group encourages consumers to eat fruits and vegetables, even those on the "Dirty Dozen" list. Even so, many consumers are concerned about pesticide residues, and apples have come under scrutiny many times. Perhaps the largest public relations issue arose in the 1980s when activists, aided by celebrities such as Meryl Streep, contended that daminozide, known by its trade name "Alar," led to increased cancer risks for children.

Approved for orchard use in 1968, daminozide is a growth regulator. It slows fruit growth and prevents apples from dropping from trees before they are ripe, a common problem with Red Delicious strains. For some red strains, it improved color and helped apples retain firmness and crispness. Alar offered potential economic benefits. In 1984, one Washington study estimated that Alar would increase profits up to $224.4 million thanks to reduced crop losses and extended storage times.[18] By the 1970s, studies by the University of Nebraska Medical Center and the National Cancer Institute questioned the safety of daminozide. When heated, daminozide breaks down into its component parts, including UDMH (unsymmetrical 1,1-dimethylhydrazine), a substance that the US Department of Health and Human Services National Toxicology Program currently lists as "reasonably anticipated to be a human carcinogen."[19] In 1985, the EPA began a review to determine whether Alar should stay on the market. The agency estimated that if Alar were banned, the apple industry would lose $30 million and up to 35 percent of the crop. The Washington State Horticultural Association argued, in comments filed with the EPA, that "as an industry, we must have the use of Alar to survive." Alar producer Uniroyal claimed that the product was safe. It asked the EPA to withhold action until the company could complete its own animal studies, scheduled to finish by 1988.[20] Citing a lack of scientific evidence, the EPA postponed the review.

Although still permitted, daminozide use declined because of pressure from environmental and consumer advocacy groups, such as the Natural Resources Defense Council (NRDC) and Ralph Nader's organization Public Citizen. In March 1986, Tree Top, a grower-owned cooperative that at the time was the world's largest processor of apple juice, announced that it would not purchase apples treated with growth regulators. Several other major retailers and processors including Heinz, Gerber, Welch, Seneca, and Mott's also stopped purchasing apples sprayed with daminozide. That July, the Washington State Apple Commission asked growers to stop using Alar until further notice. In the mid-1980s, 20 to 30 percent of Washington's crop ended up at processing plants like Tree Top. Growers also recognized the potential economic and public relations consequences of continued Alar use. Many growers, though not all, complied with the commission's recommendation.[21]

Unfortunately for Washington growers, that was not the end of the story. In 1989, the NRDC published a report on the effects of pesticides in preschool-age children, reigniting the debate over Alar. The report argued that relative to weight, preschoolers had a greater exposure to pesticides than adults, in part because preschoolers consumed more grape juice, apple juice, and applesauce than adults. Although the report emphasized the cumulative effect of twenty-three different pesticides "known to have adverse health effects" in a person's diet, media coverage focused on Alar.[22]

In February, the CBS show *60 Minutes* aired a segment titled "'A' Is for Apple," which opened with a picture of a skull and crossbones carved into a red apple. Although it mentioned other pesticides, the report focused on apples and Alar. Journalist Ed Bradley interviewed representatives from the EPA, NRDC, Harvard Medical School, and Consumers Union, which does research for *Consumer Reports*. Interviewees did not all agree with the NRDC's report, but they did agree about the potential danger of accumulated pesticides in children's bodies. Though major processors had stopped purchasing apples sprayed with daminozide, test results from a 1988 Consumers Union study found traces of daminozide in two-thirds of thirty-two apple products tested. Janet Hathaway of the NRDC charged that the EPA was not doing enough to remove what she called "the most potent cancer causing chemical in our food supply." Dr. Jack Moore of the EPA seemed defensive as he answered Bradley's questions about EPA processes for removing chemicals from the market.[23] The report left viewers with the impression that the EPA did not care about consumer safety, even though the EPA was in the process of banning daminozide before the show aired.[24]

Apple growers quickly felt the effects of the *60 Minutes* report. Taiwan stopped importing American apples. By May, total sales and prices were down by 20 percent. In response, the Washington State Fruit Commission pulled over $70,000 of advertising from CBS and its affiliates. The USDA, EPA, and FDA issued statements assuring the public that apples were safe. Most Washington growers had stopped using the product after the EPA started its review in 1985. Derl Derr, president of the

International Apple Association, said growers were directed not to use daminozide on the 1989 crop. Growers typically sprayed daminozide in June or July. The media controversy erupted well before crops were sprayed, deterring any remaining users. The EPA estimated that only 5–15 percent of the 1988 crop was sprayed with daminozide, contrary to the NRDC's estimates of 38 percent. The Processed Apple Institute, representing producers of processed apple products, challenged the Consumers Union study featured on *60 Minutes*. With a much larger sample size of 4,623 samples, the institute found only 8 that contained daminozide. In June, Uniroyal, the manufacturer of Alar, voluntarily suspended domestic sales and offered refunds to growers who had purchased Alar for the 1989 season.[25]

The Department of Agriculture spent $1.5 million to purchase apples and reduce the surplus created by the Alar scare, but the damage was done. Prices fell to a low of seven dollars for a forty-two-pound box, below the break-even price of twelve dollars per box. The USDA estimated that Washington growers lost $125 million in the six months after the scare. In the aftermath, many argued that the dangers of daminozide were overblown. Findings by Britain's Advisory Committee on Pesticides and the California Department of Food and Agriculture found minimal cancer risks from apples sprayed with daminozide. Uniroyal's studies showed that daminozide caused fifty cases of cancer in a population of one million, 80 percent fewer than indicated by the NRDC study, but a high enough rate for the EPA to ban it. Growers filed suit against the NRDC and CBS for the damage done to the industry. The case was ultimately dismissed. "We didn't set out to hurt apple farmers," said NRDC deputy director Frances Beinecke in a statement to the *New York Times*. "The original report was about pesticides in more than 20 kinds of food. What happened was, the media simplified it and focused on apples. We are concerned and not happy about the consequences to those growers who were hurt." Growers saw the situation differently. They had already acted to stop Alar use, three years before the damning *60 Minutes* report. As Timothy Egan reported, they "consider themselves environmentalists and resent the Johnny-come-latelies in Washington, who, in their eyes, are hurting them by discovering the dangers of chemicals long after they had already acted."[26]

Washington's apple industry recovered from the Alar scare. Even so, the scare highlights the challenges of hyperindustrialized agricultural production. Apple growers, like other farmers, must balance pesticides' effect on the environment, the health of trees, crop yields, quality of the final product, profitability, and consumer expectations. It is tempting to argue that growers stopped using dangerous chemicals only when pressured by consumers or government agencies to change their practices. The reality of agricultural chemicals is more complicated. Growers care deeply about their orchards, but they also want to produce a marketable product, which requires environmental intervention. Agriculture by its very nature changes the environment, although some agricultural practices are more invasive and damaging than others. In the case of Alar, the costs outweighed the benefits. Most Washington growers responded quickly and discontinued its use in 1986. In the end, it did not matter because growers in other regions used Alar. Washington growers learned early on that their individual actions had the potential to affect the entire state's reputation. In today's global economy, actions of apple growers in other parts of the country, or even the world, can affect the industry's reputation.

One positive outcome of the Alar scare was that it pushed more growers toward organic production. Organic production has increased in the twenty-first century in response to consumer demand. "People want to eat organics. And why is that? Is that the education of people? Is it a popularity thing?" said Mark Hambelton, organic coordinator for McDougall & Sons in Wenatchee. "I mean, I think those are the things we don't really know the answer to. But as a business growth plan we're obviously going to do what the consumer wants."[27] While it may seem counterintuitive to use "organic" and "industrial" in the same sentence, today's organic apple production is characterized by specialized processes and expertise, an emphasis on economic profitability, and the goal of large-scale production, all components of industrial agriculture. In 2017, Washington produced 90 percent of all organic apples grown in the United States, a total of 13.3 million boxes, which accounted for 8.4 percent of all fresh apples consumed in the United States. From 2010 to 2018, the number of certified organic acres in Washington nearly doubled, from 14,790 to 28,473, and experts estimate that organic acreage and sales will continue to increase in the coming years.[28]

While some growers have switched to organic production, others have reduced chemical usage in other ways. In the late 1960s and early 1970s, integrated pest management (IPM) arose in response to farmers' need for more efficient, cost-effective, and environmentally friendly pest management. IPM explores biological options that can reduce the need for sprays. Over the last fifty years it has been applied to agricultural, municipal, and urban pest control.[29] Apple growers continue to use a cocktail of sprays, but IPM has provided alternatives. In the 1960s, entomologists began researching the role of predatory insects in orchards. Stan Hoyt, an entomologist at TFREC, focused on spider mites, whose populations exploded after the advent of DDT. Hoyt realized that DDT killed a predatory mite, *Typhlodromus*, also known as "typh." By the 1970s, Washington growers had begun using healthy typh colonies to control spider mites. In the 1990s and early 2000s, only 24 percent of Washington apples were treated annually with miticides, compared to 76 percent of Michigan apples and 70 percent of New York apples. Growers have also found success using pheromone traps and sprays to disrupt codling moths' life cycles. Today, 85 to 90 percent of Washington growers use pheromone traps or sprays. Biological controls are also used for some species of leafhoppers and leaf miners. New research has shown promising results with pheromone-based mating disruption in San Jose scale.[30] A survey of Washington growers' pesticide use from 2007 to 2009 found that every dollar spent on high-risk pesticides resulted in an additional cost of fifty-two cents to address secondary infestations that resulted from killing natural predators. The survey also found that growers who combined IPM with low-risk pesticides spent an average of 55 percent less on pest control.[31] In a hyperindustrialized system that values efficiency, switching to IPM methods makes good economic sense and has the added benefit of being better for the environment and consumers.

Growers face an ongoing battle fighting pests and diseases in the monoculture orchard environment, just as their predecessors did over a hundred years ago. Over time, insects develop pesticide resistance. In recent years, growers have seen a resurgence in codling moth infestations, despite the use of biological controls. Global warming is also changing habitats and may bring new pests and diseases. IPM offers some solutions, but for the time being, sprays are still an integral part of commercial apple production for most apples grown in the state. Today pesticides are highly regulated. In 1996, Congress passed the Food Quality Protection Act, which mandated the review and reregistration of all pesticides. Federal and state regulations limit the amount and timing of sprays. Washington State University developed a "Decision Aid System" to provide orchard management recommendations. Computer-based models use weather data and information on ten insects and four tree fruit diseases to help growers fine-tune their spraying regimens.[32]

Organophosphates are the most recent group of pesticides to come under public scrutiny. In 2019, seven states sued the EPA to ban chlorpyrifos, a broad-spectrum organophosphate associated with neurological problems. California and New York have already banned the chemical. Washington growers rarely use chlorpyrifos, but some worry that bans might limit their ability to fight future infestations. Alternatives may not work as effectively, or they may be more dangerous than the chemical that was banned. "Most public debate just focuses on ban or keep," said David Epstein, an entomologist and vice president for scientific affairs for the Northwest Horticultural Council. "It doesn't have to be one polar end or the other." Epstein worried that the courts and activists did not fully understand or trust the EPA's scientific review process.[33] In 2020, the Washington state senate passed a bill banning chlorpyrifos. The bill was rewritten in the house to allow the state's Department of Agriculture to finish its safety review and provide funding to research alternatives. Governor Jay Inslee vetoed the bill, citing budget concerns related to COVID-19.[34] Chlorpyrifos is under EPA review, scheduled to finish in 2022. The outcome remains to be seen.

Organophosphates are not the first agricultural chemicals whose safety has been questioned, nor will they be the last. Researchers continue to look for new solutions to orchard management problems, including nonchemical interventions, such as disease-resistant rootstocks and fruit varieties. Some researchers are also reexamining heirloom apples for their genetic diversity.[35] Their rediscovery is a possible antidote to the monocultures created by industrial agriculture. David Benscoter, a retired FBI investigator who lives in eastern Washington, became interested in forgotten apple varieties after helping a neighbor pick fruit from a tree in her backyard. No one could identify the variety, so Benscoter started searching. From coast to coast over the course of the nation's history, an estimated seventeen thousand varieties have been grown, and thirteen thousand have been lost.[36] Many varieties remained unknown beyond the individual farmer's homestead, while others became features of the American food landscape. Benscoter is one of many horticulturists searching for heirloom varieties. Some heirloom seekers are motivated by the hunt. Others search with a more serious purpose—heirlooms that have survived a century or more of neglect might hold the key to feeding humanity in the future through drought resistance, disease tolerance, or some other beneficial feature in an age of global warming and agricultural uncertainty.

Finding labor has always been a challenge for Washington growers. That is likely to continue in the near term. Apple picking is not automated, and the harvest requires between thirty-five thousand and forty thousand temporary workers each year. Until the 1980s, most of Washington's transient labor force was single men under forty, though some families continued to follow the fruit. Apple picking attracted many transient workers because it paid well relative to other crops. "I could pick twelve bins and make fifty dollars—hell, that was a lot of money back then," remembered Bill Wilson of his picking days in the 1950s.[37] The pay may have been higher than for other crops, but apple picking had its downsides. As in the 1920s and 1930s, most workers were expected to supply their own housing. Many ended up in primitive camps. In 1968, the Yakima Valley Growers-Shippers Association approached the state Department of Agriculture with a proposal to provide housing to migrant workers. The same year, the Washington State Board of Health also proposed regulations that required labor camps to have potable running water, plumbing, appliances, heating, electricity, and regular garbage collection. While the Yakima Valley Growers-Shippers Association supported improvements to housing, some growers protested. In a letter to the secretary of labor, J. M. Bloxom of the Washington Fruit & Produce Co. objected to regulations because they applied to all farmworker housing, regardless of whether the dwellings were used year-round or for only a few weeks. For example, the regulations required that dwellings provide separate rooms for parents and children. As Bloxom argued, "Motels are permitted to allow parents and children to sleep in the same room. It seems peculiarly out of place in regulations to protect the health and safety of farm workers." Other growers echoed these sentiments, but the deeper issue was cost. Many growers already had slim profit margins, and upgrades to housing for seasonal workers were costly.[38]

By the 1970s, economic conditions were pushing many smaller orchards out of business. This contributed to changes in hiring patterns. Orchards involve many fixed costs, including property taxes, sprays, and irrigation fees. In the United States today, labor represents about 17 percent of variable costs for all agriculture, but 48 percent for apple growers.[39] Labor is the one area where a grower might find cost savings. As orchards consolidated, larger operations began to hire contractors to supply crews of labor, typically immigrants from Mexico who worked for lower wages than American-born pickers. In recent years, up to 40 percent of harvest workers have come to the United States on H-2A visas as temporary agricultural workers. Over the years, activists have fought to improve conditions for agricultural workers. In the 1960s, Chicano students inspired by the work of Cesar Chavez organized labor in the Yakima Valley. The United Farm Workers (UFW) of Washington State received official recognition in the 1980s.[40]

Since then, the UFW has protested poor housing conditions, low pay, and discrimination. In the late 1990s and early 2000s, workers fought for safer working conditions and filed complaints about harmful pesticides. They participated in the World Trade Organization protests in 1999, and they worked with other labor groups to fight for fair trade practices. More recently, US immigration policy has fueled protests. As workers have protested poor conditions, growers have lobbied Congress for immigration reforms so that seasonal immigrant laborers can come to Washington safely and legally. Even with immigration reforms, agricultural labor shortages are predicted to increase. "For every 100 farmworkers today, agriculture will need 138 in 2036," writes Susan Futrell. "Yet the labor supply is projected to be short by 25 farmworkers for every 100 over that time."[41] In the last few years, tight labor markets have led to increased wages, but worries about working conditions continue, most recently with the outbreak of COVID-19.[42] Even with higher wages, labor markets are only going to get tighter.

Throughout the history of the apple industry, growers have turned to technology to improve efficiency and reduce costs. In the 1910s, technology like mechanical sprayers and new packing tables helped growers reduce labor requirements. While technology has brought cost savings to other parts of the industry, it has not reduced labor costs at harvest. As early as the 1960s, growers were experimenting with mechanizing harvests. Most machines shook trees. This worked for fruit to be canned or juiced, but it left too much bruising on fresh apples. One pneumatic harvester used air nozzles to blast fruit off trees. In tests, apples remained attached to the tree unless treated with Ethro, a chemical that makes the tree produce ethylene, which speeds ripening and makes the apple loosen from the tree.[43] None of these early machines came into use, but new robotic harvesters may provide a solution to labor costs and worker safety in the field. California-based Abundant Robotics and Israeli-based FFRobotics field-tested robotic pickers in 2019 and 2020.[44] Whether robotic apple pickers replace human pickers remains to be seen. The technology is still being tested, and it will likely be cost prohibitive for many growers at first.

As in the early twentieth century, marketing is still a major challenge for the apple industry. Hyperindustrialization has led to consolidation as cooperatives succumbed to mergers because of changes in distribution networks. In 1945, Washington had forty-one active apple cooperatives. Today, there are roughly half a dozen.[45] The Yakima Horticultural Union (the oldest cooperative in the state, known for its Blue Ribbon brand) and the Yakima Fruit Growers Association (Big "Y") merged in 1965 and rebranded as Snokist in 1967. The cooperative packed fruit until 2008 and operated warehouses and canning facilities until declaring bankruptcy in 2011 after receiving FDA citations for food safety violations. Del Monte Foods purchased the company's assets in 2012.[46] In the 1980s and 1990s, many agricultural cooperatives across the country consolidated or reorganized to improve operations. Skookum merged with Blue Bird in 1989. Office Depot now occupies the site of the former Skookum packing plant, and the building is still topped with a mechanical Skookum Indian billboard that winks at visitors.[47] In 1993, nine north-central Washington cooperatives, which previously marketed fruit through Wenoka, merged to form Majestic Valley Produce.[48] The Chelan Fruit Cooperative, the product of mergers between several cooperatives, including Blue Chelan, Trout, and Mutual Apple Growers, is one of the largest grower-owned cooperatives today, serving three hundred growers.[49]

The largest grower-owned cooperative in the state, with nearly one thousand members, is Tree Top, which processes fruit by-products including juice concentrates and purees. Before World War II, local canneries handled many types of fruit, including a portion of the state's apple crop, but companies that tried to specialize in apple by-products failed because of variations in crop size and market prices. Some years prices were so low that it was not worth growers' effort to ship culls to a processing facility. In 1960, a group of growers purchased Charbonneau Packing, later Tree Top, to address the problem of disposing of cull apples. As a grower-owned cooperative, Tree Top contracts with growers for entire crops instead of relying on culls left over at the end of the season.[50]

Tree Top's success in the processed apple market coincided with new consumer trends. Before World War II, apple juice was a seasonal treat. Between 1940 and 1970, US consumption of fresh apples declined, while per capita consumption of processed apple products increased. "Products such as applesauce, canned apples, and juice became staples on supermarket shelves," writes economist Desmond O'Rourke.[51] New processing technology produced better-flavored juice. Frozen juice concentrates, developed for the military under contract with the USDA, became available to consumers in 1946. In the 1970s, as consumption of processed apple products slowed, consumption of juice remained strong.[52] In recent years, imported frozen apple juice concentrate, especially from China, has put pressure on American manufacturers like Tree Top. Today, apples are still America's most consumed fruit, but about half of that consumption is in juice form.[53]

Though consumers are purchasing more juice, most of Washington's fruit is still packed fresh. Today's technology is more sophisticated than the automated washing machines of the 1920s. Much of the packing process is mechanized. Machinery reduces labor needs and has made specialized positions such as packers and box makers a relic of the past. In the 1950s and 1960s, driven by the cost of raw materials and changes to supermarket distribution systems, the apple industry phased out the iconic apple boxes that have since become popular collectors' items. Instead, they packed apples in cardboard trays, fiberboard boxes, and cellophane bags.[54] Wood shortages during World War II prompted the first USDA studies on using fiberboard or corrugated cardboard boxes. Fiberboard boxes had been in limited use for about ten years by the time the war broke out, but they came into wider use in the 1950s as boxes were redesigned with ventilation and bracing to withstand long-term storage. Wooden receptacles are still used during harvest since fiberboard boxes do not handle moisture.[55]

New box designs allowed fruit to be held in storage for several months. More importantly, the development of controlled-atmosphere storage extended shelf life even further. Controlled-atmosphere storage works by using sealed storage chambers to remove oxygen from the atmosphere, which is replaced with nitrogen or some other gas to slow apples' respiration and rate of decay. This allows apples to be stored several months longer than was possible with conventional cold storage. In the 1910s, Franklin Kidd and Cyril West began the first systematic studies of controlled-atmosphere storage in their laboratories in Cambridge, England. Their research inspired American scientists, including F. W. Allen of the University of California, Davis, and R. M. Smock of Cornell, to test the commercial possibilities of controlled-atmosphere storage for the American fruit industry. Washington's first controlled-atmosphere storage warehouse was built in Yakima in 1958. Since then, controlled-atmosphere storage has become the standard storage method for apples, making it possible to purchase apples year-round.[56]

Just as technology transformed storage, it also transformed transportation. By the 1950s, trucking offered a new transportation option, severing the industry's long-standing relationship with railroads. By the late 1930s some trucks were outfitted with refrigeration units, but mechanically refrigerated trucks were still rare. Without refrigeration, growers could use trucks for only short hauls within the Northwest. From the railroads' perspective, trucks were initially a minor annoyance that affected only local traffic. Though trucking provided a cheaper transportation option for short hauls, it was not regulated, leaving growers with no protection if fruit was damaged in transit. Unregulated trucking, argued the Washington Produce Shippers Association, "constitutes the gravest menace of the day to adequate farm returns and to the security of farm income." The association demanded that truckers be subjected to "every tax, license, permit, regulation, inspection, limitation of hours, safety requirement, bond, insurance, quarantine, marketing agreement, and to every other restriction and disability imposed upon us by State and Federal laws for the protection of the farmer and the general public."[57]

During World War II, trucking fell by the wayside, in part because gasoline and tire rationing added to the cost. After the war, trucks offered serious competition to rail transportation. By 1955, trucks handled about 20 percent of Wenatchee fruit shipments. Not all growers wanted to switch to trucks. Ironically, regulations created to protect shippers restricted the railroads' ability to evolve with new packing technologies. The Hamilton Fruit Company in Wenatchee, for example, shipped everything by rail in the late 1940s, but by the 1953–54 season, it shipped 38 percent of its fruit by truck. Companies like Hamilton switched from wooden boxes to fiberboard boxes, but railroads could not ship fiberboard boxes because tariff rules dictated the allowable types of shipping containers.[58] The company did not want to ship by truck, but it felt it had no choice because of the railroad's "continued negligence, inflexibility, and customer-be-damned philosophy."[59] It took several years to change the tariff rules, and in the meantime, many shippers had no choice but to use trucks.

The rise of trucking diminished the railroads' role in the apple industry. In the early 1900s, railroad leaders like James J. Hill, Louis Hill, and Howard Elliott eagerly supported the apple industry. They dreamed of a land filled with small, irrigated farms, run by independent farmer-businesspeople. Their companies took an active interest in promoting the industry and attracting new orchardists to central Washington. By the 1950s, the apple industry had come a long way from the early days when inexperienced growers struggled to establish profitable orchards. Railroads were no longer the sole means of transportation. The apple industry had developed its own marketing and distribution networks. It did not need the support provided by railroads in previous decades. For their part, railroad companies had moved beyond the town-and-industry-building ethos of the late nineteenth and early twentieth centuries. Successive generations of rail executives saw transportation as the primary connection between railroads and the industries they served.

Consumer shopping habits also drove changes after the war. National chain supermarkets with self-service replaced small, independent grocery stores. Kroger stores highlight this transformation. In 1930, Kroger operated 5,500 stores, very few of which were self-serve, with sales of

$286 million. By 1952, Kroger had consolidated to 1,900 stores, 95 percent of which were self-serve, with sales of over $1 billion. As Americans moved to the suburbs after the war, people made fewer trips to the store. Though consumers tended to purchase more groceries with each trip, they preferred purchasing smaller quantities of apples rather than whole boxes. Chains like Kroger implemented a streamlined retailing model. Under the old system, the jobs of purchasing and selling fruit were separate. The purchasing agent was responsible for monitoring only wholesale prices, not retail prices. Under the new system, the merchandiser handled produce from the time it was purchased until it was sold to the consumer. Integrating wholesale and retail sides of the business allowed Kroger stores to manage their inventories more efficiently. According to Rodgers N. Brown, vice president for Wesco Foods Company, a Kroger subsidiary, Kroger purchased Delicious and Winesap apples from Washington because it knew consumers would buy them. "If you were a football coach, you wouldn't pick players for the team that were weak and lacked ability," he explained. Studies showed that consumers made approximately 40 percent of all fruit and vegetable purchases on impulse. Since stores were self-serve, Kroger encouraged impulse buys by creating eye-catching displays.[60] "Gone is the individual salesmanship of the clerk and in its place we have such strange sounding phrases as 'impulse buying' and 'eye appeal,' etc.," lamented Big Y sales manager Ray Forman.[61] Shiny Red Delicious apples were especially suited to the "eye appeal" that attracted postwar consumers.

The growth of supermarket chains pushed small distributors out of business as stores preferred to make larger purchases from a single distributor. *Better Fruit*'s 1938 annual directory listed 246 Washington-based shippers that could supply boxcars of apples. As of 2020, the Washington Apple Commission's directory lists sixty-nine packers and suppliers, of which twenty-three are sales agents. Although the number of packers and suppliers has decreased, many operations are still family or grower owned, and some have deep roots in the state. A few, such as Gilbert Orchards and Roche Fruit, date back to the beginnings of the apple industry and are still held by the families who started them over one hundred years ago. "And so we see one of the middlemen being cut out of the chain of distribution—the very thing that many students of

Apple display, Furr's Supermarket, Westminster, Colorado, 1962. In the postwar years, grocery store displays became an important advertising method. *Collections of the Yakima Valley Museum.*

marketing farm products had been advocating," remarked Forman. Though growers had fewer buyers and distributors to choose from, as Forman pointed out, chain stores were good buyers. They "have highly trained merchandising personnel, schooled in the proper way to take care of fresh fruits," and "they are easy to reach when assistance is needed in moving a surplus." From Forman's perspective, the disadvantages of few buyers outweighed the advantages of chain supermarkets.[62]

The consolidation of retailers and distribution outlets that Forman witnessed in the 1950s continues today. Rather than a decentralized network of regional fruit distributors, Washington's apple industry deals with a handful of distributors and large chain stores. Mergers such as Albertsons Companies' 2014 acquisition of Safeway or Amazon's 2017 acquisition of Whole Foods have further reduced the number of retailers.

Albertsons, the nation's second largest grocery store chain after Kroger, also controls Jewel-Osco, Vons, and several other regional chains. Likewise, Kroger owns Fred Meyer, QFC, Harris Teeter, and other stores that until the 1980s and 1990s were independent regional chains. The consolidation of retail outlets limits growers' autonomy, but it has created a more streamlined system of distribution.

Growers have always been at the mercy of consumer markets. Today's conversations about marketing are similar to those from the past. In the late 1940s, the Washington Apple Commission redoubled its advertising to repair the damage done to the reputation of Washington apples during the war. The commission worried about competition from other fruits. Citrus production increased over 300 percent between 1937 and 1947. Banana imports were up over a million stems from their prewar levels.[63] To encourage housewives to purchase apples, the commission funded scientific studies to prove the health benefits of apples and revived the old slogan "an apple a day keeps the doctor away" for the campaign. Images of robust youngsters biting into Washington apples drove home the message. In 1948, the commission brought together shippers, advertisers, wholesalers, retailers, and home economists for a series of meetings in thirty-five cities where the commission introduced the new campaign and solicited feedback.[64] The commission learned that from the retail perspective, poor quality hurt sales. "I am quite sure that if the consumer hadn't gotten a taste of that mealy, soggy, large, poor apple," opined Mr. Strock of Boston, "you would not have run into this condition."[65]

These themes are still relevant today. The Washington Apple Commission continues to market apples on behalf of the state's growers. In 2019, Washington Apple Commission president Todd Fryhover reported that Kroger's sales had declined 11 percent over the past five years. Apples still face competition from other fruit. Kroger reported increased sales of oranges, grapes, and berries during the period when apple sales decreased. Although health is still a cornerstone of apple advertising, new trends such as keto diets have hurt sales. Finally, in an echo of the early industrial era, Fryhover warned that consumers have too much variety. In the last twenty years, the number of apple varieties available in grocery stores has exploded. For some who remember the days when shoppers could choose between red, yellow, or green, this is a welcome change, but other consumers find the choice confusing. After World War II, the commission solved the quality issue through dealer and consumer education. It exhorted dealers to handle fruit gently with the "Don't be a Bruiser" campaign and reminded shoppers to store their apples in the refrigerator. Fryhover's solution for today's quality problem is to "eliminate poor eating apples" by growing varieties that consumers actually want to eat, a solution that would have been familiar to growers of earlier generations.[66]

After World War II, the Delicious apple reigned as king as the apple consumers wanted to eat, but times have changed. New varieties are taking its place. Though Washington's climate is ideal for growing Red Delicious, they can be tasteless and mushy if picked at the wrong time, leaving consumers with a disappointing product. In the 1980s and 1990s, new commercial varieties provided competition. Developed in Australia in 1868, Granny Smith apples offered a tart, flavorful alternative to Red Delicious. US growers started producing Granny Smith apples in the early 1980s. By the early 1990s, growers were producing Gala apples, which originated in the 1930s in New Zealand, and Fuji apples, which originated in Japan in the 1930s. In 1989, Granny Smith production accounted for 6.4 percent of the US total. Ten years later, Granny Smith, Gala, and Fuji production combined for over 20 percent of US production, while the share of Red Delicious production declined from 43.8 percent to 32.9 percent of the nation's total.[67]

Washington growers found it difficult to shift production to new varieties. It takes time for trees to mature and bear fruit, so removing orchards and planting new varieties is not a decision growers take lightly. By the late 1990s, however, Red Delicious prices dropped below the cost of production, and many growers found themselves on the verge of bankruptcy. In October 2000, President Bill Clinton signed a $138 million relief package for apple growers to compensate for this market loss. In an interview with the *New York Times*, Bruce Grim, chair of the Washington State Apple Commission, called the relief package a "Band-Aid." "Unless we change the economics of the industry," he continued, "we're going to be in trouble." Likewise, Kraig Naasz, president of the US Apple Commission, lamented the government bailout. "We pride ourselves on independence from the government," he explained.

"In order to ask for help, you have to admit that things are going worse than you ever imagined."[68] The market collapse of Red Delicious apples pushed growers to plant different varieties in response to consumer trends. At its peak in the late 1980s, Red Delicious accounted for 75 percent of Washington's production. Today 34 percent of Washington apples are Red Delicious, followed by Gala at 19 percent, Fuji at 13 percent, and Granny Smith at 12 percent. Washington also produces other commercial varieties including Golden Delicious, Cripps Pink, Honeycrisp, and Braeburn.[69]

The apple industry has diversified over the last twenty years, and it is still on the lookout for the next big variety that will increase sales. Washington State University spent over twenty years developing the new Cosmic Crisp apple, which debuted in stores in late 2019. A cross between the Enterprise and Honeycrisp varieties, the Cosmic Crisp is "ultra-crisp, very juicy and has a good balance of sweetness and tartness," according to Kate Evans of WSU's breeding program.[70] With a $10 million advertising budget, news of Cosmic Crisp appeared in national media outlets, creating enormous buzz for the new variety. WSU is not alone. In recent years, the industry has patented and trademarked many new varieties, including Jazz, Opal, Pacific Rose, and SweeTango. While apple consumption has not increased, consumers are willing to pay more for new proprietary varieties, and under some licensing agreements, breeders receive royalties for every tree purchased.[71] Just as Red Delicious pushed older varieties such as Ben Davis and Wagener off the market, so too are new varieties edging out Delicious. Consumer tastes will continue to drive the market as the industry looks for the next big seller.

Much has changed since growers planted Washington's first commercial orchards in the 1890s. If growers from those early days visited a modern orchard, they would recognize the basic structure of apple production, though the level of industrialization would probably surpass their wildest expectations. Apples are still sprayed, picked, packed, and shipped, but much of the process is automated and the machinery more sophisticated. The hyperindustrialization of apple production requires an even greater reliance on agricultural experts with specialized training in horticulture, entomology, plant pathology, plant breeding, economics, and marketing. Today's growers manage orchards with greater precision than in the past. Gone are the days when growers applied extra sprays, just in case.

Looking toward the future, the apple industry faces many challenges. Hyperindustrialization has accelerated consolidation. Over the last ten years, the number of independent growers has declined 64 percent. Medium-sized operations are being squeezed, dividing the industry into large-scale operators who can afford the latest technology and smaller specialized orchards that focus on proprietary varieties or organic production.[72] Climate change may bring new insect infestations or tree diseases. Erratic weather patterns can damage trees at critical moments. Water scarcity will become a concern as low snowfall and early snowmelt reduce the amount of water available for summer irrigation. Researchers are looking for ways to adapt. New varieties of apples that can withstand higher summer temperatures are just one of many research avenues. Such varieties could prove vital to Washington growers in the future.[73]

The industrial apple—shiny, red, worm-free—was one small part of the larger social trends that led to the demise of the corner grocery store, the local fruit peddler, and the home orchard. Industrial agriculture grew alongside the industrialization of other manufactured products as Americans moved to cities, away from farming and toward different opportunities. The railroads, packinghouses, warehouses, and distributors of a century ago laid the foundations of our current food system. Advances in industrial agriculture enabled American consumers to purchase fresh food year-round. By the 1950s, consumers could purchase cellophane bags of apples in supermarkets alongside packages of iceberg lettuce and oranges, all transported thousands of miles so consumers could have fresh produce out of season. Consumers prized appearance, convenience, and low cost. For those who remembered an era when most fresh produce was not available year-round, it must have been a delight.

Despite current cultural nostalgia for a time when Americans ate locally, seasonally, and organically, Americans have been eating industrially for well over a century. Social values shift with each new generation. Consumers have more information at their fingertips than ever, and while low cost and convenience are still important, so too are flavor and environmental impact. We cannot go back in time to an era when small farmers and home gardens fed the nation, but industrial practices can and do change. Consumer preferences drive changes in food production, as evidenced by the recent shift to organic production. Over the last century, Washington's apple industry has continued to evolve, and growers have adopted new practices and technologies as they proved profitable and efficient, just as early orchardists also experimented with all aspects of apple growing and production. I like to think they would be happy to see that the spirit of innovation lives on in today's industry.

Notes

INTRODUCTION

1. Evelyn Revelli, "What an Apple Could Tell Us," ca. 1947–48, Yakima Valley Growers-Shippers Association Records, Manuscripts, Archives, and Special Collections, Washington State University Libraries, Pullman (hereafter cited as MASC).

2. "Agriculture: A Cornerstone of Washington's Economy," Washington State Department of Agriculture, https://agr.wa.gov/washington-agriculture; USDA National Agricultural Statistics Service press release, August 12, 2020, https://www.nass.usda.gov/Statistics_by_State/Washington/Publications/Fruit/2020/FR08_1.pdf.

3. Stoll, *Fruits of Natural Advantage*, xv; Sackman, *Orange Empire*, 28; Farmer, *Trees in Paradise*, xxviii.

4. Vaught, *Cultivating California*, 14.

5. Fitzgerald, *Every Farm a Factory*, 23.

6. Washington Crop and Livestock Reporting Service, *Washington Tree Fruits*, 2.

7. "Bryan's 'Cross of Gold' Speech: Mesmerizing the Masses," History Matters: The U.S. Survey Course on the Web, November 14, 2021, http://historymatters.gmu.edu/d/5354/.

8. Folger and Thomson, *Commercial Apple Industry*, 8, 30.

9. Watsonville, California, averaged 2.78 million bushels a year, southern Idaho 1.89 million, Hood River 1.6 million, and Colorado 1.49 million. Folger and Thomson, *Commercial Apple Industry*, 79.

10. Folger and Thomson, *Commercial Apple Industry*, 8.

11. Robbins, *Colony and Empire*, 71–72.

12. White, *Railroaded*, xxv–xxvi.

13. Worster, *Rivers of Empire*, 179.

14. Worster, 4.

15. "The Rich History of Washington Apples," Washington Apple Commission, 2021, https://bestapples.com/washington-orchards/history/#:~:text=The%20average%20size%20of%20a,during%20the%20peak%20of%20harvest.

CHAPTER 1

1. Patty Hastings, "Vancouver's Old Apple Tree Dies at Age 194," *Columbian* (Vancouver, WA), June 27, 2020; Cardwell, "First Fruits of the Land, Part I," 28–29.
2. Cardwell, "First Fruits of the Land, Part I," 33.
3. *Vancouver Independent,* October 21, 1880; May 17, 1883; September 13, 1883; *Olympia Tribune,* April 11, 1892; "Seattle and King County Day," *Seattle Post-Intelligencer,* September 13, 1892.
4. Luce, *Washington State Fruit Industry,* 3.
5. *Malus domestica* is used as a synonym for *Malus pumila,* but according to the Integrative Taxonomic Information System, maintained through the partnership of several US government agencies, *Malus domestica* is not the accepted taxonomic term. Integrative Taxonomic Information System, "*Malus domestica* Borkh," ITIS Report, accessed October 19, 2020, https://www.itis.gov/servlet/SingleRpt/SingleRpt?search_topic=TSN&search_value=516655#null.
6. Juniper and Mabberley, *Story of the Apple,* 34, 50.
7. Juniper and Mabberley, 56.
8. Juniper and Mabberley, 46–50.
9. Some of the earliest evidence of grafting trees is from Persia 2,500 years ago. Juniper and Mabberley, *Story of the Apple,* 91; Morgan and Richards, *New Book of Apples,* 11–21.
10. Morgan and Richards, *New Book of Apples,* 23–26.
11. Edward Johnson, *Wonder-Working Providence of Sion's Savior in New England* (1654; repr., Andover, MA: Warren F. Draper, 1867), 174–75; Ott, *Pumpkin,* 32–33, 39.
12. Diamond, "Migrations," 76.
13. Morgan and Richards, *New Book of Apples,* 70.
14. Beech, *Apples of New York,* 9–10.
15. Beech, 12–13; Dolan, *Fruitful Legacy,* 14, 24.
16. Dolan, *Fruitful Legacy,* 32.
17. Haley, "Johnny Appleseed," 830.
18. Kerrigan, *Johnny Appleseed,* 6.
19. Juniper and Mabberley, *Story of the Apple,* 169–70.
20. Kerrigan, *Johnny Appleseed,* 13.
21. Price, *Johnny Appleseed,* 40.
22. Quoted in Tyrrell, *Sobering Up,* 138.
23. Morgan and Richards, *New Book of Apples,* 153–54.

NOTES TO CHAPTER 1

24. Tyrrell, "Temperance and Economic Change," 46–47.
25. Morgan and Richards, *New Book of Apples*, 154.
26. Tyrrell, "Temperance and Economic Change," 50.
27. Beech, *Apples of New York*, 11–12; Warren, "Apple Industry," 249, 254.
28. Gibson, *Farming the Frontier*, 16–17, 24–25.
29. Gibson, 10–14, 32, 36–37.
30. Cromwell, *Short History*, 4.
31. Whitman, *My Journal*, 50.
32. Erigero, *Cultural Landscape Report*.
33. *Vancouver Independent*, May 17, 1883; Rose, "How Native Farmers."
34. "Historical Trees," *Olympia Tribune*, April 11, 1892.
35. Whitman, *My Journal*, 50.
36. Miner, "Century of Washington Fruit," 6; Gibson, *Farming the Frontier*, 39.
37. Gibson, *Farming the Frontier*, 154.
38. Marvin M. Richardson, *The Whitman Mission* (Walla Walla, WA: Whitman Publishing, 1940), cited in Vandevere, "History of Irrigation in Washington," 13–14.
39. Gibson, *Farming the Frontier*, 159.
40. Boening, "History of Irrigation," 261–62.
41. Lyman, *Illustrated History*, 154; *Vancouver Independent*, October 21, 1880; Boening, "History of Irrigation," 262.
42. Luce, *Washington State Fruit Industry*, 5–6; Boening, "History of Irrigation," 262–63.
43. Rose, "How Native Farmers"; Meinig, *Great Columbia Plain*, 134, 138.
44. In the mid-1990s, the Yakama Nation changed the spelling of its tribal name to better reflect its pronunciation. Older works use the "Yakima" spelling, and "Yakima" is used for the town and the surrounding valley.
45. Meinig, *Great Columbia Plain*, 159–68.
46. Cardwell, "First Fruits of the Land, Part I," 32.
47. According to biographer David Diamond, Henderson Lewelling changed his name to Luelling sometime near the end of 1850. Both spellings are common in accounts and records in Oregon and California. Diamond, "Migrations," 1, 191–93; Duruz, "Notes on the Early History," 90.
48. Barlow, "Reminiscences of Seventy Years," 276–77.
49. Diamond, "Migrations," 217–20, 226, 235–36.
50. Seth Lewelling, "Pioneers of Fruits: Early Horticulture in Oregon," *Oregonian* (Portland), October 16, 1892.
51. Lewelling, "Pioneers of Fruits."
52. Diamond, "Migrations," 284.
53. Cardwell, "First Fruits of the Land, Part I," 35–36.
54. Quoted in Conlin, *"Bacon, Beans, and Galantines,"* 90.
55. Conlin, 96.

56. Cardwell, "First Fruits of the Land, Part I," 37.
57. Cardwell, 35, 40.
58. Diamond, "Migrations," 282.
59. Lewelling, "Pioneers of Fruits."
60. Cardwell, "First Fruits of the Land, Part I," 40.
61. Adams, "Historical Background," 37–38.
62. Lyman, *Illustrated History*, 154.
63. Meinig, *Great Columbia Plain*, 211.
64. Meeker, *Pioneer Reminiscences*, 111.
65. *Illustrated History of Klickitat*, 152.
66. *Illustrated History of Klickitat*, 157.
67. "Oldest Apple Trees," *Yakima Herald*, October 21, 1908; Luce, *Washington State Fruit Industry*, 6–7; Boening, "History of Irrigation," 264–65.
68. Boening, "History of Irrigation," 264; Luce, *Washington State Fruit Industry*, 5, 7–9.
69. Lyman, *Illustrated History*, 155; Locati, *Horticultural Heritage*, 19.
70. "The Decay of Orchards," *Albany State Rights Democrat*, October 2, 1869.

CHAPTER 2

1. Sheller, *Blowsand*, 1–3.
2. Meinig, *Great Columbia Plain*, 103.
3. Meinig, 288.
4. Lemons and Tousley, "Washington Apple Industry," 176.
5. Arthur Gunn to Thomas Burke, June 13, 1892, Thomas Burke Papers, Special Collections, University Archives Division, University of Washington, Seattle. For more on the construction of railroads in the Pacific Northwest, see Lewty, *To the Columbia Gateway* and *Across the Columbia Plain*.
6. In 1918, North Yakima was renamed Yakima, and the original site of Yakima was renamed Union Gap.
7. Lewty, *Across the Columbia Plain*; Schwantes and Ronda, *West the Railroads*, 114; Lyman, *History of the Yakima Valley*, 394–401.
8. Burke to William Watson, May 16, 1892, Thomas Burke Papers.
9. Hull, *History of Central Washington*, 534.
10. Howard, "Following the Colonists," 531.
11. Scott, *Reluctant Farmer*, 5.
12. The national population increased from 38.5 million in 1870 to 62.6 million in 1890. Urban populations increased from 9.9 million in 1870 to 22.1 million in 1890. US Census Bureau, *United States Summary*, 14–15.
13. Frederick J. Turner, "The Significance of the Frontier in American History (1893)," American Historical Association, https://www.historians.org/about-aha-and-membership/aha-history-and-archives/historical-archives/the-significance-of-the-frontier-in-american-history.

NOTES TO CHAPTER 2

14. Quoted in Pisani, *To Reclaim a Divided West*, 290–91.
15. Quoted in Pisani, 286.
16. "Settling the Irrigated Lands," Washington Irrigation Institute, ca. 1914, Northern Pacific Railway Company Records, President's Subject File 19-J2, Minnesota Historical Society, St. Paul (hereafter cited as MHS).
17. For more on the development of irrigation in Wenatchee, see Van Lanen, "'It was a time.'"
18. Sheller, *Courage and Water*, 11.
19. Fahey, *Inland Empire*, 87–99; "Tragedy at Tacoma," *San Francisco Call*, April 13, 1895.
20. Burke to Don Carlos Corbett, April 14, 1892; C. H. Warren to Andrew Woods, May 19, 1892; Burke to T. J. Hyman, May 24, 1892, letterpress books, Thomas Burke Papers.
21. Shotwell, *Shotwell Story*, 25.
22. Wenatchee Development Company Board of Trustees meeting minutes, April 9, 1896, quoted in Mitchell, *Flowing Wealth*, 9.
23. Gunn to Burke, June 15, 1896; September 7, 1898, Thomas Burke Papers.
24. Gunn to Burke, June 16, 1896, Thomas Burke Papers.
25. Contract between Lake Superior Company and Great Northern Railway Company, 1899, Thomas Burke Papers.
26. Strom, *Profiting from the Plains*, 41, 53.
27. Robert Farrington to James J. Hill, May 26, 1911, Great Northern Comptroller's Files, box 132.D.8.4F, MHS.
28. Gellatly, *History of Wenatchee*, 55–56.
29. Contract between Wenatchee Canal Company and Wenatchee Development Company, May 19, 1902, Thomas Burke Papers.
30. Charles F. Brown to Burke, April 25, 1902, Thomas Burke Papers.
31. Bright, *Apples Galore!*, 19.
32. Fahey, *Inland Empire*, 91–94; Coulter, "Victory of National Irrigation," 104–13; "List of Irrigation Projects along the Line of Northern Pacific Railway in State of Washington, and Acreage in Cultivation, October 1922," Northern Pacific Railway Company Records, President's Subject File 19-J2, MHS.
33. Hill, *Highways of Progress*, 201.
34. Ed M. Foy, "A Brief Description of Wenatchee Valley," *Better Fruit* 1, no. 1 (July 1906): 16.
35. Mickelson, *Northern Pacific Railroad*, 97–98.
36. Yakima Commercial Club, *Yakima Valley Washington*, 56–57, 60.
37. Wenatchee Investment Company, articles of incorporation, July 1, 1891, Thomas Burke Papers.
38. Edwards, "Irrigation in Eastern Washington," 113.
39. Fiege, *Irrigated Eden*, 172.
40. *Granger and the Yakima Valley*, 3.
41. "Irrigation Enterprise," *Yakima Herald*, February 2, 1889.

42. *Soil, Sunshine, Water: Prosser the Apple City in the Heart of the Yakima Valley* (n.p., n.d.), Yakima Valley Museum; Edwards, "'Early Morning,'" 79–80.

43. Similar promotional brochures were also used to promote irrigated orchard land in British Columbia's Okanagan Valley, a region also known for apple production. Bennett, "Blossoms and Borders," 71–73.

44. Quoted in White, "Main Street on the Irrigation Frontier," 96.

45. Quoted in White, 96.

46. Vaught, *Cultivating California*, 21; quoted in Bennett, "Blossoms and Borders," 79.

47. Channing, *Child Labor*, 5.

48. In 1919, before the passage of the alien land bill, 119 Japanese farmers had leases on the Yakama Reservation totaling 6,334 acres, with 160 acres in fruit. Heuterman, *Burning Horse*, 23, 31–32; Iwata, *Planted in Good Soil*, 524–25; Wyman, *Hoboes, Bindlestiffs*, 95.

49. Joseph E. Wing, "Washington State College at Pullman," *Better Fruit* 3, no. 4 (October 1908): 30.

50. "Rich in Lands," *Yakima Herald*, February 2, 1889.

51. Anderson, *Charles F. Keiser*, 11–12.

52. *Granger and the Yakima Valley*.

53. "The Fruit Growing Industry in Washington," *Better Fruit* 3, no. 5 (November 1908): 17; "White Salmon—a Developing Fruit District," *Better Fruit* 2, no. 7 (January 1908): 14. See also Luce, *Washington State Fruit Industry*, 7.

54. Worster, *Rivers of Empire*, 179.

55. Worster, 170.

56. Sheller, *Blowsand*, 4–7, 49.

57. Fahey, *Inland Empire*, 90.

58. Coulter, "New Settlers," 10–21; Sheller, *Courage and Water*, 121.

59. Fahey, *Inland Empire*, 94–95.

60. Yakima Commercial Club, *Yakima Valley Washington*, 29.

61. Fortier, *Irrigation of Orchards*, 25.

62. Vaught, *Cultivating California*, 116–17.

63. In the 1920 census, Okanogan County recorded 12 Japanese residents, Kittitas County 26, Benton County 37, and Yakima County 771.

64. Zaragoza, "Apple Capital," 119–21.

65. Anderson, *Pioneers of North Central Washington*, 425–28.

66. Jackson, *Yakima's Past*, 24.

67. Anderson, *Pioneers of North Central Washington*, 559.

68. Washington Irrigation Institute to Franklin K. Lane, Secretary of the Interior, August 31, 1914, Northern Pacific Railway Company Records, President's Subject File 19-J2, MHS.

69. "True Independence Is Orchardists' Lot," *Better Fruit* 1, no. 6 (December 1906): 14.

70. Gunn to Burke, February 1, 1904; Burke to Melville Stone, February 3, 1904; Gunn to Burke, February 3, 1904, Thomas Burke Papers.

71. Fortier, *Irrigation of Orchards*, 33–34.

72. Oscar M. Morris, "Fruit Growing and Diversified Farming," *Better Fruit* 8, no. 6 (December 1913): 21.

73. Thatcher, *Washington Soils*, 53–54; editorial, *Better Fruit* 8, no. 6 (December 1913): 20.

74. L. S. Smith, "The Fruit Grower Should Diversify," *Better Fruit* 8, no. 1 (July 1913): 37.

75. Arthur G. B. Bouquet, "Intercropping Vegetables in the Commercial Orchard," *Better Fruit* 8, no. 6 (December 1913): 17.

76. Hill, *Highways of Progress*, 36.

77. Editorial, *Better Fruit* 8, no. 1 (July 1913): 22.

78. Smith, "Fruit Grower Should Diversify," 35–36.

79. "Settling the Irrigated Lands," Washington Irrigation Institute, ca. 1914, Northern Pacific Railway Company Records, President's Subject File 19-J2, MHS.

80. Washington Crop and Livestock Reporting Service, *Washington Tree Fruits*, 2.

81. Each car represents 630 boxes of apples. Freeman, "Apple Industry," 170.

82. "Orchard Development in the Yakima Valley," *Better Fruit* 2, no. 8 (February 1908): 11–13.

CHAPTER 3

1. Sheller, *Blowsand*, 108–9.

2. Anderson, *Pioneers of North Central Washington*, 66.

3. Anderson, 399.

4. For a full treatment of the development of agricultural extensions and land-grant institutions, see Scott, *Reluctant Farmer*.

5. Washington Agricultural College and School of Science, *Report of Farmers' Institute*, 21, 23.

6. Stoll, *Fruits of Natural Advantage*, 20.

7. William A. Taylor, "Marketing, Storage and Transportation," *Better Fruit* 2, no. 3 (September 1907): 21.

8. "Early Orchards Had All Kinds of Apples," *Big "Y" Bulletin* 16, no. 6 (April–May 1937): 4.

9. F. A. Huntley, "Choice Varieties—Peculiar Condition of Soil and Climate," *Better Fruit* 8, no. 1 (July 1913): 27.

10. Fletcher, *Nursery Stock*, 30.

11. *First Biennial Report, State Board of Horticulture of the State of Washington for the Years 1891–1892* (Olympia: O. C. White, 1893), 117–19, box 5, Washington State Department of Agriculture Records.

12. Balmer, *Report on Damage*, 11, 19.
13. Fletcher, *Planting Orchards*, 16–17.
14. Overholser, "Production and Marketing Problems," 90.
15. F. A. Huntley, "Choice Varieties, Etc.," *Better Fruit* 8, no. 2 (August 1913): 41–43.
16. Beech, *Apples of New York*, 69.
17. Huntley, "Choice Varieties, Etc.," 41.
18. "Large Sized Apples Handicap," *Better Fruit* 25, no. 8 (February 1931): 32, 42.
19. "Washington Horticulturists Meet," *Better Fruit* 25, no. 7 (January 1931): 7–8.
20. Tove Danovich, "The Red Delicious Apple Is an Atrocity. Why Are We Growing Billions of Pounds of Them Each Year?," *New Food Economy*, March 13, 2018.
21. Niraj Chokshi, "The Long, Monstrous Reign of the Red Delicious Apple Is Ending," *New York Times*, August 29, 2018.
22. *Apple Stark "Delicious,"* 3–4.
23. Huntley, "Choice Varieties, Etc.," 42.
24. Ferree, *History of Fruit Varieties*, 1–2; Huntley, "Choice Varieties, Etc.," 42.
25. *Richared: The Delicious Supreme*, 3–9.
26. "A New Race of Red Apples," *Better Fruit* 25, no. 6 (December 1930): 1; "Solid Red Apples," *Better Fruit* 25, no. 5 (November 1930): 13; Ralph Sundquist to Stark Bro's Nurseries, November 27, 1928, box 4, Ralph R. Sundquist Papers, MASC; A. R. Chase, "Trends of Deciduous Fruits," in *Proceedings of the Twenty-Seventh Annual Meeting of the Washington State Horticultural Association* (Yakima, WA, December 1–3, 1931), 93–100, box 6, Washington State Department of Agriculture Records.
27. Lerner, "Plant Patent Act of 1930," 643.
28. "Fruit Patent Law," *Better Fruit* 25, no. 8 (February 1931): 36.
29. Chase, "Trends of Deciduous Fruits," 93–100.
30. Dr. Auchter, "National and International Aspects of Fruit Growing," in *Proceedings of the Twenty-Seventh Annual Meeting*, 63–69.
31. Melander, *Wormy Apple*, 8.
32. A. B. Crodley, "The Destructive San Jose Scale," *Better Fruit* 1, no. 6 (December 1906): 4.
33. "Spraying for Scale," *Yakima Republic*, March 31, 1899; Piper, *Insect Pests*, 40.
34. Beech, *Apples of New York*, 13–14.
35. Melander, *Wormy Apple*, 5.
36. Piper, *Insect Pests*, 5–65.
37. Stoll, *Fruits of Natural Advantage*, 109.
38. Orlando Beck, "Pests of the Orchard," *Yakima Republic*, February 3, 1899.
39. Piper, *Insect Pests*, 9.
40. Whorton, *Before Silent Spring*, 20–24.
41. Johnson, "Early History," 67–79.

NOTES TO CHAPTER 3   239

42. Lawrence, *Apple Scab*, 5, 11.
43. Melander and Beattie, *Penetration System*, 27.
44. E. L. Stewart, "My Experience in the Use of Dust Spray," *Better Fruit* 1, no. 11 (May 1907): 6–7; David R. McGinnis, "Fruit Raising in the Upper Columbia Valley," *Better Fruit* 2, no. 2 (August 1907): 5.
45. Sheller, *Blowsand*, 195.
46. Melander and Beattie, *Penetration System*, 18.
47. Mendenhall, *Orchards of Eden*, 155.
48. Crodley, "Destructive San Jose Scale," 6.
49. George Wright, "Suggestions to Apple Growers of the Northwest," *Better Fruit* 8, no. 3 (September 1913): 30.
50. Crodley, "Destructive San Jose Scale," 6.
51. Act Providing against the Adulteration of Paris Green, *Session Laws of the State of Washington, Seventh Session* (1901), chap. 22.
52. Act Relating to Horticulture, *Session Laws of the State of Washington, Fourteenth Session* (1915), chap. 166.
53. Seftel, "Government Regulation," 379–80; Stoll, *Fruits of Natural Advantage*, 102, 112.
54. *First Biennial Report, State Board of Horticulture*, 1, 5–6, 16, 24.
55. *First Biennial Report, State Board of Horticulture*, 4–5, 12, 34.
56. Act Relating to Horticulture, *Session Laws of the State of Washington, Session of 1897*, chap. 109; Act for the Promotion of Fruit Growing and Horticulture, *Session Laws of the State of Washington, Eighth Session* (1903), chap. 133.
57. *Yakima Republic*, March 10, 1899.
58. "Inspectors Say Infected Trees Must Go," *Better Fruit* 1, no. 11 (May 1907): 14.
59. *Second Biennial Report, State Board of Horticulture of the State of Washington for the Years 1893–1894* (Olympia, WA: O. C. White, 1895), 35, box 5, Washington State Department of Agriculture Records.
60. *Second Biennial Report, State Board of Horticulture*, 35.
61. *First Biennial Report, State Board of Horticulture*, 15.
62. "Wormy Apples Destroyed at Yakima Depot," *Wenatchee Daily World*, November 15, 1905.
63. *Cases Determined in the Supreme Court of Washington* (Seattle: Bancroft-Whitney, 1908), 49:307–9.
64. *First Report of the Department of Agriculture of the State of Washington*, 60–63, box 5, Washington State Department of Agriculture Records.
65. A. L. Roberts, "The Colorado Fruit Growers Endorse Arsenate of Lead," *Better Fruit* 1, no. 1 (July 1906): 10.
66. Melander, *Wormy Apple*, 10.
67. Melander, *Control of Codling Moth*, 7.
68. Whorton, *Before Silent Spring*, 39.
69. Whorton, *Before Silent Spring*, 31–33; Heald et al., *Arsenic Spray Residue*, 5.
70. Whorton, *Before Silent Spring*, 68–69.

71. W. P. Headden, "Effect of Arsenical Poisoning on Fruit Trees," *Better Fruit* 3, no. 7 (January 1909): 13–22.

72. E. D. Ball, "Is Arsenical Spraying Killing Our Fruit Trees," *Better Fruit* 3, no. 11 (May 1909): 21.

73. "A. I. Hall Disagrees with Dr. Headden on the Arsenical Poisoning of Fruit Trees," *Better Fruit* 3, no. 11 (May 1909): 33.

74. "Notes from the Oregon Experiment Station," *Better Fruit* 3, no. 4 (October 1908): 17; Whorton, *Before Silent Spring*, 123–25.

75. Whorton, *Before Silent Spring*, 133–34; "Find Arsenic in American Apples," *New York Times*, November 26, 1925.

76. "Find Arsenic in American Apples," *New York Times*, November 26, 1925; "Arsenic in U.S. Apples Alleged in London," *Washington Post*, November 28, 1925.

77. "Arsenic in Imported Apples," *Times* (London), January 23, 1926; "Arsenic on Imported Apples," *Times* (London), February 4, 1926; "Arsenic on American Apples," *Times* (London), February 9, 1927; "Arsenic on Apples," *Times* (London), March 25, 1926; "British Spurn Our Apples: Fear of 'Poisoned' Fruit Causes Demand to Drop 60 Per Cent," *New York Times*, April 7, 1926.

78. "Arsenic in Apples—Kent Growers' Assurance to the Public," *Times* (London), March 22, 1926; "Arsenic on Apples: Fruit Traders' Views," *Times* (London), March 24, 1926.

79. "Arsenic on Fruit," *Times* (London), March 29, 1926.

80. "British Spurn Our Apples: Fear of 'Poisoned' Fruit Causes Demand to Drop 60 Per Cent," *New York Times*, April 7, 1926.

81. Whorton, *Before Silent Spring*, 141–42, 173.

82. "Shortages Follow Gluts in Apple Exports," *Better Fruit* 20, no. 7 (January 1926): 8; "Northwest Apple Exports Shown," *Better Fruit* 21, no. 3 (September 1926): 6; Ernest C. Potts, "Northwest's Horticultural Year Reviewed," *Better Fruit* 20, no. 8 (February 1926): 8.

83. J. W. Hebert, "Arsenate of Lead Situation," in *Proceedings of the Twenty-Second Annual Meeting of the Washington State Horticultural Association*, 8, box 5, Washington State Department of Agriculture Records.

84. Hebert, "Arsenate of Lead Situation," 8.

85. The maximum residue allowed was 1/100 of a grain per pound. J. R. Neller, "Spray Residue Removal from Apples," in *Proceedings of the Twenty-Second Annual Meeting*, 28–36; R. H. Robinson and Henry Hartman, "The Removal of Spray Residue from Apples and Pears," in *Proceedings of the Twenty-Second Annual Meeting*, 94–103.

86. Ernest C. Potts, editorial, *Better Fruit* 21, no. 6 (December 1926): 12.

87. "'Arsenic Apple' Scare Ended," *Washington Post*, December 13, 1926; "Fruit Tree Spraying," *Times* (London), November 23, 1926.

88. "Box Lunch Inquiry Begun," *Los Angeles Times*, September 22, 1927; "War on American Apples," *New York Times*, January 18, 1931; "Rumania Bars California Apples," *New York Times*, August 21, 1931.

NOTES TO CHAPTER 4   241

89. "Woman's Death May Not Be Due to Eating Pear," *Seattle Times*, August 27, 1934; "Fruit Spray Poisoning," *Seattle Star*, August 27, 1934; "The Facts about Kinsman's Death," *Wenatchee Daily World*, September 6, 1934.

90. Dr. Irving S. Cutter, "Today's Health Talk—Arsenic Poisoning," *Washington Post*, April 10, 1936.

91. Robinson and Hartman, "Removal of Spray Residue," 94–103.

92. *Report of Conference concerning Spray Residue Regulations of Food & Drug Administration*, Spokane, WA, May 31, 1933, box 67, Yakima Valley Growers-Shippers Association Records, 1917–1981, MASC.

93. "Study of the Effect of Lead Arsenate Exposure on Orchardists and on Consumers of Sprayed Fruit," box 25, Washington State Department of Agriculture Records.

94. In the mid-1930s, for example, tolerances were set at 0.018 grain per pound for lead and 0.01 grain per pound for arsenic. Growers asked for a minimum lead tolerance of 0.025 grain per pound for lead. "Spray Residue Cut on Apples and Pears," *Skookum News* 10, no. 2 (February 1936): 1; Bert L. Baxer to Ivan L. Plette, December 26, 1934, box 67, Yakima Valley Growers-Shippers Association Records, 1917–1981, MASC.

95. Suggestions of the Yakima Valley Growers' Spray Residue Committee, February 12, 1927, box 5, Ralph R. Sundquist Papers, MASC; Edward C. Johnson, "Forward without Lead in Codling Moth War," *Skookum News* 9, no. 9 (October 1935): 1, 4; "Lead Residue Ruling Presents Difficulties," *Big "Y" Bulletin* 12, no. 12 (April–May 1933): 1; "Fluorine Compounds Now under U.S. Ban," *Big "Y" Bulletin* 12, no. 11 (March 1933): 3.

96. *Report of Conference concerning Spray Residue Regulations of Food & Drug Administration*, Spokane, WA, May 31, 1933; William H. Horsley to J. W. Hebert et al., October 20, 1937, box 67, Yakima Valley Growers-Shippers Association Records, 1917–1981, MASC.

CHAPTER 4

1. C. L. Durkee to Louis Hill, July 31, 1912, Great Northern Railway Company Records, President's Subject File 4369, MHS.

2. Beech, *Apples of New York*, 11–12.

3. Ohio ranked second, with 10.8 million, and Pennsylvania third, with 9 million. Warren, "Apple Industry," 249–50.

4. Gellatly, *History of Wenatchee*, 164.

5. Folger and Thomson, *Commercial Apple Industry*, 8; Warren, "Apple Industry," 251.

6. Pennsylvania ranked third, with $7.9 million worth of orchard products, and Ohio fourth, with $6.1 million. Warren, "Apple Industry," 253–54.

7. Warren, "Apple Industry," 254.

8. By 1906, Washington's output had grown to 3 million bushels of apples, and in 1910, growers harvested 5.8 million bushels, with projected increases as several thousand acres of newly planted land came into production. Overholser, "Production and Marketing Problems," 87.

9. Northwest Fruit Exchange, *A Way to Sell Apples* (n.p.: Northwest Fruit Exchange, 1913), Northern Pacific Railway Company Records, President's Subject File 1787, MHS.

10. Warren, "Apple Industry," 307.

11. Maynard, *Marketing Northwestern Apples*, 28.

12. Maynard, 24–27.

13. Maynard, 30–31.

14. C. I. Lewis, "Shipping the Apple—from Orchard to Market," *Better Fruit* 2, no. 3 (September 1907): 11.

15. Commission Merchants Act, *Session Laws of the State of Washington*, Tenth Session (1907), chap. 139.

16. "Seattle Commission Men and the New Paulhamus Law," *Ranch* (Seattle), July 1, 1907; "Commission Men to Dodge," *Evening Statesman* (Walla Walla), July 24, 1907; "Will Ignore the Paulhamus Bill," *Ranch* (Seattle), May 15, 1907; "Commission Men Take Out State Licenses," *Evening Statesman* (Walla Walla), July 27, 1907; "Commission Pirates Will Ignore the Law," *San Juan Islander* (Friday Harbor), May 8, 1907; "Commission Houses," *Ellensburg Dawn*, November 5, 1907; "Free to Farmers and Fruitgrowers," *Ranch* (Seattle), March 1, 1908.

17. Fahey, *Inland Empire*, 112–13.

18. Interview with James S. Crutchfield, December 20, 1912, Northern Pacific Railway Company Records, President's Subject File 1787, MHS.

19. U. Grant Border, "Co-operation in Advertising the Apple," *Better Fruit* 8, no. 3 (September 1913): 16.

20. H. C. Sampson, "Seventeen Reasons Why a Cooperative Central Selling Agency of the Fruit Growers of the American Northwest Is a Necessity" (paper presented at the Second National Conference on Marketing and Farm Credits, Chicago, April 14–17, 1914), Northern Pacific Railway Company Records, President's Subject File 1787, MHS. Italics in original.

21. Erdman, *California Fruit Growers Exchange*, 6.

22. Tufts, "Rich Pattern," 218.

23. Erdman, *California Fruit Growers Exchange*, 7–9.

24. Erdman, 11–12.

25. Stoll, *Fruits of Natural Advantage*, 74–75.

26. "Cooperation," *Better Fruit* 5, no. 6 (December 1910): 44; E. H. Shepard, "Necessity and Benefits of Associations for Fruit Growers," *Better Fruit* 1, no. 7 (January 1907): 15–18; G. Harold Powell, "California Fruit Growers' Exchange," *Better Fruit* 9, no. 6 (December 1914): 27–28.

NOTES TO CHAPTER 4   243

27. W. H. Paulhamus, "Importance of Fruit Growers Associations," *Better Fruit* 1, no. 1 (July 1906): 3–4.

28. "How to Form Fruit Growers' Associations," *Better Fruit* 1, no. 9 (March 1907): 3–13.

29. E. H. Shepard, "Common Sense Applied to the Fruit Industry," *Better Fruit* 8, no. 1 (July 1913): 7–9.

30. Erdman, *California Fruit Growers Exchange*, 9.

31. E. H. Shepard, "The Northwest Fruit Industry," *Better Fruit* 8, no. 5 (November 1913): 12.

32. Yakima County Horticultural Union, articles of incorporation, June 1902, and corporate minutes, January 31, 1913, Snokist Collection, Yakima Valley Museum; Maynard, *Marketing Northwestern Apples*, 62–63.

33. About 150 growers were on the waiting list in 1920. Maynard, *Marketing Northwestern Apples*, 65.

34. Maynard, *Marketing Northwestern Apples*, 66–68.

35. Maynard, 36.

36. Maynard, 37–40.

37. C. I. Lewis, "Shipping the Apple—from Orchard to Market," *Better Fruit* 2, no. 3 (September 1907): 5.

38. Maynard, *Marketing Northwestern Apples*, 19.

39. Landis and Brooks, *Farm Labor*, 30; Scroggs, "Labor Problems," 38; US Department of Labor, *Women in the Fruit Growing*, 29.

40. Channing, *Child Labor*, 5.

41. Landis and Brooks, *Farm Labor*, 63.

42. Scroggs, "Labor Problems," 48.

43. US Department of Labor, *Women in the Fruit Growing*, 84.

44. Channing, *Child Labor*, 9.

45. Wyman, *Hoboes, Bindlestiffs*, 88–90; "School Notes," *Leavenworth Echo*, November 9, 1917; Channing, *Child Labor*, 15.

46. US Department of Labor, *Women in the Fruit Growing*, 41.

47. Landis and Brooks, *Farm Labor*, 45.

48. *Vashon Island News-Record*, November 4, 1921.

49. US Department of Labor, *Women in the Fruit Growing*, 41, 45.

50. "All the Comforts of Home," *"Big Y" Bulletin* 1, no. 1 (April 1920): 4; US Department of Labor, *Women in the Fruit Growing*, 44–46.

51. Interview with James S. Crutchfield, December 20, 1912, Northern Pacific Railway Company Records, President's Subject File 1787, MHS.

52. "Standard of Fruit Grades for Yakima Valley," *Better Fruit* 3, no. 4 (October 1908): 25.

53. "Grade Rules for North Pacific Fruit Distributors, Season 1914," *Better Fruit* 9, no. 2 (August 1914): 11, 29; Bailey, *Field Notes on Apple Culture*, 62.

54. Levenstein, *Revolution at the Table*, 39–41.

55. Van Buren, "Apple Grading Law," 670.
56. Folger and Thomson, *Commercial Apple Industry*, 331.
57. Act Relating to Horticulture, *Session Laws of the State of Washington, Fourteenth Session* (1915), chap. 166.
58. Horticulture, *Session Laws of the State of Washington, Extraordinary Session* (1920), chap. 141.
59. Caldwell, *Evaporation of Apples*, 9.
60. Warren, "Apple Industry," 351–53.
61. E. F. Benson to Thomas Cooper, February 26, 1913, Northern Pacific Railway Company Records, President's Subject File 1787, MHS.
62. "The Dry Yard Is the Only Place for Culls," *Better Fruit* 3, no. 5 (November 1908): 28.
63. W. M. Kohagen, "A General Statement about the Labor Needs of the Tree Fruit Industry and Labor's Relation to Agriculture," box 15, Yakima Valley Growers-Shippers Association Records, 1917–1981, MASC.
64. Maynard, *Marketing Northwestern Apples*, 18, 21.
65. "Apple Packing Schools," *Better Fruit* 5, no. 4 (October 1910): 54.
66. US Department of Labor, *Women in the Fruit Growing*, 35–37, 145–46, 155; Max G. Fultz, "Do Fruit Men Hire Too Many Women?," *Better Fruit* 19, no. 9 (March 1925): 10.
67. "Big Y to Try Out Sizing Machines," *"Big Y" Bulletin* 1, no. 2 (May 1920): 1.
68. "Grade Rules for North Pacific Fruit Distributors, Season 1914," *Better Fruit* 9, no. 2 (August 1914): 11, 29; "Grander Association Protest against Bill," *Better Fruit* 3, no. 6 (December 1908): 37.
69. C. I. Lewis, "Shipping the Apple—from Orchard to Market," *Better Fruit* 2, no. 3 (September 1907): 6–8.
70. Lewis, 5–13.
71. Folger and Thomson, *Commercial Apple Industry*, 330.
72. Bailey, *Field Notes on Apple Culture*, 60–62.
73. The Watsonville District in Northern California is generally credited with introducing the first box, which measured 9¾ × 11 × 20¼ inches. Tufts, "Rich Pattern," 180.
74. Dolan, *Fruitful Legacy*, 70; Bright, *Apples Galore!*, 98–99.
75. Waugh, *American Apple Orchard*, 161–63.
76. Ralph Sundquist, "Origins of the Northwest Apple Box: A Review of Early Documents in History Northwest Apple Industry," DBX_120, Director's Apple History Project, Yakima Valley Museum.
77. The standard Northwest box was 2,173½ cubic inches. An Act to Establish a Standard Barrel and Standard Grade for Apples When Packed in Barrels, and for Other Purposes, Public Law 252, *U.S. Statutes at Large* 62 (1912): 250–51; F. Walden, "The Apple Box Question," *Ranch* (Seattle), June 15, 1912; F. Walden, "Standardizing the Apple Box," *Ranch* (Seattle), August 15, 1912.

78. International Apple Shippers' Association, *Grade and Standardization Laws*, 195.

79. "A Way to Sell Apples," Northwest Fruit Exchange, April 1913, Northern Pacific Railway Company Records, President's Subject File 1787, MHS.

80. H. C. Sampson, "Seventeen Reasons Why a Cooperative Central Selling Agency of the Fruit Growers of the American Northwest Is a Necessity" (paper presented at the Second National Conference on Marketing and Farm Credits, Chicago, April 14–17, 1914), Northern Pacific Railway Company Records, President's Subject File 1787, MHS.

81. E. H. Shepard, "Common Sense Applied to the Fruit Industry," *Better Fruit* 8, no. 1 (July 1913): 8.

82. Sampson, "Seventeen Reasons Why."

83. "How to Form Fruit Growers' Associations," *Better Fruit* 1, no. 9 (March 1907): 3–4.

84. Ellison, "Cooperative Movement," 80–81.

85. J. Woodworth to Charles Donnelly, August 29, 1927, Northern Pacific Railway Company Records, President's Subject File 365–42, MHS.

86. Cronon, *Nature's Metropolis*, 234.

87. Thompson, Church, and Jones, *PFE*, 57, 61; Kujovich, "Refrigerator Car," 466; Freidberg, *Fresh*, 66–67, 133–34.

88. White, *Great Yellow Fleet*, 12, 16–17.

89. Thompson, Church, and Jones, *PFE*, 60–61.

90. By 1924, Pacific Fruit Express operated 32,800 cars, Fruit Growers Express operated 16,266 cars, Western Fruit Express operated 5,123 cars, and the Northern Pacific operated 4,768 cars. "Refrigeration Test Trip, June 19th to July 1st, 1924, conducted by the Standardization Department of the California Fruit Exchange," box 28, Yakima Valley Growers-Shippers Association Records, 1917–1981, MASC; White, *Great Yellow Fleet*, 20.

91. Mechanically refrigerated railcars did not come into use until the mid-1950s. Iced refrigerated cars were not completely phased out until the 1970s. Entze, "Importance of the Refrigerated Rail Car."

92. The number of cars originated by all rail carriers in the country grew from 4,582,537 in 1899 to 19,726,069 in 1919, a 330 percent increase in traffic. These numbers do not provide a clear correlation to the increased use of refrigerated cars because they include not only cars carrying all fresh fruits and vegetables, but also those carrying dried and canned products. However, these figures indicate the tremendous growth of the fruit and vegetable industries in the first decades of the twentieth century. Dummeier, "Marketing of Pacific Coast Fruits," 11.

93. Data on the number of cars shipped from Washington State vary. The Northern Pacific, Great Northern, Washington State Department of Agriculture, and US Department of Agriculture all report different figures for the period in question. *First Report of the Department of Agriculture of the State of Washington to the Governor* (Olympia, WA, 1914), 76, box 5, Washington State Department

of Agriculture Records; *Second Report of the Department of Agriculture of the State of Washington to the Governor* (Olympia, WA, 1916), 119–21, box 5, Washington State Department of Agriculture Records; *Third Biennial Report of the Department of Agriculture of the State of Washington to the Governor* (Olympia, WA, 1918), 132, box 5, Washington State Department of Agriculture Records; US Department of Agriculture, *Yearbook of Agriculture 1935* (Washington, DC: Government Printing Office, 1935), 469.

94. William P. Kenney to J. M. Gruber, December 18, 1915, Great Northern Railway Company Records, President's Subject File 6267, MHS.

95. Nationwide, railroads owned 14,500 cars in 1900 and over 39,000 cars by 1910. White, *Great Yellow Fleet*, 12; Thomas Cooper, "The Relation of the Producer and the Railroad in Marketing Farm Products" (paper given at the First Annual Short Course, Agriculture and Horticulture, Yakima, Washington, February 20, 1913), Northern Pacific Railway Company Records, President's Subject File 1787, MHS; William P. Kenney to J. M. Gruber, December 18, 1915, and J. M. Gruber to Louis W. Hill, November 24, 1915, Great Northern Railway Company Records, President's Subject File 6267, MHS.

96. "Car Shortage Stirs Wenatchee," *Wenatchee Daily World*, November 1, 1913.

97. "Wenatchee Car Famine Broken," *Spokesman Review* (Spokane, WA), November 2, 1913.

98. W. C. Watrous to Carl R. Gray, November 11, 1913, Great Northern Railway Company Records, President's Subject File 6159, MHS.

99. "General Fruit Notes of Northwest Sections," *Better Fruit* 3, no. 5 (November 1908): 30.

100. Assistant to President to W. D. Scott, November 5, 1913; J. M. Gruber to C. H. Unwin, March 5, 1914; J. M. Gruber to H. H. Parkhouse, August 28, 1914; J. M. Gruber to Ralph Budd, September 21, 1914; J. M. Gruber to Ralph Budd, February 24, 1915; Ralph Budd to G. H. Emerson, August 19, 1915; G. H. Emerson to Ralph Budd, September 8, 1915, Great Northern Railway Company Records, President's Subject File 7096, MHS.

101. A. Crowl to Louis Hill, December 7, 1915; J. M. Gruber to Ralph Budd, January 5, 1916, Great Northern Railway Company Records, President's Subject File 7096, MHS.

102. J. M. Gruber to Ralph Budd, January 5, 1916; memo, March 20, 1918; W. J. Mooney to I. C. Watrous, June 17, 1919, Great Northern Railway Company Records, President's Subject File 7096, MHS

103. Thompson, Church, and Jones, *PFE*, 9.

104. W. H. Wilson to J. M. Rapelje, January 6, 1923; W. H. Wilson to Charles Donnelly, February 2, 1923; Chief Engineer to Charles Donnelly, March 6, 1923; W. H. Wilson to J. M. Rapelje, November 17, 1922, Northern Pacific Railway Company Records, President's File 1094–19, MHS; H. C. James Jr. to J. M. Rapelje,

NOTES TO CHAPTER 4   247

July 15, 1924, Northern Pacific Railway Company Records, President's File 1094–15, MHS; Charles Donnelly to Howard Elliott, January 29, 1923, Northern Pacific Railway Company Records, President's File 1094–14, MHS.

105. Thompson, Church, and Jones, *PFE*, 345.

106. George C. Stiles, "Hints to Shippers and Receivers of Fruit," *Better Fruit* 1, no. 8 (February 1907): 16–19.

107. J. G. Woodworth to C. B. Cooper, November 7, 1912, Northern Pacific Railway Company Records, President's Subject File E 134, MHS.

108. Yakima Valley Fruit Growers Association to Ira P. Englehart, December 27, 1912, and Ira P. Englehart to George T. Reid, January 6, 1913, Northern Pacific Railway Company Records, President's Subject File E 134, MHS.

109. George T. Reid to E. C. Blanchard, February 10, 1913, Northern Pacific Railway Company Records, President's Subject File E 134, MHS.

110. Maynard, *Marketing Northwestern Apples*, 13.

111. R. W. Clark to Jule M. Hannaford, August 20, 1918, Northern Pacific Railway Company Records, President's Subject File 1787-8, MHS.

112. I. L. Plette to R. H. Aishton, August 20, 1918, Northern Pacific Railway Company Records, President's Subject File 1787-8, MHS.

113. Maynard, *Marketing Northwestern Apples*, 83–84.

114. Duddy, *Cold Storage Industry*, 4–7.

115. In 1898, cold-storage warehouses held an estimated 800,000 barrels of apples. Five years later, storage had increased to 2,300,000 barrels. Beech, *Apples of New York*, 14.

116. "To the Public," *Yakima Herald*, February 17, 1904; "Ice Plant in Operation," *Wenatchee Daily World*, May 8, 1907.

117. Ramsey et al., *Handling and Storage*, 2.

118. Warehouse photograph, *Better Fruit* 1, no. 9 (March 1907): 8.

119. C. L. Durkee to Louis Hill, July 31, 1912, Great Northern Railway Company Records, President's Subject File 4369, MHS.

120. Thomas Cooper, "The Relation of the Producer and the Railroad in Marketing Farm Products" (paper given at the First Annual Short Course, Agriculture and Horticulture, Yakima, Washington, February 20, 1913), Northern Pacific Railway Company Records, President's Subject File 1787, MHS.

121. Cooper, "Relation of the Producer."

122. C. W. Burnham to Louis Hill, December 14, 1911, Great Northern Railway Company Records, President's Subject File 4369, MHS.

123. Wenatchee Fruit Growers Union et al. to Carl R. Gray, September 14, 1912; Carl R. Gray to Wenatchee Fruit Growers Union et al., September 17, 1912, Great Northern Railway Company Records, President's Subject File 4383, MHS.

124. Cooper, "Relation of the Producer."

125. Howard Elliott to George T. Reid, April 2, 1913, Northern Pacific Railway Company Records, President's Subject File 1787, MHS.

126. Elliott based his estimated gross on ten thousand outbound fruit cars charged $200 each for shipping. Howard Elliott to George T. Reid, April 2, 1913, Northern Pacific Railway Company Records, President's Subject File 1787, MHS.
127. George Reid to Jule M. Hannaford, April 22, 1914, Northern Pacific Railway Company Records, box 134.B.16.8.F, MHS.
128. Duddy, *Cold Storage Industry*, 13, 95.
129. Zaragoza, "Apple Capital," 85–90.
130. Stoll, *Fruits of Natural Advantage*, 83.

CHAPTER 5

1. U. Grant Border, "Co-operation in Advertising the Apple," *Better Fruit* 8, no. 3 (September 1913): 18.
2. "Boxed Apple and Nearby Markets," *Fruit Trade Journal and Produce Record*, January 6, 1923.
3. Leach, *Land of Desire*, 3–4.
4. Trachtenberg, *Incorporation of America*, 130.
5. Leach, *Land of Desire*, 40–41; Trachtenberg, *Incorporation of America*, 136–37.
6. Levinson, *Great A&P*, 76–78, 125.
7. Trachtenberg, *Incorporation of America*, 135–36.
8. Erdman, *California Fruit Growers Exchange*, 24.
9. "Winesap Apples to President," *Wenatchee Daily World*, May 18, 1909; "President Enjoys Apples," *Wenatchee Daily World*, June 2, 1909; "Mme. Bernhardt Eats Local Apples," *Wenatchee Daily World*, August 29, 1912.
10. Louis Hill to M. O. Tibbits, February 3, 1908, Great Northern Railway Company Records, President's Subject File 4369, MHS.
11. Howard Elliott to Robert Jones, April 19, 1913, Northern Pacific Railway Company Records, President's Subject File 1787, MHS.
12. Jule M. Hannaford to W. F. Gwin, June 24, 1913, Northern Pacific Railway Company Records, President's Subject File 1787, MHS.
13. "King of Apple Bids You Come," foreword to *Third National Apple Show, Spokane, WA, November 14–19, and Chicago, November 28–December 4* (pamphlet), Great Northern Railway Company Records, President's Subject File 4464, MHS.
14. *National Apple Show Bulletin and Premium List* 2, no. 1 (July 1909), Second Exhibition, November 15–20, Spokane, WA, Great Northern Railway Company Records, President's Subject File 4464, MHS.
15. Harry J. Neely to Louis Hill, November 16, 1908, Great Northern Railway Company Records, President's Subject File 4464, MHS.
16. Harry J. Neely to Louis Hill, December 15, 1908, Great Northern Railway Company Records, President's Subject File 4464, MHS; Unknown to A. M. Cleland, December 14, 1908, Northern Pacific Railway Company Records, President's Subject File 1427-A, MHS; *National Apple Show Bulletin* 1, no. 4 (January

1909): 1–16, Northern Pacific Railway Company Records, President's Subject File 1427-A, MHS.

17. H. M. Gilbert to Howard Elliott, December 19, 1908, Northern Pacific Railway Company Records, President's Subject File 1427-A, MHS.

18. Harry J. Neely to Louis Hill, November 16, 1908, Great Northern Railway Company Records, President's Subject File 4464, MHS; "Charles H. Barnes Praises Apples Show," *Yakima Herald*, December 9, 1908.

19. "Cost Him $2000 to Win the Prize," *Yakima Herald*, December 16, 1908.

20. "Wenatchee First," *Yakima Herald*, December 16, 1908; "Yakima Man Sore Because He Lost Prize," *Wenatchee Daily World*, December 14, 1908.

21. "Wenatchee Goes Wild with Enthusiasm" and "What the Big Victory Means to the Valley," *Wenatchee Daily World*, December 12, 1908.

22. "Gilbert Apples Going to London," *Yakima Herald*, December 23, 1908; "Apples to New York and England," *Wenatchee Daily World*, December 14, 1908.

23. Louis Hill to E. F. C. Van Dissel (VP Apple Show), June 12, 1909, Great Northern Railway Company Records, President's Subject File 4464, MHS.

24. Louis Hill to Harry J. Neely, October 21, 1909; Harry J. Neely to Louis Hill, October 25, 1909, Great Northern Railway Company Records, President's Subject File 4464, MHS; W. I. Moody to Howard Elliott, November 1, 1909, Northern Pacific Railway Company Records, President's Subject File 1427-A, MHS; James L. Gibson of Simons, Shuttleworth & French Co. to Louis Hill, October 13, 1909, Great Northern Railway Company Records, President's Subject File 4464, MHS.

25. H. M. Gilbert to Howard Elliott, September 9, 1909; Howard Elliott to Ren Rice, September 13, 1909; Howard Elliott to Ren Rice, September 18, 1909; E. F. Cartier Van Dissel to Howard Elliott, October 12, 1909, Northern Pacific Railway Company Records, President's Subject File 1427-A, MHS; "Accepts Rules; Will Exhibit," *Yakima Herald*, October 13, 1909; *National Apple Show Bulletin and Premium List* 2, no. 4 (December 1909), Great Northern Railway Company Records, President's Subject File 4464, MHS.

26. "Hill Support Withdrawn from Spokane Apple Show," *Wenatchee Daily World*, August 18, 1910.

27. Ren Rice to Louis Hill, June 7, 1910, Great Northern Railway Company Records, President's Subject File 4464, MHS.

28. H. M. Gilbert to Elliott, March 22, 1910, Northern Pacific Railway Company Records, President's Subject File 1427-B, MHS.

29. H. N. Kennedy, General Agent, to Howard Elliott, December 13, 1910, Northern Pacific Railway Company Records, President's Subject File 1427-B, MHS.

30. Jule M. Hannaford to Louis W. Hill and E. D. Sewall, April 30, 1914, Northern Pacific Railway Company Records, President's Subject File 1427-E, MHS; Louis W. Hill to Waldo Paine, August 8, 1911, Northern Pacific Railway Company Records, President's Subject File 1427-D, MHS.

31. George Reid to J. D. Farrell and H. B. Earling, September 29, 1915, Northern Pacific Railway Company Records, President's File E-119, MHS.
32. Waldo Paine to Jule M. Hannaford, May 22, 1918, Northern Pacific Railway Company Records, President's Subject File 1427-E, MHS.
33. "Long Live King Pip IX! Apple Monarch Summons All to Week of Festivities," *Spokesman Review* (Spokane, WA), November 19, 1916.
34. "The Seattle Apple Show," *Yakima Valley Progress* 3 (January 1922): 14.
35. J. C. Roth to R. A. Jennings, March 7, 1913, Northern Pacific Railway Company Records, President's Subject File 1787, MHS.
36. W. W. Butler to Thomas Cooper, May 24, 1911, Northern Pacific Railway Company Records, President's Subject File 1787, MHS.
37. W. F. Gwin to Howard Elliott, June 13, 1913, Northern Pacific Railway Company Records, President's Subject File 1787, MHS.
38. U. Grant Border, "Co-operation in Advertising the Apple," *Better Fruit* 8, no. 3 (September 1913): 16, 19.
39. Union Pacific, *150 Recipes for Apple Dishes*.
40. Both U. Grant Border and H. E. Shepard mentioned this book in their addresses to the International Apple Shippers' Convention in 1913. Border credited the book to a "Miss Mackey" of Washington State College in Pullman. Another version with many of the same recipes was republished in 1918 under the title *Housekeeper's Apple Book* when Mackay was an instructor of domestic economy at Schenley High School in Pittsburgh, Pennsylvania. The revised version contained more information on the nutritional value of the apple than the 1913 edition. Border, "Co-operation in Advertising the Apple," 16; H. E. Shepard, "The Northwest Fruit Industry," *Better Fruit* 8, no. 5 (November 1913): 15; Mackay, *Housekeeper's Apple Book*.
41. Mackay, *Housekeeper's Apple Book*, 1–3.
42. Mackay, *Two Hundred and Nine Ways*, 14, 22.
43. Gordon, *Comic Strips*, 32.
44. Gordon, 48, 55.
45. *Wenatchee Daily World*, September 20, 1912.
46. "About Fruit and Fruit People," *Better Fruit* 8, no. 5 (November 1913): 39.
47. *New York Times*, October 11, 1925.
48. *New York Times*, October 22, 1914.
49. *New York Times*, October 19–21, 1914.
50. Fahey, *Inland Empire*, 114; "Last Bite: The Amazing Saga of the Skookum Logo," *Good Fruit Grower*, April 1, 2007, https://www.goodfruit.com/last-bite-30/.
51. Ellison, "Cooperative Movement," 86–87.
52. "The Skookum Injuns," Skookum Packers Association, 1927, author's collection.
53. Melanie Eastman, "Everything Skookum: Let the Conversation Begin," *Wenatchee World*, May 5, 2016; Lyn Kelley, "Tribal Leader to Share 'The Indian

Side of the Story' at Wenatchee Valley Museum and Cultural Center," *Gazette-Tribune* (Oroville, WA), May 6, 2016; "The Skookum Indian," *Wenatchee World*, July 3, 2008.

54. No. 15614, United States of America, Department of the Interior, Patent Office, March 28, 1911, box 8, Elon James Gilbert Papers, 1890–1977, MASC.

55. "Big Y Advertising for 1920 Announced," *"Big Y" Bulletin* 1, no. 3 (June 1920): 1.

56. "Annual Report of General Manager," *"Big Y" Bulletin* 3, no. 5 (February 1923): 4.

57. "Use Big Red Apple as Wenatchee Trademark," *Wenatchee Daily World*, October 4, 1912.

58. Interview with James S. Crutchfield, December 20, 1912, Northern Pacific Railway Company Records, President's Subject File 1787, MHS.

59. "Synopsis of Agents' Reports Relative to Market Standing and Reputation of Wenatchee and Yakima Valley Apples," February 1914, Northern Pacific Railway Company Records, President's Subject File 1787, MHS.

60. Jule M. Hannaford to C. C. Burdick, March 25, 1914, Northern Pacific Railway Company Records, President's Subject File 1787, MHS.

61. J. A. Warman, "Cooperation among the Apple Growers," *Northwest Fruit Grower* 3, no. 5 (November 1921): 41.

62. "Skookum Displays Distributed during 1919–1920," *Northwest Fruit Grower* 1, no. 1 (July 1920): 22.

63. "Skookum," *Northwest Fruit Grower* 3, no. 6 (December 1921): 18.

64. "More Co-operation Needed," *Northwest Fruit Grower* 1, no. 4 (October 1920): 24.

65. Herbert B. Cash, *Annual Report on Publicity, Results and Awards for 1923 National Apple Week* (International Apple Shippers' Association), Great Northern Railway Company Records, President's Subject File 11270, MHS.

66. Newsletter, November 10, 1923, International Apple Shippers' Association, Great Northern Railway Company Records, President's Subject File 11270, MHS.

67. Memo to employees, October 30, 1930, Northern Pacific Railway Company Records, President's Subject File 356–42, MHS; menus, Great Northern Railway Company Records, Advertising and Publicity Department, Files 1048 and 1049, MHS.

68. Menu, Great Northern Railway Company Records, President's Subject File 648, MHS.

69. Northern Pacific General Passenger Dept. to R. G. Phillips, International Apple Shippers' Association, December 6, 1922, Northern Pacific Railway Company Records, President's Subject File 356–42, MHS; B. O. Johnson to R. W. Clark, General Traffic Manager, October 20, 1927, Northern Pacific Railway Company Records, President's Subject File 356–42, MHS.

70. "Annual Report on Publicity, Results and Awards for 1923 National Apple Week," Great Northern Railway Company Records, President's Subject File 11270, MHS.

71. Jim Beaver, "Jack Holt Biography," Internet Movie Database, accessed July 29, 2019, https://www.imdb.com/name/nm0392442/bio?ref_=nm_ov_bio_sm; Gary Brumburgh, "Billie Dove Biography," Internet Movie Database accessed July 29, 2019, https://www.imdb.com/name/nm0235521/bio?ref_=nm_ov_bio_sm.

72. *Wenatchee Daily World*, November 12, 1938.

73. C. W. Moore to Loren H. Milliman, editor of *Better Fruit*, November 7, 1938, Great Northern Railway Company Records, President's Subject File 11270, MHS.

74. Newsletter, International Apple Shippers' Association, November 10, 1923, Great Northern Railway Company Records, President's Subject File 11270, MHS.

75. Yakima Valley Traffic and Credit Association Committee on National Apple Week, 1927 Apple Week publicity scrapbook, MASC; "Huge Apple Pie Costing $1000 Is Produced Today," *Yakima Daily Republic*, October 15, 1927.

76. "Arsenic in American Apples," *Times* (London), April 1, 1892; Sampson Morgan, "Arsenic in American Apples," *Times* (London), April 2, 1892; "They Like Our Apples: English People Refuse to Be Frightened by an Arsenic 'Scare,'" *Washington Post*, August 1, 1892.

77. "'Apples for Health' Plan Framed," *Better Fruit* 21, no. 4 (October 1926): 8.

78. Ralph Budd to Charles Donnelly and Carl R. Gray, June 14, 1927, Northern Pacific Railway Company Records, President's Subject File 365–42, MHS.

79. William P. Kenney to Ralph Budd, June 1, 1927, Great Northern Railway Company Records, President's Subject File 12569, MHS.

80. Shapiro, *Perfection Salad*, 71–72.

81. Levenstein, *Revolution at the Table*, 153–54.

82. Union Pacific, *150 Recipes for Apple Dishes*, 5–6.

83. "Apple Men of 3 States Ready to Act," *Seattle Daily Times*, March 19, 1927; "Northwest Backs Fruit Men's Plan," *Seattle Post-Intelligencer*, March 19, 1927; "Kipp Plan Adopted by Apple Growers," *Oregonian* (Portland), March 19, 1927; Luthene C. Gilman to Ralph Budd, March 19, 1927, Great Northern Railway Company Records, President's Subject File 12334, MHS.

84. George Reid to Luthene C. Gilman, H. B. Earling, and Arthur A. Murphy, August 23, 1927, Northern Pacific Railway Company Records, President's Subject File 365–42, MHS.

85. Carl R. Gray to Ralph Budd with cc to Charles Donnelly, June 21, 1927, Northern Pacific Railway Company Records, President's Subject File 365–42, MHS.

86. George Reid to W. E. Coman, July 7, 1927, Northern Pacific Railway Company Records, President's Subject File 365–42, MHS.

NOTES TO CHAPTER 6   253

87. J. Woodworth to Charles Donnelly, August 29, 1927, Northern Pacific Railway Company Records, President's Subject File 365–42, MHS.

88. William P. Kenney to Ralph Budd, January 27, 1928, Great Northern Railway Company Records, President's Subject File 12490, MHS.

89. Wayne K. Davis, "Big Apple Advertising Body Organized," *Better Fruit* 21, no. 1 (July 1926): 8.

90. "Northwest Apples to Be Preferred," *"Big Y" Bulletin* 7, no. 9 (July 1927): 1, 6.

91. H. A. Glen to J. L. Burnham, Western Traffic Manager, March 22, 1928, Northern Pacific Railway Company Records, President's Subject File 365–42, MHS.

92. "Advice Asked on $5 for Campaign," *"Big Y" Bulletin* 8, no. 2 (December 1927): 1.

93. Correspondence indicates that the Northern Pacific pledged support to Apples for Health, provided that the other major railroads also pledged funds. By 1928, this condition had not been met, and the Northern Pacific closed its file on the matter. J. G. Woodworth, memorandum, July 10, 1928, Northern Pacific Railway Company Records, President's Subject File 365–42, MHS.

94. J. L. Burnham to R. W. Clark, General Traffic Manager, March 26, 1928, Northern Pacific Railway Company Records, President's Subject File 365–42, MHS.

95. The carload numbers for bananas are an estimated equivalent since bananas were shipped in steamships and measured in bunches or tons. Charles E. Durst, "Bananas as a Competitor of American Grown Fruit," *Better Fruit* 23, no. 1 (July 1928): 5. For more on the history of the banana industry, see Koeppel, *Banana*.

96. "Editorial Notes," *Better Fruit* 25, no. 1 (July 1930): 14.

97. Earl R. French, "Consumer Demand for Apples in New York City," *Better Fruit* 23, no. 2 (August 1928): 7–8.

98. "Pacific Northwest Carlot Apple Shippers and Their Brands," *Better Fruit* 23, no. 2 (August 1928): 26–28.

CHAPTER 6

1. "Virginia Writer Has Sad Slant on Apples," *"Big Y" Bulletin* 11, no. 6 (May 1931): 7.

2. "The Apple Situation," *Better Fruit* 24, no. 6 (December 1929): 13.

3. Charles E. Durst, "Apple Prices, High or Low?," *Better Fruit* 25, no. 4 (October 1930): 14–15.

4. "Sell Apples . . . Apple Week," *Better Fruit* 25, no. 5 (November 1930): 5.

5. "Selling Apples by Jobless," *Better Fruit* 25, no. 6 (December 1930): 11.

6. Joseph Sicker to G. R. Merritt, November 24, 1930, Northern Pacific Railway Company Records, President's Subject File 1787, MHS.

7. "Apples Furnish Jobs to Hungry Thousands," *"Big Y" Bulletin* 10, no. 12 (November 1930): 2–3.

8. "Apple Sellers No Longer Need Charity," *"Big Y" Bulletin* 11, no. 1 (December 1930): 1; "Sell Apples in Yakima Too," *"Big Y" Bulletin* 11, no. 1 (December 1930): 2.

9. American Fruit Growers, "Thirteenth Annual Report to the Stockholders," June 30, 1933, Northern Pacific Railway Company Records, President's Subject File 1787-12, MHS.

10. Gwin, White & Prince to Wenoka and Pinnacle Growers, January 31, 1935, Northern Pacific Railway Company Records, President's Subject File 1787-12, MHS.

11. Agricultural Marketing Act of 1929, Public Law 10, 71st Cong., 1st Sess. (June 15, 1929), 11–19.

12. "Big Y Helps in Forming Board," *"Big Y" Bulletin* 9, no. 11 (October 1929): 1, 5.

13. "Meeting the Farm Board," *"Big Y" Bulletin* 9, no. 12 (November 1929): 2–3; "Marketing Aim of Law," *"Big Y" Bulletin* 10, no. 2 (January 1930): 1, 4–5.

14. Ellison, "Marketing Problems," 104.

15. Ellison, 105–6; "New Tariff Is Sales Barrier," *"Big Y" Bulletin* 10, no. 9 (July 1930): 1.

16. Valgren, "Agricultural Credits Act," 443; Edwy B. Reed, "How Federal Land Banks Serve the Farmer," *Better Fruit* 24, no. 5 (November 1929): 8.

17. J. W. Hebert, "Outlook Not Favorable," *"Big Y" Bulletin* 11, no. 4 (March 1931): 12.

18. Luthene C. Gilman to William P. Kenney, February 19, 1932; Thomas Balmer to Gilman, March 1, 1932, Great Northern Railway Company Records, President's Subject File 13574, MHS.

19. E. M. Willis to Charles Donnelly, March 7, 1932, Northern Pacific Railway Company Records, President's Subject File 11-10, MHS.

20. "Finance Group Designates 17 Loan Agencies," *St. Paul Pioneer Press*, February 8, 1932; "Loans Get O.K. of New Group," *Spokesman Review* (Spokane, WA), February 18, 1932.

21. "Reconstruction Finance Corporation Recognizes Northwest Fruit Ex.," *Chicago Packer*, February 27, 1932; William P. Kenney to Luthene C. Gilman, February 4, 1932; Ralph Budd to William P. Kenney, February 29, 1932; Luthene C. Gilman to William P. Kenney, March 4, 1932; Luthene C. Gilman to J. A. Lengby, March 11, 1932, Great Northern Railway Company Records, President's Subject File 13574, MHS.

22. Luthene C. Gilman to William P. Kenney, March 11, 1932, Great Northern Railway Company Records, President's Subject File 13574, MHS.

23. William P. Kenney to Luthene C. Gilman, March 21, 1932, Great Northern Railway Company Records, President's Subject File 13574, MHS.

24. Leuchtenburg, *Franklin Roosevelt*, 258.

NOTES TO CHAPTER 6   255

25. Undated report, ca. 1932, Northern Pacific Railway Company Records, President's Subject File 11–10, MHS.

26. W. F. Gwin to Luthene C. Gilman, March 20, 1932, Great Northern Railway Company Records, President's Subject File 13574, MHS.

27. Thomas Balmer to Luthene C. Gilman, March 1, 1932, Great Northern Railway Company Records, President's Subject File 13574, MHS.

28. H. M. Gilbert to H. E. Jones, March 8, 1932, Northern Pacific Railway Company Records, President's Subject File 11–10, MHS.

29. "Hebert Gives Report on Big Y Operations," *"Big Y" Bulletin* 12, no. 11 (March 1933): 4–5, 7.

30. "Railroads Take Stock in Yakima Fruit Loan Body," *Yakima Morning Herald*, March 22, 1932.

31. Luthene C. Gilman to William P. Kenney, March 28, 1932, Great Northern Railway Company Records, President's Subject File 13574, MHS.

32. C. W. White, General Manager Wenatchee District Cooperative Association to William P. Kenney, March 26, 1932, Great Northern Railway Company Records, President's Subject File 13574, MHS.

33. William P. Kenney to Luthene C. Gilman, September 7, 1932; Luthene C. Gilman to William P. Kenney, September 10, 1932, Great Northern Railway Company Records, President's Subject File 13574, MHS.

34. William P. Kenney to Luthene C. Gilman, March 30, 1932, Great Northern Railway Company Records, President's Subject File 13574, MHS.

35. William P. Kenney to Luthene C. Gilman, May 26, 1932, Great Northern Railway Company Records, President's Subject File 13574, MHS.

36. Luthene C. Gilman to William P. Kenney, July 23, 1932, Great Northern Railway Company Records, President's Subject File 13574, MHS.

37. George H. Bradshaw to W. E. Coman, October 14, 1932, Northern Pacific Railway Company Records, President's Subject File 11–10, MHS.

38. William P. Kenney to Luthene C. Gilman, June 24, 1932, Great Northern Railway Company Records, President's Subject File 13574, MHS.

39. Volney T. Boaz, "Through My Spectacles," *Better Fruit* 27, no. 3 (September 1932): 7.

40. Rufus Woods to Ralph Budd, William P. Kenney, Luthene C. Gilman, and W. E. Coman, December 29, 1934, Northern Pacific Railway Company Records, President's Subject File 1787–12, MHS.

41. Ralph Budd to Rufus Woods, January 9, 1935, Northern Pacific Railway Company Records, President's Subject File 1787–12, MHS.

42. Luthene C. Gilman to William P. Kenney, May 24, 1932; Luthene C. Gilman to William P. Kenney, May 28, 1932, Great Northern Railway Company Records, President's Subject File 13574, MHS.

43. Luthene C. Gilman to Rufus Woods, December 31, 1935, Northern Pacific Railway Company Records, President's Subject File 1787–12, MHS.

44. "Tie These Strings to Your Bank Book," *Better Fruit* 27, no. 11 (May 1933): 10; Bright, *Apples Galore!*, 66–67.

45. Carl R. Gray, Charles Donnelly, and William P. Kenney to Mr. Miller, February 27, 1933, Great Northern Railway Company Records, President's Subject File 13574, MHS.

46. "R.F.C. Would Aid Apple Growers," *Spokesman Review* (Spokane, WA), February 8, 1933; Luthene C. Gilman to William P. Kenney, March 22, 1933, Great Northern Railway Company Records, President's Subject File 13574, MHS.

47. Washington Crop and Livestock Reporting Service, *Washington Tree Fruits*, 2.

48. A. B. Chase, County Agent, to E. C. Leedy, Ag. Dev. Agent, October 13, 1932, Great Northern Railway Company Records, President's Subject File 13769, MHS.

49. A. C. Rich, "Cutting Costs with an Axe," *Better Fruit* 27, no. 8 (February 1933): 14.

50. "An Old Fashioned Farm," *"Big Y" Bulletin* 12, no. 3 (May 1932): 2.

51. Donald L. Saunders, "Make Your Orchard Supply Your Table," *Better Fruit* 27, no. 10 (April 1933): 10.

52. Farm Credit Administration, "History of FCA and the FCS," accessed November 3, 2020, https://www.fca.gov/about/history-of-fca#historyfcafcs; Bright, *Apples Galore!*, 68–70.

53. Lowitt, *New Deal and the West*, 138–39.

54. Quoted in Lowitt, 139.

55. Lowitt, 140, 178.

56. Lowitt, 142.

57. E. C. Leedy to William P. Kenney, September 12, 1932, Great Northern Railway Company Records, President's Subject File 13769, MHS.

58. Roza Irrigation District, "History of the Roza," accessed November 2, 2020, https://www.roza.org/about-us/history-of-the-roza/; Bureau of Reclamation, "Projects and Facilities," accessed November 2, 2020, https://www.usbr.gov/projects/facilities.php?state=Washington; Simonds, *Columbia Basin Project*, 31, 65–66.

59. Lowitt, *New Deal and the West*, 143.

60. Newbill, "Farmers and Wobblies," 80–82, 85; Daniel, "Wobblies on the Farm," 170.

61. Landis and Brooks, *Farm Labor*, 18, 32.

62. Daniel, "Wobblies on the Farm," 174.

63. Landis and Brooks, *Farm Labor*, 8.

64. Blanchard, *Caravans to the Northwest*, 43.

65. Newbill, "Farmers and Wobblies," 83–84.

66. Landis and Brooks, *Farm Labor*, 18, 32, 41–42, 64, 71; Lowitt, *New Deal and the West*, 142.

67. "To Harvest or Not to Harvest," *Better Fruit* 27, no. 3 (September 1932): 8.

68. Irving W. Smith, "Delicious as the Keystone Variety," *Skookum News* 10, no. 2 (February 1936): 3.

69. A. W. Peterson, "The Central Sales Exchange Plan for Apples," *Better Fruit* 27, no. 9 (March 1933): 3.

70. William E. Berney, "Let's Control the Surplus," *Better Fruit* 27, no. 9 (March 1933): 3.

71. Ellison, "Marketing Problems," 107–8.

72. Washington Agricultural Adjustment Act, *Session Laws of the State of Washington Passed at the Extraordinary Session* (1933), chap. 12.

73. "Public Hearing with Reference to a Proposed Marketing Agreement Embodying Code of Ethics, Rules of Fair Practice and Prices in the Marketing of Deciduous Tree Fruits" (Ellensburg, WA, July 20, 1934), box 13, Washington State Department of Agriculture Records.

74. "Order 128 Relating to the Marketing of Deciduous Tree Fruits for the State of Washington" (August 11, 1934), box 23, Washington State Department of Agriculture Records.

75. "Public Hearing with Reference to a Proposed Marketing Agreement."

76. "Public Hearing with Reference to a Proposed Marketing Agreement."

77. Editorial, *Better Fruit* 10, no. 2 (August 1935): 10.

78. Levinson, *Great A&P*, 88–89, 100.

79. "Safeway Stores Help Growers Move Apple Surplus," *Better Fruit* 30, no. 6 (December 1935): 16.

80. "President's Report, 1935," Skookum Packers Association, Skookum Records Collection 83–15, box 1, folder 9, Wenatchee Valley Museum and Cultural Center.

81. J. M. Crawford to W. E. Coman, June 4, 1936, Northern Pacific Railway Company Records, President's Subject File 43–17, MHS.

82. M. S. Foster to Luthene C. Gilman, June 1, 1936, Northern Pacific Railway Company Records, President's Subject File 43–17, MHS.

83. C. E. Chase, lecture, Idaho State Horticultural Association Convention, Boise, ID (February 4, 1937); C. E. Chase to Walter J. Robinson, November 2, 1937, box 25, Washington State Department of Agriculture Records.

84. Editorial, *Better Fruit* 30, no. 10 (April 1936): 14.

85. W. E. Coman to Charles Donnelly, June 6, 1936, Northern Pacific Railway Company Records, President's Subject File 43–17, MHS.

86. J. M. Crawford to W. E. Coman, June 4, 1936, Northern Pacific Railway Company Records, President's Subject File 43–17, MHS.

87. "Industrial Advertising," *Wenoka Arrowhead* 5, no. 3 (September 1935): 6; "Cooperatives Endorse Industrial Program," *Skookum News* 10, no. 6 (June 1936): 1.

88. "Big Y Rejects Industry Plan," *"Big Y" Bulletin* 15, no. 12 (July–August 1936): 1.

89. W. E. Coman to Charles Donnelly, August 5, 1936, Northern Pacific Railway Company Records, President's Subject File 47–13, MHS.

90. "Growers Sign in Advertising Move," *Yakima Daily Republic*, July 2, 1936; "$200,000 Ahead for Apple Ads," *Spokesman Review* (Spokane, WA), August 4, 1936; "Advertising Plan Becomes Reality," *Yakima Daily Republic*, August 13, 1936; *Yakima Daily Republic*, August 25, 1936.

91. George W. Coburn, "Report on Sales and Marketing Statistics," Skookum Packers Association, Skookum Records Collection 83–15, box 1, folder 10, Wenatchee Valley Museum and Cultural Center.

92. "Cooperatives Vote against Joining Move," *Yakima Daily Republic*, June 3, 1936; "PNF Planned Big Advertising and Selling Campaign," *Better Fruit* 31, no. 1 (August 1936): 6; "Doc Apple," *"Big Y" Bulletin* 16, no. 2 (October–November 1936): 6.

93. Washington State Apples, Inc., *Annual Report, August 1936–July 1937*, 4–5, 8–9.

94. C. E. Chase, lecture, Idaho State Horticultural Association Convention, Boise, ID (February 4, 1937), box 25, Washington State Department of Agriculture Records.

95. "'37 Apple Ad Sign-Up Opens," *Wenatchee Daily World*, January 14, 1937; "Minority Group Blocks Move to Push Fruit Sale," *Yakima Morning Herald*, February 24, 1937.

96. "Committee of Fifteen May Support Compulsory Advertising Law," *Wenatchee Daily World*, February 12, 1937.

97. "Apple 'Ad' Commission Proposed," *Wenatchee Daily World*, February 25, 1937.

98. "Fruit Producers Support Bill to Promote Apples," *Yakima Morning Herald*, February 26, 1937.

99. "Senate Gets Apple Ad Bill," *Wenatchee Daily World*, March 2, 1937.

100. "Senate Approves New State Apple Advertising Bill," *Yakima Morning Herald*, March 4, 1937; "Governor Gets Apple 'Ad' Bill," *Wenatchee Daily World*, March 4, 1937; "Apple 'Ad' Bill Signed," *Wenatchee Daily World*, March 18, 1937.

101. State Apple Advertising Commission Act, *Session Laws of the State of Washington, Twenty-Fifth Session* (1937), chap. 195.

102. Editorial, *Better Fruit* 31, no. 9 (April 1937): 12.

103. "Everyone Contributes to Industrial Advertising," *Wenoka Arrowhead* 7, no. 1 (May 1937): 2.

104. Editorial, *Better Fruit* 31, no. 11 (June 1937): 12.

105. Washington State Apples, Inc., *Annual Report, August 1936–July 1937*, 1; Washington State Apple Advertising Commission, *Season's Report, August 1937–July 1938*, 4.

106. Washington State Apple Advertising Commission, *Season's Report, August 1937–July 1938*, 5, 25.

NOTES TO CHAPTER 6

107. Agriculture Experiment Station Established at Wenatchee Act, *Session Laws of the State of Washington, Twenty-Fifth Session* (1937), chap. 25.
108. Luce, *Washington State Fruit Industry*, 33; Bright, *Apples Galore!*, 29–34.
109. Bright, *Apples Galore!*, 32–34.
110. Lowitt, *New Deal and the West*, 37.
111. E. H. Sargent, "Financing Needs: The Wenatchee-Okanogan Fruit District of the State of Washington," January 1937, Great Northern Railway Company Records, President's Subject File 15272, MHS.
112. Thomas Balmer to William P. Kenney, March 3, 1938, Great Northern Railway Company Records, President's Subject File 15272, MHS.
113. James S. Crutchfield to William P. Kenney, April 22, 1938, Great Northern Railway Company Records, President's Subject File 15272, MHS.
114. James S. Crutchfield to William P. Kenney, April 23, 1938, Great Northern Railway Company Records, President's Subject File 15272, MHS.
115. William P. Kenney to Thomas Balmer, April 23, 1938, Great Northern Railway Company Records, President's Subject File 15272, MHS.
116. William P. Kenney to Thomas Balmer, August 19, 1938, Great Northern Railway Company Records, President's Subject File 13574, MHS.
117. "Counter Attack Launched on War," *Better Fruit* 34, no. 4 (October 1939): 3.
118. "Hebert Discusses Market Situation," *"Big Y" Bulletin* 17, no. 3 (September 1939): 1–2.
119. "Army to Buy 12,000,000 Boxes," *Better Fruit* 37, no. 2 (August 1942): 3.
120. "Apple Named 'Victory Food' Special October 5–31," *Better Fruit* 37, no. 4 (October 1942): 9.
121. Special Letter No. 1545 to Members of the International Apple Association, October 6, 1944, Great Northern Railway Company Records, President's Subject File 13362, MHS.
122. "Gwin Finds Big Y Apples at Guam," *"Big Y" Bulletin* 20, no. 11 (March 1945): 2.
123. W. W. Prince to Balmer, December 9, 1944, Great Northern Railway Company Records, President's Subject File 14364, MHS.
124. "Big Y Labor Policy," *"Big Y" Bulletin* 12, no. 6 (August 1932): 2; "Big Y Jobs to Big Y Workers in Valley," *"Big Y" Bulletin* 18, no. 6 (August–September 1941): 1.
125. "Plans Are Announced to Alleviate Farm Labor Shortages," *Skookum News* 16, no. 2 (April 1942): 2; "Volunteers Help Pick Apple Crop," *"Big Y" Bulletin* 19, no. 4 (October–November 1942): 1.
126. "Commission Takes Lead in Drive for Harvest Labor," *Better Fruit* 37, no. 3 (September 1942): 7; "Apple Corps Saves Apple Crop," *Better Fruit* 37, no. 5 (November 1942): 3; Balmer to Gavin, October 27, 1942, Great Northern Railway Company Records, President's Subject File 14364, MHS; "'42 Apple Crop Saved, Says U.S. Farm Aid," *Seattle Post-Intelligencer*, November 21, 1942.

127. "Labor Supply for 1943 Concerns Growers," *"Big Y" Bulletin* 19, no. 5 (December 1942–January 1943): 3.

128. "Apple Crop Harvesting Favorable," *Seattle Post-Intelligencer*, October 31, 1943; "Save the State's Apple Crop," *Seattle Post-Intelligencer*, October 2, 1944.

129. "Homefront Mobilizing Again," *Better Fruit* 38, no. 4 (October 1943): 3; Gamboa, *Mexican Labor and World War II*, 50, 57, 65; "Manager's Report," *"Big Y" Bulletin* 20, no. 10 (January–February 1945): 7.

130. "Valley Residents Sign for Harvest," *"Big Y" Bulletin* 19, no. 8 (April–May 1943): 1, 4–5; "15,000 Yakima Valley People Pledge Aid in Fruit Harvest," *Better Fruit* 37, no. 12 (June 1943): 19.

131. "'Green' Workers Need Training," *Better Fruit* 38, no. 4 (October 1943): 6; "14 Year Old Girl Handled 12-Foot Ladder," *Better Fruit* 38, no. 4 (October 1943): 11.

132. "War Shortages Add to Burden of Pest Control," *"Big Y" Bulletin* 19, no. 6 (February 1943): 3; "Manager's Report," *"Big Y" Bulletin* 20, no. 3 (February 1944): 4; Ivan L. Plette to Bert L. Baker, January 21, 1942, box 24, Yakima Valley Growers-Shippers Association Records, 1917–1981, MASC; "Container Problem Grows Acute," *Better Fruit* 37, no. 12 (June 1943): 3.

133. "Hebert Reviews Ceiling Sales," *"Big Y" Bulletin* 20, no. 2 (January 1944): 1.

134. "Hebert Discusses O.P.A. Apple Order," *"Big Y" Bulletin* 20, no. 3 (February 1944): 1.

135. "Bill Brown Reports on Bulk Shipments," *Better Fruit* 38, no. 7 (January 1944): 14.

136. "California Handler Opposes Bulk Cars," *Better Fruit* 38, no. 12 (June 1944): 17, 20; C. E. Chase, "Washington Industry Faces Difficulty," *Better Fruit* 38, no. 9 (March 1944): 17.

137. *Ladies' Home Journal*, February 1945.

138. "Food Business Undergoing Many Changes in Wartime," *Better Fruit* 35, no. 12 (June 1942): 8–10; Safeway advertisement, *Better Fruit* 38, no. 3 (September 1943): 19.

139. "Quality Apples," *Better Fruit* 39, no. 4 (October 1944): 13.

CHAPTER 7

1. D. L. Mansell, "Apple Pie Order," *Canton (OH) Repository*, 1946, box 70, Yakima Valley Growers-Shippers Association Records, 1917–1981, MASC.

2. C. E. Chase, "Washington Industry Faces Difficulty," *Better Fruit* 38, no. 9 (March 1944): 17.

3. "Lancaster Tells of Marketing Changes," *"Big Y" Bulletin* 22, no. 4 (March 1947): 5.

4. Ficken, "Rufus Woods," 75–78.

5. Pitzer, "A 'Farm-in-a-Day,'" 2, 5–6.

6. The Yakima Valley, which includes Benton, Kittitas, and Yakima Counties, has 69,117 acres in production with 47.6 million bearing trees. The Columbia Basin, which includes Adams, Franklin, and Grant Counties, has 64,910 acres in production with 53.5 million trees. Wenatchee, which includes Chelan, Douglas, and Okanogan Counties, has 34,021 acres in production with 17.5 million trees. "Columbia Basin Project," Bureau of Reclamation, November 16, 2020, https://www.usbr.gov/pn/grandcoulee/cbp/index.html; USDA/National Agricultural Statistics Service, *Washington Tree Fruit Acreage Report, 2017*, November 8, 2017, https://www.nass.usda.gov/Statistics_by_State/Washington/Publications/Fruit/2017/FT2017.pdf.

7. Washington Crop and Livestock Reporting Service, *Washington Tree Fruits*, 2.

8. Bright, *Apples Galore!*, 34; Wenatchee Tree Fruit Research and Extension Center, Washington State University, "About," accessed November 21, 2020, http://tfrec.cahnrs.wsu.edu/about/.

9. Luce, *Washington State Fruit Industry*, 59; Emily E. Hoover and Richard Marini, "Understanding Apple Tree Size; Dwarf, Semi-Dwarf and Standard," Extension Foundation, August 22, 2019, https://apples.extension.org/understanding-apple-tree-size-dwarf-semi-dwarf-and-standard/.

10. Shannon Dininny, "Trellis Guide for High Density Planting in the Works," *Good Fruit Grower*, August 16, 2016, https://www.goodfruit.com/trellis-guide-for-high-density-plantings-in-the-works/.

11. Guy K. Ames, "Dwarfing Apple Rootstocks: Pros and Cons," National Center for Appropriate Technology, December 27, 2019, https://www.ncat.org/pros-and-cons-of-dwarfing-apple-rootstocks/; Shannon Dininny, "Which Apple Rootstock Should You Grow With?," *Good Fruit Grower*, February 10, 2016, https://www.goodfruit.com/which-apple-rootstock-should-you-grow-with/; Morris and Luce, *Orchard Crowding*, 30–34; Ross Courtney, "Growing by the Acres," *Good Fruit Grower*, December 27, 2017, https://www.goodfruit.com/growing-by-the-acres/#:~:text=Apple%20trees%20stand%20at%20825,Wenatchee%20and%20the%20Yakima%20Valley.

12. National Agricultural Statistics Service, US Department of Agriculture, "Washington Apples 1889–2010," https://www.nass.usda.gov/Statistics_by_State/Washington/Publications/Historic_Data/fruit/apples.pdf; Cascadia Capital LLC, *Washington Tree Fruit Industry*.

13. Jill Scheffer, "Cleaning Up: New Model Remedies for Contaminated Historic Orchard Lands," Department of Ecology, State of Washington, June 3, 2021, https://ecology.wa.gov/Blog/Posts/June-2021/Learn-about-our-new-model-remedies-for-cleaning-up; Hood, "Apple Bites Back," 475.

14. Bright, *Apples Galore!*, 48–50; Berry-Caban, "DDT and Silent Spring," 19.

15. Conis, "Beyond Silent Spring."

16. Bright, *Apples Galore!*, 50.

17. Bright, 52.

18. Anton S. Horn, "Alar Can Improve Production Methods, Yields and Quality," *The Packer*, December 28, 1968, Northwest Horticultural Council Records, 1951–1976, MASC; Bright, *Apples Galore!*, 228–29.

19. US Department of Health and Human Services, National Toxicology Program, *14th Report on Carcinogens*, November 3, 2016, https://ntp.niehs.nih.gov/whatwestudy/assessments/cancer/roc/index.html#toc1.

20. The EPA based its figures on crop losses alone, whereas the earlier Washington study also accounted for the economic benefits of extended storage. Patricia Picone Mitchell, "Daminozide: A Chemical Controversy in the Orchards," *Washington Post*, October 2, 1985.

21. Bright, *Apples Galore!*, 232–33; Philip Shabecoff, "Hazard Reported in Apple Chemical," *New York Times*, February 2, 1989.

22. Sewell and Whyatt, *Intolerable Risk*, 2–4.

23. *60 Minutes*, "'A' Is for Apple" (originally aired February 26, 1989), https://www.youtube.com/watch?v=7mwrWgqF4Ac.

24. Philip Shabecoff, "Hazard Reported in Apple Chemical," *New York Times*, February 2, 1989.

25. Timothy Egan, "Yakima Valley Journal: Farming without Alar, Suffering with the Rest," *New York Times*, March 24, 1989; "Fruit Growers Pull Commercials to Protest Report by CBS on Alar," *New York Times*, May 7, 1989; Philip Shabecoff, "3 U.S. Agencies, to Allay Public's Fears, Declare Apples Safe," *New York Times*, March 17, 1989; Warren E. Leary, "Test Data Differ on Ripening Agent," *New York Times*, March 30, 1989; Philip Shabecoff, "Apple Industry Says It Will End Use of Chemical," *New York Times*, May 16, 1989; Philip Shabecoff, "Apple Chemical Being Removed in U.S. Market," *New York Times*, June 3, 1989.

26. "Government Will Buy Apples Left Over from Scare on Alar," *New York Times*, July 8, 1989; Timothy Egan, "Apple Growers Bruised and Bitter after Alar Scare," *New York Times*, July 9, 1991; Timothy Egan, "Yakima Valley Journal: Farming without Alar, Suffering with the Rest," *New York Times*, March 24, 1989.

27. Dominick Bonny, "From Alar to Organics," *Wenatchee Business Journal* 24, no. 11 (November 2010): 6.

28. David Granatstein and Elizabeth Kirby, "Recent Trends in Certified Organic Tree Fruit in Washington State: 2018," Washington State University Extension Service, April 2019, http://tfrec.cahnrs.wsu.edu/organicag/wp-content/uploads/sites/9/2019/04/WA_OrgTreeFruit_ann_rev2018.pdf.

29. "Landscape IPM: History of IPM," Texas A&M AgriLife Extension, accessed September 2, 2020, https://landscapeipm.tamu.edu/what-is-ipm/history-of-ipm/.

30. "Calculating the Value of Biological Control," *Good Fruit Grower*, April 1, 2013, https://www.goodfruit.com/calculating-the-value-of-biological-control/; Melissa Hansen, "Codling Moth Mating Disruption Reaches a Milestone," *Good Fruit Grower*, March 5, 2015, https://www.goodfruit.com/codling-moth-mating-disruption-reaches-a-milestone/; Matt Milkovich, "San Jose Scale Befuddled by

Pheromones," *Good Fruit Grower*, March 9, 2020, https://www.goodfruit.com/san-jose-scale-befuddled-by-pheromones/; Geraldine Warner, "New Pests Threaten IPM," *Good Fruit Grower*, March 5, 2014, https://www.goodfruit.com/new-pests-threaten-ipm/.

31. "Good to Know: Reflections on the Elder Statesmen of Apple and Pear IPM," *Good Fruit Grower*, March 1, 2020, https://www.goodfruit.com/good-to-know-reflections-on-the-elder-statesmen-of-apple-and-pear-ipm/; "Apple-Spider Mite," *Pacific Northwest Pest Management Handbook*, https://pnwhandbooks.org/insect/tree-fruit/apple/apple-spider-mite; "Calculating the Value of Biological Control," *Good Fruit Grower*, April 1, 2013, https://www.goodfruit.com/calculating-the-value-of-biological-control/.

32. "WSU Decision Aid System," WSU Tree Fruit, Washington State University, accessed September 11, 2020, http://treefruit.wsu.edu/tools-resources/wsu-decision-aid-system-das/.

33. Ross Courtney and T. J. Mullinax, "Growers Tracking Chemical Controversies Measure for Measure," *Good Fruit Grower*, December 26, 2019, https://www.goodfruit.com/growers-tracking-chemical-controversies-measure-for-measure/.

34. Don Jenkins, "Coronavirus Budget Hit Nixes Chlorpyrifos Review in Washington," *Capital Press*, April 9, 2020, https://www.capitalpress.com/ag_sectors/research/coronavirus-budget-hit-nixes-chlorpyrifos-review-in-washington/article_010866ee-79c3-11ea-baf2-9379ab3da151.html.

35. Geraldine Warner, "Insect-Resistant Varieties," *Good Fruit Grower*, October 1, 2012, https://www.goodfruit.com/insect-resistant-varieties/.

36. Kirk Johnson, "Hunting Down the Lost Apples of the Pacific Northwest," *New York Times*, May 29, 2017.

37. Futrell, *Good Apples*, 155; Sonneman, *Fruit Fields in My Blood*, 31.

38. News release, State Department of Agriculture, October 11, 1968; "Proposed Rules and Regulations of the State Board of Health Sanitation and Labor Camps" (October 4, 1968), chap. 248–60; J. M. Bloxom to Willard Wirtz, August 1, 1968, all in box 1, Northwest Horticultural Council Records, 1951–1976, MASC.

39. Futrell, *Good Apples*, 150.

40. Oscar Rosales-Castañeda, Maria Quintana, and James Gregory, "A History of Farm Labor Organizing, 1890–2009," Seattle Civil Rights and Labor History Project, University of Washington, accessed December 3, 2020, https://depts.washington.edu/civilr/farmwk_history.htm.

41. Futrell, *Good Apples*, 150.

42. Sonneman, *Fruit Fields in My Blood*, 15; Castañeda, Quintana, and Gregory, "History of Farm Labor Organizing."

43. "Special Report on Machine Harvesters," *American Fruit Grower*, September 1969, 9–11; Charles Kerr, "Apple-Shaking Machine Undergoes Experiment," *Wenatchee Daily World*, September 18, 1969.

44. Dan Wheat, "Quest for Robotic Apple Pickers Nearing Fruition," *Capital Press*, November 18, 2020, https://www.capitalpress.com/ag_sectors/orchards_nuts_vines/quest-for-robotic-apple-pickers-nearing-fruition/article_0b6a2992-29e5-11eb-9444-57f69b64fff0.html.

45. Heckman and Goldsborough, *Cooperative Marketing*, 67; Ross Courtney, "Finding Success the Cooperative Way," *Good Fruit Grower*, January 24, 2018.

46. "Big Y Brand Bulletin to the Trade," July 9, 1965, box 5, Yakima Valley Growers-Shippers Association Records, 1917–1981, MASC; "Snokist Focuses on Cannery," *Good Fruit Grower*, April 1, 2008; Molly Rosbach, "Snokist Announces Bankruptcy Filing," *Tri-City Herald* (Kennewick, WA), December 9, 2011; "Del Monte Foods Completes Acquisition of Snokist Growers' Assets," *Food Processing Technology*, June 7, 2012, https://www.foodprocessing-technology.com/uncategorised/newsdel-monte-foods-acquires-snokist-growers/.

47. "The Skookum Indian," *Wenatchee World*, July 3, 2008.

48. Wadsworth, *Cooperative Restructuring*, 5, 26; Linda Barta, "Old News—Leman Named Sportsman of the Year," *Wenatchee World*, April 12, 2018.

49. Jonelle Mejica, "Chelan Fruit Announces New Interim CEO," *Good Fruit Grower*, December 18, 2018.

50. Stratton, *Tree Top*, ix–xiii.

51. O'Rourke, *World Apple Market*, 14.

52. "Frozen Concentrated Citrus Juice Process Covered by Public Service Patent," *Fruit Products Journal and American Food Manufacturer* 28, no. 7 (March 1949): 195; O'Rourke, *World Apple Market*, 15.

53. "Food Availability and Consumption," USDA Economic Research Service, accessed January 10, 2020, https://www.ers.usda.gov/data-products/ag-and-food-statistics-charting-the-essentials/food-availability-and-consumption/.

54. "A Report to Cooperators: Shipping Golden Delicious Apples in Cell and Tray Packs," 1965, box 162, Yakima Valley Growers-Shippers Association Records, 1917–1981, MASC.

55. "Wooden vs. Fiberboard Box Discussed by Hort. Expert," *Better Fruit* 38, no. 11 (May 1944): 22; "Fibreboard Boxes Undergoing Tests," *Better Fruit* 38, no. 6 (December 1943): 15.

56. Bright, *Apples Galore!*, 191–94, 196.

57. Washington Produce Shippers Association, Inc., "Produce Shippers Lead Truck Fight," June 29, 1939, box 30, Washington State Department of Agriculture Records.

58. "Outline of Suggested Procedure to Arrange for the Acceptance of New Fibreboard Containers for Fresh Fruits, Fresh or Green Vegetables, Melons and Berries (Not Cold-Packed nor Frozen) Under the Railroads' Test Shipment Procedures," Circular Letter No. 1, prepared by the National Container Committee, January 31, 1956, Great Northern Railway Company Records, President's Subject File 14364, MHS.

NOTES TO CHAPTER 7   265

59. J. M. Budd to W. T. Faricy, May 20, 1955; memo, Hamilton Fruit Company, Wenatchee to J. M. Budd, I. B. Pool, and C. E. Finley, January 8, 1954, Great Northern Railway Company Records, President's Subject File 14364, MHS.

60. Rodgers N. Brown, "Merchandising Pioneering" (annual meeting of the Washington State Horticultural Association, Yakima, WA, December 10, 1952), Great Northern Railway Company Records, Agricultural Development Department File 403–1, MHS.

61. "Forman Examines Selling in a Changing World," *"Big Y" Bulletin* 26, no. 8 (February 1954): 6.

62. "Report of Ray Forman, Sales Manager," *"Big Y" Bulletin* 27, no. 9 (February–March 1956): 8.

63. Dinner meeting by Apple Marketing Committee, Boston, January 6, 1948, box 90, Yakima Valley Growers-Shippers Association Records, 1917–1981, MASC.

64. Washington State Apple Advertising Commission, *Apple Commission Reports*, 13; Washington Apple Marketing Mission, January 1, 1948, Yakima Valley Growers-Shippers Association Records, 1917–1981, box 90, MASC.

65. Dinner meeting by Apple Marketing Committee, Boston, January 6, 1948, box 90, Yakima Valley Growers-Shippers Association Records, 1917–1981, MASC.

66. Todd Fryhover, "Retail Has Much to Say . . . Are We Listening?," *Good Fruit Grower*, October 1, 2019, https://www.goodfruit.com/fryhover-retail-has-much-to-say/.

67. USDA Economics, Statistics and Market Information System, "U.S. Apple Statistics," accessed December 22, 2020, https://usda.library.cornell.edu/concern/publications/1j92g7448?locale=en.

68. Timothy Egan, "'Perfect' Apple Pushed Growers into Debt," *New York Times*, November 4, 2000.

69. WSU Tree Fruit, "Varieties—Apple," accessed December 22, 2020, http://treefruit.wsu.edu/web-article/apple-varieties/.

70. "Move Over, Honeycrisp: New Apple to Debut at Grocery Stores," *Oregonian* (Portland), October 19, 2019, https://www.oregonlive.com/pacific-northwest-news/2019/10/move-over-honeycrisp-new-apple-to-debut-at-grocery-stores.html.

71. Cosmic Crisp, "History," accessed January 8, 2020, https://cosmiccrisp.com/cosmic-crisp-story/; "Want to Grow These Apples? You'll Have to Join the Club," *Morning Edition*, National Public Radio, November 10, 2014, https://www.npr.org/sections/thesalt/2014/11/10/358530280/want-to-grow-these-apples-youll-have-to-join-the-club; Futrell, *Good Apples*, 101–2.

72. Cascadia Capital LLC, *Washington Tree Fruit Industry*, 12.

73. "Changing Climate Impacts Northwest," *Good Fruit Grower*, January 22, 2016, https://www.goodfruit.com/changing-climate-impacts-northwest/; Kate Prengaman, "Hot New Varieties for Hot Climates," *Good Fruit Grower*, June 25, 2019, https://www.goodfruit.com/hot-new-varieties-for-hot-climates/.

Bibliography

MANUSCRIPT COLLECTIONS

Elon James Gilbert Papers, 1890–1977. Manuscripts, Archives, and Special Collections (MASC), Washington State University Libraries, Pullman.
Great Northern Railway Company Records. Minnesota Historical Society (MHS), St. Paul.
Northern Pacific Railway Company Records. Minnesota Historical Society (MHS), St. Paul.
Northwest Horticultural Council Records, 1951–1976. Manuscripts, Archives, and Special Collections (MASC), Washington State University Libraries, Pullman.
Ralph R. Sundquist Papers, 1909–1980. Manuscripts, Archives, and Special Collections (MASC), Washington State University Libraries, Pullman.
Skookum Records Collection. Wenatchee Valley Museum and Cultural Center, Wenatchee, WA.
Snokist Collection. Yakima Valley Museum, Yakima, WA.
Thomas Burke Papers. Special Collections, University Archives Division, University of Washington, Seattle.
Washington State Department of Agriculture Records. Washington State Archives, Olympia.
Yakima Valley Growers-Shippers Association Records, 1917–1981. Manuscripts, Archives, and Special Collections (MASC), Washington State University Libraries, Pullman.

AGRICULTURAL BULLETINS AND REPORTS

Apple Industry, Other Fruits and Nuts. Portland, OR: Portland Chamber of Commerce, 1911.
The Apple Stark "Delicious." Louisiana, MO: Stark Bro's Nurseries and Orchards Co., 1909.

267

Balmer, John A. *Pruning Orchard Trees*. Agricultural Experiment Station Bulletin 25. Pullman: State College of Washington, 1896.

———. *A Report on Damage to Fruit Trees Caused by the Severe Freeze of Nov. 26–27–28, 1896*. Agricultural Experiment Station Bulletin 30. Pullman: State College of Washington, 1897.

Caldwell, Joseph S. *Evaporation of Apples*. Agricultural Experiment Station Bulletin 131. Pullman: State College of Washington, 1916.

Cascadia Capital, LLC. *Washington Tree Fruit Industry: Marketing Trends and Analysis 2020*. http://www.cascadiacapital.com/wp-content/uploads/2020/03/WA-Tree-Fruit-Industry-Trends-Analysis-2020-vPRINT.pdf.

Channing, Alice. *Child Labor in Fruit and Hop Growing Districts of the Northern Pacific Coast*. US Department of Labor Bulletin 151. Washington, DC: Government Printing Office, 1926.

Erdman, Henry E. *The California Fruit Growers Exchange: An Example of Cooperation in the Segregation of Conflicting Interest*. New York: American Council Institute of Pacific Relations, 1933.

Fletcher, Stevenson W. *Nursery Stock for Washington Orchards*. Agricultural Experiment Station Bulletin 53. Pullman: State College of Washington, 1902.

———. *Planting Orchards in Washington*. Agricultural Experiment Station Bulletin 52. Pullman: State College of Washington, 1902.

Fortier, Samuel. *Irrigation of Orchards*. US Department of Agriculture Farmers' Bulletin 404. Washington, DC: Government Printing Office, 1910.

Granger and the Yakima Valley. Granger, WA: Granger Commercial Club, n.d.

Hampson, Chester C. *Apple Prices Received by Washington Growers*. Agricultural Experiment Station Bulletin 326. Pullman: State College of Washington, 1936.

———. *Cost of Shipping Point Marketing Services for Apples in Washington*. Agricultural Experiment Station Bulletin 312. Pullman: State College of Washington, 1935.

Hampson, Chester C., and E. F. Dummeier. *Washington Apple Prices and Costs of Shipping Point Market Services*. Agricultural Experiment Station Bulletin 242. Pullman: State College of Washington, 1930.

Heald, F. D., J. R. Neller, F. L. Overley, and H. J. Dana. *Arsenical Spray Residue and Its Removal from Apples*. Agricultural Experiment Station Bulletin 213. Pullman: State College of Washington, 1927.

Heckman, John H., and George H. Goldsborough. *Cooperative Marketing of Apples in the United States*. Farm Credit Administration Bulletin 55. Washington, DC: US Department of Agriculture, November 1948.

International Apple Shippers' Association. *Grade and Standardization Laws, United States and Canada*. Rochester, NY: International Apple Shippers' Association, 1923.

Landis, Paul H., and Melvin S. Brooks. *Farm Labor in the Yakima Valley, Washington*, Rural Sociology Series in Farm Labor No. 1, Bulletin 343. Pullman: State College of Washington Agricultural Experiment Station, December 1936.

Lawrence, William H. *Apple Scab in Eastern Washington.* Agricultural Experiment Station Bulletin 75. Pullman: State College of Washington, 1906.

———. *Three Common Insect Pests of Western Washington.* Agricultural Experiment Station Bulletin 65. Pullman: State College of Washington, 1904.

Mackay, L. Gertrude. *The Housekeeper's Apple Book: Over Two Hundred Ways of Preparing the Apple.* Boston: Little, Brown, 1917.

———. *Two Hundred and Nine Ways of Preparing the Apple.* Spokane, WA: Shaw and Borden, ca. 1912.

Melander, Axel L. *The Codling Moth in Eastern Washington.* Agricultural Experiment Station Bulletin 81. Pullman: State College of Washington, 1907.

———. *The Control of the Codling Moth.* Agricultural Experiment Station Bulletin 103. Pullman: State College of Washington, 1911.

———. *The Wormy Apple.* Agricultural Experiment Station Bulletin 68. Pullman: State College of Washington, 1905.

Melander, Axel L., and R. Kent Beattie. *The Penetration System of Orchard Spraying.* Agricultural Experiment Station Bulletin 106. Pullman: State College of Washington, 1913.

Melander, Axel L., and Eldred Llewellyn Jenne. *The Codling Moth in the Yakima Valley.* Agricultural Experiment Station Bulletin 77. Pullman: State College of Washington, 1906.

Miller, George H., and S. M. Thomson. *The Costs of Producing Apples in Wenatchee Valley Washington.* US Department of Agriculture Bulletin 446. Washington, DC: Government Printing Office, 1917.

Morris, Oscar M. *Studies in Apple Storage.* Agricultural Experiment Station Bulletin 193. Pullman: State College of Washington, 1926.

Morris, Oscar M., and William A. Luce. *Orchard Crowding, Its Effects and Remedies.* Agricultural Experiment Station Bulletin 200. Pullman: State College of Washington, 1925.

Piper, Charles V. *Insect Pests of the Garden, Farm, and Orchard.* Agricultural Experiment Station Bulletin 17. Pullman: State College of Washington, 1895.

Portland Young Men's Christian Association. *Apple Growing in the Pacific Northwest: A Condensation of Lectures, Experiments, and Discussions Conducted by the Education Department of the Portland, Oregon, Young Men's Christian Association.* Portland, OR: Young Men's Christian Association, 1911.

Powell, G. Harold, and S. H. Fulton. *The Apple in Cold Storage.* US Department of Agriculture Bureau of Plant Industry Bulletin 48. Washington, DC: Government Printing Office, 1905.

Ramsey, H. J., A. W. McKay, E. L. Markell, and H. S. Bird. *The Handling and Storage of Apples in the Pacific Northwest.* US Department of Agriculture Bulletin 587. Washington, DC: Government Printing Office, 1917.

Rees, Ralph W. *Apple Survey of the United States and Canada.* New York: Department of Agricultural Relations of the New York Central Lines, 1926.

Richared: The Delicious Supreme. Wenatchee, WA: Columbia and Okanogan Nursery Company, ca. 1928.

Sewell, Bradford H., and Robin M. Whyatt. *Intolerable Risk: Pesticides in Our Children's Food.* Natural Resources Defense Council, February 27, 1989.

Thatcher, Roscoe W. *Washington Soils.* Agricultural Experiment Station Bulletin 85. Pullman: State College of Washington, 1908.

Union Pacific. *150 Recipes for Apple Dishes.* N.p.: Union Pacific, 1924.

US Census Bureau. *United States Summary, 2010: Population and Housing Unit Counts.* Washington, DC: US Government Printing Office, 2012.

US Department of Agriculture. *Sales Methods on Policies of a Growers' National Marketing Agency.* Bulletin 1109. Washington, DC: Government Printing Office, 1923.

US Department of Labor. *Women in the Fruit-Growing and Canning Industries in the State of Washington.* Bulletin of the Women's Bureau 47. Washington, DC: Government Printing Office, 1926.

Van Buren, B. D. "The Apple Grading Law." In *The Fruit Industry in New York State*, 669–78. Bulletin 79. Albany: New York State Department of Agriculture, 1916.

Wadsworth, James J. *Cooperative Restructuring, 1989–1998.* Rural Business Cooperative Service, Report 57. US Department of Agriculture, November 1998.

Waller, Osmar L. *A Report on Irrigation Conditions in the Yakima Valley, Washington.* Agricultural Experiment Station Bulletin 61. Pullman: State College of Washington, 1904.

Warren, G. F. "The Apple Industry." In *An Apple Orchard Survey of Wayne County, New York*, 241–362. Cornell University Agricultural Experiment Station Bulletin 226. Ithaca, NY: Cornell University, 1905.

Washington Agricultural College and School of Science. *Report of Farmers' Institute, Held at Colton, Washington.* Agricultural Experiment Station Bulletin 2. Olympia, WA: O. C. White, 1892.

Washington Crop and Livestock Reporting Service. *Washington Tree Fruits.* Seattle: Washington Crop and Livestock Reporting Service, 1952.

Washington State Apple Advertising Commission. *The Apple Commission Reports, Fall 1945.* Wenatchee and Yakima: Washington State Apple Advertising Commission, 1945.

———. *Season's Report, August 1937–July 1938.* N.p.: Washington State Apple Advertising Commission, 1938.

Washington State Apples, Inc. *Annual Report, August 1936–July 1937.* N.p.: Washington State Apples, Inc., 1937.

Waugh, Frank A. *The American Apple Orchard: A Sketch of the Practice of Apple Growing in North America at the Beginning of the Twentieth Century.* New York: Orange Judd, 1917.

Wenatchee Commercial Club. *Chelan County, Washington: Home of the Big Red Apple.* Wenatchee, WA: Wenatchee Commercial Club, 1908.

Wickson, Edward J. *Irrigation Practice among Fruit Growers on the Pacific Coast.* US Department of Agriculture Office of Experiment Stations Bulletin 108. Washington, DC: Government Printing Office, 1902.

Yakima Commercial Club. *Yakima Valley Washington.* North Yakima, WA: Yakima Commercial Club, 1912.

BOOKS

Adams, Frank. "The Historical Background of California Agriculture." In *California Agriculture*, edited by Claude B. Hutchison, 1–50. Berkeley: University of California Press, 1946.

Anderson, Eva G. *Charles F. Keiser: The Pioneer with a Yen for Work.* Wenatchee, WA: Wenatchee Daily World, 1954.

———. *Pioneers of North Central Washington.* Wenatchee, WA: Wenatchee World, 1980.

Bailey, Liberty Hyde, Jr. *Field Notes on Apple Culture.* New York: Orange Judd, 1911.

Beech, Spencer A. *The Apples of New York.* Vol. 1. Albany, NY: J. B. Lyon, 1905.

Blanchard, John. *Caravans to the Northwest.* Boston: Houghton Mifflin, 1940.

Bright, Al C. *Apples Galore! The History of the Apple Industry in the Wenatchee Valley.* Wenatchee, WA: DMI, 1988.

Conlin, Joseph Robert. *"Bacon, Beans, and Galantines": Food and Foodways on the Western Mining Frontier.* Las Vegas: University of Nevada Press, 1986.

Cronon, William. *Nature's Metropolis: Chicago and the Great West.* New York: W. W. Norton, 1991.

Dolan, Susan. *Fruitful Legacy: A Historic Context of Orchards in the United States with Technical Information for Registering Orchards in the National Register of Historic Places.* National Park Service. Washington, DC: Government Printing Office, 2009.

Duddy, Edward A. *The Cold Storage Industry in the United States.* Chicago: University of Chicago Press, 1929.

Erigero, Patricia C. *Cultural Landscape Report.* Vol. 2. Fort Vancouver National Historic Site, National Park Service, 1992. https://www.nps.gov/parkhistory/online_books/fova/clr/clr.htm.

Fahey, John. *The Inland Empire: Unfolding Years, 1879–1929.* Seattle: University of Washington Press, 1986.

Farmer, Jared. *Trees in Paradise: A California History.* New York: W. W. Norton, 2013.

Ferree, David C., ed. *A History of Fruit Varieties: The American Pomological Society, One-Hundred and Fifty Years, 1848–1998.* Yakima, WA: Good Fruit Grower Magazine, 1998.

Ficken, Robert E. *Washington Territory.* Pullman: Washington State University Press, 2002.

Fiege, Mark. *Irrigated Eden: The Making of an Agricultural Landscape in the American West*. Seattle: University of Washington Press, 1999.

Fitzgerald, Deborah. *Every Farm a Factory: The Industrial Ideal in American Agriculture*. New Haven, CT: Yale University Press, 2003.

Folger, J. C., and S. M. Thomson. *The Commercial Apple Industry of North America*. New York: Macmillan, 1921.

Freidberg, Susanne. *Fresh: A Perishable History*. Cambridge, MA: Belknap Press of Harvard University Press, 2009.

Futrell, Susan. *Good Apples: Behind Every Bite*. Iowa City: University of Iowa Press, 2017.

Gamboa, Erasmo. *Mexican Labor and World War II: Braceros in the Pacific Northwest, 1942–1947*. Austin: University of Texas Press, 1990.

Gellatly, John A. *History of Wenatchee: The Apple Capital of the World*. Wenatchee, WA: Wenatchee Bindery and Printing, 1958.

Gibson, James R. *Farming the Frontier: The Agricultural Opening of the Oregon Country, 1786–1846*. Seattle: University of Washington Press, 1985.

Gordon, Ian. *Comic Strips and Consumer Culture, 1890–1945*. Washington, DC: Smithsonian Institution Press, 1998.

Heuterman, Thomas. *The Burning Horse: Japanese-American Experience in the Yakima Valley, 1920–1942*. Cheney: Eastern Washington University Press, 1995.

Hill, James J. *Highways of Progress*. New York: Doubleday, 1910.

Hull, Lindley M. *History of Central Washington*. Spokane, WA: Shaw and Borden, 1929.

An Illustrated History of Klickitat, Yakima, and Kittitas Counties. Chicago: Interstate, 1904.

Iwata, Masakazu. *Planted in Good Soil: The History of the Issei in United States Agriculture*. Vol. 2. New York: Peter Lang, 1992.

Jackson, Gary, ed. *Yakima's Past*. Vol. 3 of *Remembering Yakima by Those Who Were There*. Yakima, WA: Golden West, 1977.

Johnson, Edward. *Wonder-Working Providence of Sion's Savior in New England*. Andover, MA: Warren F. Draper, 1867. First published 1654. Page references are to the 1867 edition.

Juniper, Barrie E., and David J. Mabberley. *The Story of the Apple*. Portland, OR: Timber Press, 2006.

Kerrigan, William. *Johnny Appleseed and the American Orchard: A Cultural History*. Baltimore: Johns Hopkins University Press, 2012.

Koeppel, Dan. *Banana: The Fate of the Fruit that Changed the World*. New York: Hudson Street Press, 2008.

Leach, William. *Land of Desire: Merchants, Power, and the Rise of a New American Culture*. New York: Pantheon Books, 1993.

Lerner, Adrienne Wilmoth. "Plant Patent Act of 1930." In *Biotechnology: In Context*, vol. 2, edited by Brenda Wilmoth Lerner and K. Lee Lerner, 643–44. Detroit: Gale, 2012.

BIBLIOGRAPHY

Leuchtenburg, William E. *Franklin Roosevelt and the New Deal.* New York: Harper and Row, 1965.

Levenstein, Harvey A. *Revolution at the Table: The Transformation of the American Diet.* New York: Oxford University Press, 1988.

Levinson, Marc. *The Great A&P and the Struggle for Small Business in America.* New York: Hill and Wang, 2011.

Lewty, Peter J. *Across the Columbia Plain: Railroad Expansion in the Interior Northwest, 1885–1893.* Pullman: Washington State University Press, 1995.

———. *To the Columbia Gateway: The Oregon Railway and the Northern Pacific, 1879–1884.* Pullman: Washington State University Press, 1987.

Locati, Joe, J. *The Horticultural Heritage of Walla Walla County, 1818–1977.* College Place, WA: Color Press, 1978.

Lowitt, Richard. *The New Deal and the West.* Bloomington: Indiana University Press, 1984.

Luce, William A. *Washington State Fruit Industry: A Brief History.* N.p., 1972.

Lyman, William Denison. *History of the Yakima Valley, Washington Comprising Yakima, Kittitas, and Benton Counties.* Vol. 1. N.p.: S. J. Clark, 1919.

———. *An Illustrated History of Walla Walla County, State of Washington.* San Francisco: W. H. Lever, 1901.

Malone, Michael P. *James J. Hill: Empire Builder of the Northwest.* Norman: University of Oklahoma Press, 1996.

Marshall, John. *Washington Apple Country.* Portland, OR: Graphic Arts Center, 1995.

Martin, Alice A. *All about Apples.* Boston: Houghton Mifflin, 1976.

Maynard, Harold H. *Marketing Northwestern Apples.* New York: Ronald Press, 1923.

Meeker, Ezra. *Pioneer Reminiscences of Puget Sound.* Seattle: Lowman and Hanford Stationery and Printing, 1905.

Meinig, Donald W. *The Great Columbia Plain: A Historical Geography, 1805–1910.* Seattle: University of Washington Press, 1995.

Mendenhall, Nancy. *Orchards of Eden: White Bluffs on the Columbia, 1907–1943.* Seattle: Far Eastern Press, 2006.

Mickelson, Sig. *The Northern Pacific Railroad and the Settling of the West.* Sioux Falls, SD: Center for Western Studies, 1993.

Mitchell, Bruce. *Flowing Wealth: The Story of Water Resource Development in North Central Washington, 1870–1950.* Wenatchee, WA: Wenatchee Daily World, 1967.

Morgan, Joan, and Allison Richards. *The New Book of Apples.* London: Ebury Press, 1993.

Morrisey, Katherine. *Mental Territories: Mapping the Inland Empire.* Ithaca, NY: Cornell University Press, 1997.

Okie, William Thomas. *The Georgia Peach: Culture, Agriculture, and Environment in the American South.* New York: Cambridge University Press, 2016.

O'Rourke, A. Desmond. *The World Apple Market.* New York: Food Products Press, 1994.

Ott, Cindy. *Pumpkin: The Curious History of an American Icon.* Seattle: University of Washington Press, 2012.

Parkin, Katherine J. *Food Is Love: Advertising and Gender Roles in Modern America.* Philadelphia: University of Pennsylvania Press, 2006.

Pisani, Donald J. *To Reclaim a Divided West: Water, Law, and Public Policy, 1848–1902.* Albuquerque: University of New Mexico Press, 1992.

Price, Robert. *Johnny Appleseed: Man and Myth.* Bloomington: Indiana University Press, 1954.

Relander, Click, and George M. Martin. *Yakima, Washington Jubilee, 1885–1960.* Yakima, WA: Yakima Diamond Jubilee, Inc., n.d.

Robbins, William G. *Colony and Empire: The Capitalist Transformation of the American West.* Lawrence: University Press of Kansas, 1994.

Sackman, Douglas Cazaux. *Orange Empire: California and the Fruits of Eden.* Berkeley: University of California Press, 2005.

Schwantes, Carlos A., and James P. Ronda. *The West the Railroads Made.* Seattle: University of Washington Press, 2008.

Scott, Roy V. *The Reluctant Farmer: The Rise of Agricultural Extension to 1914.* Urbana: University of Illinois Press, 1971.

Shapiro, Laura. *Perfection Salad: Women and Cooking at the Turn of the Century.* New York: Modern Library, 2001.

Sheller, Roscoe. *Blowsand.* Portland, OR: Metropolitan Press, 1963.

———. *Courage and Water: A Story of Yakima Valley's Sunnyside.* Portland, OR: Binfords and Mort, 1952.

Shotwell, Harry I. *The Shotwell Story.* Wenatchee, WA: Wenatchee Daily World, 1953.

Simonds, William Joe. *The Columbia Basin Project.* Denver, CO: Bureau of Reclamation History Program, 1998.

Sonneman, Toby F. *Fruit Fields in My Blood: Okie Migrants in the West.* Moscow: University of Idaho Press, 1992.

Spargo, L. Darlene, and Judy Artley Sandbloom. *Pioneer Dreams . . . Histories of Washington Territorial Pioneers.* Wenatchee, WA: Native Daughters of Washington Territorial Pioneers, 2004.

Steele, Richard F. *History of North Washington: Illustrated History of Stevens, Ferry, Okanogan, and Chelan Counties.* Spokane: Western History Publishing, 1904.

Stoll, Steven. *The Fruits of Natural Advantage: Marketing the Industrial Countryside in California.* Berkeley: University of California Press, 1998.

Stratton, David. *Tree Top: Creating a Fruit Revolution.* Pullman: Washington State University Press, 2010.

Strom, Claire. *Profiting from the Plains: The Great Northern and Corporate Development of the American West.* Seattle: University of Washington Press, 2003.

Thompson, Anthony W., Robert J. Church, and Bruce H. Jones. *PFE, Pacific Fruit Express: The World's Largest Refrigerator Car Company.* Wilton, CA: Central Valley Railroad Publications, 1992.

Tufts, Warren P. "The Rich Pattern of California Crops." In *California Agriculture*, edited by Claude B. Hutchison, 113–238. Berkeley: University of California Press, 1946.
Trachtenberg, Alan. *The Incorporation of America: Culture and Society in the Gilded Age*. New York: Hill and Wang, 1982.
Tyrrell, Ian R. *Sobering Up: From Temperance to Prohibition in Antebellum America, 1800–1860*. Westport, CT: Greenwood Press, 1979.
———. "Temperance and Economic Change in the Antebellum North." In *Alcohol, Reform and Society: The Liquor Issue in Social Context*, edited by Jack S. Blocker Jr., 45–68. Westport, CT: Greenwood Press, 1979.
Vaught, David. *Cultivating California: Growers, Specialty Crops, and Labor, 1875–1920*. Baltimore: Johns Hopkins University Press, 1999.
Wiebe, Robert. *The Search for Order, 1877–1920*. New York: Hill and Wang, 1967.
White, John H. *The Great Yellow Fleet: A History of American Railroad Refrigerator Cars*. San Marino, CA: Golden West Books, 1986.
White, Richard. *Railroaded: The Transcontinentals and the Making of Modern America*. New York: W. W. Norton, 2011.
Whitman, Narcissa Prentiss. *My Journal, 1836*. 7th ed. Fairfield, WA: Ye Galleon Press, 2004.
Whorton, James. *Before Silent Spring: Pesticides and Public Health in Pre-DDT America*. Princeton, NJ: Princeton University Press, 1974.
Worster, Donald. *Rivers of Empire: Water, Aridity, and the Growth of the American West*. New York: Oxford University Press, 1985.
Wyman, Mark. *Hoboes, Bindlestiffs, Fruit Tramps, and the Harvesting of the West*. New York: Hill and Wang, 2010.

ARTICLES

Barlow, William. "Reminiscences of Seventy Years." *Oregon Historical Quarterly* 13 (September 1912): 240–86.
Berry-Caban, Cristobal S. "DDT and Silent Spring, Fifty Years After." *Journal of Military and Veterans Health* 19, no. 4 (October 2011): 19–24.
Boening, Rose M. "History of Irrigation in the State of Washington." *Pacific Northwest Quarterly* 9, no. 4 (1918): 259–76; 10, no. 1 (1919): 21–45.
Cardwell, J. R. "The First Fruits of the Land, Part I." *Oregon Historical Quarterly* 7, no. 1 (1906): 28–51.
———. "The First Fruits of the Land, Part II." *Oregon Historical Quarterly* 7, no. 2 (1906): 151–62.
Conis, Elena. "Beyond Silent Spring: An Alternate History of DDT." Science History Institute. February 14, 2017. https://www.sciencehistory.org/distillations/beyond-silent-spring-an-alternate-history-of-ddt.

Coulter, Calvin Brewster. "The New Settlers on the Yakima Project." *Pacific Northwest Quarterly* 61, no. 1 (1970): 10–21.

———. "The Victory of National Irrigation in the Yakima Valley, 1902–1906." *Pacific Northwest Quarterly* 42, no. 2 (April 1951): 99–122.

Cromwell, Robert J. *A Short History of the "Old Apple Tree," Located in the Old Apple Tree Park, Vancouver National Historic Reserve, Vancouver, Washington, Compiled from Various Historical Sources.* Northwest Cultural Resources Institute Short Report 34. Vancouver, WA: National Park Service, September 2010.

Daniel, Cletus E. "Wobblies on the Farm: The IWW in the Yakima Valley." *Pacific Northwest Quarterly* 65, no. 4 (October 1974): 166–75.

Dimitri, Carolyn. "Contract Evolution and Institutional Innovation: Marketing Pacific-Grown Apples from 1890 to 1930." *Journal of Economic History* 62, no. 1 (2002): 189–212.

Duruz, Willis P. "Notes on the Early History of Horticulture in Oregon." *Agricultural History* 15, no. 2 (April 1941): 84–97.

Edwards, G. Thomas. "'The Early Morning of Yakima's Day of Greatness': The Yakima County Agricultural Book of 1905–1911." *Pacific Northwest Quarterly* 73, no. 2 (April 1982): 78–89.

———. "Irrigation in Eastern Washington, 1906–1911: The Promotional Photographs of Asahel Curtis." *Pacific Northwest Quarterly* 72, no. 3 (July 1981): 112–20.

Ellison, Joseph Waldo. "The Beginnings of the Apple Industry in Oregon." *Agricultural History* 11, no. 4 (October 1937): 322–43.

———. "The Cooperative Movement in the Oregon Apple Industry, 1910–1929." *Agricultural History* 13, no. 2 (April 1939): 77–96.

———. "Marketing Problems of Northwestern Apples, 1929–1940." *Agricultural History* 16, no. 2 (April 1942): 103–15.

Fahey, John. "Irrigation, Apples, and the Spokane Country." *Pacific Northwest Quarterly* 84, no. 1 (1993): 7–18.

Ficken, Robert E. "Rufus Woods, Wenatchee, and the Columbia Basin Reclamation Vision." *Pacific Northwest Quarterly* 87, no. 2 (Spring 1996): 72–81.

Freeman, Otis W. "Apple Industry of the Wenatchee Area." *Economic Geography* 10, no. 2 (1934): 160–71.

Haley, W. D. "Johnny Appleseed—a Pioneer Hero." *Harper's New Monthly Magazine* 43, no. 258 (November 1871): 830–36.

Hood, Ernie. "The Apple Bites Back: Claiming Old Orchards for Residential Development." *Environmental Health Perspectives* 114, no. 8 (August 2006): 471–76.

Howard, Randall R. "Following the Colonists: An Account of the Great Semiannual Movement of Homeseekers." *Pacific Monthly* 23 (1910): 520–33.

Johnson, George Fiske. "The Early History of Copper Fungicides." *Agricultural History* 9, no. 2 (April 1935): 67–79.

Kujovich, Mary Yeager. "The Refrigerator Car and the Growth of the Dressed Beef Industry." *Business History Review* 44, no. 4 (Winter 1970): 460–82.
Lemons, Hoyt, and Rayburn D. Tousley. "The Washington Apple Industry I: Its Geographic Basis." *Economic Geography* 21, no. 3 (1945): 161–82.
Miller, Elbert E., and Richard M. Highsmith Jr. "Geography of the Fruit Industry of Yakima Valley, Washington." *Economic Geography* 25, no. 4 (October 1949): 285–95.
Newbill, James G. "Farmers and Wobblies in the Yakima Valley, 1933." *Pacific Northwest Quarterly* 68, no. 2 (April 1977): 80–87.
Ormsby, Margaret A. "Fruit Marketing in the Okanagan Valley of British Columbia." *Agricultural History* 9, no. 2 (April 1935): 80–97.
Pitzer, Paul C. "A 'Farm-in-a-Day': The Publicity Stunt and the Celebrations That Initiated the Columbia Basin Project." *Pacific Northwest Quarterly* 82, no. 1 (January 1991): 2–7.
Relander, Click. "The Battleground of National Irrigation." *Pacific Northwest Quarterly* 52, no. 4 (October 1961): 144–50.
Rose, Mary. "How Native Farmers Shaped the Northwest Apple Industry, Part 1: Origins." Confluence Project. July 17, 2019. https://www.confluenceproject.org/library-post/how-native-farmers-shaped-the-northwest-apple-industry-part-1-origins/.
Seftel, Howard. "Government Regulation and the Rise of the California Fruit Industry: The Entrepreneurial Attack on Fruit Pests, 1880–1920." *Business History Review* 59, no. 3 (1985): 369–402.
Valgren, V. N. "The Agricultural Credits Act of 1923." *American Economic Review* 13, no. 3 (September 1923): 442–60.
White, W. Thomas. "Main Street on the Irrigation Frontier: Sub-urban Community Building in the Yakima Valley, 1900–1910." *Pacific Northwest Quarterly* 77, no. 3 (July 1986): 94–103.
Zeisler-Vralsted, Dorothy. "Reclaiming the Arid West: The Role of the Northern Pacific Railway in Irrigating Kennewick, Washington." *Pacific Northwest Quarterly* 84, no. 4 (1993): 130–39.

DISSERTATIONS, THESES, AND CONFERENCE PAPERS

Bennett, Jason Patrick. "Blossoms and Borders: Apples in a Modern Countryside in the Pacific Northwest, 1890–2001." PhD diss., University of Victoria, 2008.
Diamond, David. "Migrations: Henderson Luelling and the Cultivated Apple, 1822–1854." PhD diss., Northern Arizona University, 2005.
Dummeier, Edwin F. "The Marketing of Pacific Coast Fruits in Chicago." PhD diss., University of Chicago, 1926.
Entze, Marc A. "The Importance of the Refrigerated Rail Car to Pacific Northwest Agriculture." Paper presented at the Pacific Northwest History Conference, Tacoma, WA, April 20, 2007.

Mabbott, Leslie LaVerne. "A History of the Wenatchee-Okanogan Apple Industry Prior to 1930." Master's thesis, State College of Washington, 1940.

Miner, Grace Edith. "A Century of Washington Fruit." Master's thesis, University of Washington, 1926.

Overholser, E. L. "Production and Marketing Problems of Apples in the States of Washington and New York Contrasted." Paper presented at the Thirty-Second Annual Meeting of the Washington State Horticultural Association, Yakima, WA, December 7–9, 1936.

Scroggs, Joseph Campbell. "Labor Problems in the Fruit Industry of the Yakima Valley." Master's thesis, University of Washington, 1937.

Vandevere, Emmett Kaiser. "History of Irrigation in Washington." PhD diss., University of Washington, 1948.

Van Lanen, Amanda L. "'It was a time when the promoter promoted': Irrigation Projects in Wenatchee, Washington, 1890–1908." Master's thesis, Washington State University, 2004.

Zaragoza, Tony. "Apple Capital: Growers, Laborers and Technology in the Origins of the Washington State Apple Industry." PhD diss., Washington State University, 2007.

Index

advertising: and Apples for Health, 163–66, 167, 168, 253n93; and "Big Y" brand, 154–55, 167–68, 170; and branding, 139, 140–41, 142, 151, 152–55, 158, 169–70; and celebrity endorsements, 160; and comic strips, 151–52; for commission houses, 100; and consumers, 138, 139–40, 141, 149, 150, 155, 156, 169–70, 173, 190–91, 192, 204–5, 228; and "Farmer-Consumer Campaign," 190–91; of fruit, 140–42, 149, 153, 154–55, 188; and growers' cooperatives, 170, 171, 188, 192–93; and International Apple Shippers' Association, 149–50; and James J. Hill, 154; and land promotion, 147; and National Apple Day, 158; and National Apple Show, 148; and national marketing campaigns, 148–50, 154–55, 158, 166–67, 192–95; newspapers and other methods of, 149–50, 153, 157, 159, 160–61, 172, 196, 201; and Northwest Fruit Exchange, 194; in *Northwest Fruit Grower*, 156–57; and Pacific Northwest Boxed Apples, 167–68; and Pacific Northwest Fruits (PNF), 192, 193, 194–95, 196; and promotion of apples, 141, 159, 165, 169, 226; and promotion of trade, 188; racism in, 153–54; on radio, 194, 196; and railroads, 141–42, 159–61, 163–67, 168, 253n93; and sales, 137, 150, 151, 157, 194; and Skookum Packers Association, 154, 155, 194; and state advertising commission, 171, 194; and statewide marketing, 190, 192, 197; and supermarkets, 225; and Washington growers' campaigns, 169–70, 193–95; and Washington State Apples, 194–95, 196; and Washington State Fruit Commission, 213; and Wenatchee, Wash., 149, 152, 155–156, 160–61; and Wenatchee Okanogan Federation (Wenoka), 194, 196; and Yakima, Wash., 149. *See also* National Apple Show

agriculture: and Agricultural Marketing Act, 173–74, 175; and chemical use, 16, 77, 79, 92, 94–95, 210–17, 220, 241n94; and class, 54; and Columbia Basin Project, 208–9; and credit corporations, 176–77, 179; and credit for rural farmers, 175; and cultivation of Old World crops, 22; and DDT use, 77, 94–95; and Depression, 184–85; development of, 62; and domestication of plants for humans, 5; and eastern orchards, 9, 20–21; and farmers as businesspeople, 8–9, 12, 53, 65–66, 182, 223; and fruit prices, 189; and fruit production, 1, 3, 5, 6–11, 21, 26, 53, 62, 66, 67; and fungicides, 81; and grafting of trees, 6, 21; and Grand Coulee Dam, 208; and growing wheat, 54–55, 109; and harvest labor, 201–3; and horticultural societies, 6, 7, 21, 26, 30, 65, 92, 122, 189, 211, 212, 217; and Hudson's Bay Company's farming, 25–26; and industrialization, 5–9, 13, 15–16, 24, 65, 73, 163, 186, 206–8, 209, 210, 215, 216, 220, 221, 228–30; and intercropping, 62–64; and

279

agriculture (*continued*)
irrigation, 3, 4, 5, 41, 51, 53, 54–59, 65, 66, 208–9; and labor, 9, 12–13, 61, 195; and landownership, 6, 8, 22, 23, 24; and marketing, 3–4, 5; and Native Americans, 154; and New Deal, 183–84; and Northern Pacific Department of Agriculture, 47–48; and Northwest Fruit Growers' Association, 57; and nurseries, 21, 22, 23; and organic products, 15, 215, 230; and pesticides, 5, 80, 210–16; and plant patents, 74; and price of imported produce, 139; and production of monocultures, 6, 8, 15; and professionalism, 12, 67, 69, 104; and Reconstruction Finance Corporation (RFC), 176–80; and rural American values, 65, 69; and science, 3, 23, 53, 65, 66, 69, 76, 77, 86; and secondary crops or animals, 64; and soil, 5, 66; and specialty crops, 57, 69; and sprays, 77–80; and technology, 65–66; and temporary migrant workers, 219; and tree-growing techniques, 12, 68–69; in United States, 4; in Walla Walla, 35; in Washington State, 3, 109; and western orchards, 9, 143; and Works Progress Administration, 197; world's fairs as platform for, 142. *See also* Hudson's Bay Company; Jefferson, Thomas; monoculture; United States Department of Agriculture (USDA)

apples: acreage of, 61, 67, 209, 215; and Ahtanum mission, 36; and Alar use, 211–15; and American apples, 89, 90, 91–92, 149, 163, 172, 173, 175; and American International Apple Association, 175; and American Pomological Society, 146, 163; and America's roots, 1, 4, 6, 17–21, 22, 224; and apple cider, 20, 21, 23, 69, 115; and apple cookery, 149, 150, 159–62, 194, 206, 250n40; arrival of in Washington, 7, 17–19, 36–37; and arsenic, 77, 81, 86–92, 94, 117, 163, 166, 169, 241n94; Asian and European history of, 20–21; books about, 6, 150, 153, 160; boxed, 167–68, 172, 174, 175, 188, 191, 200, 203–4, 221–22, 244n77; and brokers, 100, 171; and colonization, 6, 75; and Columbian Exchange, 20; and commercial nurseries, 33; cost of, 4, 9, 33, 35, 38, 76; and crab apples, 20, 29, 31; and culls, 116, 189–90, 200, 221; and Delicious apples, 73–74, 75, 161, 164, 188, 200, 212, 224, 227–28; and Depression, 94, 170, 171–75, 188, 197, 200; and domestication of plants, 5; and federal regulations, 120–21; and fruit markets, 99–100, 140; and fruit's condition, 107, 108, 112–20, 205, 224, 226, 227; and fungicides, 77–78; grading system for, 113–18, 138, 189; and grafting of trees, 6, 20, 21, 23, 30–32, 33, 36; and Granny Smith, Gala, and Fuji apples, 227, 228; and growers' cooperatives, 102–7, 117, 121–22, 149, 176, 212, 220–21; and health, 164–65, 169, 195, 205, 211–22, 213, 214, 226, 250n40; home use of, 34, 37, 67, 69–70, 72, 141, 143; ideal temperature for, 133–34, 229; and industrialization, 39, 68, 118, 229–30; and industry standards, 68, 114–21, 137; inspection of, 114, 115, 131–32; and International Apple Shippers' Association, 102, 158, 160, 164, 200, 250n40; and irrigation, 15, 28, 39, 41–42, 68, 209; and labor, 171, 200–203; and land-grant colleges and universities, 6–7, 69, 95; and landownership, 21; and lead, 93, 94–95; and local markets, 97, 98; *Malus pumila* species of, 19, 20, 231n5; *Malus sieversii* species of, 20; marketing of, 3–4, 14, 55, 67, 68, 71, 73–75, 91, 95, 96–99, 102–7, 113, 121, 122–23, 135, 137, 138, 141, 146, 148, 156–57, 158, 166, 172–73, 174, 181, 188, 190, 195–6, 207–8, 220–21, 224–25, 226, 228; maturation of, 72, 220; national and global markets for, 37–39, 90, 97, 98, 104, 105, 137, 174–75, 213, 215; and Northern Pacific Railway, 156; and Northwest Fruit Exchange, 153; and other fruits, 3, 4, 21, 22, 23, 26, 27, 31, 55, 56, 60, 64, 92, 98, 107–8, 110, 112, 116, 150, 153, 155, 169, 200, 207, 226, 229; and other vegetables, 64, 92; in Pacific Northwest, 17–18, 24, 26, 33–39, 55–56, 60–61, 66, 90–91, 98, 121, 125–26, 147, 152–53, 163; packing of, 116–21, 122, 123, 137, 138, 143, 145, 153, 156, 168, 204, 208, 224, 228;

and planting from seed, 21, 22, 23, 26; price of, 72, 97, 98, 99–100, 102, 103, 106, 119–20, 121, 137, 145, 150, 168, 171, 172, 178, 181, 184, 187, 188, 189–90, 192, 198, 200, 203, 204, 213, 214, 221, 229; production of, 1, 3–11, 14, 15, 16, 20–21, 23, 24, 33, 34, 39, 61, 65, 66, 72, 74, 90, 92, 97, 98, 99, 102, 108–12, 133, 138, 142, 153, 163, 164, 171, 173, 178, 181, 187, 189, 192, 194, 198, 206–7, 209, 215–16, 227–28, 230; and pruning, 10, 13, 68, 75, 94, 99, 107, 176, 178, 180, 181–82; and rail transportation, 150, 178, 179–81, 198–199, 229; and refrigeration, 133, 205, 207, 227; romantic notions about, 1, 17; and science, 209; and seeds at Fort Vancouver, 26, 27; Starking apples, 74; storage of, 20, 55, 70, 72, 73, 74, 91, 96, 97, 98, 100, 102, 112, 123, 129, 131, 132–35, 136, 137, 138, 141, 171, 174, 200, 203, 212, 222; and supermarkets, 3, 140, 190–91, 194, 205, 207, 208, 223–27; and urban growth, 6, 10, 22, 24; varieties of, 6, 7, 10, 15, 19–20, 21, 30, 32, 33, 61, 67–75, 86, 111, 115, 117, 141, 143, 146, 147, 150, 153, 188, 200, 204, 209, 217–18, 226–28, 229; and World War II era, 199–205, 206. *See also* advertising; agriculture; growers' cooperatives; New York State; Oregon; transportation; Washington State
Atwater, Wilbur O., 165

Bailey, Liberty Hyde, Jr., 114, 118–19.
Barlow, William, 30–31
Better Fruit: and apple boosting, 138; and apple packing, 118; and apple's competition, 169; articles on railroads, 123, 131; and commission houses, 100; and consumers' budgets, 172; and crop diversity, 65; editors of, 105–6, 169, 180, 193; founding of, 104; growing information in, 108; and harvest labor, 202; and marketing, 188; and Washington Apple Commission, 195–96; and Washington-based shippers, 224
Blalock, Nelson G., 38
British Columbia, 104, 129
Bryan, William Jennings, 8
Budd, Ralph, 164

Burbank, Luther, 74
Burke, Thomas, 48–49

California: and arsenic poisoning, 91; and brokers, 103; and California Fruit Growers Exchange, 103, 122, 140–41, 169; and California oranges, 3, 4, 140–41; and chemical use, 217; citrus industry in, 3, 57, 98, 103, 112, 138, 140; and commercial orchards, 9, 37, 76, 103; and Edenic imagery, 3; and fruit production, 182, 204; and growers' cooperatives, 103, 104; growers in, 3, 7, 12, 13, 14, 60, 61, 82, 103–4, 136–37, 174; and harvest workers, 187; importance of capitalist class to, 11; irrigated lands in, 54; landscape of, 69; Luelling nurseries in, 32, 33; migrants in, 184, 185; and miners' food demands, 32–33; orchards in, 4, 7, 13, 32, 34, 98; and packing apples, 117, 119; pest control in, 82; and rail transportation, 24, 124; San Francisco in, 156; and San Jose scale, 75–76; and seedlings, 31; and Southern California Fruit Exchange, 103; University of California, 76; and Watsonville, 10
Chapman, John (Johnny Appleseed), 1, 6, 22, 23, 24, 37
Chavez, Cesar, 219
cider, 20, 21, 23, 69, 115, 189
Clinton, Bill, 227
Colorado, 10, 87, 118, 225
Commission Merchants Act (Paulhamus Bill), 100–101
Crutchfield, James S., 101–2
Crutchfield, Woolfolk & Gibson, 101–2

Elliott, Howard, 146, 147
Environmental Protection Agency (EPA), 211, 212, 213, 214, 217

Federal Farm Board, 174
Florida, 3
Food and Drug Administration, 86, 91, 94, 213, 220

Granger, Walter N., 47, 48, 53–54
Great Northern Railway, 42–44, 46–47, 96, 126, 127, 129–30. *See also* Washington State

growers' cooperatives, 102–7, 117, 121–23, 133, 134, 136–37. *See also* advertising; apples; Washington State

Hill, James J., 48, 49, 51, 65, 141, 144, 223
Hill, Louis, 141, 143–44, 146, 147, 148, 223
Hoover, Herbert, 74, 176, 177
Hudson's Bay Company: and apple production, 19, 26; Captain Aemilius Simpson of, 26; and European crops, 27; Fort Vancouver of, 17, 18, 19, 25–26, 27, 28, 39; and George Simpson, 25, 26; and John McLoughlin, 25–26, 27, 28; in Pacific Northwest, 17, 18, 19, 24–27

Idaho: and cold-storage warehouses, 133; commercial apple districts in, 10; discovery of gold in, 35, 36; and Dust Bowl migrants, 184; and growers' cooperatives, 104, 122, 158; and Henry and Eliza Spalding, 27; and Idaho Territory, 35; missionaries in, 27; and Pacific Northwest Regional Planning Commission, 183–84; silver mines in, 43
Industrial Workers of the World (IWW), 185–87
Inslee, Jay, 217
Interstate Commerce Commission (ICC), 181, 189

Jefferson, Thomas, 8, 21, 22, 37, 53
Jungle, The (Sinclair), 114

Keiser, Charles, 55, 61, 62

Lewis and Clark Expedition, 18
Luelling, Henderson, 30, 31, 32–33, 233n47

Martin, Clarence, 195
Miller, Philip, 37
missionaries, 27–30, 31
monoculture, 6, 8, 15, 62, 216, 217
Montana, 35, 128, 146, 158, 183–84
Morrill Land-Grant Act, 6–7, 24, 69

Nader, Ralph, 212
National Apple Show, 142–48, 150
National Apple Week, 1, 158–63, 194, 206

New York State: and apple markets, 90, 141, 167; and apple production, 6, 10, 19, 24, 37, 97, 98, 99, 167; and chemical use, 217; and cold-storage warehouses, 133, 136; commercial orchards in, 76; consumers in, 169–70; cull apples in, 115; Delmonico's restaurant in, 150; Gerrit Smith of, 23; and grades of apples, 114–15; growers in, 9, 10, 97, 146; and National Apple Show, 144, 146; and New York Apple Week, 172–73; New York City in, 100, 155, 167, 169, 172; and New York Land and Irrigation Show, 121; and Union Pacific Railway, 124; and Wenatchee apples, 152
Northern Pacific Railway, 42–43, 44, 46–48, 112, 130, 136. *See also* Washington State

Ohio, 23, 139
orchards: abandonment of, 182, 184, 209; acreage of, 15, 60, 85, 109, 182, 210; business of, 12, 13, 14, 15, 57, 58, 60, 61–62, 63, 67, 68, 76, 96–97, 219; capital needed for, 59–60, 61; and chemical sprays, 68, 76–82, 210–17; and cider making, 6; and colonization, 20–21; and commercial orchards, 4, 6, 7, 9–10, 17, 19, 22, 24, 30, 34, 36–37, 39, 70, 76, 97, 103, 228; during Depression, 14, 197–99, 209; development of, 6–11, 12, 13–15, 17, 20–21, 66; and development of railroads, 11, 12, 14, 15; and dwarf rootstocks, 209–10; and eastern orchards, 4, 9, 10, 20–21, 87, 97, 98; expert advice on, 69–70, 209, 210; and fruit production, 51, 57, 60, 186, 209–10; and growing information, 7, 12, 60, 68–69, 209–10; and harvesting, 61, 201–3, 208, 210, 218, 219, 220; and impact of weather, 72, 210, 229; and industrialization, 7, 9, 14–15, 34, 42, 207, 209–10, 219–20; industry standards for, 12, 13, 14, 112–19; inspection of, 82–85, 107; and irrigation, 9, 10, 12, 27, 28, 36, 37, 39, 41–42, 46, 51, 59–60, 72, 95, 98, 181–82, 219, 229; and labor disputes, 185–86; labor in, 12–13, 60–61, 66, 85–86, 93, 107–12, 200–203, 218–19, 220; and landownership, 61–62; and

INDEX

land prices, 51, 52, 60; lead arsenate residue in, 197, 210, 211; and local markets, 35, 38, 39; management of, 13, 15, 60, 67–68, 69, 107; and marketing, 12, 13, 14, 15, 56; in Milwaukie, Ore., 31; national and global markets of, 37; and National Apple Week, 158; in nineteenth century, 1, 3, 9, 10, 24, 34, 66, 97; and orchard management, 81, 85, 95, 96, 97, 117, 208, 209, 217, 228–29; in Oregon Territory, 30–31; and peaches, 185; and pest control, 7, 9, 12, 13, 60, 66, 85; and pesticides, 79–80, 81, 219; planting of trees in, 13, 60, 68–69; promotional literature about, 67; and pruning, 12, 13, 60, 61, 69; romantic notions about, 1, 9, 12; and science, 7, 9, 13, 14, 87, 99; and settlement of land, 37; and Skookum Packers Association, 153, 154; spraying of, 13, 60, 79, 80–81, 82, 83, 84, 90, 95, 96, 99, 100, 107, 137, 176, 178, 180, 181–83, 198, 199, 214, 217, 219, 228, 229; and temperance movement, 23; and transportation, 11; twentieth-century planting, 4, 9–10, 210; in United States, 4, 9–10, 22, 23; and urban markets, 10, 14, 22, 97, 98; and Walla Walla Valley, 38; and western orchards, 7, 9–14, 22, 27, 34, 87, 97–98, 160; after World War II, 207. *See also* New York State; Oregon; pests; transportation; Washington State

Oregon: Agricultural Experiment Station in, 81, 88; and arsenic, 90; and cold-storage warehouses, 133; Columbia River in, 37; commercial nurseries in, 7, 33; and Dust Bowl migrants, 184; fruit production of, 7, 10, 18, 26, 27, 33, 37, 38, 90; and growers' cooperatives, 104, 122; growers in, 14, 32, 33, 90–91, 144, 158, 174; and harvest workers, 187; Hood River in, 37, 57, 122, 144, 169; landownership in, 54; Luelling nurseries in, 31–32; Oregon City in, 26; and Oregon colleges, 91, 100, 108; and Oregon Trail, 29, 30, 31, 35; and Oregon-Washington Railroad and Navigation Company, 130, 148; and Pacific Northwest Regional Planning Commission, 183–84; Portland, 101, 112, 122, 125, 133, 191; settlement in, 54, 55–56; State Horticultural Society of, 18; Willamette Valley in, 7, 27, 29–30, 31, 33–36, 38, 41, 43. *See also* missionaries

Oregon-Washington Railroad and Navigation Company (OWR&N), 130, 148

Outcault, Richard, 151, 152

pests: and arsenic, 77, 81, 86–92, 94, 117, 163; and blight infestation, 85–86; codling moth, 75–76, 77, 78, 81, 86, 88, 89, 94, 163, 197, 211, 216; control of, 7, 9, 12, 13, 60, 66, 68, 69, 76–77, 81–84, 85, 89, 94–95, 209, 210–11, 216; damage from, 75, 76, 114, 115; and DDT use, 210–11; insects in orchards, 216, 217, 229; and inspection law, 132; integrated management of, 216; and lead arsenate residue, 93–94, 197; and pesticides, 60, 76, 77, 80–81, 83, 86–91, 92, 93–95, 198, 203, 208, 210–15, 214, 216–17; and San Jose scale, 75, 81, 216; and sprays, 68, 69, 75, 76, 80–81, 83–84, 86, 87–88, 90–94, 180, 182, 203, 211, 216–17; and woolly aphids, 83. *See also* orchards

Prince, Robert, 21

Roosevelt, Franklin, 183, 189
Roosevelt, Theodore, 141, 153

Sievers, Johann, 20
"Significance of the Frontier in American History, The" (Turner), 44
Simpson, George, 25, 26
Smith, Hiram "Okanogan," 37
Spalding, Henry, 27, 28, 29
Sundquist, Ralph, 74
Swift, Gustav, 124

Taft, William Howard, 141
Texas, 10
transportation: and brokers, 102; cost of, 5, 72, 82, 98, 99, 101, 116, 119, 123–24, 128, 130, 134, 136, 137, 167, 173, 181, 188–89, 200, 203, 223; and credit corporations, 181; and federal regulations, 8, 123, 135; and Fruit Growers Express, 125, 127, 245n90;

transportation (*continued*)
and fruit markets, 38, 39, 98, 101, 102, 116; and fruit's condition, 70–71, 75, 116, 130–33, 204; and intermediaries' role, 13–14, 99, 105; and International Apple Shippers' Association, 123; and interstate trade, 120, 181; and irrigation, 44, 47, 49; and land and water's convergence, 11; and National Apple Show, 144; networks of, 24, 39, 96, 137, 139; and Northwest Fruit Exchange, 142; of out-of-season fruit, 207; and Pacific Fruit Express, 130, 245n90; and rail transportation, 3, 8, 11, 12, 13, 14, 15, 24, 38, 39, 40, 41–44, 46–48, 49, 51–52, 55, 96, 97, 98, 99, 102, 103, 105, 123–32, 134–37, 138, 141–42, 144, 146, 147–48, 167, 176–77, 180–81, 188–89, 200, 208, 222, 245n90, 245n92, 245n93, 246n95; and refrigeration, 15, 98, 124–31, 133, 134, 135, 138, 200, 245n91; and San Jose scale, 76; by ship, 32, 34, 39, 138; and shipping, 66, 94, 96, 98–99, 104, 108, 112, 116, 118, 121, 122, 123, 124–27, 130–32, 133, 134–36, 138, 153, 169, 170, 171, 172, 173, 176, 177, 179, 200, 203–4, 224, 228; and in-transit storage, 133–36; and trucks, 15, 208, 222–23; and Union Pacific, 124, 125; and urban markets, 4, 24, 124; and Walla Walla Valley, 38; on waterways, 25, 32, 42; and Wenatchee, 145; during World War I, 132. *See also* Hill, James J.; Washington State
Turner, Frederick Jackson, 44

United States Department of Agriculture (USDA): and Alar use, 213, 214; and arsenic levels, 88, 91, 163; Cooperative Research Extension of, 197; creation of, 6; and farmers' professionalism, 24; and frozen juice for military, 221; and growing information, 84, 95; and Kipp Plan, 166; and pesticides, 80; and planting alfalfa, 64; and Pure Food and Drug Act, 121; and rail transportation, 245–46n93; and regulations, 90; researchers at, 13, 197; and science, 80, 197, 209; War Board of, 201; and William A. Taylor, 70
United States Railroad Administration, 132

Virginia, 37

Washington, George, 21
Washington Irrigation Institute, 62, 65
Washington State: Agricultural Experiment Station in, 81, 197; and Alar use, 215; apple-growing districts of, 4–5, 10, 11, 14, 18–19, 36–37, 102, 122, 141, 149, 155, 158, 160; apple industry in, 3, 4, 5, 7, 9, 10–14, 15, 18–19, 39, 66, 67–68, 90, 97, 98, 101, 102, 123, 242n8; and Big Y cooperative, 174, 175, 193, 203–4; Board of Horticulture, 71, 82, 83, 85; and bud spot mutations, 73–74; Chinese residents, eviction of, 61; citrus in, 11; climate of, 4–5, 12, 35–36, 39, 41, 56, 68, 75, 80, 197, 210; and cold-storage warehouses, 133, 135, 136; Columbia Basin, 41, 208, 209, 210, 261n6; and commercial varieties, 74–75, 116; and Commissioner F. A. Huntley, 71, 73; and Department of Agriculture, 190, 217, 218; Department of Horticulture, 13, 83, 86; and Depression, 149, 171, 175, 182, 184–88, 190, 191–92, 197; and Dust Bowl migrants, 184, 185, 188; and Edenic imagery, 3; fruit production of, 5, 7, 11–12, 14, 53, 54, 55, 56–57, 69, 71, 79, 82, 106–7; and gold mining boom, 36; and grades of apples, 113–18; and Great Northern Railway, 42–43, 44, 46–47, 96, 126, 127, 129–30, 134–35, 136, 141, 144, 155, 167, 177, 178, 180; and growers' cooperatives, 102–7, 121–22, 131, 134, 135, 136–37, 142, 149, 154, 155, 157–58, 170, 174, 175–76, 178–79, 190–92, 195–96, 208, 220–21; growers in, 3–4, 5, 8, 9, 12–13, 14, 15, 16, 19, 36, 56, 59, 60, 61, 66–74, 75, 76, 77, 79–101, 102, 103–6, 107, 110, 111, 113, 115, 121, 123, 130–32, 135, 136–37, 138, 145, 146, 147, 148, 149, 154, 155, 156–58, 160, 161, 167, 168–78, 180–82, 185, 186–93, 195, 197–98, 203–4, 205, 207–8, 212–14, 216; and growing information, 83–84; and hops, pears, and other fruit, 5, 107–8, 109, 110, 112, 155, 185; Horticultural Society of, 147; industrialization process in, 12, 15, 44; and investment in land companies, 11, 42–43, 44, 46; and irrigation, 11–12, 40, 41–42, 44, 45–54,

INDEX

56–59, 60, 61, 68, 184–85, 208; Japanese population of, 61, 110, 236n48; and Kipp Plan, 164; laborers in, 60–61, 109–12, 117, 185–88, 200–203, 208; and landownership, 11, 12, 40, 54, 58, 60; Luelling nurseries in, 32; and marketing, 5, 12, 14, 102–7; and mining in Washington Territory, 34–35; and national apple sale, 172; and New Deal, 183, 187; and Newlands Reclamation Act, 50; and Northern Pacific Railway, 42–43, 44, 46–47, 48, 112, 130, 136, 141, 147–48, 167, 245n90; and Northwest Fruit Exchange, 156, 157–58, 178, 180; and orchard inspectors, 83, 84–85; and organic apples, 215–16; and Pacific Northwest Regional Planning Commission, 183–84; and production costs, 4, 5; promotional literature about, 69; Pullman in, 80, 250n40; and Red Wolf, 18, 28, 29; and science, 5, 14, 80, 81; Seattle in, 43, 46, 92, 101, 112, 125, 148, 155, 162, 178, 191, 201; settlement in, 40–44, 46, 47, 51, 52–53, 54, 57, 58, 60, 67, 96; and Skookum Packers Association, 154, 155, 156, 158, 169–70, 174, 191–92, 193, 220; soil of, 64, 68, 197, 210; and specialty crops, 69; Spokane, 43, 46, 83, 128, 142, 143, 147, 148, 175, 176, 177, 181, 201, 208; and spraying trees, 81, 85; Sunnyside in, 40, 46, 48, 58, 59, 66, 79, 85, 190; Supreme Court of, 84–85; and treaties with Indian tribes, 29; and Tree-Top cooperative, 221; and urban markets, 55, 99; and U.S. military purchases of apples, 199–200; volcanic soil of, 4–5, 41, 56; and Walla Walla Valley, 43, 54–55, 117, 122; Washington Agricultural Adjustment Act, 189, 190; Washington Apple Commission, 122, 195, 226; Washington State Apple Commission, 195–96, 197, 201, 204–5, 207, 212–13, 227; and Wenatchee Okanogan Federation (Wenoka), 196; and western land brochures, 51–53, 55, 56, 57, 60; wheatland of, 55, 109; during World War II, 14; and Yakama and Colville reservations, 61. *See also* National Apple Show; Wenatchee, Wash.; Yakima, Wash.

Washington State College (WSC): Agricultural College of, 69; and business of farming, 64; certification from, 83; and commercial apple varieties, 71; Department of Domestic Economy at, 150; experiment station of, 72, 197; field research station of, 57, 197; and home gardens, 183; and infestations of pests, 75, 76; and lead arsenate, 91; and National Apple Show, 143; in Pullman, 250n40; scientists at, 84; and spraying trees, 77–78, 79, 86

Washington State University, 209, 217, 228

Wenatchee, Wash.: and advertising, 55, 190; agricultural research station in, 196; Apple Blossom Festival in, 148; as Apple Capital, 40, 155; apple cooperatives of, 106–7; and apple-packing schools, 117; and apple production, 4, 10, 66, 68, 106–7, 126–28, 149, 152, 155–56, 210, 261n6; and apple sales, 172; and branding, 169; and Buster Brown label, 152; and cold-storage warehouses, 133; and Columbia & Okanogan Nursery Co., 74; and Columbia Ice, 129–30; and Columbia River, 41; Conrad Rose of, 116; and crop loans, 176; and Delicious apples, 73, 74; and emergency loan funds, 183; and fruit grades, 189; fruit harvest in, 111–12; and George Batterman, 62; and gold mining boom, 36; and Great Northern Railway, 11, 42–43, 48–49, 127–28, 142, 178–79, 180, 199; and growers' cooperatives, 105, 122, 174; growers in, 141, 174, 178, 179–80, 199, 202; irrigation in, 44, 46, 48–49, 50, 63; and labor, 201, 202; and lead poisoning, 93; Mike Horan of, 145, 146; and National Apple Show, 144–45, 146, 147; and Northwest Fruit Exchange, 177; orchards in, 37, 63, 210; and packing apples, 118, 120, 154; and pears and peaches, 155; settlement in, 35–36, 47; and Skookum Packers Association, 171, 188; and sugar beets, 63–64; transportation to, 42, 44; tree removal in, 182; USDA Cooperative Research Extension in, 197; and Wenatchee Canal Company, 50; and Wenatchee-Columbia Fruit Company, 152; and

Wenatchee, Wash. (*continued*)
  Wenatchee Commercial Club, 155; and Wenatchee Development Company, 43, 48, 49; and Wenatchee Okanogan Federation (Wenoka), 190, 192, 193. *See also* Keiser, Charles
West Virginia, 171
Whitman, Marcus, 27, 28, 29, 31
Whitman, Narcissa, 27, 29, 31

Yakima, Wash.: and Ahtanum Creek mission, 28; as Apple Capital, 40, 155; and apple-packing schools, 117, 187; and apple production, 4, 10, 28, 35, 36, 66, 126, 149, 155, 156, 168, 172, 209, 210, 261n6; and apple sales, 172, 191; and Big Y cooperative, 171, 178, 220; and branding, 169; climate of, 35–36; and cold-storage warehouses, 133; and credit corporations, 180; and crop loans, 176; and Delicious apples, 73; and Fred Raymond, 61–62; and fruit grades, 189; growers in, 193; H. M. Gilbert of, 144–45, 146, 147, 180; and irrigation, 36, 41, 44, 46, 47–51, 53, 59; Japanese farmers in, 54; and labor, 109, 110, 185–87, 201, 202, 218; and National Apple Show, 144–45, 146, 147; National Apple Week in, 1, 159, 161–63, 206; and Northern Pacific, Yakima, and Kittitas Irrigation Company, 47–48; and Northern Pacific Railway, 11, 42, 43, 47–48, 126, 128, 132, 135–36, 141, 142, 146, 155; and Oregon-Washington Railroad and Navigation Company, 130, 136; population of, 52; produce of, 55, 94, 122, 155, 210; and rail transportation, 131, 141; settlement in, 35–36, 41, 47, 50, 53–54; Snokist, 220; spraying in, 79, 86, 93–94, 182; storage facility in, 222; transportation to, 42, 44; tree removal in, 182; and Union Pacific Railway, 178; and Yakama Nation, 29, 233n44; and Yakama Reservation, 41, 50, 54, 236n48; and Yakima Commercial Club, 146, 149; and Yakima County Horticultural Union, 106, 113, 116, 171, 174, 178, 190, 220; and Yakima Fruit Growers Association, 106, 117, 122, 130, 132, 136, 154, 190, 191, 220; and Yakima Project, 184; Yakima Valley, 36, 41, 47, 50–51, 53, 54, 155, 178, 185, 186, 187, 218, 233n44, 261n6

www.ingramcontent.com/pod-product-compliance
Lightning Source LLC
Chambersburg PA
CBHW020832160426
43192CB00007B/622